Reform in Russia and the U.S.S.R.

Reform in Russia and the U.S.S.R.

Past and Prospects

Edited by

Robert O. Crummey

University of Illinois
Urbana and Chicago

Publication of this book was supported in part by a grant from the
Ford Foundation and the Center for Russian and East European
Studies, University of Michigan.

This book is printed on acid-free paper.

Library of Congress Cataloging-in-Publication Data

Reform in Russia and the U.S.S.R. : past and prospects / edited by
Robert O. Crummey.
    p.   cm.
    Bibliography: p.
    Includes index.
    ISBN 0-252-01612-2 (alk. paper)
    1. Soviet Union—Politics and government. 2. Soviet Union—
Politics and government—1917- I. Crummey, Robert O.
DK60.R44 1989
947.084—dc19   88-39451
                                           CIP

Contents

Acknowledgments

Acknowledgment of our collective debts must begin with thanks to the Ford Foundation for its generous support of the Conference on Reform in Russia and the U.S.S.R., which took place in Ann Arbor in April of 1986, and for the publication of this volume. The Center for Russian and East European Studies of the University of Michigan provided funding and organizational support without which the meeting could not have taken place. The Horace H. Rackham School of Graduate Studies and the Office of the Vice-President for Research at the University of Michigan also provided indispensable financial backing.

Many individuals contributed to this book. Alexander Yanov deserves the credit for developing the idea for the conference and, through his writings, posing the questions with which the participants wrestled. William G. Rosenberg organized the meeting and provided sage advice and moral support throughout the process of editing this volume. I also owe a debt of gratitude to each and every one of the participants in the Ann Arbor conference who offered the group their enthusiasm, their insights, and their understanding. Moreover, two members of the team, David L. Ransel and Daniel Field, shared helpful hints from their long experience as editors. I am indebted to our staffs in Ann Arbor and Davis—particularly Marisha Ostafen and Sherryl Fawx, who typed much of the manuscript; Austin Jersild, the editorial assistant; and Eric Duskin, who compiled the guide to further reading at the end of the volume.

Introduction

ROBERT O. CRUMMEY

Since the late sixteenth century, when Giles Fletcher characterized the Muscovite Russian monarchy as "plain tyrannical,"[1] many foreign observers and native commentators have drawn attention to the predominance of authoritarian forms of rule in Russia's history. On a number of occasions, Russian leaders have attempted to make social relations more equitable and governmental institutions more responsive to the needs of elite groups in society or the population as a whole. Time and again, would-be reformers attempted to win a voice in the governing of the country and freedom from governmental arbitrariness for themselves and those in whose name they spoke. On many occasions, they failed completely; when they succeeded, the changes in the structure of government and in social relations were often less profound than they probably would have liked.

Nevertheless, the reformers' policies and projects represent much more than interesting and courageous attempts to swim against the current of Russian institutional history. Campaigns for reform and their limitations and failures tell us much about the social relations, habits of institutional behavior, and modes of political thinking that have shaped the Russian political tradition. Moreover, for this very reason, study of reform in Russia, remote and recent, illuminates the present contours of politics in the U.S.S.R. and suggests the conditions under which the Soviet system of government—in many ways the heir of the Russian past—might undergo significant change.

With this in mind, thirty-two scholars gathered at the University of Michigan in April, 1986, to examine the history and prospects of reform in Russia and the U.S.S.R.[2] Long before *perestroika* became a household word, Alexander Yanov had presented the idea of such a conference to his colleagues at the Center for Russian and East European Studies at the University of Michigan. Under the leadership of William G. Rosenberg, the center secured the Ford Foundation's support for the venture and the process of organizing began. As part of the preparation for the meeting, Yanov and Rosenberg circulated to the participants a "Conference Proposal"—based in part on the theories advanced in Yanov's earlier writings—which urged them to reflect on Russia's "total experience with reform," to examine the pressures for and the impediments to it in various historical periods, and to weigh the prospects for reform in the contemporary Soviet Union.[3]

Collectively, the participants in the conference made an extraordinary group. Rarely, if ever, have historians of late medieval and modern Russia, political scientists specializing in Soviet affairs, and scholars of other socialist societies come together to examine a common subject from their differing vantage points. This book is a record of their common venture; all of them have contributed to the shaping of its arguments.

The most obvious sign of the assembled scholars' varied backgrounds and preconceptions is the wide range of meanings which they attached to the pivotal word, "reform," itself. According to the *Oxford English Dictionary,* reform is "the amendment or altering for the better of some faulty state of things, especially of a corrupt or oppressive political institution or practice."[4] Almost all of the authors in this collection accept this formulation. For a number of them it is definition enough.

Attempts to articulate more detailed or more precise notions of "reform" revealed the differences of opinion among the participants. Few of them would argue with Alexander Dallin's sensible clarification of what "reform" does and does not mean. As distinct from "revolution," he suggests, " 'reform'... must denote significant change *within* the existing system." It is not merely "changes of policy which require neither structural changes nor the redistribution of power and which can readily be reversed," nor does it imply "a replacement of the existing regime." A program of reform, he cautions, may improve the functioning of the prevailing political and institutional system without improving the lot of the citizens within it.[5]

In his recent book, *The Dilemma of Reform in the Soviet Union,* Timothy J. Colton makes a helpful distinction between "radical reform," "minimal reform," and "moderate reform." "Radical reform" he characterizes as "all-encompassing change containing as an essential component the restructuring of the country's political institutions and central, legitimating beliefs and myths." By way of contrast, "moderate reform" entails significant changes in the machinery, personnel, and policies of government, but it does not aim at changing society's basic political structures and traditions.[6] In his terms, most of the reforms discussed in this volume would fit into his "moderate" category, although a few, such as the Great Reforms of the 1860s and perhaps some of Gorbachev's recent initiatives, approach the "radical" end of Colton's spectrum. Moreover, it is the conviction of such authors as Walter M. Pintner that, in the Russian political tradition, apparently radical programs of reform may introduce less fundamental long-term change than an observer might assume at first glance.

Other authors in the collection offer more controversial suggestions. Some, like Pintner and Robert O. Crummey, prefer to stress the overtone of conscious action that the word "reform" has had historically in both Anglo-American and Russian contexts. A reform, in their view, is a conscious step toward a preconceived goal or an attempt to reshape government or society according to some general principles. Their emphasis puts them at the opposite pole from other contributors, notably Alexander Yanov who insists that political leaders can institute "unconscious reforms," measures that have profound consequences they never intended or foresaw.

Alexander Yanov brings to the discussion a particularly detailed definition of "reform." In his books and essays, he has presented a thought-provoking model of Russian political development which examines the attempts, beginning in the sixteenth century, to reform the prevailing system of government. "Reform," in a Russian context, he defines as "a set of socio-economic and institutional changes opening up the system for political modernization and/or moving it" in that direction.[7] The nations which have achieved "political modernization" have succeeded, among other things, in:

1. Legalizing and institutionalizing political opposition as part of the normal functioning of government.
2. Basing their governments on the principle of separation of powers.
3. Abolishing state censorship of intellectual and cultural pursuits.
4. Separating church from state.
5. Integrating the working class into the political structure of society by legitimizing independent trade unions.
6. Getting rid of their empires.
7. Allowing citizens to choose a country of residence without considering emigration treason.

Russia, Yanov argues, has not followed the Western path. As he puts it, "By the end of the second Christian millennium all European nations with the exception of Russia (and those under her political or ideological influence) achieved political modernization."[8] Instead of steady progress toward this goal, Russia's political and social history since the sixteenth century has taken the shape of a cycle, consisting of periods of harsh autocratic rule, followed by (often abortive) attempts at reform, then periods of stagnation.[9] Russia thus remains, in Yanov's terms, "an anomalous case in the European family of nations," a pre-modern actor on the modern political stage.[10]

One reason for the persistent failure of reform attempts, Yanov argues, was the lack of an adequate social base. In fact, programs of reform were designed, in part, to create one. In each case, the social thrust of aborted reform was an attempt "to open the system for the formation of an economically sound and politically articulated middle class."[11] Without the support of a middle class, he suggests, any attempt at political reform in Russia is doomed.

Whatever their precise formulations, most authors in this collection have proceeded on certain assumptions about the nature of reform in Russia and the U.S.S.R. In studying successful or abortive reform, they have concentrated on political, institutional, and legal matters. Many probably would agree with Daniel T. Orlovsky's contention that reform in Russia has usually taken either of two forms. Some reforms, he suggests, have been institutional changes designed to improve the effectiveness of the governmental administration for its own sake and, in some instances, for the well-being of the population. Most other more radical reforms have aimed at limiting the arbitrary power of the monarch or central bureaucracy or at increasing "self-government," giving men and women a greater share in the decisions which govern their lives. By and large, however, social reform is conspicuous by its absence. Several authors in the collection emphasize the glacial pace of change in social relations and perceptions in Russia, even in eras of dramatic institutional or cultural reform. Economic issues come into play chiefly in the Soviet period when management of a state-controlled economy became one of the principal functions of the bureaucracy.

All this may seem to give these essays a distinctly Whiggish flavor. At the same time, the authors would surely insist, the fault lies not in their perceptions but in the nature of government and society in Muscovite and Imperial Russia, because, as both governors and governed realized, significant changes in economic and social relations could take place not through reform but spontaneously or through revolution.

In spite of these common assumptions—to which the careful reader will undoubtedly find exceptions—this volume has no "party line" on the definition of the word "reform." Instead, we have accepted the authors' varied understandings of "reform" in general and in a specific Russian context as a fact of scholarly discourse and a welcome invitation to future reflection and discussion. Moreover, the book is not a debate about the validity of any single model or formulation or a dissection of the theories of any particular author. It is intended to be a many-sided examination of past and future reform in Russia. As the discerning reader will note, Yanov's ideas stimulated the reflections of some of the other contributors but do not dominate their thinking or dictate their conclusions. All of them reject some features of his model; many frankly disagree with the fundamental assumptions on which he constructed it.

Definitions and models aside, the essays reflect the remarkable variety of the writers' interests, approaches, and opinions. Some are detailed monographic studies, while others are brief syntheses of broad subjects. The authors' styles range from traditional academic reticence to polemical bluntness. The choice of topics likewise represents the authors' collective diversity. The essays range over time from the sixteenth century to the present, but they do not claim to constitute a survey of the history of reform in Russia. For one thing, a number of important subjects—for instance, the reforms and attempted reforms of the late seventeenth century, the reigns of Peter the Great and Alexander I, and 1905—for a variety of reasons had to be left out.

The first two essays in the collection deal with the issue of reform during the Muscovite period of Russian history. Crummey's essay on the reign of Ivan IV (1533-84) can best be understood when set against the arguments in Yanov's book, *The Origins of Autocracy: Ivan the Terrible in Russian History.* In Yanov's view, Ivan's reign was the turning point in Russian history. The reforms of the first years of the tsar's majority allowed the country to begin moving toward political modernization along with the other major European states. Ivan's subsequent reign of terror, the *oprichnina,* however, abruptly reversed the direction of Russia's historical development and threw it into the futile cycles of reform, counterreform, and stagnation which have characterized its history since that time.[12] By way of contrast, Crummey argues that the reforms of the 1550s were well-conceived incremental measures designed to increase the ability of the tsar's government to mobilize the human and material resources of Russian society. The oprichnina, he argues, pursued the same broad objective—greater governmental control over society—but by pathologically brutal and destructive means. In his view, the decisive changes which set Russia on the road to autocracy were not the wild but short-lived experiments of the oprichnina, but the far more gradual processes of subjugating the aristocracy and creating a bureaucratic administration and a class of noble military servitors, loyal to and dependent on the crown.

Continuing his investigation of Muscovite political culture in a somewhat different vein, Crummey sees the attempts during the Time of

Troubles (1605-13) to limit the arbitrary power of the monarch not as programs of reform in a modern sense, but as attempts by elite groups to spare themselves a recurrence of the persecutions of Ivan IV's reign. The court aristocracy of Muscovy had no desire or need to change the structure of the tsardom which they both served and dominated. Moreover, given the narrow parameters of Muscovite political thinking, fundamental institutional or legal reform was virtually inconceivable.

The reforms of Peter I introduced major changes into Russia's political and administrative institutions, but they did little to alter the social relations and attitudes which his subjects brought with them from Muscovite times. As a consequence, the eighteenth-century Russian nobility by and large had as little interest in political reform as their Muscovite forebears had. In his examination of the crisis of 1730, David L. Ransel argues that the attitudes of the vast majority of the nobles doomed efforts to limit the monarch's arbitrary power. With a history of dependence on the crown and no tradition of corporate rights, most nobles preferred the unfettered rule of an autocrat to the only alternatives they could imagine—government by an oligarchy of aristocrats or social chaos.

Toward the end of the century, Catherine the Great tried her best to break her nobles and other social leaders of these traditional habits of passivity and dependency. Summarizing the policies of one of the most energetic and articulate rulers of the century, John T. Alexander concludes that she genuinely attempted to "liberalize" her rule, "to encourage a greater measure of initiative and self-directed activity on the part of responsible elements of society, the nobility above all."[13]

Pintner's overview of the Great Reforms of the mid-nineteenth century emphasizes how difficult it was for any leaders of Imperial Russia to promulgate and implement fundamental reforms of institutions and society. While not wishing to disregard the reformers' real achievements—above all the emancipation of the serfs and the creation of a new system of courts—Pintner argues that the reforms did not change Russian institutions and society as radically as historians have sometimes assumed. To mention the most obvious example, the new institutions and social relations the reforms fostered rarely touched the world in which the peasants continued to live.

The Russian revolutions of 1917 ushered in profound changes in many spheres of national life. New conditions presented new challenges. At the same time, old dilemmas reappeared in new guises. In a wide-ranging analysis of the Provisional Government's attempts to restructure governmental institutions in the middle months of 1917, Daniel T. Orlovsky points out how difficult it is to interest people in any kind of reform in a climate of utopian revolutionary expectations. More specifically, the new government's program of restructuring the local administration came to grief for two reasons. It failed to win the support of the "lower middle strata" of Russian society, newly active in politics. Moreover, old habits proved hard to break: the new government, like its imperial predecessor, tended to encumber its officials "with legal codes of behavior," while the officials themselves preferred to rely on their charisma and exercise unfettered authority in the traditional manner.

The recent flowering of historical scholarship on the first years of the Soviet regime has led, among other things, to reexaminations of the period of the New Economic Policy. Lewis Siegelbaum portrays the 1920s as a decade of ferment and experimentation—in other words, reform. He sees in the ideological and political conflicts of the time a fundamental reassessment of the historic relationship between a powerful Russian state and an immature society. The changing aspirations and demands of "society"—the industrial workers and peasants—contributed at least as much to a redefinition of the relationship between "state" and "society" as the arguments and political maneuvers of Party intellectuals and activists. In the end, in Stalin's "revolution," the state swallowed society, thus, in a sense, returning to the traditions of Imperial Russia in a particularly simplified, brutal form. Nevertheless, the 1920s remain an inspiration for would-be Soviet reformers because of their climate of openness and the willingness of government and society honestly to confront "inconvenient facts."

The last three historical essays deal with Nikita Khrushchev's attempts to reform the Soviet Union in the late 1950s and early 1960s. At first glance, three examinations of so brief a period of recent history may appear excessive. The years of Khrushchev's leadership are exceptionally important for our purposes, however, because, until very recently, his were the most serious attempts to reform the Soviet system shaped by Stalin. They are thus the immediate predecessor of Gorbachev's campaign of reform and a test of his prospects for long-term success as a reformer. An examination of Khrushchev's successes and failures also raises the perennial question of the relationship between international politics and Soviet reform. To what extent did the policies of the Western powers determine his fate and how, by analogy, should the Western powers respond to Gorbachev?

Yanov portrays Khrushchev as a genuine reformer, some of whose policies had even more radical implications than he realized. Khrushchev's domestic reforms, he argues, amounted to a program of political modernization; unfortunately, the intransigent foreign and military policy of the United States made his position as leader of the U.S.S.R. untenable. In their analysis of Khrushchev's campaign to reduce the size and political power of the Soviet military, George Minde and Michael Hennessey reach a similar conclusion. They argue that, throughout his years in power, Khrushchev championed reductions in Soviet troop strength and attempted to limit the U.S.S.R.'s nuclear arsenal to levels appropriate for a policy of minimum deterrence. As the years passed, his military policy encountered increasing resistance from the leaders of the Soviet armed forces who looked with understandable dismay at the rapid growth of America's nuclear forces under President Kennedy. These pressures at home and from abroad—combined with the disastrous failure of his economic policies—fatally weakened him and, after his fall from power, his successors quickly reentered the international arms race.

William Taubman sees matters in a different light. He argues that, while unquestionably the champion of reform at home, Khrushchev pursued an aggressive foreign policy which gave American leaders little choice but to respond as they did. In rebuttal, Yanov insists that, on balance, Khrushchev's foreign policy aimed at reducing international tensions; American policymakers, however, consistently misunderstood his more dramatic initiatives and overreacted to them. Just beneath the surface of the argument lies a fundamental disagreement on the extent to which the foreign policy of the United States can or should be tailored to encourage reformist leaders within the U.S.S.R.

In spite of their variety, the historical papers reveal a number of recurring patterns and tendencies in Russia's experience with political and institutional reform. In other words, their authors collectively offer insights into Russian political culture. At the same time, they have no desire to propound a series of reductionist truisms of the "Russians are like that" variety.

Collectively, the essays on Russian and Soviet history stress the weak social and legal foundations for reform. In comparison to western Europe, the country's middle class, however we define that term, was small and vulnerable to governmental manipulation. Moreover, there was no tradition of estates or legal corporations independent of the state. On the contrary, historians of Russian politics and society stress the entrenched power of evolving administrative elites with a vested interest in preserving the status quo from which their privileges derived.

Moreover, the historical essays suggest, certain widespread attitudes have persisted in Russia—and not only there—with remarkable tenacity. As in other societies, Russians have tended to pull together in the face of danger, real or imagined, from other countries. In Russia, however, this sense of common purpose has extended to an inclination to view all criticism of or opposition to existing arrangements as a threat to the common good. The concept of loyal opposition makes little sense in a Russian context and a would-be reformer can easily be branded a traitor. Time and again, moreover, most members of the ruling elite have interpreted proposals for legal or institutional reform as the self-interested action of a clique or faction whose only real purpose is its own aggrandizement. Overcoming such a heritage is no easy matter.

What are the prospects for reform in the U.S.S.R.? Most of the authors of the historical essays in this collection are inclined toward pessimism. Although the historical essays make clear Russia's leaders have sometimes succeeded in enacting real reforms—incremental changes in law and institutional practice which have significantly improved the performance of the government or the quality of life for the population as a whole—they provide many examples of opportunities missed and reform initiatives wrecked on the rocks of popular indifference or hostility or the resistance of powerful groups in society to the loss of their privileges. Equally threatening to significant reform is the ease with which initiatives for change can be sucked into the morass of traditional administrative habits and ways of thinking. A number of the contributors argue that the strength of tradition makes fundamental change in the Soviet system of government unlikely in the near future. For example, in explaining the limited success of the reformers of the 1860s, Pintner points, above all, to the imperial government's failure to accept the peasants as full members of society.

Some observers of the contemporary scene, however, are more optimistic. Summarizing Gorbachev's achievements up to the summer of 1987, Colton credits him with undertaking a remarkably wide-ranging program of reform designed to bring into being a more productive and open society. Gorbachev, he argues, has learned on the job and, in the process, has become committed to an increasingly radical vision of reform; at the same time, he has shown no inclination to question such foundations of the Soviet system as centralized economic planning and the political monopoly of the Communist party. Still, Gorbachev's regime has done remarkable things. Under his leadership, the Soviet government has greatly stretched the parameters of permitted public discussion and cultural expression, begun to make the economy more responsive to market forces and the needs of consumers, curbed the arbitrary power of Party and government officials, and taken steps to recognize and channel the entrepreneurial talent and public spiritedness of ordinary Soviet citizens.[14]

For the moment, then, Gorbachev's well-wishers have good reasons for optimism. Yet, as even his most enthusiastic admirers realize, the long-term success of his campaign of reform is by no means assured. Colton cautions that Gorbachev may not yet realize the potentially disruptive implications of some of his reform measures. In addition, he points out, there is no doubt that Gorbachev's policies have aroused powerful currents of opposition, not the least among officials whose jobs, privileges, and style of life may be at stake.

As many of the papers make clear, the fate of programs of reform in the U.S.S.R. depends in part on the international situation. What, then, could the United States do to advance the cause of reform in the U.S.S.R.? Yanov argues that, by a subtle combination of flexibility and determination in its foreign policy, the government of the United States could strengthen the hand of aspiring reformers in the Soviet Union. In a more circumspect tone, Dallin, after reviewing changing American attitudes toward reform in the U.S.S.R., suggests "the United States must define, for its own purposes, what kinds of reform in the Soviet Union it favors and why."[15] Changing the Soviet system must never be the official business of the United States. No nation has the right to reshape another. At the same time, Dallin concludes, better understanding of the prospects for change in the U.S.S.R. and its consequences will help U.S. policymakers respond appropriately to future Soviet reform programs.

This book, then, presents no easy insights on the political future of the U.S.S.R. Moreover, as the contributors are well aware, the future direction of Soviet state and society is for its own leaders and peoples to decide. At the same time, on our shrinking planet the fate of each nation concerns us all.

Assuming that reform in the Soviet Union is desirable—for its own citizens if not necessarily for us—what can outsiders do to advance its cause? First, we can strive for a better understanding of the Russian past that helps shape the Soviet present. Second, we can encourage our governments to make clear, creative, and flexible responses to Soviet foreign and domestic policy. Finally, we must accept the fact that, if the leaders of the U.S.S.R. work to make government and society more open, responsive, and productive, they will do so in their own ways and for their own purposes, not ours.

NOTES

1. Giles Fletcher, "Of the Russe Commonwealth," in *Rude and Barbarous Kingdom,* ed. Lloyd E. Berry and Robert O. Crummey (Madison, Wisc., 1968), p. 132.

2. John T. Alexander, Timothy J. Colton, Robert O. Crummey, Alexander Dallin, Daniel Field, Zvi Gitelman, Stephen Goldstein, Hugh F. Graham, Michael Hennessey, Jerry F. Hough, Aron Katsenelenboigen, Bennett Kovrig, Brenda Meehan-Waters, Alfred G. Meyer, George F. Minde II, Sidney Monas, Daniel T. Orlovsky, Walter M. Pintner, David L. Ransel, Hans Rogger, William G. Rosenberg, Teodor Shanin, Lewis H. Siegelbaum, Dina Spechler, Ronald Grigor Suny, Roman Szporluk, William Taubman, Robert C. Tucker, Lynne Viola, Alexander Yanov, Elizabeth Zelensky, and William Zimmerman.

3. "Conference Proposal: Is the Soviet Union Reformable?" (Prepared for the Conference on Reform in Russia and the Soviet Union, University of Michigan, April 4-6, 1986).

4. *The Oxford English Dictionary,* 12 vols. (Oxford, 1933), 8:347.

5. Alexander Dallin, "Reform in Russia: American Perceptions and U.S. Policy," pp. 252-53, herein.

6. Timothy J. Colton, *The Dilemma of Reform in the Soviet Union* (New York, 1986), pp. 4-5.

7. Alexander Yanov, "Russian Reform: To Be or Not to Be?" (Prepared for the Conference on Reform in Russia and the Soviet Union, University of Michigan, April 4-6, 1986), p. 18.

8. Letter of Alexander Yanov to Robert O. Crummey, September 27, 1987.

9. See, in particular, Alexander Yanov, *The Origins of Autocracy: Ivan the Terrible in Russian History* (Berkeley and Los Angeles, 1981), especially pp. 52-67, and his "The Drama of the Time of Troubles," *Canadian/American Slavic Studies* 12 (1978):1-59, particularly pp. 1-7, where he labels the three phases of the cycle "pseudodespotism," "Time of Troubles," and "pseudoabsolutism."

10. Yanov to Crummey, September 27, 1987.

11. Yanov, "Russian Reform," p. 34.

12. Yanov, *Origins.*

13. John T. Alexander, "Catherine II's Efforts at Liberalization and Their Aftermath," pp. 78-79, herein.

14. Timothy J. Colton, "Gorbachev and the Politics of System Renewal," herein. Another helpful summary of Gorbachev's reforms is Gail W. Lapidus, "Gorbachev and the Reform of the Soviet System," *Daedalus* 116 (Spring, 1987):1-30.

15. Dallin, "Reform in Russia," p. 253, herein.

Reform under Ivan IV:
Gradualism and Terror

ROBERT O. CRUMMEY

The stormy reign of Ivan IV has aroused intense passions and has set off lively controversy. There can be no question, however, that his government made reforms, if by that we mean conscious efforts to improve the functioning of the administration and its ability to mobilize the material and human resources of Russian society. In the last two decades, several important books and articles have analyzed Ivan's reforms individually or collectively; one particularly helpful contribution to the literature bears the simple title *Reformy Ivana Groznogo* (*The Reforms of Ivan the Terrible*).[1]

Establishing that point, however, only begins the discussion. Historians differ strenuously on virtually every important issue in the interpretation of the reign, including the identity of the reformers.[2] Any discussion of Ivan's reforms must grapple with a wide range of vexing questions. What were the most important goals of Ivan's government in making them? Were they primarily attempts to make the tsar's government more systematic and effective? What were their social objectives and implications? Were they intended to strengthen particular social groups?

In addition, any comprehensive overview of the reign necessarily includes an examination of the relation of the reforms of Ivan's early adult years to the *oprichnina,* the restructuring of the army and administration and the accompanying reign of terror that gave Ivan his notoriety in Russia's historical memory. Did the oprichnina represent a radical departure from earlier policies? Or was it an attempt to achieve the same goals as before, only with far more radical methods?

This essay will focus on the political dimension and implications of the reforms or, in Alexander Yanov's vocabulary, the extent to which they can be viewed as steps toward "political modernity."[3] At the same time, we must be careful not to denature the reforms by pulling them out of their sixteenth-century milieu or distort our understanding of them by examining them through an anachronistic conceptual apparatus. In other words, we must avoid the danger of reading into these measures a conscious theory of reform or a comprehensive program for restructuring governmental institutions or social relations. Rather, to appreciate their impact and significance in their own time, the reforms must be seen in the total context of governmental activity, including war and diplomacy, set against the structure of governmental institutions and society.

Before examining the reforms themselves, we must thus remind ourselves of the circumstances in which they took place. In the century before Ivan IV's accession, the territory under the control of the princes of Moscow had expanded very rapidly, and the great noble clans of the realm had largely been assimilated into the political and social network of the Moscow court. At the same time, the administrative system had not kept pace with the explosive territorial expansion.

Ivan's childhood and youth provide dramatic evidence of both the aspirations and weaknesses of the Muscovite polity. Nominally inheriting the throne at the age of three, Ivan lived through a stormy regency in which the leading boyar clans fought for preeminence at his court and control over the machinery of government. Only the young tsar's marriage to a representative of one of them, Anastasiia Romanova, provided the focal point around which the court clans could put their interrelationships in order.[4] On a more positive note, Ivan's coronation as tsar in 1547 marked the culmination of the efforts of Muscovite churchpeople to demonstrate that the Eastern Orthodox sovereign was the equal of any ruler on earth.

Once stability returned to the court and administration and an adult monarch occupied the throne, a single concern dominated the government's activity—Kazan'. Officials gathered men and supplies for the conquest of Muscovy's Islamic neighbor to the east, and ecclesiastical polemicists proclaimed a crusade to free suffering Christians from the oppression of the unbelievers. Military and ideological mobilization finally brought victory in 1552.

Against this background, Ivan IV and his advisers undertook their reforms. They left behind few programmatic statements of their intentions as reformers.[5] The very word "reform" would probably have rung strangely in their ears. Nevertheless, a regime that stages the first coronation of the ruler with an imperial title, issues a new law code, and conducts a comprehensive review of the state of the church intends to inspect and, if necessary, repair the institutional and ideological foundations of society. Moreover, there seems to have been a widespread perception within the ruling elite that changes had to be made. Reform began during the "boyar rule" of Ivan's childhood and continued through Ivan's life-threatening illness in 1553 to about 1560. Finally, the reforms to a considerable extent form a coherent pattern in that many of the government's measures are clearly interrelated.

The concrete objectives of Ivan and his advisers in making the reforms, judging by their actions, were primarily to bring consistency and order to the church and the royal courts, strengthen the army, and make the royal administration more efficient and less corrupt. Within these broad rubrics, we can distinguish several general types of reform measures.

First, in the early 1550s, Ivan's government made a number of detailed technical reforms that might be characterized as "housekeeping" in state and church. In putting its house in order, Ivan's government issued a new law code (*sudebnik*) in 1550. The act of promulgating a legal codex symbolized the regime's determination to assert its authority over its subjects by systematizing legal norms and procedures. Yet, while the sudebnik fixed prevailing administrative and legal practice in written form, it did not depart radically from current norms. To mention one frequently cited example, Article 98 stipulated that the monarch was to consult his boyars about any future additions to the code—a formalization of centuries-old custom. Like the Code of 1497 from which it drew many provisions, the Code of 1550 was essentially a procedural manual for conducting investigations and trials. Moreover, its concrete provisions were generally conservative, although certain provisions echoed the government's other reform measures.[6]

In a similar vein, the *"Stoglav"* church council of 1551 was the centerpiece of a campaign, supported by the tsar's government, to bring greater order and discipline to the liturgical and moral life and administration of the Eastern Orthodox church and to set limits to its acquisition of lands.[7]

Second, in mobilizing for an all-out assault on Kazan', Ivan's government gave highest priority to strengthening the army. In no sense did its reforms involve a systematic restructuring of the tsar's forces; they consisted instead of piecemeal attacks on specific problems. Nevertheless, their cumulative effect was substantial. First the government attacked the most destructive feature of precedence ranking (*mestnichestvo*), the tendency of aristocratic commanders to refuse to do their duty for fear that carrying out their assignments would lower their future standing and that of their family. Commanders' quarrels over precedence had already undermined the regime's first campaigns against Kazan'.[8] The government's solution in 1550 was to promulgate a set of regulations governing the relationships among commanders in the field. While on campaign all officers were to recognize the commander-in-chief of the central regiment as their superior, and the relationships of his principal subordinates were formalized two-by-two. The commander of the right wing, for example, was to be the equal of the commanders of the advance and rear guards but superior to the commander of the left wing. More generally, the decree stipulated that an officer's assignment could not be used as a precedent for future precedence disputes.[9]

The decree's significance should not be exaggerated. The government made no attempt to attack the mestnichestvo system as such; on the contrary, precedence relationships in the following century became increasingly complex and litigation more frequent. More to the point, the decree failed in its primary mission—to eradicate disputes while the army was on campaign. The military records from the remainder of the sixteenth century report many such quarrels.

In preparation for the assault on Kazan', Ivan's government created a new military force with concentrated firepower that complemented the noble cavalry. In 1550, Ivan IV ordered the formation of six companies of musketeers (*strel'tsy*), who fought primarily on foot with the latest firearms. In a certain sense, these units amounted to a small standing army since the men served throughout the year and received a salary from the royal treasury. In the subsequent century and a half, the strel'tsy played a vital role in the Muscovite armed forces. They helped greatly in besieging strong fortresses like Kazan' and gave the Muscovites a better chance in battle against up-to-date European armies. From the beginning, the strel'tsy, who lived in urban centers when not on campaign, took on the role of garrison troops and police.

At about the same time, Ivan's government attempted to provide lands near Moscow for one thousand military servitors. The idea behind the proposal was reasonable enough. Estates near the capital were at a premium since they allowed a servitor to live on his lands within easy ride of Moscow or alternately in the city, provisioned by his nearby peasants. Whether Ivan's officials were actually able to find enough land suitable for distribution under these conditions is a subject of intense debate among historians.[10] Whatever its concrete achievements, the government's motive was clear—to strengthen the upper echelons of the service nobility.

The "decree on service" in 1556 set norms for the nobles' military obligations. According to its provisions, the owner of any estate—

whether held on hereditary or *pomest'e* (conditional on service) tenure—
had to appear for muster himself and bring with him one fully equipped
cavalryman for every one hundred *chetverti* (about four hundred acres) of good land which he owned.[11] As with so many of Ivan's
reforms, the measure gave concrete expression to a well-established
assumption—that all members of the traditional warrior caste of Muscovy were obligated to fight for the sovereign when summoned.

In short, the military reforms addressed specific problems of the army.
Judging by the army's performance in battle, the results were mixed.
Kazan' and other eastern outposts fell to Ivan's troops, but after decades
of alternating victories, setbacks, and stalemates, the Muscovite armies
that invaded Livonia suffered bitter defeat. The social implications of
the reforms were also ambivalent; they made clear the government's
concern for the well-being of the noble cavalrymen who made up most
of the army while simultaneously telling them bluntly that they had to
serve at its convenience.

Third, in Ivan's early adult years, the central administration grew
and assumed more distinct organizational forms. Since the fifteenth
century, a small number of officials had served at the Muscovite court
in essentially non-military functions; however, according to a number
of historians, not until the 1550s did the proto-bureaucratic chanceries
(*prikazy*) take shape. Certainly, a number of the most important chanceries in the bureaucratic system of the seventeenth century—the
Posol'skii (Foreign Office), Razriadnyi (Military Records), Pomestnyi
(Landholding), and Razboinyi (Anti-Brigandage) Prikazy—were already in place in Ivan's lifetime. These administrative offices, consisting
of a director and his staff of clerks, kept increasingly elaborate records
of the government's most important activities and thus considerably
increased its control over the country and its resources, above all the
tsar's military servitors and the estates that supported them.[12]

Last, and perhaps most significant of all, was the reform of the local
administration of justice and tax collection. Banditry flourished in many
parts of the country in sixteenth-century Muscovy, and the governors
(*namestniki*) sent out from Moscow were unable or unwilling to put
an end to it. The urgency of the problem must have been obvious,
since the government took the first steps to deal with it in 1539 in the
midst of the political struggles of Ivan's minority. Beginning in that
year, the royal government issued charters to the population of particular
districts (*guby*), especially in northern Russia, instructing them to select
elders (*starosty*) who were to be responsible for assembling posses and
on their own authority arresting and hanging highwaymen and other
notorious characters. Rather than reporting to the provincial governor,

the district elders were to be accountable directly to the appropriate officials in Moscow.[13]

These ruthlessly simple arrangements worked above all to the advantage of the royal administration in the capital. Its officials undoubtedly increased their ability to supervise the administration of justice in the provinces since the district elders were strictly accountable to them. The reform placed the elders in an ambivalent position. On the one hand, they gained sweeping powers to deal with troublemakers and were presumably happy to have the central administration's support in doing so. At the same time, as their oath of office made clear, their responsibilities were onerous. For their part, the great nobles of the court who served as provincial governors can hardly have regretted losing functions that brought them little but trouble.

Ivan's government clearly saw the advantages of the new system for, over the next decades, it introduced district elders to more and more areas of the country. The idea that the royal government would function more effectively if it made local elites responsible for their own fate produced an even more sweeping reform of the local administration within a few years. In the mid-1550s, a series of decrees created a new group of officials (the *zemskie starosty*), drawn primarily from the merchants and prosperous peasants, to serve as tax collectors. Like the guba elders, they at first appeared in a few localities, particularly in the northernmost regions of the country, ostensibly in response to the petitions of local leaders.[14] In the mid-sixteenth century, the north was a productive laboratory for administrative experiments because its population, which consisted mainly of peasants, merchants, and churchpeople, was enjoying a period of unprecedented prosperity. In 1555, Ivan's government created a radically new system of administration by extending the network of zemskie starosty across much of the realm. In the next few years, thanks to the creation of the two new types of local officials, governors of the old type (namestniki) disappeared from most parts of the country.

Once again, apparent decentralization served to increase the effectiveness of the central bureaucracy. Unlike the old governors, the local merchants or peasants who received the onerous job of collecting taxes from their fellow citizens had little to gain from cheating the royal exchequer under whose supervision they functioned. In addition, the taxpayers paid twice the previous rate for the privilege of taxing themselves. By way of contrast, Ivan's noble courtiers—the men who had normally served as governors—probably saw the change as a boon. They no longer had to spend time administering remote and often poor districts and, in compensation for the loss of this dubious privilege, they received monetary payments from the treasury's increased revenue.[15]

Parallel with the new system of local administration were new modes of establishing national priorities with the support of social elites. In Ivan's reign, as before, the tsar and his inner circle of boyars constituted the nerve center of the government. In the first years of his majority— beginning in 1549 according to one version[16]—he and his advisers summoned assemblies of his leading subjects, known in later generations as the *zemskii sobor* or "assembly of the land," to gain their support for governmental policy. Over the course of the next century, the zemskii sobor met at irregular intervals, when summoned by the tsar. Its composition was equally unpredictable. Sometimes it consisted only of the boyars and the leaders of the church; on other occasions, the government reached out to include members of the lesser nobility who happened to be in Moscow and perhaps even merchants and artisans from the capital.[17]

Even though at the height of its development this institution bore a rough resemblance to the parliaments or national estates of the monarchies of western Europe, it would be a mistake to view it as an embryonic representative institution. With rare exceptions in the early seventeenth century, as Kliuchevskii pointed out long ago, the zemskii sobor served not as the authentic voice of Muscovy's leading citizens but as a means by which the government mobilized the support of its leading servitors. Even the most widely representative zemskii sobor of Ivan's reign, the assembly of 1566, did not meet to decide whether to continue the war with Poland; instead, it was called to lend its support to decisions that the tsar and his advisers had already made.[18]

As a result of Ivan's reforms, the so-called middle classes of Muscovite society—the provincial nobles and merchants—undeniably played a more prominent role in public life than before. At the same time, it would be a mistake to see their participation in the zemskii sobor and the local administration as the germ of representative government. The modern word which is most applicable to these institutional arrangements of the mid-sixteenth century is "mobilization." Nobles and merchants were invited to support the government and work for it, not to help it make basic decisions about the future development of government and society. Participation had its price.

For these reasons, it is misleading to look to Ivan's reforms for signs of political modernization or convergence with emerging western European patterns of representative government or civil rights. The institutional scope, legal implications, and social impact of the reforms of the 1540s and 1550s were quite limited. Although a veritable golden age in comparison with the horrors to come, the reform period of the reign was a time of freedom only in the most relative sense. The creation of institutions of political mobilization went hand in hand with the increasingly rigid codification of ecclesiastical ideology and the repression of religious dissenters.

However we interpret the period of reforms, the oprichnina (1565-72) represents something dramatically different. Where it fits in a discussion of political reform is not easy to determine. The narrative sources describing the dramatic scenes Ivan IV staged in the first weeks of 1565 demonstrate that he intended to make radical changes in his mode of governing. Nevertheless, the word "reform" seems a singularly inappropriate characterization of the oprichnina for at least two reasons. The tsar's statements and gestures—and his subsequent actions—showed that he intended to make not gradual but sudden and dramatic changes in the body politic. Moreover, the changes he made can scarcely be interpreted as steps to improve the administration of the realm or better the lot of downtrodden groups in society.

Before briefly reviewing the central features of the oprichnina, we should remind ourselves of the international background against which it took place. At the very beginning of 1558, Ivan had sent his troops into Livonia. After initial victories, the Muscovite advance had slowed to a halt, and, by 1565, the country was locked in an exhausting and apparently endless war against a coalition of European rivals led by Poland and Sweden. The oprichnina sprang from a military and diplomatic stalement and the frustrations which it produced.

Thanks to the detailed studies of several Soviet scholars, the central features of the oprichnina's structure and activities are well known.[19] From the beginning, Ivan made clear that, in order to escape from the clutches of the boyars and chancery officials and the leaders of the church whom he collectively accused of treason, he intended to create for himself a separate administration, court, and army. To support himself and the men who would serve in these new institutions, the tsar took direct personal control of substantial areas of the country, selected primarily for their promise as sources of tax revenues.[20] In the oprichnina lands in central Muscovy, Ivan undertook a review of the nobility. Those who satisfied him of their loyalty joined his private army; those who failed the test had their lands confiscated and were forced to find new estates outside of the oprichnina's boundaries.

Oddly enough, Ivan arranged for the Boyar Council to administer the *zemshchina* (the areas of the country outside of his private principality) and report to him only the most important matters of state.

Thus, Muscovy suddenly found itself with two administrations, two armies, and two separate groups of territories, one ruled directly by Ivan IV and the other by the aristocrats of his old court.[21]

The oprichnina's most notorious feature was a reign of terror designed to purge those whom Ivan regarded as his enemies. On a number of occasions during the course of the seven-year experiment, groups of prominent courtiers and officials were executed on charges of treason, often with bloodcurdling brutality. Many times the victims were not only men of prominence but also their more obscure male kin and, on some occasions, their retainers and servants.

The roster of Ivan's victims included prominent aristocratic court- iers—both princes and non-titled servitors—leading chancery officials; Metropolitan Filipp, the head of the church; other prominent clergy; and Vladimir Andreevich of Staritsa, head of the only cadet branch of the ruling dynasty. Most startling of the victims was an entire city— Novgorod—which oprichnina troops occupied and sacked with great loss of life after Ivan accused its population of treasonous negotiations with the Poles.[22] Finally, as students of more recent reigns of terror have come to expect, the oprichnina devoured its own leaders; Ivan's most prominent advisers and officials mounted the scaffold in their turn.

For more than a century, historians have debated the meaning of these actions.[23] Those who come closest to characterizing the oprichnina as an attempt at reform argue that Ivan was attempting a project of "social engineering" designed to break the power of the great princely clans of the court and strengthen the middle classes of Muscovite so- ciety—the provincial service nobility and the urban elite.[24] A more recent restatement of this general position argues that, in purging Vla- dimir Andreevich and Metropolitan Filipp and in sacking Novgorod, Ivan was attempting, however misguidedly, to destroy the remnants of "feudal fragmentation" in Muscovite society.[25] The proponents of both positions see the oprichnina as a continuation of Ivan's earlier reforms with more violent methods.

These interpretations have some distinct merits. In one episode, as a recent study emphasizes, the tsar uprooted about two hundred nobles whose estates fell within the borders of the oprichnina and banished them to the region of Kazan'. There most of the exiles were given only very small holdings to which they received conditional title. As the proponents of the "social engineering" hypothesis point out, princes from Starodub, Iaroslavl', and Rostov—some of them powerful and wealthy—made up the largest single component of exiles.[26]

Even here, however, the data raise troubling problems for those who see the oprichnina as a kind of reform. A large number of the exiles were obscure men with little or no power either at court or in their home regions. Moreover, the tsar's treatment of the nobles of these areas was extremely inconsistent; some of the local princes were not exiled at all, and most of those banished were pardoned within about a year and allowed to return home.[27]

Recent studies have criticized the "social engineering" hypothesis on other grounds as well. If the oprichnina was an attempt to attack the aristocracy and strengthen the lesser nobility, it is difficult to explain why the social composition of the oprichnina court and that of the zemshchina were virtually identical.[28] Aristocrats and lesser nobles — sometimes members of the same clans — served in both. For these and other reasons it makes little sense to interpret Ivan's experiments as projects of conscious social engineering. The issue of aristocratic power was genuine, but Ivan's attempt to deal with it was neither realistic nor consistent.

If the oprichnina cannot be viewed as a "reform," even by the most elastic use of that word, was it a "counterreform"? Use of the latter term is justified only if we regard the reforms of the 1550s as steps toward political modernization in a Western sense. Moreover, "counterreform" implies that the reforms were reversed or that the oprichnina was directed against the middle classes of Muscovite society who presumably benefited from the earlier changes. Most recent historians would accept the general proposition that, in the oprichnina, the tsar and his inner circle of advisers were aiming at the same goal they had pursued earlier — more effective control over the population and lands of the realm. In addition, the new institutions created in the reform period continued to do their work. The district elders functioned well into the seventeenth century, and the zemskii sobor went on meeting intermittently. Indeed, the liveliest assembly of the sixteenth century took place in 1566 in the midst of the oprichnina.

The social impact of Ivan's experiment was extremely ambiguous. Some lesser nobles suffered death or loss of their lands, while others thrived. The experience of the merchants was equally complex. At one extreme, Ivan favored the wealthy northern regions with their merchant and peasant population by including them in his private principality. On the other, he ravaged Novgorod, the wealthiest trading city of his realm, and executed many of its people.

These observations in no way undermine the common sense judgment that there was a world of difference between the reforms of the 1550s and the oprichnina. The differences lie, however, not so much in the objectives of royal policy or their social implications as in the impatience and brutality with which the oprichnina regime pursued them and in the devastating consequences of its actions.

The indiscriminate and often sadistic methods of the oprichnina regime appear to reflect more than anything else the complex and troubled personality of its leader, Ivan IV. A number of historians have suggested that Ivan suffered from paranoia in the oprichnina years. Some of his actions during the period, including his request for a guarantee of political asylum in England, dramatically testify to his exaggerated concern for his own safety.[29] At times, burdened by his fears and chronic illness, he seems to have been obsessed with the need to escape from the dangers of leadership in one way or another.[30]

To put it bluntly, the meaning of the oprichnina is to be sought above all in the realm of psychology. Ivan IV created the oprichnina to keep himself and his realm safe from enemies, real and imagined. Individual paranoia begot social pathology; the tsar's desperate search for security destroyed his subjects' confidence in the order and predictability of life. Years of absurd denunciations, sudden arrests, and horrifying executions left Muscovite society numb and made Ivan IV the terrible and awe-inspiring figure of literature and legend.

However real the substance of Ivan's fears, the social, economic, and political results of the oprichnina were a genuine disaster. Although it did not revolutionize social relations in Muscovy or destroy the princely aristocracy or any other social group, it killed off a wide variety of Russians, ranging from aristocrats to the poorest artisans, peasants, and domestics. One can easily imagine the demoralization and shock of those who survived the whirlwind. Moreover, the oprichnina's operations contributed to the economic decline and social dislocation of much of Muscovy, particularly the Novgorodian lands. The sack of the great trading city contributed significantly to its rapid decline into a run-of-the-mill provincial town. The depredations of Ivan's bodyguards, combined with natural disasters and rising taxes to feed the war in Livonia, forced thousands of peasants to flee from their ancestral homes to the remote forests, the open steppe, or the estates of the wealthiest landlords who could offer them minimal protection and support. Their action, in turn, forced the government to set legal limits on their movement in order to protect the interests of the poorer service nobles and the royal treasury. The enserfment of the peasantry was in sight.

As a program of political reform or enforced social change—if it was ever intended as such—the oprichnina was a dismal failure. After 1572, just as before, the tsar ruled in collaboration with the aristocratic clans of his court. Many individual aristocrats perished alongside their fellow citizens of humbler rank, but their surviving kin in most cases succeeded

in preserving their clans' position next to the throne, where they were joined by parvenues like the Godunovs who had risen to prominence as *oprichniki*. Moreover, as noted, the oprichnina made virtually no lasting impact on the institutional structure of the Muscovite state.[31] The central bureaucratic administration continued to grow, the local elders to function, and the zemskii sobor to meet.

Finally, the shattering experience of the oprichnina made leading Muscovites leery of reform of any kind. Except for their reactions to the tidal wave of peasant flight, the regimes that ruled Muscovy for several decades after 1572 showed little of the creativity of Ivan's government in the 1550s. Even the collapse of the administration and the unravelling of society during the Time of Troubles produced no significant change in the structure or legal foundation of government or in social relations. Only in the mid-seventeenth century, under the pressure of international military and diplomatic competition, did Aleksei Mikhailovich and his advisers return to the kind of incremental reform measures that had marked the early years of Ivan the Terrible's reign.

The nature, course, and fate of the reforms of Ivan IV offer much food for reflection about the prospects for reform of Russian institutions and society in our own day. Some of the lessons of Ivan IV's reign are almost too obvious to mention. A political system in which a monarch or ruling clique exercises power unchecked by legal limitations, competing institutions, or independent social forces is dangerous to the well-being of the ruled. "Harebrained schemes" implemented through terror are likely to have disastrous consequences for rulers and ruled alike. Beyond such truisms, how are we to appraise the impact of Ivan's reforms and of the oprichnina?

Yanov has suggested that the oprichnina was the point at which Russian political culture decisively turned toward authoritarianism and away from political modernization. To make such a case, one must show that Russia had the potential to develop along western European lines until 1565 and that the oprichnina destroyed that potential. In social terms, if we follow Yanov's categories, we must argue that the middle classes of Muscovite society were growing in power and independence until the oprichnina fatally weakened them.

Neither position can be maintained without very serious qualifications. The oprichnina's impact on the middle classes, the lesser nobility and merchants, was ambiguous; for example, the tsar and his minions ravaged the commercial city of Novgorod but left the new system of local administration, staffed largely by local nobles and merchants, intact. The primary reasons why the merchants and lesser nobles failed to become a middle class in the Western sense were the former were too few and weak outside of the far north, and the latter were dependents of the crown.

Moreover, although the reforms of the 1540s and 1550s made a number of beneficial alterations in the workings of the Muscovite administration and army and strengthened the middle classes of Russian society in some ways, they did not change the fundamental structure of the Muscovite government or alter social relations significantly. In 1565 there were no constitutional inhibitions or social or institutional barriers to prevent the creation of the oprichnina. Instead, the primary limitation on the monarch's freedom of action was the tight network of aristocratic court clans with their traditional monopoly of high office, their notions of social precedence and honor, and their matrimonial interconnections. The oprichnina cut some of the threads of this spider's web but did not destroy it.

Speculation about the emotional and intellectual consequences of political acts is a particularly dangerous undertaking. Nevertheless, I would suggest the oprichnina's primary impact on the development of Russian political culture was probably its contribution, along with defeat in the Livonian War and the foreign occupations in the Time of Troubles, to a climate of fearful conservatism — a paralyzing fear of the risks involved in any significant reforms — which gripped all leading groups in Muscovite society in the first decades of the seventeenth century.

In its methods and many of its specific actions, the oprichnina was an aberration, a bloody detour on the road of Russia's political development. In its general objectives, however, it did not represent a repudiation of the goals of the regimes of the young Ivan IV and his predecessors. Muscovite autocracy rested on the cooptation of the aristocratic clans of east Russia into the imperial political and social system, the creation of numerous lesser nobility as military servitors and dependents of the monarchy, and the creation of a rudimentary but crudely effective bureaucracy. All three of these processes began long before Ivan IV's reign and went on through the years of reform and the oprichnina. It was in this sense that Ivan's reign constituted a milestone in the development of the Russian autocracy.

NOTES

1. A. A. Zimin, *Reformy Ivana Groznogo* (Moscow, 1960). See also N. E. Nosov, *Stanovlenie soslovno-predstavitel'nykh uchrezhdenii v Rossii* (Leningrad, 1969).

2. Since Muscovite times, there has not even been a consensus on the locus of decision-making authority at Ivan's court. Scholars have most commonly assumed that the tsar ruled as well as reigned from the time he reached the age of consent. A persistent minority opinion, however, argues that an inner circle of royal relatives and advisers governed in Ivan's name, at least during the so-called period of reform, roughly 1547-60. Since we have very little information about the inner workings of Ivan's regime, it is probably safest to assume that the balance of power within the inner circles of government changed as the tsar passed through the successive stages of life and counselors and favorites came and went.

The notion that Ivan's advisers ruled in his name up until the 1560s first appears in the letters traditionally attributed to Ivan and Prince A. M. Kurbskii, published in *The Correspondence between Prince A. M. Kurbsky and Tsar Ivan IV of Russia, 1564-1579,* ed. and trans. J. L. I. Fennell (Cambridge, 1955), and *Perepiska Ivana Groznogo s Andreem Kurbskim,* ed. Ia. S. Lur'e and Iu. D. Rykov (Leningrad, 1979). For a dramatic recent statement of this view, see Edward L. Keenan, "Vita: Ivan Vasil'evich, Terrible Czar; 1530-84," *Harvard Magazine* 80, no. 3 (1979):48-49.

3. For a brief presentation of Yanov's model of political modernity, see his essay, "In the Grip of the Adversarial Paradigm: The Case of Nikita Sergeevich Khrushchev in Restrospect," herein.

4. For the latest—and particularly illuminating—analysis of court politics during Ivan's minority, see Nancy Shields Kollmann, *Kinship and Politics: The Making of the Muscovite Political System, 1345-1547* (Stanford, 1987), pp. 161-79.

5. For a partial exception, see *Pamiatniki Russkogo Prava,* 8 vols. (Moscow, 1952-63), 4:575-76 (hereafter *PRP*).

6. For the text of the sudebnik, see *PRP,* 4:233-61. See also Zimin, *Reformy,* pp. 348-65, and Horace A. Dewey, "The 1550 *Sudebnik* as an Instrument of Reform," *Jahrbücher für Geschichte Osteuropas* 10 (1962):161-80.

7. The most readily available edition of the text describing the council's activities is *Stoglav,* ed. E. D. Kozhanchikov (St. Petersburg, 1863). See also Jack Edward Kollmann, Jr., "The Moscow Stoglav ('Hundred Chapters') Church Council of 1551" (Ph.D. dissertation, University of Michigan, 1978). The text of the provisions on ecclesiastical landholdings is reprinted in *PRP,* 4:523-24.

8. S. O. Shmidt, *Stanovlenie rossiiskogo samoderzhavstva: Issledovanie sotsial' no-politicheskoi istorii vremeni Ivana Groznogo* (Moscow, 1973), pp. 262-307.

9. *PRP,* 4:582-83.

10. Ibid., pp. 581-82; Zimin, *Reformy,* pp. 366-71. Zimin argues that, in spite of its good intentions, Ivan's government could not carry out the reform for lack of available land. As he points out, relatively few of the men named in the project are listed in the cadastres of the Moscow region in subsequent decades.

11. *Polnoe sobranie russkikh letopisei,* 39 vols. to date (St. Petersburg, Moscow, 1841-), 13:268-69 (hereafter *PSRL*); Zimin, *Reformy,* pp. 437-40.

12. Zimin, *Reformy,* pp. 328-33, 421-22, 449-60; see also Peter Bowman Brown, "Early Modern Bureaucracy: The Evolution of the Chancellery System from Ivan III to Peter the Great, 1478-1717" (Ph.D. dissertation, University of Chicago, 1978), pp. 57-60. Some scholars, notably A. K. Leont'ev, in *Obrazovanie prikaznoi systemy upravleniia v Russkom gosudarstve: Iz istorii sozdaniia tsentral'nogo gosudarstvennogo apparata v kontse XV-pervoi polovine XVI v.* (Moscow, 1961), argue that the prikazy emerged earlier and more gradually over the first decades of the sixteenth century.

13. *PRP,* 4:176-88; Zimin, *Reformy,* pp. 253-58.

14. *PRP,* 4:188-97.

15. Nosov, *Stanovlenie,* pp. 240-526; Zimin, *Reformy,* pp. 422-36; Edward L. Keenan's review of Nosov's *Stanovlenie* in *Kritika* 7 (1970-71):67-96.

Why, a sceptical reader may ask, was the restructuring of the local administration not undertaken earlier if its benefits were so obvious to all concerned? What we know about Muscovy in Ivan IV's time—Nosov's meticulously assembled data, for example—suggests at least two interconnected answers. First, the local elites—minor nobles, merchants, and wealthy peasants—who provided its personnel seem to have emerged slowly in numbers sufficient to support the reform over the course of the late fifteenth and first half of the sixteenth centuries. Second, reform requires leaders determined to make significant changes in political, economic, legal, or social relations; its actions in other spheres indicate that Ivan's government in the 1550s was just such a regime.

16. *PRP,* 4:575-76.

17. Shmidt, *Stanovlenie,* pp. 120-261.

18. V. O. Kliuchevskii, *Sochineniia,* 8 vols. (Moscow, 1956-59), 2:373-95; A. A. Zimin, *Oprichnina Ivana Groznogo* (Moscow, 1964), pp. 159-211. Some participants in the assembly of 1566 voiced their opposition to the government's policy of continued war—the only known instance in Ivan's reign.

19. For a convenient summary of the actions of Ivan's government during the oprichnina, see Robert O. Crummey, *The Formation of Muscovy, 1304-1613* (London and New York, 1987), pp. 161-72.

20. S. B. Veselovskii, *Issledovaniia po istorii oprichniny* (Moscow, 1963), pp. 156-63, 167-77.

21. *PSRL,* 13:391-95; Zimin, *Oprichnina,* pp. 127-34; R. G. Skrynnikov, *Rossiia nakanune "smutnogo vremeni"* (Moscow, 1981), pp. 83-87.

22. See Robert O. Crummey, "New Wine in Old Bottles? Ivan IV and Novgorod," *Russian History* 14 (1987):61-76.

23. On the historiography of the reign, see Robert O. Crummey, "Ivan the Terrible," in *Windows on the Russian Past,* ed. Samuel H. Baron and Nancy W. Heer (Columbus, Ohio, 1977), pp. 391-403.

24. For the best known statement of this view, see the works of S. F. Platonov, for example, *Ocherki po istorii Smuty v moskovskom gosudarstve XVI-XVII vv.* (St. Petersburg, 1910), pp. 131-50, and his *Ivan the Terrible,* trans. Joseph L. Wieczynski (Gulf Breeze, Fla., 1974).

25. This is the central theme of Zimin, *Oprichnina.*

26. R. G. Skrynnikov, *Nachalo oprichniny* (Leningrad, 1966), pp. 271-98; Skrynnikov, *Rossiia nakanune "smutnogo vremeni,"* pp. 89-94. Skrynnikov's interpretation of the oprichnina is complex and combines elements of several earlier schools of interpretation with new insights of his own.

27. Veselovskii, *Issledovaniia po istorii oprichniny,* pp. 149-55.

28. V. B. Kobrin, "Sostav oprichnogo dvora Ivan Groznogo," in *Arkheograficheskii Ezhegodnik za 1959 god* (Moscow, 1960), pp. 16-91.

29. For a review of the evidence, see Crummey, *Formation,* p. 166.

30. In addition, as I have argued elsewhere, some of Ivan's targets in the oprichnina—the Staritsa appanage and Novgorod—were the ghosts of once threatening opponents which had been subdued by his immediate predecessors and thus could offer him no real resistance. Crummey, "New Wine." On Ivan's paranoia, see also Richard Hellie, "In Search of Ivan the Terrible," in Platonov, *Ivan the Terrible,* pp. ix-xxxiv.

31. P. A. Sadikov, *Ocherki po istorii oprichniny* (Moscow and Leningrad, 1950), stresses the development of the central administrative chanceries, especially the revenue-gathering chetverti, as a result of the oprichnina.

"Constitutional" Reform during the Time of Troubles

ROBERT O. CRUMMEY

The search for a usable past is a legitimate exercise. Those who undertake it, however, have goals distinctly different from those scholars who attempt to understand the past in its own terms. To be sure, twentieth-century men and women cannot travel to another society in another age—seventeenth-century Russia, for example—without the cultural baggage, the political and philosophical assumptions, of their own time and place. Nevertheless, the purposes of historians and historical polemicists are essentially different.

Writing a paper on "constitutional" reform during the Time of Troubles by definition means projecting nineteenth- and twentieth-century categories and concerns back into the seventeenth century. First of all, I question whether the concept of "reform," in the sense of a conscious restructuring of governmental institutions or social relations, would mean very much to medieval men and women. That, of course, is not to say that pre-modern governments were not capable of taking practical steps to solve particular problems or achieve particular goals. In Russian history, the reforms of Ivan IV's government in the 1540s and 1550s are an obvious case in point. Second, in the Russian case, seventeenth-century writers who recorded the turbulent events which took place between 1598 and 1613 paid very little attention to changes in the structure and functioning of government. They were far more interested in other matters—the struggle of Orthodox Muscovites to preserve their political independence and religious heritage from the attacks of Polish Roman Catholics, for example.[1]

The subject also, by implication, introduces the elusive notion of "political culture," "the system of empirical beliefs, expressive symbols, and values which defines the situation in which political action takes place." In other words, it forces us to deal with the "subjective orientation to politics."[2]

Interest in the so-called constitutional agreements which rulers of the Time of Troubles made with their subjects began in the nineteenth century. Solov'ev gave them substantial attention but ultimately dismissed them as temporary expedients without lasting significance.[3] V. O. Kliuchevskii took over his teacher's scheme of interpretation and transformed it into the striking statement that still dominates thinking on the subject. In his view, conservative leaders of Muscovite society made three serious attempts to limit the tsar's freedom of action by obliging him to observe the due process of the law and decide matters of national policy only in consultation with his most prominent subjects, the members of the Boyar Council or, in some cases, the *zemskii sobor* (assembly of the land). At his accession in 1606, Tsar Vasilii Shuiskii made these guarantees to his people and sealed the bargain with an exchange of oaths. Then, in 1610, groups of boyars included such terms in the two agreements they made with King Sigismund III that were designed to enthrone his son, Władysław, as tsar. Finally, Mikhail Romanov, on ascending the throne in 1613, gave a written guarantee that he would consult the boyars on all important matters.[4]

Kliuchevskii's use of sources was thorough but highly selective. A number of narrative sources mention Shuiskii's compact with his subjects, and several texts of the new tsar's proclamation and the people's oath of allegiance have come down to us.[5] There is also ample solid evidence of the conditions under which the Tushino boyars led by M. G. Saltykov and later the leaders of the "boyar government" in Moscow accepted Władysław as tsar.[6] As for Mikhail's purported compact with the boyars, however, no contemporary record survives; it is mentioned only in much later underground or foreign sources. Most important was Kotoshikhin's exposé of Muscovite life and institutions written in exile in Sweden.[7] Interestingly enough, Kliuchevskii limited his treatment of attempts at reform during the Time of Troubles to documents describing the relations between tsars and their leading subjects; his discussion left aside the ways in which the leaders of the movements of national revival—first Liapunov and Trubetskoi and then Minin and Pozharskii—made decisions and attempted to administer the realm. These interesting arrangements did not address his concerns since, being obviously temporary, they had no long-range constitutional significance.

In his classic monograph on the *Smuta* (Troubles), S. F. Platonov took a very different tack. In keeping with his general approach to the period, he interpreted the statements defining the rulers' responsibilities to their subjects in sociological terms, as the temporary expedients adopted by competing factions or social groups. Most were issued by and for the group of powerful boyar clans which, by tradition, stood around the throne of the tsars. Platonov placed particular stress on precisely those documents which to Kliuchevskii had least significance, namely the regulations issued in 1611 by Prokopii Liapunov and the other leaders of the first national movement. Although Liapunov's forces were a motley crew ranging from renegade boyars to cossacks and runaway slaves, he argued, his policies were designed to satisfy his more conservative supporters, the provincial nobles and prosperous towns-people who wanted to reaffirm the prevailing structure of state and society founded on serfdom.[8]

Historians of Muscovy thus once again find themselves weighing familiar historiographical alternatives. Whose views—Kliuchevskii's or Platonov's—are more instructive about Muscovite politics? Or were the conclusions of both correct given their presuppositions?[9] Before deciding, we must, of course, look at what the documents do and do not say.

According to a number of sources, Vasilii Shuiskii publicly swore to respect the rights of his subjects when he became tsar in May, 1606. The most common version of the text contains several revealing stipulations. It begins with an assertion that the new ruler had ascended the throne by hereditary right since he was a descendant of Riurik, Aleksandr Nevskii, and the princes of Suzdal'. Since he wished to bring peace and well-being (*blagodenstvo*) to his realm, he promised to judge his subjects justly and honestly and to protect them from "all kinds of arbitrariness (*oto vsiakogo nasil'stva*)." In particular, he promised not to condemn to death the relatives of anyone accused of a crime or confiscate their property without a proper trial by the tsar and the Boyar Council (*"ne osudia istinnym sudom s boiary svoimi"*). The document implies—but does not explicitly state—that the principal accused will be accorded due process. Shuiskii extended the same guarantees to merchants and traders (*"gosti"* and *"torgovye liudi"*) and their families. Finally, he made a firm commitment to expose and punish false witnesses.[10]

The *Novyi letopisets* (*New Chronicler*), written after the Romanovs had consolidated their rule, summarizes Shuiskii's oath in simpler and more colorful language. "I will not do anything bad (*nikakova durna*) to anybody without consultation (*bez soboru*). If the father is guilty, nothing will be done to the son; if the son is guilty and his father did not know about it, nothing evil will be done to the father." With whom the monarch is to consult is not made clear. The chronicle adds that the boyars and others told Shuiskii not to take such an oath since the action was unprecedented in the history of the Muscovite state.[11] Why the boyars objected is a matter of dispute. By stressing the public circumstances in which Shuiskii made his pledge and the chronicler's choice of the word *"sobor"* (council, assembly), Kliuchevskii argued that the new tsar promised the zemskii sobor a regular voice in political and judicial affairs, thus, in effect, impinging on the boyars' traditional prerogatives. In Platonov's opinion, the chronicler simply meant what he wrote—the oath was unnecessary to the boyars since it restated traditional principles.[12]

The coup d'état which overthrew Shuiskii in July, 1610, left the imperial throne vacant. No native aristocrat emerged to fill the void. All the same, there was no lack of candidates. Courtiers of the Second False Dmitrii had earlier in the year made a treaty with King Sigismund III of Poland setting the conditions under which his son, Prince Władysław, might become tsar.[13] After Shuiskii's fall, the Polish candidacy won wide support among the traditional leaders of Muscovite society, who were desperate to preserve their position amid widening political and social chaos. A group of boyars, led by M. G. Saltykov, concluded a treaty with the king's representative in Moscow, Hetman Żółkiewski.[14]

The text of the treaty of August 17, 1610, is remarkably similar to an earlier pact which the king concluded with certain of Shuiskii's opponents on February 14 of the same year. Many of the two treaties' stipulations, for example, arose naturally from the immediate situation—the candidacy of a Polish, Roman Catholic prince for the throne of the tsars. Under Władysław, relations between Muscovy and Poland would be reconstituted on a new footing: the two powers would support one another against common enemies and open their borders to each other's merchants. In addition, Żółkiewski promised that Władysław would preserve Eastern Orthodoxy and respect its leaders. He also pledged that the prince would honor Muscovite institutional traditions and not tamper with existing social arrangements. Except under very special circumstances, Poles were not to replace Russians in positions of authority within Muscovy.

Crucial was the treaties' insistence that the new tsar would abide by the legal traditions of the Muscovite state and the *Sudebnik* (Law Code) of 1550. Specifically, Żółkiewski promised, Władysław would consult the boyars on all important matters of national policy. Without the consent of the Boyar Duma, no one was to be imprisoned, have his estates confiscated, or his rank changed without cause. No one was to be guilty by association; wives and children, for example, were not to suffer for the sins of husbands and fathers. Moreover, the treaty specifically recognized the right of other Muscovites to a voice in national politics. If the boyars and "all the land" (in other words, the zemskii sobor) wanted to change the law to improve the judicial system, they were free to do so. In addition, if the leaders of the Orthodox church, the boyars, or other leading laymen had objections to the stipulations of the treaty, the new tsar would discuss these concerns with all of these groups and "the whole land."

As events unfolded, the boyars' treaty with Żółkiewski proved to be only a statement of good intentions and aspirations. Władysław's candidacy quickly foundered on the rock of his father's ambition and missionary zeal; the Muscovite ambassadors who went to the king to negotiate the details of his accession found themselves prisoners of war. The treaty is nevertheless significant, in part because of what it tells us about the goals of the men who made it.

The decree issued by the leaders of the first national movement on June 30, 1611, had radically different objectives. Most of its detailed stipulations express two sentiments—disdain for the boyars and a longing for a strong, stable government. First, Liapunov and his associates promised their lesser noble followers economic justice. In particular, they announced their intention to confiscate estates unjustly seized by boyars and those which Sigismund III had granted to his Russian supporters. They vowed to distribute these lands to patriotic rank-and-file nobles beginning with the most needy. Second, to carry out these tasks and to bring order to the realm, the movement's leaders committed themselves to reestablishing the central administrative chanceries (*prikazy*) which had recently fallen into decay.[15]

The document says comparatively little about the political structure of the realm and the administration of justice. Its implications, however, are remarkably radical. It opens with the statement that the members of the national movement from boyars down to provincial servitors (*"deti boiarskie vsekh gorodov"*), cossacks, and various other servitors had chosen Liapunov, Prince D. T. Trubetskoi, and Hetman I. M. Zarutskii as their leaders and promised to obey them. The council of leaders was to act as a government (*"buduchi v pravitel'stve"*) and to give justice. These "boyars," however, were not to pass sentences of death or exile without the approval of the "land." Moreover, the document concludes, if these leaders do not do their job, the "land" would replace them with others (*"nam vseiu zemleiu vol'no Boiar i Voevod peremeniti, i v to mesto vybrati inykh, pogovoria so vseiu zemleiu"*).[16]

The implications of the "boyars'" proclamation are clear and startling: in the temporary government of the first national movement, sovereignty resided in the whole militia, the entire "land." At the same time, the long-term significance of these arrangements is unclear. The primary purpose of the movement of national revival was to expel the Poles from Moscow and restore the monarchy. Until it achieved these goals, any administrative measures or legal guarantees were, by definition, temporary. Since the movement fell apart on the verge of victory, we will never know what its leaders would have done after they had selected a new tsar.

The second national movement, under the leadership of Minin and Pozharskii, succeeded where its predecessor had failed. In 1613, after intricate negotiations and lobbying, the "land" chose Mikhail Romanov as tsar. Notwithstanding Kotoshikhin's claims, it is most unlikely that the new monarch repeated Vasilii Shuiskii's public guarantees to his subjects. If he had, the narrative and documentary sources of his own day would probably have mentioned them.[17] Indeed, it is possible that later authors confused the circumstances of Shuiskii's accession with Mikhail's. More significant for our purposes, the sources which do mention such promises give very few specifics: Kotoshikhin claimed that all rulers after Ivan IV until Aleksei Mikhailovich promised not to execute anybody without due process and to consult the Boyar Duma on all important matters.[18] By and large, seventeenth-century tsars ruled according to these precepts; the practices of their government, however, appear to derive not from any formal commitments to their subjects but from the structure and personal composition of the court and central administration under the first Romanovs.

What were the main concerns of the "reformers" of the Time of Troubles? Most fundamental, the promises of Shuiskii and Żółkiewskii in Władysław's name reflected a reaction against the arbitrariness and use of guilt by association by Boris Godunov and, by implication, Ivan IV.[19] Members of the ruling elite of Muscovite society yearned for guarantees that, if they fell into disfavor, they and their closest relatives would receive a hearing before the Boyar Council and if innocent would not be sentenced to death or exile. Shuiskii, in particular, stressed the need to protect the innocent wives, parents, children, and brothers of accused traitors. No one, however, questioned the right of the tsar to accuse any of his subjects, even the most powerful boyars, of treason and order their execution if, following due process of the law, they were found guilty.

As Platonov correctly pointed out, these declarations and agreements were the work of the inner circle of boyar clans at the Muscovite court which had traditionally advised the tsars, led their armies, governed the provinces, and lorded it over the rest of society. Under Ivan IV and Godunov, the boyars' power and prominence had made them especially vulnerable to royal caprice. Understandably, the network of boyar clans, bloodied but not destroyed by the *oprichnina,* used every chance to protect its members from the horrors of the recent past.[20]

Two of their best opportunities came with the accessions of Shuiskii and Mikhail Romanov, charter members of the boyar elite. These men and their kin knew first hand what it cost to fall into royal disfavor. In 1606, the boyars received formal public guarantees. If the testimony of the *Novyi letopisets,* a later work of Romanov propaganda, can be trusted, they advised against such an unprecedented public statement, probably arguing their need for personal security could be met without it. Certainly, if this was their reasoning, seventeenth-century experience proved them correct. By and large, the Romanovs respected the lives and property of their leading subjects—many of whom were also their kin by marriage. In the comparatively rare cases in which members of the Boyar Duma were executed or exiled, the government of the new dynasty took great pains to observe due legal process.[21]

The proclamations and arrangements which we have examined, however, reflected far more than the simple self-interest of the boyar clans. Shuiskii's oath promised the merchants and traders that their relatives too would no longer suffer from guilt by association. Yanov has suggested that this provision arose from the boyars' awareness that, if they were to enjoy the protection of the law, they would have to extend it to others.[22] This hypothesis projects onto the boyars modern modes of thought, crediting them with a broader, more comprehensive view of political life than the sources of the time reflect. To explain the promise to the leaders of urban society, we should look instead at the specific political circumstances of the time.

The documents reflect the chaotic conditions in Muscovy between 1606 and 1611. Shuiskii's oath was part of the desperate campaign of a weak, conservative regime of dubious legitimacy to win the allegiance of as many Muscovites as possible. The boyars who negotiated with Żółkiewski and the leaders of the first national movement felt the same pressure to win supporters to their cause. In both of the latter instances, moreover, Saltykov, Liapunov, and their fellows knew that their mandate was temporary; their primary purpose was to fill a vacancy on the throne. Thus, it seems the promises and commitments which they made were temporary expedients designed to deal with an immediate emergency or appeals for support. They do not represent attempts to make basic changes in the structure and functioning of the autocracy.

The authors of these documents described them as the reaffirmation of native tradition. Were they in fact? To which tradition did they return? The rhetorical assertion that the tsars consulted the boyars on administrative and legal questions runs through the *sudebniki* (legal codes) of 1497 and 1550 and occurs regularly in the decrees of Ivan IV's government, particularly during the 1550s. As Article 98 of the Sudebnik of 1550 puts it, "If there are new matters and they are not recorded in this Code, they are to be dealt with according to the Sovereign's report and with the assent of all of the boyars. And these matters are to be added to this Code."[23] As far as we know, previous Muscovite rulers, including Ivan IV, regularly met with the members of the Boyar Duma who were in the capital.[24] Who actually decided the direction of Muscovite domestic and foreign policy is, of course, another matter. It is entirely possible that the Duma only gave formal assent to decisions actually made by an inner circle of royal advisers and favorites. In institutional terms, however, the Duma functioned as the highest judicial instance of the realm and, through the most powerful chancery officials (the *dumnye d'iaki*), oversaw the operations of the prikazy (chanceries).

As we might expect, the promises of the tsars or would-be tsars to their subjects appeal to a generalized past. Their authors unequivocally rejected the abuses of royal power during the oprichnina and the reign of Boris Godunov. It is much harder to tell what they had in mind when they alluded to the "good old days" before the recent horrors. The best guess would appear to be the early years of Ivan IV's majority before the oprichnina. The references to the zemskii sobor, an institution which began to take shape in the 1550s, certainly support this supposition.[25]

What were the ideas about government underlying the concrete promises of the rulers of the Troubles? The most common image is that of a just tsar who rules with the consent of the Boyar Duma and on the most important issues perhaps consults the zemskii sobor. A far more radical vision fleetingly appears in Liapunov's compact with his followers. In this case, the nation in arms was the locus of political authority: the men who made up the national movement's forces had chosen their leaders and, if necessary, could dispense with them and appoint others. Given the temporary nature of their mission, however, it is impossible to say whether Liapunov or any of his followers aspired to realize this vision in a restored Muscovite polity.

More broadly speaking, was there *any* body of theory or abstract model of a just polity behind the commitments of Muscovite leaders during the Troubles? Daniel Rowland's work on the political theory of the writers of the historical tales on the Smuta strongly suggests that even the most sophisticated Muscovites lacked the intellectual background and training necessary to develop cogent abstractions about politics. The most interesting reflective accounts of the Time of Troubles—Ivan Timofeev's *Vremennik* (*Chronograph*), for example—as political theory more closely resemble the writings of western Europeans of Carolingian times than the treatises of their own contemporaries.[26]

In more concrete terms, did contemporary Polish theory or political practice play any role in the formulation of these treaties and public declarations? More than a century ago, S. M. Solov'ev suggested, for example, that the First False Dmitrii and his Polish followers brought to Muscovy the peculiar notion the innocent should not be punished for the sins of their guilty kin.[27] There is, however, no direct evidence of Polish influence on the political statements of the Time of Troubles and little suggesting that possibility, apart from the presence of many Poles in Muscovy—as hated enemies. More to the point, the political structure and modes of constitutional thought of the neighboring Slavic monarchies were radically different. Polish magnates and gentlemen took for granted rights and privileges their Muscovite counterparts could scarcely imagine.[28]

Did the guarantees and arrangements of the Time of Troubles actually change the nature of the autocracy and, if so, in what concrete ways? The documents which we are discussing were written in moments of extreme emergency and spoke primarily of a return to the national political tradition. Yet, in pre-modern times, fundamental reform often occurred when temporary expedients took root and ambitious rulers often justified novel policies as the restoration of traditional practices.

The impact of the promises of the regimes of the Troubles thus must be examined from two directions. First, the act of stating, orally or in writing, that the tsars' leading subjects had minimal legal rights and a voice in important matters of state made it more difficult for future regimes to ignore those rights. The boyars were quite right in 1606, and so in a limited sense was Kliuchevskii. Shuiskii had indeed set a dangerous precedent. At the same time, there were, of course, no institutions or social groups which could force an unwilling ruler to abide by his predecessors' commitments.

Second, how did the Romanov autocrats of the seventeenth century actually behave when they ascended the throne? To begin with, as noted, the monarchs of the new dynasty sentenced very few prominent men to death or exile and then only through due legal process of a sort. Summary executions were a thing of the past—or future. The new regime, moreover, usually distinguished between the guilty and their innocent kin. In some instances, however—the case of M. B. Shein, for example—sons, including those far from the scene of the supposed crime, suffered exile for the father's failings.

The Muscovite system of government under the first Romanovs is a fascinating mixture of elements. Throughout the seventeenth century, the tsar and a small circle of boyar advisers and in-laws formed the hub of the administration. The chanceries—an embryonic bureaucracy—took care of the day-to-day business of the government. At the same time, following the traditions articulated in the documents of the Time of Troubles, the tsar went through the ritual of consultation with the Boyar Duma on all important matters and frequently mobilized the support of the provincial nobility and urban elites by calling together a zemskii sobor. The same groups also expressed their needs and grievances through such other channels as collective petitions.[29] The so-called middle groups in society did not use their voices to press for corporate rights or a restructuring of the body politic. Instead, they campaigned for a single goal—the full enserfment of the manorial peasants and the concomitant fettering of the townspeople. Once they achieved these objectives in the Law Code of 1649, they disappeared from the political scene. In the second half of the century, the tsar and his inner circle essentially ruled bureaucratically without public consultation with his subjects.[30]

The Time of Troubles and the accession of a new dynasty thus brought temporary changes in the balance of elements within the Muscovite political system but did not lead to any far-reaching change in the autocracy inherited from the fifteenth and sixteenth centuries. Yet ironically, the years of the Troubles seemed the perfect time for experiment and reform since the old order had collapsed and men were desperate for any political solution that would restore peace and order. Moreover, groups such as the provincial nobles, which had little or no voice in the decision-making centers of the old monarchy, had become a force with which any potential ruler had to reckon.

Why, then, did the opportunity to reform the autocracy lead to so little fundamental change? In the broadest terms, the answer lies in Muscovite political culture. The concept of "political culture" attempts to explain why people of different cultural backgrounds—Americans, Filipinos, or Ethiopians—prefer to be governed by quite different institutions and react very differently to political events. The explanation, the proponents of the theory would argue, is to be found in the attitudes inculcated into members of the particular cultural community in the home and school and by their participation in political life. To apply the concept to Russian society centuries ago poses many problems. For one thing, we know very little about the ways in which Muscovite children were reared.

In spite of the difficulties, I would put forward a few working hypotheses. First, to judge from the events of the Time of Troubles, Muscovy had several political cultures, not one. The cossacks' values and political instincts, for example, set them apart from the rest of society. Whether Muscovite nobles, townspeople, and peasants shared a common political culture is more difficult to say.[31] It is an issue we can safely sidestep, however, since the political statements we are examining represented the values of boyars or prominent provincial nobles.

Second, the political culture of Muscovite nobles stressed loyalty to clan or family and to the broader political and religious community symbolized by the monarch. It is entirely likely that Muscovites emerged from childhood with a strong awareness of the sinfulness of human nature and thus a tendency to distrust their fellow men and women.[32] Moreover, they undoubtedly had a hierarchical vision of society, surely a comforting assumption for men born to dominate their social inferiors. They owed their primary allegiance to their clan[33] and the throne. A Muscovite noble passed into adulthood when he formally enrolled in the tsar's army or entourage, usually at the age of fifteen. Thereafter service to the monarch was his raison d'être and the foundation of his economic security and social standing. Moreover, in a world in which the Muscovite state was the only major Eastern Orthodox power and was surrounded by Roman Catholic, Protestant, and Moslem rivals, defense of the faith and loyalty to the crown were synonymous—a point which the tsars' pronouncements and ecclesiastical propaganda repeatedly emphasized. In short, the nobles' identity and place in the world depended on the maintenance of this structure and these reinforcing values. They thus were unlikely to tamper with the institutions and traditions of a strong monarchy. They were even less likely to envision the possibility of legal limits on the tsar's prerogative or noble corporate rights.

There are other, more concrete reasons why the promises and projects of the Time of Troubles offered little and changed even less. First, a stable society threatened by radical change in its social structure, moral values, or international standing may be open to sweeping reforms; but in a society that has already fallen into chaos, people long for order and predictability above all. Such societies, I would suggest, are inclined to be very conservative in mood and intent, if not in practice. Certainly, the voluminous writings of contemporaries and near-contemporaries on the Time of Troubles reflect a profound desire to preserve the cultural and religious heritage and political system of their country.

Second, as noted, those writings do not display a level of political thinking high enough to envision reform in any abstract sense and do not reveal any ideal types other than the autocracy of Ivan IV without the excesses of the oprichnina.[34] Moreover, just as in later times,[35] any proposal for reform appeared to most prominent Russians to be the attempt of the sponsoring clan, clique, or party to gain more power for itself. All those outside the inner circle of reformers felt that they had little to gain and much to lose if the proposed reforms were enacted.

Third, foreign models were probably either inappropriate or unattractive to the leaders of Muscovite society. Linguistically and geographically, the Polish model was the most accessible. That model had several drawbacks, however. Emotionally, it was inextricably tied to militant Roman Catholicism and the personal and dynastic ambitions of Sigismund III. Moreover, as Hans-Joachim Torke has recently observed, in practice it meant magnate domination over a weak royal authority and over society. Such a system had little to offer the rank-and-file provincial nobility and leading townspeople of Muscovy—the kind of hardheaded men who spearheaded the two movements of national revival.[36]

Fourth, the Muscovite equivalent of the Polish magnates—the great boyar clans of the tsars' court—occupied a very different position in society. They had no regional power base; in many cases, by the early seventeenth century, they owned little or no land in their region of origin.[37] Their power derived, above all, from their position as leaders of an increasingly centralized system of administration and social and economic rewards. Power and wealth derived not from resistance to royal power but from exploiting the power of the tsar's office for individual and clan profit.[38] The boyar clans, then, had little interest in limiting the royal prerogative. They did, however, have good reasons for wanting guarantees that they and their kin would not be treated harshly and capriciously.

Fifth, as historians of many periods have pointed out, Muscovite and Imperial Russian society had no legal corporations or estates which might have insisted on their rights and set limits to the power of the crown. In addition, the main social groups or classes exhibited little solidarity or awareness of their collective self-interest. In fact, the most powerful social groups appear to have been remarkably fragmented. In the sixteenth and seventeenth centuries, the boyar clans fought one another for positions of power behind or beside the throne.[39] Historians have often remarked, for example, that Ivan IV encountered no organized resistance when he attacked individual members of the court aristocracy. Moreover, when one clan amassed considerably more power than its rivals, the latter banded together to put its members in their place.[40] This pattern of behavior suggests that the boyars feared above all the emergence of an "overmighty" clan of royal favorites who might bar the rest of them from access to the tsar and the offices and rewards which he alone could grant. It is therefore impossible to see how any boyar clan or the boyars collectively could have made significant changes in the structure of the Russian government.

The provincial nobles were an equally unpromising agent of change. Their conduct during the Troubles suggests that they were divided along economic and regional lines. The comparatively prosperous Riazan' nobles struggled to restore social and political order, while the petty military servitors of the southern frontier districts repeatedly threw in their lot with rebels against the government in Moscow. Moreover, like the boyars, the provincial nobles' attitudes were the product of long service to the monarchy; when it fell, their leaders could envision no alternative but to restore it along traditional lines. Then, under the Romanovs, they used their limited opportunities to pursue a single goal—serfdom—which ultimately served to strengthen the government's control over all its subjects.

A final point should be made. The Muscovite autocracy was not an unchanging monolith; its methods of governing the realm and the background and qualifications of the men who made it function gradually changed over time. Within the broad limits of Muscovite institutional traditions and the values and attitudes of the men who ruled, challenges elicited a variety of creative responses. At the same time, given those limits, constitutional reform in a modern sense was impossible for political and social reasons; indeed, it was hardly even conceivable.

What do these obscure events of long ago suggest about the reformability of Russia in the foreseeable future? First, reform must arise from within Russian society and appear as the embodiment of its shared values and traditions. Projects and proposals that openly espouse foreign models or clearly reflect the aspirations of the non-Russian peoples of the U.S.S.R. are likely to encounter widespread opposition in all strata of the Russian population. Second, to be accepted any reform proposal must appear to benefit the entire community, not just a faction or clique. Third, any reform must be rooted in a coherent vision of a new and better political and legal order. Finally, as Yanov has often suggested, reform in practice is likely to begin as a series of incremental changes within an essentially authoritarian system. Such changes are most likely to occur in response to widely perceived domestic needs at a time when the community is comparatively stable and foreign rivals do not threaten its very survival. At the beginning of the seventeenth century, chaos at home and threats of annihilation from abroad impelled Russia's leaders to reassert the legitimacy of an authoritarian system of rule. The same conditions would probably elicit the same response in our own day.

NOTES

1. By "constitutional" reform, I mean a deliberate change in the legal and institutional relations between ruler and ruled. The vague but evocative German word *"verfassung"* is a rough equivalent of "constitutional" in the present context.

The historical tales on the Time of Troubles have been collected in *Russkaia istoricheskaia biblioteka,* 39 vols. (St. Petersburg and Leningrad, 1872-1927), 13 (hereafter *RIB*), and analyzed in S. F. Platonov, *Drevnerusskiia skazaniia i povesti o smutnom vremeni XVII veka, kak istoricheskii istochnik* (St. Petersburg, 1913). There are separate editions of the *Vremennik Ivana Timofeeva,* ed. O. A. Derzhavina (Moscow and Leningrad, 1951), and *Skazanie Avraamiia Palitsyna,* ed. O. A. Derzhavina and E. V. Kolosova (Moscow and Leningrad, 1955). The extended version of one of the texts, the so-called *Inoe Skazanie,* does contain the text of Vasilii Shuiskii's oath to his subjects. *RIB,* 13:72.

2. Lucian W. Pye and Sidney Verba, eds., *Political Culture and Political Development* (Princeton, N.J., 1965), p. 513.

3. S. M. Solov'ev, *Istoriia Rossii s drevneishikh vremen,* 29 vols. in 15 books (Moscow, 1959-66), Book 4, pp. 459-60, 556-59, 582-83, 643-46; Book 5, pp. 256-57.

4. V. O. Kliuchevskii, *Boiarskaia duma drevnei Rusi* (Moscow, 1909), pp. 353-82.

5. *Sobranie gosudarstvennykh gramot i dogovorov,* 5 vols. (Moscow, 1813-28), 2:299-300 (no. 141), 302-4 (no. 144), (hereafter *SGGD*); *Akty, sobrannye v bibliotekakh i arkhivakh Rossiiskoi imperii Arkheograficheskoiu ekspeditsieiu,* 4 vols. (St. Petersburg, 1836), 2:102-3 (no. 44), (hereafter *AAE*); *Polnoe sobranie russkikh letopisei,* 39 vols. to date (St. Petersburg, Moscow, 1841–), 24:213-14 (hereafter *PSRL*). See also *PSRL,* 14:69.

6. *Akty, otnosiashchiesia k istorii Zapadnoi Rossii,* 5 vols., (St. Petersburg, 1846-53), 4:314-18 (no. 180), (hereafter *AZR*); *SGGD,* 2:390-99 (no. 165); Stanislaw Żółkiewski, *Zapiski Getmana Zholkevskago o Moskovskoi voine,* ed. P. A. Mukhanov (St. Petersburg, 1871), Prilozheniia [Appendices], pp. 41-48 (no. 20).

7. Grigorij Kotošixin, *O Rossii v carstvovanie Alekseja Mixajloviča. Text and Commentary,* ed. and trans. A. E. Pennington (Oxford, 1980), pp. 139-40.

8. S. F. Platonov, *Ocherki po istorii Smuty v moskovskom gosudarstve XVI-XVII vv.* (St. Petersburg, 1910), pp. 283-87, 402-4, 437-38, 472-85. R. G. Skrynnikov makes essentially the same point in *Minin i Pozharskii* (Moscow, 1981), pp. 206-7.

9. Alexander Yanov, *The Origins of Autocracy: Ivan the Terrible in Russian History* (Berkeley and Los Angeles, 1981), pp. 269-79.

10. *SGGD*, 2:299-300.

11. *PSRL*, 14:69.

12. Kliuchevskii, *Boiarskaia duma*, pp. 363-65; Platonov, *Ocherki*, pp. 285-87. Kliuchevskii's argument is open to two technical objections. First, the term "sobor" occurs in only one of the many versions of the story and in a relatively late and literarily elaborate source at that. Second, if the chronicler had intended to refer to the zemskii sobor, he more likely would have used a phrase such as "the whole land."

13. *AZR*, 4:314-18; Żółkiewski, *Zapiski, Prilozheniia*, pp. 41-48.

14. Żółkiewski, *Zapiski, Prilozheniia*, pp. 41-48. Using the treaty of February as a base, the editor carefully indicates the passages omitted from the second accord. See also *SGGD*, 2:391-405, 440-44; *AAE*, 2: 280-84.

15. N. M. Karamzin, *Istoriia gosudarstva rossiiskago*, 12 vols. in 6 (St. Petersburg, 1892-97), 12:131-36 (second pagination). The document specifically mentions tax-collection agencies (the Bol'shoi Dvorets, the Bol'shoi Prikhod, the Chetverti); the Pomestnyi Prikaz, which registered and regulated landholding; and police agencies, the Razboinyi and Zemskii Prikazy.

16. Ibid., p. 136.

17. It is, of course, possible that, once securely in power, the new regime attempted to suppress all records of such promises. Certainly in their propaganda, the Romanov tsars presented themselves as rulers by hereditary right because of their family's marriage ties with the old dynasty. They thus owed their throne to God, not to their subjects.

18. Kotošikhin, *O Rossii*, p. 139.

19. Shuiskii's oath explicitly mentioned the excesses of Boris but not those of Ivan IV, perhaps because the latter was unquestionably a legitimate tsar while the former could be labelled a usurper.

20. Following Kliuchevskii's suggestions, S. B. Veselovskii forcefully argued that the oprichnina destroyed individual boyars and their immediate families but not the great boyar clans as units or as an elite group. See his *Issledovaniia po istorii oprichniny* (Moscow, 1963). My own studies have led me to similar conclusions. See Robert O. Crummey, *Aristocrats and Servitors: The Boyar Elite in Russia, 1613-1689* (Princeton, N.J., 1983), and "The Fate of Boyar Clans, 1565-1613," *Forschungen zur osteuropäischen Geschichte* 38 (1986):241-56.

21. On the execution or exile of Duma members see, Crummey, *Aristocrats and Servitors*, p. 225, n. 46.

22. Yanov, *The Origins of Autocracy*, pp. 278-79.

23. *Pamiatniki russkogo prava*, 8 vols. (Moscow, 1952-63), 4:260 (hereafter *PRP*). See also *PRP*, 3:346; 4:356, 363, 375-78, 413; *Tysiachnaia kniga 1550 g. i dvorovaia tetrad' 50-kh godov XVI v.*, ed. A. A. Zimin (Moscow and Leningrad, 1950), p. 53.

24. Giles Fletcher, "Of the Russe Commonwealth," in *Rude and Barbarous*

Kingdom, ed. Lloyd E. Berry and Robert O. Crummey (Madison, Wisc., 1968), p. 157.

25. In this connection, Yanov's distinction between the absolutism of Ivan III and the autocracy of Ivan IV is misleading since it relies on an exaggeratedly positive assessment of Ivan III's rule and the growth of the Muscovite economy in the sixteenth century and passes over the more positive features of Ivan IV's reign. I find two other distinctions between "absolutism" and "autocracy" unconvincing. Even after the purges of the oprichnina, I am convinced, a strong hereditary aristocracy survived and continued to dominate Muscovite politics and society. As for "ideological pluralism," its scope was extremely limited and had disappeared altogether by the mid-1550s. Ivan III may have tolerated the Judaizers for a time, but he ordered their execution. See Alexander Yanov, "The Drama of the Time of Troubles, 1725-1730," *Canadian-American Slavic Studies* 12 (1978):1-59, particularly pp. 6-7.

26. Daniel Rowland, "The Problem of Advice in Muscovite Tales about the Time of Troubles," *Russian History* 6 (1979):259-83; Rowland, "Muscovite Political Attitudes as Reflected in Early Seventeenth-Century Tales about the Time of Troubles" (Ph. D. dissertation, Yale University, 1976).

27. Solov'ev, *Istoriia,* 5:460.

28. For a convenient summary, see A. Gieysztor, S. Kieniewicz, E. Rostworowski, J. Tazbir, and H. Wereszycki, *History of Poland,* 2d. ed. (Warsaw, 1979), pp. 145-79 (by Tazbir and Rostworowski).

29. See Hans-Joachim Torke, *Die staatsbedingte Gesellschaft im Moskauer Reich* (Leiden, 1974). In this limited sense, Platonov's oft-repeated assertion that the middle classes of Muscovite society emerged victorious from the Time of Troubles has considerable merit. At the same time, we should note that, even under Tsar Mikhail, the remnants of the great boyar clans dominated Muscovite politics and that the limited political participation of the provincial nobility ended in mid-century, as soon as the peasants were fully enserfed. See S. F. Platonov, *The Time of Troubles,* trans. John T. Alexander (Lawrence, Kans., 1970), pp. 164-69.

30. Torke has given this late-seventeenth-century form of government the suggestive label "autocratic absolutism."

31. In a recently published essay, Edward L. Keenan argues that the boyar clan and the peasant village were the focal points of two distinct political cultures, which shared a number of central features: an obsession with individual and collective survival, a strong sense of collective identity, and a profound distrust of outsiders. See Edward L. Keenan, "Muscovite Political Folkways," *Russian Review* 45 (1986):115-81.

32. Donald N. Levine makes this point about Amhara society in pre-revolutionary Ethiopia in Pye and Verba, *Political Culture,* pp. 256-61. Parallels between these two eastern Christian societies, Ethiopia and Russia in earlier times, should be explored further.

33. Nancy Shields Kollmann's book, *Kinship and Politics: The Making of the Muscovite Political System, 1345-1547* (Stanford, 1987), makes this point forcefully.

34. Or, in Yanov's terminology, "absolutism." In spite of the power of Yanov's rhetoric, I still prefer to use the word "autocracy" for the unlimited rule of the Muscovite tsars expressed in the symbols of Eastern Orthodox Christianity and "absolutism" for the European-clothed government of the eighteenth and nineteenth centuries whose leaders justified their exercise of power by "reason of state." Whichever label we prefer, we must, I believe, apply it equally to the political and institutional realities of the reigns of Ivan III, Ivan IV during the "reform period" of the 1550s, and Aleksei Mikhailovich.

35. See David L. Ransel, *The Politics of Catherinian Russia: The Panin Party* (New Haven, Conn., 1975).

36. *Handbuch der Geschichte Russlands,* 3 vols. to date (Stuttgart, 1976–), 2:51.

37. The gradual separation of the great princely clans from their ancestral homelands appears to have been taking place in the course of the sixteenth century. For one important example, see Crummey, *Aristocrats and Servitors,* p. 120. S. V. Rozhdestvenskii, *Sluzhiloe zemlevladenie v Moskovskom gosudarstve XVI veka* (St. Petersburg, 1897), pp. 148-204, points out some prominent clans preserved their family "nests" into the seventeenth century. That fact, however, does not prove ownership of their ancestral estates was the source of their power, as R. G. Skrynnikov seems to imply in *Nachalo oprichniny* (Leningrad, 1966), pp. 281-88. Far more significant, in my view, is the fact that the most powerful of the Suzdal' princes, whose fate Skrynnikov discusses, held prominent positions at the court of Ivan IV.

38. The behavior of the most powerful boyar clans during the minority of Ivan IV illustrates the situation particularly well.

39. See, for example, the essays of Gustave Alef, collected in *Rulers and Nobles in Fifteenth-Century Muscovy* (London, 1983); Nancy Shields Kollmann's dissertation "Kinship and Politics: The Origin and Evolution of the Muscovite Boyar Elite in the Fifteenth Century" (Ph.D. dissertation, Harvard University, 1980); Ann M. Kleimola's articles, including "The Changing Face of the Muscovite Aristocracy, the Sixteenth Century: Sources of Weakness," *Jahrbücher für Geschichte Osteuropas* 25 (1977):481-93, and "Status, Place and Politics: The Rise of Mestnichestvo during the *Boiarskoe Pravlenie,*" *Forschungen zur osteuropäischen Geschichte* 27 (1980):195-214; and the studies of Robert O. Crummey, summarized in *Aristocrats and Servitors.*

40. Two separate studies make this point forcefully in explaining Ivan III's disgrace of the Patrikeevs in 1499: Gustave Alef's unpublished paper, "The Fall of the Patrikeevs: Eshchë Raz," and Kollmann's dissertation, "Kinship and Politics," pp. 482-521.

The Government Crisis
of 1730

DAVID L. RANSEL

The events of the early weeks of 1730 have attracted the attention of historians interested in the reform of the Russian political system. Historians of the liberal or Kadet school have shown the greatest interest in this attempt to impose restrictions on the rule of the new monarch, Empress Anna, because in their view this action came close to being a "Glorious Revolution" for the Russian nobility and so a harbinger of their own efforts in the twentieth century to bring a constitutional order to Russia. Alexander Yanov revives much of the liberals' schema of Russian development while rejecting its Whiggish implications of movement toward ever greater freedom and democracy. His notion of "political modernization" seems to incorporate two developments: the limitation of autocratic power by the upper nobility and the liberalization of commercial life accompanied by the growth of a middle class. Although these developments are not necessarily compatible, they have occurred at various times in Russian history either singly or in combination and then suffered defeat at the hands of a resurgent autocracy or confiscatory taxation policy. Yanov asks if there is something in the events of 1730 and the preceding period of rule by the Supreme Privy Council that could guide modern analysts to a solution for breaking the cycle of reform and reaction and leading Russia to a sustainable form of limited government and political liberty.[1]

To attempt to answer this question, we must first understand what the reformers of 1730 wished to achieve. Then we can ask whether the conditions that frustrated this attempt are still present. I hasten to add that I shall leave the answer to the last question to those more expert than I in the recent history of the Russian and Soviet state.

Background of the Election

It is important first to reconstruct as clearly as possible the course of the events in question. Confusion about the character and sequence of actions taken in connection with the crisis has been common. Recent archival research by the Soviet scholar G. A. Protasov clears up many aspects of the record, and it is his reordering of the evidence that I follow in this reconstruction.

There is no question, of course, that it was the death of the young Emperor Peter II on the night of January 18-19, 1730, that touched off the crisis. Since Peter had left no heir, the Supreme Privy Council—the highest executive body of the realm—decided to elect Duchess Anna of Courland as successor to the throne. At the same time the Council drew up a number of "Conditions" to which Anna had to agree in accepting the crown. The Conditions left all important decisions of government in the hands of the Council. The Council then dispatched three deputies to carry the offer to the duchess. Before doing so, members of the Council had informed high-ranking officers in the military and civil service of their action, and word slipped out in time for some officials opposed to the plans of the Council to send their own representative to Courland to warn Anna that the Conditions did not reflect the wishes of the Russian people but only the will of an oligarchic faction.

Although the immediate source of the crisis was the unexpected death of the young emperor, the institutional context in which his death occurred complicated the situation. Legal and administrative changes arising from the Petrine reform era set the scene for the struggle in 1730.

Most important was Peter the Great's law of 1722 decreeing that succession to the throne was dependent on appointment by the reigning emperor.[2] Having disposed of his own son Aleksei and fearing that the government might fall into the hands of conservatives, Peter intended to appoint a successor who could be trusted to continue his work of modernization.[3] Ironically, Peter I's own death struck so suddenly that he did not have time to name a successor. A number of his closest collaborators therefore resolved the issue by rousing the guard regiments of the capital to declare themselves in favor of Peter's second wife Catherine. A semi-literate Baltic peasant woman who before her marriage to Peter went by the name of Marta Skavronskaia, Catherine could not rule by herself. She had risen to her high station by her ability to govern Peter the Great's passions, not his empire. Prince Aleksandr

Menshikov, himself an upstart and earlier patron of Catherine, took control of affairs for her. Soon, however, this powerful favorite overplayed his hand and turned his former friends and collaborators against him.

Since the Petrine Senate proved too weak to control Menshikov, dissatisfied members of the new elite joined with some of the older families and persuaded Catherine to erect a new high government institution between the Senate and the monarch. This was the Supreme Privy Council, established in February, 1726. Its composition reflected the designs of its proponents. The purpose was to bring Menshikov's authority within an institutional framework that would both dilute and control it and to strike a compromise between members of opposing factions. Instead of being a dictator, Menshikov was now one member of a council of seven. Four others were Petrine servitors (Petr Tolstoi, Fedor Apraksin, Gavriil Golovkin, Andrei Osterman); another was Catherine's son-in-law, Duke Karl Friedrich of Holstein; and the other was Prince Dmitrii Golitsyn, the leading representative of the old aristocracy.

Over the next few years, the composition of the Council became increasingly aristocratic. After the death of Catherine in 1727 and the accession of Peter II, a series of cabals eliminated Menshikov, Tolstoi, and Apraksin. In the meantime, the ancient Dolgorukii clan had acquired seats in the Council by virtue of personal ties to the new monarch. By the time of Peter II's death, the Council was composed of Dmitrii Golitsyn, two Dolgorukiis, Golovkin, and Osterman. In the following days, the councilors coopted two more members of the Dolgorukii family and another Golitsyn. Since the one foreigner, Osterman, excused himself from meetings during the 1730 interregnum, the Council that elected Anna and imposed the Conditions was made up almost exclusively of two aristocratic families.

This composition cast suspicion on the right of the Council to name a new ruler and to set restrictions on her power. But with the young emperor gone and the Senate reduced in authority—even its name had been changed from "Governing Senate" to "High Senate"—the Council stood unchallenged as the loftiest political institution. There was no organized political body to oppose it, no succession law to which disaffected groups could appeal, and no obvious and willing candidate around which a party could form. These circumstances, as much as any recognized authority or power of the Council, made its action possible. It alone among the central government institutions was in a position to act.

The Struggle for Power

The Conditions were the work of Dmitrii Golitsyn.[4] They bound the new empress not to marry or designate an heir. The choice of an heir was to belong to the Council. Further, the empress could not declare war or conclude peace without the Council's consent. Nor could she levy new taxes; promote persons to positions above the rank of colonel; deprive nobles of life, property, or honor without trial; grant hereditary lands or villages; promote Russians or foreigners to court offices; or spend state revenues. Anna had to indicate her agreement with these points by affixing her signature to the Conditions and then pledging to abide by them or be deprived of the Russian throne.[5] The Council constructed the pledge to give the appearance that Anna volunteered these limitations and was not submitting to demands from a state institution. Under this guise, the Council later announced the Conditions to the nobility. For her part, Anna, who until that time had been a pawn in the game of Baltic politics and had no fortune, influence, or clear title to the Russian throne, agreed to the Conditions and left for Moscow.[6]

The Conditions had been hastily drawn up after the death of Peter II, and upon reflection the Council wrote a codicil that gave consideration to the needs of other estates. The main provisions of the codicil included: (1) regulation and easing of the nobility's service in the army and navy; (2) reestablishment of free trade for merchants and in general an end to restrictions on commerce; (3) easing of the taxation burdening agriculture and the peasantry; and (4) reestablishment of the church's rights of landholding so that bishops might exercise full governance of their bishoprics and monasteries might exercise governance of their estates.[7] This codicil marked a first stage of the Council's consideration of the state government structure, but the Council unwisely did not release this document or even announce its intention to consider further the character of government institutions and policy.

In the meantime, the news of the Council's election of Anna and its imposition of restrictions on her rule spread through the city and sparked debate and protest among the nobility. In addition to the noble officials of the capital, a large number of nobles from surrounding towns and provinces were on the scene, having assembled for the anticipated marriage of Peter II and having stayed on to assist at his funeral. Although the details of the Council's coup d'état remained vague, the nobles understood the substance well enough and evidently resented what they perceived as a usurpation of the supreme power. Even before Anna arrived and the Conditions were officially announced, some nobles drew up their own project for the future government of Russia, a project that called for the abolition of the Supreme Privy Council.

This "outline" or project of the "society," as it has variously been called, evidently appeared before the end of January and had the character of a manifesto of protest. The drafters did not yet know the Conditions and therefore could not pose specific objections to each of the points. They simply challenged the whole procedure.[8] The project included nine points:

1. The Senate should be expanded to thirty members with the empress presiding and having three votes; there should be no Supreme Privy Council.
2. Routine business should be carried out by ten members (of the Senate?) delegated each year; but all members are to consult on matters of state.
3. Members of the Senate should be chosen by ballot (*chrez balatirovan'e*), but no more than two persons should be from a single family.
4. The army should be under the Military Collegia, the guard under the Senate.
5. Court officials are to be appointed (*vybrat'*) anew.
6. The nobility is to fill by balloting the vacancies occurring in the Senate, the presidencies of Collegia, and the governorships, and the Senate should not interfere in the elections.
7. Henceforth a Diet (*seim*) should devise, and society confirm, whatever is necessary for the reform and welfare of the state.
8. Noblemen should not be appointed to the military ranks of private and artisan, but special companies should be established for them, and for those in the navy, units of marine guards.
9. The rule of entail in matters of inheritance should be abrogated and complete freedom given to the parents; and, if there are no parents left, the inheritance is to be divided in equal shares.[9]

In addition to reacting against the Supreme Privy Council and voicing demands about inheritance law and state service, the drafters were wrestling with the issue of how persons are chosen for high offices. It is far from clear, however, what they were getting at. Peter I had introduced the practice of balloting to fill vacancies in state offices, and the procedure would therefore have been familiar. But the project said nothing about who was entitled to participate in the balloting for these high offices. The term "seim" in Article 7 evidently referred to a policy-making body, not an electoral one. Use of the term "seim" is itself significant, for it indicates that the drafters were looking to models abroad, in Poland and Sweden, rather than to earlier assemblies in Russia, which they would have referred to as a *sobor* (assembly) or a *sovet vseia zemli* (council of the whole land). Finally, the project expressed no objection to the choice of Anna as empress, while it clearly wanted an end to the Supreme Privy Council or any other body that included more than two members from a single family.

Council deliberations on the character of the new government continued, spurred on no doubt by the protests emerging among the nobility and also by the anticipated arrival of the empress from Mitau. In the period from January 31 to February 2, preceding the arrival of the empress and the announcement of the Conditions, a lengthy and detailed, if incomplete, project was drafted in the Council offices.[10] This "form of government" had two parts. The first part repeated the Conditions and rehearsed the circumstances of the death of Peter II and election of Empress Anna that had given rise to them. The second part dealt with procedures for filling vacancies in high government posts, general principles of government, and indications of policy, in the following order. (1) Vacancies in the Council were to be filled by a vote of the Council and the Senate. The empress would confirm the vote. No foreigners and no more than two members of a single family could be elected to the Council. On important matters the Council would consult with the Senate, the *generalitet* (civil and military officials of the first four ranks), members of the collegia, and the high nobility (*znatnoe shliakhetstvo*). Council members were to work within the law and to bear criminal responsibility for illegal acts they might commit. (2) The church was to govern its properties as before, and the Economy Collegium was to be abolished. Procedures for replacing and judging members of the Holy Synod were noted. (3) The Senate's position as subordinate to the Council was confirmed, and the number of senators was left open. (4) The principle of appointment to the Senate, collegia, chanceries, and other government offices of worthy persons from the generalitet and high nobility was enunciated, and "the entire nobility would be shown due respect as in other European states and given consideration and care by Her Imperial Majesty." (5) The nobility was to be freed of service in the lower ranks and placed in special cadet regiments so that they could begin services as officers. (6-7) Non-nobles were to have the right to rise through the ranks to nobility and chancery workers were to advance by merit and loyal service. Peasants and dependent people were not permitted to work in government service. (8) Immediate family members and relatives of persons convicted of crimes were not to be harmed or deprived of their property. (9-10) The military was to be kept in good condition, salaries were to be paid on time, promotion was to be by merit and not by favoritism or bribery, and soldiers and sailors were not to be overworked or treated rudely. (11) Baltic nobles were to retain their rights, and foreigners were to be treated fairly. (12) Merchants were to be shown respect, and restrictions on trade were to be lifted. (13) Peasants were not to be overburdened with taxes. (14) Laws were to be established for the common good. (15) The capital was to be in "Moscow and nowhere else."[11]

For all its eloquence about legality and concern for other groups, this form of government proposal included no modification of the structure implied in the Conditions. The Supreme Privy Council remained the leading institution, with no change in its size or composition. The Council was apparently aiming to reassure other groups that their positions, persons, and property were secure and that at least the most highly placed people would be consulted on matters directly affecting their interests. The statements about good order in the military, timely pay, and fairness in promotion reflected the Council's knowledge of widespread concern about the disarray in just these areas of government during the preceding three years. The mention of other groups followed the same lines as those in the earlier codicil. The expression used to designate this draft — "form of government" — may have reflected the interest of D. M. Golitsyn in Sweden, where the constitution was known by the same term, *"regeringsform."* Yet, even if this document had been made public, it could not have provided a foundation for a constitutional order in Russia unless many more members of the elite had been able to conceptualize power in terms of institutional responsibilities and constraints rather than, as they evidently did, in terms of personal authority and kinship links.

Before the Council finished filling in all the details of this plan, news arrived of Anna's favorable reply to the invitation to become empress, and the Council called a meeting to announce the Conditions and the empress's acceptance of the crown. The meeting took place on February 2 and included about eighty high-ranking members of the military and civil officialdom. Tension ran high. Some members anticipated that Anna may have repulsed the Council's offer and insisted on full autocratic prerogatives. That hope dissolved quickly when they learned that a vocal supporter of autocratic restoration, Pavel Iaguzhinskii, had been arrested as the assembly was convening.[12] Other persons expected that the Council might invite them to join in establishing a new government order based on participation by the ranking nobility. The Council's presentation likewise failed to satisfy this hope.

Prince Golitsyn began the meeting by reading the Conditions and the letter from Anna, previously prepared by the Council, announcing her voluntary submission to them. Then Golitsyn delivered a brief address praising the empress's graciousness and droning on about how all true patriots sought the country's prosperity and well-being. An awkward silence ensued. Golitsyn tried a few times to warm up his audience by speaking of the bright future in store for the country, but each time his words were greeted by a stony silence. The members of the Council whispered uncomfortably among themselves. Then Golitsyn turned back to the audience and declared that if no one cared to speak, there was nothing left but to thank the monarch for her graciousness and adjourn. Suddenly, a quiet voice broke from the assembly: "I am quite confused as to how the empress could have got it into her head to write such a thing." Again silence. Finally, Prince Aleksei Mikhailovich Cherkasskii screwed up enough courage to ask: "What form is the government going to take in the future?" Here was a question that required a direct answer from the Council, and Golitsyn was prepared for it. He responded that the officials present "could, in seeking the general welfare and prosperity of the state, themselves write a project and submit it the following day."[13]

In the next few days the nobility submitted a number of projects or "opinions" to the Council. The first of these and the one receiving the largest number of signatures was designated by Protasov as the project of the 361, the number of signers. It came to the Council on February 5 and contained ten articles that can be divided into two general sections. Half of them touched the organization of the government and called for: (1) a High Government of twenty-one persons; (2) a Senate of eleven (variant: one hundred) members; (3) voting on important offices by the ranking officials and nobility with a quorum of no less than one hundred, and the listing of no more than one candidate from a single family; (4) no more than two persons from the same family in the High Government and Senate counted together; and (5) important state affairs to be decided by consultation among the High Government, Senate, general officers, and nobility.[14] The intent of these articles was transparent. As in the earlier "society" project that emerged from the same circle of nobles, the drafters sought to dilute the power of the Council and restrain it in some vague fashion with the cooperation of the ranking officers and the nobility. Although they did not define the mechanism for the nobility's participation, their desire to expand the High Government to three times the current size of the Council and their insistence on preventing the dominance of powerful families made clear that they did not trust the Golitsyns and Dolgorukiis to represent their interests.

The second half of the project catalogued a number of grievances and requests. The signers asked for a reduction of obligatory service to twenty years, abrogation of the requirement to serve as sailors and artisans, an orderly system of pay and promotions in the military, compensation for retired or wounded military personnel, and an examination of inheritance laws. One article even requested relief of the burdens on the clergy, merchants, and peasants. In other words, much like the "society" project that preceded it, this one was at once a proposal for government reform directed against the Council and a petition for redress of grievances.

The project of the 361 was followed by five more proposals from smaller groups of nobles and two individuals, altogether representing fifty-five additional signers.[15] The Council itself apparently generated these additional opinions by suggesting that those who disagreed with the 361 project might submit proposals of their own. Not suprisingly, these subsequent opinions were more solicitous of the Council than was the project of the 361, and they seem to have been efforts to find a compromise between the position of the Council and the 361. The most favorably disposed toward the Council was the "project of the 15," sometimes called the "generalitet project" because its signers were military and civil officers of general rank. It asked for an expansion of the Council to twelve or thirteen members, consultation with the general officers and the nobility on more important issues, and procedures for filling vacancies in the Council by election, including an assembly of general officers of the military and civil service of not less than seventy persons and no more than two persons from any single family. A key statement on governance provided that "everything that will be needed in the future to complete the statutes concerning the state administration or the commonweal must be confirmed by the common counsel and wish of the Supreme Privy Council, the general officers, and the nobility."[16] The rest of the project repeated the usual desires for reduced service obligations, timely pay, and the like.

Brenda Meehan-Waters has analyzed an important dimension of this project that is not obvious in the language alone—the personal and family networks tying the signers of the project to members of the Supreme Privy Council and the court. In pointing out the role of the leaders of prominent noble families in drafting all the projects, Meehan-Waters provided a glimpse into the strivings of the various personal and clientage groupings that underlay the projects and revealed the importance of family links in the Russian nobility's notions of power.[17] Recognition of this fact is also apparent in the strictures expressed in the anti-Council projects against representation by more than one or two members of a family.

The Council did not sit idle in the face of the proposals from the 361 and the 15. The second of these proposals reached the Council on February 7, and evidently within the next three days members of the

Council made changes in the form of government draft that they had been working on earlier. The changes reveal the Council's willingness to compromise with the opposition. The Council was not prepared to accept an expansion of its membership to twenty-one, as the project of the 361 wished, but it did write in an expansion to twelve members and the provision that new members would be elected. The electoral assembly would be limited to members of the Council, the Senate, and the general officers in the civil and military services in the capital at the time of an election. But a further condition was set on the election: half the members of the Council would have to be from the aristocracy and half from the nobility (*"Vsegda odna polovina iz famil'nykh, a drugaia iz shliakhetstva"*). The same arrangement applied to the Senate; half the membership was supposed to be from the old families and half from the nobility.[18] In short, the Council moved some way toward meeting the wishes of the opposition but at the same time inserted provisions that would guarantee the old families (*famil'nye*) a share of power equal to that of the nobility of rank (*chinovnaia znat'*).

As events unfolded and opinions continued to come in from other groups of nobles, the Council took the further step of drawing up a list of procedures that would establish a small constitutional assembly and allow for consultation by representatives of recognized social groups and government offices. This document, found among the papers of the Council, is entitled "Means by which the affair of such importance and benefit to the people and the state might be better founded and made more orderly and firm." Only recently published in full in Russian, it appears here for the first time in English and consists of seven points that can be readily summarized. (1) "The first and main point is that the entire Great Russian nobility (in the capital) . . . should agree unanimously for themselves and on behalf of those not present that they would all be of one voice and that no one could in any way abstain from this agreement no matter what his service, rank, or family status." (2) They would by unanimous agreement elect twenty to thirty good men and true to draft a new order for the fatherland. (3) This assembly would elect from its ranks two persons who would not have a vote but would be responsible for maintaining good order and taking the votes. (4) This assembly would draft everything that pertains to the governance of the state and whatever they might consider to the benefit of the fatherland. If the Council and Senate offer recommendations, the assembly should consider them and draft what it decides is proper. (5) When the assembly considers the affairs of the church, the military, the merchants, or other groups, it should have four to six elected representatives from the group in question come before it. (6) If property matters are before the assembly, it should call in the president and two or three members of the appropriate collegium for advice just as in the case of the church, the military, and the merchants, and the same should be done for affairs concerning other collegia. (7) "When these elected assemblymen draft and pass a measure, they should take it to the Senate, advise the senators and come to a agreement with them; then the assemblymen and senators should take the measure to the Supreme Council and all consider it together. And when the assembly, the Senate and Supreme Council have agreed on the measure, a small delegation should take it to Her Imperial Majesty to request Her confirmation."[19]

This set of procedures may have gone far toward resolving the differences between the Council and the nobles who supported the project of the 361. This at any rate was Protasov's view, since he held that an anti-autocratic spirit had seized the nobility as a whole. The question of whether the Council's new proposals would have satisfied the nobility remains moot, however, since the Council did not release its proposals or even let the public know it was contemplating constitutional procedures.

So far as is known, only one Council member, Vasilii Lukich Dolgorukii, demonstrated the political savvy required by the situation, but during most of the crisis he was not in a position to influence events. Dolgorukii had traveled to Mitau to accompany the new empress to Russia and then stayed with her outside Moscow to police her communications. When he returned to the city on February 18 and sized up the situation, he pressed the Council to act more resolutely. He wanted the form of government proposal as recently amended published.

He also suggested three ways that the Council could involve a greater number of people in the choice of leaders. He presented his ideas as a set of options, noting the advantages and disadvantages of each choice. First, he wrote, the Council and Senate could coopt a few key people from the general officer ranks in the military and civil service and could fill future vacancies through further cooption by the Council and Senate sitting together. This method, he noted, would cause the least discord.[20] Second, he proposed involving all nobles through elected representatives, who would be empowered, along with the Council members and senators, to choose candidates for the Council. Dolgorukii believed this would be popular with the entire nobility, but he feared this method would lead to "difficulties and disagreements." Third, he thought they could implement the proposal on procedures (the one entitled "Means"), which provided for an elected constitutional assembly of twenty to thirty persons, but he urged the importance of first carefully defining the rules under which the assembly would act and the affairs which it would decide. Otherwise, he warned, there would be discord in the assembly and, as a result, murmuring and criticism from the public.[21]

Return to Autocracy

While these deliberations continued in chambers, events overtook the Council. Despite Dolgorukii's urgings, the proposals being considered by the Council remained unknown to the nobility at large, and many of them began to question whether the Council's request for their opinion had not been just a dodge. The drafters of the project of the 361 and their supporters regarded themselves as the "majority," and they had reason to fear that the Council was stalling and looking for support for its own programs to avoid accepting the recommendations of the majority group. Seeing no concessions from the Council and fearful that the Council was outflanking them, the leaders of this group turned directly to the empress in the hope that she would force the Council to accept their majority proposal for the reorganization of the government.

On February 25, with Prince Aleksei Mikhailovich Cherkasskii in the lead, they presented a petition to Anna outlining the developments of the previous six weeks and saying that

> we have written down our opinions and presented them to the Supreme Privy Council with all due respect and in all humility, requesting that there be devised a safe system of government for the peace and welfare of the state in accordance with the opinion of the majority, yet, most Gracious Lady, they have still not decided on it, and the written opinions of many have not even been accepted. However, knowing Your Imperial Majesty's natural charity and desire to show favor to the whole empire, we most humbly and submissively request Your Majesty that You graciously permit an assembly of all general officers, officers, and nobles, one or two from every family, to examine the opinions submitted by us and others, to investigate all circumstances, and, *on the basis of the majority's opinion,* to devise a form of government for the state and to submit it for Your Majesty's approval.[22]

The irony is that this method of proceeding was not far from the measures the Council was then considering—with the proviso that the Council meant to exercise tight control over initiatives from below and showed no inclination to cave in to majority opinion. But secrecy, mistrust, and fear of disorder had prevented the type of communication that might have resolved the differences without appeal to the empress. This appeal gave away the whole game. By turning to Anna, the nobles not only implicitly recognized her authority over the Council and therefore over themselves, they also ensured that the struggle would be played out in the arena most favorable to those who wished a restoration of autocracy: at court with its symbols of autocratic power and its guards pledged to defend the tsar. The decision of the nobles to appeal to the empress was, however, altogether in character and spoke volumes about the prospects of limited monarchy in Russia.

From the beginning several prominent officials had been pressing for a return to autocracy. One was the former general-procurator of the Senate, Pavel Iaguzhinskii, who after offering his services to the Council and being rebuffed, joined Anna's party and encouraged her to undermine the Council. Two others were Vice Chancellor Andrei Osterman and Archbishop Feofan Prokopovich. All three men were non-Russians who had risen to high office during Peter I's reign and owed their positions to the autocrat's recognition of their talents, not to their family status. The Grand Chancellor, Golovkin, the only other member of the Council besides Osterman who was not a Golitsyn or a Dolgorukii, may also have been involved with the opposition.[23]

These men worked behind the scenes to assure a return to the former order of government. They had established secret contact with the empress and kept her informed about developments and the persons striving to restore autocracy. Occasionally, they intervened to thwart Council plans or expectations. Prokopovich, for example, persuaded the Holy Synod, of which he was a member, to include the term "Autocatrice" in the prayers for the monarch on February 3.[24] Osterman advised the Council not to publish the text of the Conditions until after Anna had arrived in Moscow. The opponents of the Council also sought to mobilize support among the rank-and-file nobility for a full restoration of autocracy. In this effort they contacted confederates in the guard regiments and asked them to pass the word, and they even released broadsides detailing arguments for their case.

One of these raised the specter of disunity and chaos:

> God forbid that instead of one autocrat there should be ten despotic and powerful families; and so we, the nobility, will be completely ruined and compelled more than ever to go worshipping idols and seeking everyone's favor. And this will not be easy to obtain; for however much agreement there may be among the most important people (i.e., aristocrats), they will of course not be without disagreements in the future. Hence, one of them may show favor, while the other, because of that, will react with anger and cause harm and ruin.[25]

The authors spoke also of how disagreements among the leaders could threaten the nation's security. In time of crisis, finances and recruitment will be subjects of dispute, and "what should be done in a week will take six months or a year to complete." And, the broadside warned, whatever is decided will not weigh on the leading men, but "we middle people will alone be left to make the payments and bear the burdens."[26]

These arguments and, apparently, assurances that the new empress would give attention to the grievances of the nobility soon brought a large number of nobles into the camp of those who wished to restore autocracy. Even when the frustrated followers of the "majority" group presented their petition to Anna in hopes of forcing the Council to back down, some of the assembled nobles shouted demands for an immediate restoration of autocracy. Support for reform was thin. When the guards entered the palace a short time after demanding restoration of full autocratic powers, the few holdouts for political participation could not prevent the others from seizing this solution to the crisis. The same afternoon, the nobles assembled at the palace produced a second petition asking Anna to resume autocratic power. It included a request to abolish the Supreme Privy Council and reestablish the Governing Senate of Peter I's time. With this support the empress ordered the text of the Conditions brought to her; she ripped them in two and thus unceremoniously put an end to the attempt at limited monarchy.

Analysis

Several political strategies operated in the events of 1730. The first was that of the initiators, Dmitrii Golitsyn and Vasilii Dolgorukii, whose apparent purpose was to limit despotism without extending political rights to more than a narrow circle of aristocrats. Political experience and knowledge of statecraft were the strengths of these two men. Both were well acquainted with the institutions of European government and the ideas upon which they were based. Golitsyn had received a good education and later spent a year and a half in Venice mastering seamanship and other arts. He could not have failed to observe the leadership of this ancient state by a venerable council. Golitsyn also possessed one of the largest private libraries in Russia, including many works on European politics and statecraft. Much of his career in service was spent in Kiev, the center of Russian intellectual life, such as it was, and the site of the office, administered by Golitsyn, for translating foreign books into Russian. After moving to the central bureaus to head the financial adminstration, Golitsyn struck up a friendship with the Holstein adventurer Heinrich Fick, who had served the Swedish government and was the main technician of the administrative reforms borrowed from Sweden and introduced into Russia toward the end of Peter I's reign. Fick would have known well the limitations imposed on royal power in Sweden after the death of Charles XII in 1718, which in their initial form resembled the Conditions of 1730 in Russia. As for Vasilii Dolgorukii, he had served abroad during most of his career. As a diplomatic representative of Russia in France, Poland, Denmark, and Sweden, he had ample opportunity to observe the mechanisms of limited monarchy.

Though Golitsyn and Dolgorukii were both descendants of ancient clans, neither was an opponent of the Petrine reforms. It is true that Golitsyn had a great appreciation of early Russian history and law; his library contained valuable chronicles and documents on Russian history, and the historian Vasilii Tatishchev sought him out for information and documentation.[27] The Swedish envoy Cedercreutz wrote of him: "Knez Dmitri Gallizin is a gentlemen fond of the old Russian system."[28] But he and Dolgorukii collaborated in much of the Petrine enterprise and advanced the cause of reform.

Indications of disaffection on Golitsyn's part first surfaced when rule fell to Marta Skavronskaia and her favorites, Menshikov and Duke Karl Friedrich. About this time the French envoy Campredon reported Golitsyn was interested in establishing a government order like that in England.[29] Picking up on the same intelligence, the English envoy Rondeau noted Golitsyn was a powerful and destabilizing presence in Russian politics. He was

> possessed of singular natural abilities improved by art and experience. An active mind, of deep forsight and penetration, with solid judgement, surpassing all men in the knowledge of russian laws and a manly eloquence, of a bold enterprising genius full of ambition and artifice, remarkably sober but in his temper haughty cruel and implacable . . . no man is more capable than he, nor any more inclined to raise and conduct a dangerous rebellion in the russian empire.[30]

Golitsyn's concern stemmed in part from a revulsion against the elevation of a commoner with a scandalous past and in part from the disarray in government after Peter I's demise.[31]

The key issue of power in the reign of Catherine I touched the regulation of delegated authority. The symbol of and vehicle for abuse of tsarist authority was the issuance of oral imperial decrees. Anyone who had the confidence of the empress could issue decrees in her name, whether or not they held a position of responsibility in the government. Persons, not institutions, ruled; normal procedures were circumvented by anyone with the opportunity to issue oral imperial decrees. The regents named upon Catherine's death ordered an end to this practice and forbade the promulgation of imperial decrees without the approval of the regency council (which included all members of the Supreme Privy Council). Since a series of cabals soon removed most of the people who had acted independently and left control in the hands of the Supreme Council, there was no urgency at that time to alter the arrangements of government. But with the prospect of a new ruler in 1730—a woman from Courland with her own entourage—the need to guard against the abuse of sovereign authority by favorites again arose, and members of the Council sought to institutionalize the kind of control they had acquired by default in the years of Peter II's reign.[32]

It is worth considering the role that the sex of the new monarch played. The regency agreement for Peter II's minority placed limits on his freedom of action but did not contemplate any restrictions on his autocratic power after he came of age. The Supreme Council would probably not have dared to impose limitations on a male ruler. Only the novelty and incidental nature of the elevation of a female, plus the general evaluation of women as incompetent, made it possible for the Council to act as it did.[33]

Golitsyn and Dolgorukii disliked despotism, but, even more than a despot, they seemed to fear the use of despotic authority by favorites. They also feared "democracy," broad political participation by the nobility as was the practice in Poland and Sweden. This is evident in Dolgorukii's remarks about the dangers and inconveniences of this kind of arrangement. The leaders of the Council sought to establish a middle way—oligarchy—but they did not seem to understand that Russian history had not given them the means to realize this third possibility. Neither the Council nor any other mechanism for limiting monarchy could work until it acquired the necessary authority. The source of this authority in Europe was legitimation by the estates of the realm, but Russia had no recognized estates in the European sense, let alone a tradition of legitimation by a constituted assembly of estates. Legitimacy derived from God acting through His viceroy the tsar. In this sense, the Council's tactic of representing the Conditions as a voluntary concession of the empress was the right one.

But when opponents challenged the Conditions and Anna ceased to play along with the fiction—she soon made appointments in violation of her promise—the Council suddenly had to cast about for another source of legitimacy. Golitsyn evidently had previously given some thought to this problem. When he announced the election of Anna the night of Peter II's death, he did so in a predetermined sequence, going to the Senate and then to the generalitet. Because the high clergy had supinely agreed to the earlier elevation of Marta Skavronskaia, Golitsyn regarded them as forfeit and did not include them. In this connection, he remarked that "estates of the realm would henceforth be the Supreme Council, the Senate, and the generalitet."[34]

The generalitet may have been the key, since one of the articles of the Conditions also referred to this group indirectly by forbidding the empress to appoint persons to ranks above that of colonel, a provision that gave the Council control over the composition of the generalitet. Possibly then, as Isabel de Madariaga speculated recently, the Council toward the end hoped to win legitimation from an "estate" made up of the body of general officers of civil and military rank.[35] It was, however, no easy matter to instill in as recent and artificial a category as the generalitet the authority to grant sovereign power. Golitsyn's knowledge of Western history and statecraft may have permitted him to conceive of a proper mechanism for legitimating a limited monarchy, but Russian history did not give him the means to bring this conception to life.

Even if Golitsyn intended to include the generalitet, he imposed a major limiting condition: the reservation of half the seats in the Council and the Senate for the "families." The most that can be said about this strategy was it may have been an attempt to marry the ancient principle of clan precedence with the newer one of earned rank. But what families did Golitsyn have in mind? The proposals generated in the Council chambers offered no definition, and no one but the Golitsyns and Dolgorukiis received an invitation to join the Council. The use of the loan word "famil'nye" suggests that Golitsyn borrowed this notion from his knowledge of Venice, whose leaders since the fourteenth century had "closed" participation on the governing council to everyone except members of certain ancient families.[36]

Whatever the case, even the Council's later proposals were concessions made under the press of battle, concessions not actually granted or publicized. Not only does the wording of the proposals remain unclear but even whether the members of the Council had agreed to offer the concessions at all. Often quoted is Dmitrii Golitsyn's remark after the failure of the coup: "The banquet was prepared, but the guests proved unworthy."[37] He may, however, have neglected to send an invitation, or, if he did, to specify what dishes were being served.

A second strategy was pursued by the supporters of the project of the 361. Although historians usually place this project together with the Conditions as part of an anti-autocratic movement for political rights, the project sought not so much political as civil rights. Its only clear political aim was to dilute the power of the oligarchs. It will be recalled that the first expression from the group behind the 361 project—the

society proposal that preceded the announcement of the Conditions—
demanded abolition of the Supreme Privy Council. The project of the
361, which had to treat the Conditions as an accomplished fact, left a
"High Government" of twenty-one persons and a Senate, both of which
would be "elected." But unlike the Council, the drafters of the 361
project made no effort to define the electorate beyond a vague reference
to the ranking officials and the nobility. Given its vagueness, the reference may have pointed to nothing more than the practice introduced
by Peter I of balloting for offices, which was altogether compatible with
autocracy. The project of the 361 was explicit, however, in its strictures
against concentrating power in a few families.

The concern for civil protections is the most striking aspect of the
project. The drafters wanted protection from the dominance of the old
families and a guarantee that the nobles of rank would be treated with
respect. This meant no service in the lowest ranks, a limitation on the
years of obligatory service, orderly pay and promotion, adequate care
when disabled or retired, and the opportunity to provide for their children by a return to traditional inheritance laws. The project made no
mention of autocratic power and posed no challenge to tsarist authority.
Nor did it question the choice of Anna. Some of the signers were, in
fact, close relatives of the new empress, persons who could expect boons
from her assumption of full autocratic power. The project of the 361
was aimed not against autocracy but against oligarchy, against the Council. It sought to build a shield for the lives and careers of nobles by
redressing the balance of power between the Council and the crown.
Russia had always had its powerful clans, which sat in the tsar's councils
and steered the administration. That was their proper role. They went
too far, however, when they usurped sovereign power.

Foreign diplomats on the scene understood the conflict. The British
envoy Rondeau reported the participants had "no true notions of limited
government. The great nobility would fain get the power in their hands,
and the little nobility and gentry are very jealous they should, and would
rather have one master than several without some way be found out
to make them easy and secure from being tyrannised by the great
families."[38] The Danish envoy Westphalen made the keen observation
that if the Council had merely chosen Anna and continued as before,
it would have retained its power and authority. But its decision to strip
the empress of her prerogatives and authorize itself to run the state
aroused the generalitet, the Senate, and the lesser nobility, which had
good reason to prefer the monarchy over an oligarchy.[39]

One of these reasons was pointed out by the chief ideologue of the
group behind the 361 project, Vasilii Tatishchev. During the discussions

at the time of the crisis, he explained the importance of the proper order in government, noting that a change in authority at the top could threaten the social order. In answering hypothetical objections to autocracy—in this instance, the objection that an absolute monarch can sometimes act evilly, not accept wise counsel, and do great harm—Tatishchev responded that

> this must be accepted as punishment from God. For it is not prudent to alter the former order just because of an exceptional case. Who would assert that if we saw some noble senselessly destroying his domain, this would be cause to deprive the entire nobility of its freedom to rule [its estates] and instead turn [the management] over to the slaves; no one would countenance that. Governance in the state must operate in the same manner at every level; the authority of the central government should correspond in some way with the authority of the nobles on their domains, as may be sufficiently demonstrated by [the example of] other countries.[40]

In other words, if the nobles wished to act as little autocrats on their estates, they had best not undermine autocracy at the top. Their security depended upon a continued correspondence between the political and the social regimes.

Hostility to a council staffed by the old aristocracy was not out of character for the nobility. The Petrine nobility evolved from the military service class of Muscovite Russia. The group was a creation of the centralizing autocracy. The tsar provided for the noblemen's support by granting them populated estates; the servicemen's interests were therefore tied to the autocracy. In contrast, the boyar magnates, who included the Golitsyn and Dolgorukii families, had often been the servicemen's social and economic rivals. The magnates had dominated the upper reaches of the state administration and had placed obstacles in the path of the servicemen's social and career advancement. The magnates had also posed an economic threat, because the aristocrats usually owned large lands with hundreds and even thousands of peasant households, whereas the great majority of servicemen held small estates populated by only a few peasant households. In the labor-short economy of Muscovite Russia, the two groups competed for a limited supply of peasant workers. This conflict was at the core of a struggle to change the laws governing serf runaways. The servicemen demanded an end to the statute of limitations on returning runaways, while the boyars resisted attempts to restrict peasant mobility, since in a fluid market peasants gravitated to the larger estates that could offer better terms. The unequal competition frequently drove the poorer servicemen to the wall. The servicemen finally won their demand when the government needed them to put down the widespread disturbances in the mid-seventeenth century. Still, the memory of this conflict was sufficiently fresh that few servicemen were likely to entrust their careers and livelihood to a sovereign council of boyars.

A lack of unity at the top also worked to the disadvantage of ordinary nobles. The Supreme Privy Council's takeover in 1730 resembled a number of previous boyar attempts to dominate the government, most notably during the regency of Ivan IV and after the death of False Dmitrii I. On both occasions the servicemen suffered great losses. Turmoil destroyed the central authority, and as a result peasant flight increased, delivering the hardest blow to the servicemen, who could ill afford the drain of labor power. If the loss of unity in central government was costly in the days before full enserfment, how much greater the cost must have appeared after this boon. As never before the state operated to the benefit of the servicemen. The government was now committed to track down serf runaways, but it could only do so if it were united and strong. To leave the oligarchs in control would not only threaten unity; it would also place command in the hands of the very magnates who would profit most from lax enforcement of the laws on serfdom.

If oligarchy broke the unity of authority in government, broader participation would further weaken it. The dualistic character of Russian thought may have made government by elected representatives virtually unthinkable, because it would have to allow for a gray area, a neutral space, rather than clear rules and a single point of view, which was the right one by definition. If authority were divided—even potentially divided—who could protect the faith and the homeland while the squabbling went on? Besides, a divided sovereignty would not resemble God's authority or, as Tatishchev pointed out, that of the nobles on their estates and in their homes. If evidence of the dangers of divided rule were needed, it lay close at hand. News arrived that the Swedes were mobilizing in Finland and planning to move on St. Petersburg, while other reports told of disorders and possible plans for secession in the Ukraine.[41]

The supporters of the project of the 361 thus rejected oligarchy, and they seemed equally determined not to govern in their own behalf. Yet it is clear that this group did not want despotism either, for they demanded respect and security of their lives and livelihood. They wanted to be consulted on the choice of a new ruler and on matters that concerned their interests directly. In their attack on the Council, they may have been groping for a division of responsibility among the autocracy, the Council, and the Senate that would prevent the emergence of a tyranny of either the monarch or the Council.

But underlying this, both hidden and revealed in the patterned expressions about tsarist solicitude, is a yearning for the tsar-father who will look after the country and its servicemen with firm and understanding leadership. Despite Peter I's efforts to implant the notion of an abstract state to which everyone, including the tsar, would owe allegiance, most Russian nobles continued to conceive of the ruler as a charismatic figure, the agent of God. This desire for security under the personal authority of a sanctified ruler ensured a sympathetic hearing for the appeals of the third political program being advanced during the crisis.

The strategy of the third group, represented by outsiders like Iaguzhinskii, Prokopovich, and Osterman, was aimed not at restoring a traditional balance between council and autocrat but at destroying the Council and returning to autocracy without conditions or concessions. The tactics included a crude appeal to the fear of disunity and chaos. This message was clear in the broadside quoted earlier. Prokopovich played to these concerns, bolstering his predictions of catastrophe with references to history and the Russian nature:

> These lords [Privy Councilors] cannot long remain in agreement; as many as be their number, so many will there be atamans battling with one another, and Russia will take on the shabby appearance it once had when, divided into many principalities, it lived in poverty. . . . The Russian people is of such a nature that only autocratic authority can preserve it; and if any other principle of authority is instituted, it will be impossible to maintain [the people] in unity and prosperity.[42]

These appeals were having an impact. The Saxon envoy Lefort heard the same alarms in his conversations with rank-and-file nobles. They asked questions: "Who is going to guarantee that with time instead of a single ruler we will not have as many tyrants as there are members in the Supreme Privy Council and that they will not by their oppression increase our slavery? We have no established laws that could guide the Council; if its members should begin to promulgate laws themselves, they could as well at any time do away with them, and Russia will be thrown into anarchy!"[43] The same concerns on the part of the nobility can be detected in the reports by other foreign envoys.[44]

The strategy of the opponents of reform worked for a number of reasons, both proximate and dispositional. They mobilized a number of resolute confederates, including Ivan Iur'evich Trubetskoi, his kinsman Aleksei Mikhailovich Cherkasskii, and members of the Saltykov clan related to the new empress. These men then took advantage of the nobility's fear and confusion—a state of mind produced by the opposition's propaganda and the Supreme Council's failure to respond publicly to the proposals of the nobles—and led the guards and three hundred noblemen up to the Kremlin to press their petition upon the empress. This bold step in the midst of confusion and doubt made the difference.

But what made this action successful was the disposition of the nobility to mistrust the oligarchs. They were determined not to be ruled by the Golitsyns and Dolgorukiis, and they were equally determined not to rule on their own behalf. A few nobles may have wished to extend political participation, but they were greatly outnumbered. The majority wished to reduce their obligations to the state. This desire was evident in the proposals submitted to the Council, and it was also manifest in the widespread practice of service dodging (*netchestvo*), which posed a continual challenge for the government.[45] Public spirit was not an outstanding characteristic of the Russian nobility. To cite one example from this period, in 1728 the government ordered the nobility to elect five delegates from each province to assist in the compilation of a new law code. By the date set for the assembly only one delegate had come voluntarily to Moscow. A month later no more than a handful of the delegates had appeared. The government finally had to send troops out to force the representatives to show up and attend to business.[46] Ordinary nobles seemed to regard participation in government as a burden. In addition to the good reasons the nobility had to support strong government, the opponents of reform could count on the aversion of the rank and file to direct participation in government.

Conclusion

The Supreme Privy Council's role as a force for "political modernization" in Yanov's sense of the term might finally be tested by a look at what the Council did while in power. To what extent did the Council modify what Yanov calls the "garrison-state dictatorship" of Peter I?[47] The answer is: not much. The changes made by the Council could scarcely be termed liberal and could not fit under any definition of "political modernization."

The Secret Chancellery was abolished in 1726 but in name only. Its functions fell to a revived Preobrazhenskii Prikaz (Office of State Investigations) and to other agencies, including the Council itself, which supervised special inquisitions. Still other inquisitorial investigations were carried out by ad hoc commissions and even by individuals like

Menshikov.[48] This chaotic situation was scarcely to be preferred to Peter's government, which at least had a regular office that bore responsibility for this unappealing work. The Council also revised Peter I's tariff law of 1724, easing trade regulations in order to sell more raw products and purchase manufactured goods. The policy was liberal only in the sense of favoring the nobility over commercial and manufacturing interests and may have slowed Russia's productive development.[49] The Council did not reestablish the office of Patriarch of the Orthodox Church or the institutions of boyar rule in the seventeenth century, unless one regards the Council itself as an updated Boyar Duma.

Two decisions by the Council of major practical and symbolic significance were the dismantling of the local government reform of Peter I and the retention of the poll tax. By 1727 the Council abandoned Peter's system of local government with its highly articulated separation of functions and responsibilities and returned to the unified system of the seventeenth century in which all power was concentrated in the hands of the governor and *voevoda* (a provincial official holding both administrative and judicial powers). In the matter of taxation the Council took the opposite approach. Instead of restoring the earlier system of tying taxation to cultivated land, which had the advantage of determining the tax burden through some measure of productivity, a commission headed by Golitsyn opted—after much deliberation, to be sure—to retain a poll tax that bore little relation to a community's ability to pay. Neither decision could be described as liberalization or political modernization.

The collapse of Russia's finances no doubt forced both these decisions. But the Council shared responsibility for the breakdown. It failed to get control of finances or plan for the future but grabbed ad hoc for the nearest revenue source to cover each contingency. By 1728-29, the government lacked money for ordinary expenses, the fleet was falling into decay, and the administration was in a state of drift.[50] It is not surprising that the nobility rejected this kind of leadership in the crisis of 1730.

To sum up, the failure of the attempt to limit the autocracy in 1730 stemmed in large part from the absence of estate institutions that could confer legitimacy on the Council or some other body. But the cause lies deeper, in the perception of authority as God-given and unitary and in the historical experience of the nobility that shaped this perception. If it is true, as the semioticians write, that Russians thought in strictly dualistic terms, the lack of intermediary corporations implied the absence of a category of thought that would have accommodated institutions of limitation and compromise. The life of society could only be conceived of either as security under autocracy or as an anarchic freedom in which the strong tyrannized the weak. This cast of mind would have found reinforcement in the experience of the nobility, which had seen in the past that divided leadership and boyar rule had harmed noble interests and weakened the country. The recent stewardship of the Supreme Privy Council may have done much to recall the chaotic times of past boyar government.

Those who wish to judge present-day possibilities for reform on the basis of this early-eighteenth-century experience should obviously not make one-to-one comparisons of the Supreme Privy Council as the Politburo, the generalitet as the Central Committee or military brass, and the middle-level Party officials as nobles. But analysts can pose questions about power relationships in a more general way. They need not ask whether Soviet citizens today have an awareness of constitutional order; the conventional knowledge about the mechanisms of limited government and constitutional protection of individual rights is expressed in the documents that define the Soviet system of governance. People know in some abstract way how limited government is supposed to operate, but, even assuming they think it a good idea, do they believe that it can operate in the U.S.S.R. (or for that matter anywhere else)? Do Soviet officials in the government and economy feel more comfortable with a system of diffused authority—a collective leadership reflecting the pluralistic competition of interest groups—or with the leadership of a charismatic party boss who enforces a discipline on subordinate bodies in line with his own program? Are those in positions of responsibility persuaded that security can be combined with freedom, that the independent action of citizens can operate within a framework of order? Are middle-level officials willing to sacrifice their power to act and to punish in the same measure that they wish to be released from the grip of those above them? In other words, have those in positions of responsibility come to trust that, in the absence of a charismatic leader who can enforce discipline, a constitutional order and the laws will protect them from the tyranny of those above them? These are minimal conditions for reform of the type that interests Yanov; they do not even go to the more fundamental issues such as protection of unpopular opinion from the tyranny of the majority. But these conditions must be met if liberal constitutionalists like Yanov hope to see Russia overcome the obstacles that stymied reform in the eighteenth century.

NOTES

1. Alexander Yanov, "The Drama of the Time of Troubles, 1725-1730," *Canadian-American Slavic Studies* 12 (1978):1-59. Soviet historians have, as

a rule, not pursued the constitutional implications of the events of that time but have seen them as a struggle of intra-class strata. See, for example, S. M. Troitskii, "Istoriografiia 'dvortsovykh perevorotov' v Rossii XVIII v.," *Voprosy istorii* 41, no. 2 (1966):38-53.

2. *Polnoe sobranie zakonov rossiiskoi imperii,* 1st series (St. Petersburg, 1830), vol. 6, no. 3,893 (February 5, 1722).

3. For recent discussion of the provenance of the document, see James Cracraft, "Did Feofan Prokopovich Really Write *Pravda Voli Monarshei?*" *Slavic Review* 40 (1981):173-93.

4. For a recent positive assessment of Golitsyn and his work, which describes him as a constitutional reformer in the Speranskii mold, see Isabel de Madariaga, "Portrait of an Eighteenth-Century Russian Statesman: Prince Dmitry Mikhaylovich Golitsyn," *Slavonic and East European Review* 62 (1984):36-60.

5. Text abbreviated slightly from that in D. A. Korsakov, *Votsarenie imperatritsy Anny Ioannovyny* (Kazan', 1880), pp. 17-18. The origin of these "points" is much disputed. Direct borrowing from Swedish codes is argued by Korsakov, *Votsarenie,* pp. 280-86; Harald Hjärne, "Ryska konstitutionsprojekt år 1730 efter svenska förebilder," *Historisk tidskrift,* no. 4 (1884):189-272; and P. N. Miliukov, *Iz istorii russkoi intelligentsii* (St. Petersburg, 1903), pp. 8-11. Other scholars find the source in earlier aristocratic bids for power: N. P. Zagoskin, *Verkhovniki i shliakhetstvo 1730-go goda* (Kazan', 1881), pp. 36-38; Walther Recke, "Die Verfassungspläne der russischen Oligarchen im Jahre 1730," *Zeitschrift für osteuropäische Geschichte* 2 (1911):37; V. O. Kliuchevskii, *Kurs russkoi istorii,* 5 vols. (Moscow, 1915), 4:354-55.

6. On Anna's political role in Courland, see Theodor Schiemann, "Eine Episode aus der Geschichte der preussisch-russischen Heiratspläne," *Historische Zeitschrift* 68 (1892):428-40.

7. As quoted in G. A. Protasov, "'Konditsii' 1730 g. i ikh prodolzhenie," *Uchenye zapiski Tambovskogo gosudarstvennogo pedagogichekogo instituta* 15 (1957):226.

8. For a detailed examination and analysis of the project's origin and dating, see G. A. Protasov, "Zapiska Tatishcheva o 'Proizvol'nom rassuzhdenii' dvorianstva v sobytiiakh 1730 g.," *Problemy istochnikovedeniia* 11 (1963):245-53; and Protasov, "Dvorianskie proekty 1730 goda (istochnikovedcheskoe izuchenie)," *Istochnikovedcheskie raboty* 2 (1971):66-72.

9. Korsakov, *Votsarenie,* p. 170. Translation modified from that in Marc Raeff, ed., *Plans for Political Reform in Imperial Russia, 1730-1905* (Englewood Cliffs, N.J., 1966), pp. 49-50.

10. This is the document (in three drafts) known in the literature as the "Oath" or "Points for an Oath." The dating is Protasov's. See his "Verkhovnyi tainyi sovet i ego proekty 1730 goda," *Istochnikovedcheskie raboty* 1 (1970):78-81.

11. As summarized in ibid., pp. 69-71; a fuller summary is in Korsakov, *Votsarenie,* appendix, pp. 13-19.

12. Iaguzhinskii had secretly advised Anna to reject the supremacy of the

Council. Details are in the dispatches of the French envoy Magnan published in N. Tourgueneff, *La Russie et les Russes,* 3 vols. (Paris, 1847), 3:386-90.

13. Description of the meeting by Feofan Prokopovich in I. A. Chistovich, *Feofan Prokopovich i ego vremia* (St. Petersburg, 1868), p. 258.

14. Text from the Grekov copy reproduced in full in Raeff, *Plans,* pp. 48-49.

15. For details, see Protasov, "Dvorianskie proekty," pp. 61-102.

16. Project published in Korsakov, *Votsarenie,* appendix, pp. 9-11, and in Raeff, *Plans,* pp. 46-48.

17. Brenda Meehan-Waters, *Autocracy and Aristocracy: The Russian Service Elite of 1730* (New Brunswick, N.J., 1982), pp. 132-48.

18. Protasov, "Vekhovnyi tainyi sovet," pp. 85-86.

19. The entire text is in Protasov, "Verkhovnyi tainyi sovet," pp. 88-89.

20. This method would, however, not have accorded with the provisions in the "form of government."

21. Quoted in Protasov, "Verkhovnyi tainyi sovet," pp. 100-1.

22. Korsakov, *Votsarenie,* pp. 271-72 (italics added).

23. The English envoy Rondeau reported this intelligence. *Sbornik Imperatorskogo russkogo istoricheskogo obshchestva,* 148 vols. (St. Petersburg, 1867-1916), 66:153 (hereafter *SIRIO*).

24. Korsakov, *Votsarenie,* p. 135.

25. This document was found in the papers of Artemii Volynskii and is sometimes attributed to him. Korsakov places it among the written protests that the Danish envoy Westphalen noted. Korsakov, *Votsarenie,* pp. 256, 264.

26. Ibid., p. 264.

27. N. Popov, *V. N. Tatishchev i ego vremia* (St. Petersburg, 1861), p. 434.

28. Quoted in Hjärne, "Ryska konstitutionsprojekt," p. 206n.

29. *SIRIO,* 64:199, 264.

30. *SIRIO,* 66:158-59.

31. Westphalen dispatch of February 5, in Korsakov, *Votsarenie,* appendix, pp. 75-76.

32. Debate has raged over whether the Supreme Privy Council in fact served prior to Peter II's death as the leading executive body. A. N. Filippov argued that the Council in 1730 was only claiming de jure the power it had already acquired de facto. See his "K voprosu o verkhovnom tainom sovete," *Russkaia mysl',* no. 6 (1896):54-79; no. 7 (1896):90-124. This view was shared by P. Golitsyn, *Pervyi Vek Senata* (St. Petersburg, 1910), pp. 72-79; M. N. Pokrovskii, *Russkaia istoriia s drevneishikh vremen,* 5 vols. (Leningrad, 1924), 2:322; and Walther Recke, "Die Verfassungspläne der russischen Oligarchen," p. 39. A. S. Alekseev disagreed and, on the basis of statistical evidence, held that the Council had fallen into disuse during Peter II's reign, leaving matters to powerful individuals. "Sil'nye persony v Verkhovnom Tainom Sovete Petra II i rol' kniazia Golitsyna pri votsarenii Anny Ioannovny," *Russkoe obozrenie* 46:641-44. V. O. Kliuchevskii adopted this view. *Kurs russkoi istorii,* 4:361. It is of some importance whether the nobility perceived the Council's power

as that of influential individuals or a legitimate state institution sanctified by tsarist decision.

33. I may be in disagreement here with the conclusions of the thought-provoking article of Brenda Meehan-Waters, "Catherine the Great and the Problem of Female Rule," *Russian Review* 34 (1975):295-307. She will at least agree that Tatishchev questioned the ability of a woman, and I believe that most other nobles were still close to the monkish views of Muscovy about the evil and incompetence of women. See, for example, the discussion in L. N. Semenova, *Ocherki istorii byta i kul'turnoi zhizni Rossii. Pervaia polovina XVIII v.* (Leningrad, 1982), pp. 142-50.

34. Westphalen dispatch of January 22, in Korsakov, *Votsarenie,* appendix, p. 72.

35. de Madariaga, "Portrait," p. 56.

36. James C. Davis, *A Venetian Family and Its Fortune, 1500-1900* (Philadelphia, 1975), pp. 1-20. The Polish senate was another possible model, if not a precise one. As a rule, only members of magnate families sat in the senate, but they did so by virtue of their office, not family entitlement—a formal distinction of some significance.

37. Korsakov, *Votsarenie,* p. 278.

38. Dispatch of February 16, *SIRIO,* 66:136-39.

39. Dispatch of March 2, in Korsakov, *Votsarenie,* appendix, p. 82.

40. "Proizvol'noe i soglasnoe rassuzhdenie i mnenie sobravshegosia shliakhetstva russkogo o pravlenii gosudarstvennom," *Utro* (Moscow, 1859), p. 374.

41. Korsakov, *Votsarenie,* pp. 253-54.

42. From his pamphlet, "O kontse Petra II," published as an addendum to "Zapiski diuka Liriiskogo," *Russkii Arkhiv* 1 1909):434-35.

43. Cited in M. M. Bogoslovskii, *Konstitutsionnoe dvizhenie 1730 g.* (Petrograd, 1918), p. 16.

44. See Rondeau, *SIRIO,* 66:136; Westphalen, in Korsakov, *Votsarenie,* appendix, pp. 76-77.

45. N. P. Pavlov-Sil'vanskii, *Gosudarevy sluzhilye liudi* (St. Petersburg, 1898), pp. 282-87.

46. V. N. Latkin, *Zakonodatel'nye komissii v Rossii v XVIII st.* (St. Petersburg, 1887), pp. 46-52.

47. Alexander Yanov, "Is Sovietology Reformable?" herein, p. 265.

48. William Slany, "Russian Central Government Institutions, 1725-1741" (Ph.D. dissertation, Cornell University, 1958), pp. 230-32.

49. E. V. Anisimov, *Vnutrenniaia politika Verkhovnogo tainogo soveta,* (Leningrad, 1975), pp. 17-19.

50. Slany, "Russian Central Government," pp. 105, 214.

Catherine II's Efforts at Liberalization and Their Aftermath

JOHN T. ALEXANDER

Is "liberalization" applicable to the basic policies pursued by Empress Catherine II during her lengthy reign (1762-96)? With appropriate qualifications (and some lingering doubts), this essay will argue for the affirmative. To be sure, the term "liberalization" may be understood in various ways depending upon the perspective adopted. No doubt Russians and Europeans in the eighteenth century understood the term differently than we do today. And their ideas probably changed after 1789. The working definition employed here will be to denote a process of political, societal, economic, and intellectual change that aimed at— and to some extent achieved—expansion of the political arena in terms of numbers of persons and types of social groups involved, kinds of issues addressed, and the means whereby those issues were made public or resolved. In terms of Alexander Yanov's theory of cycles of Russian political development, Catherine's reign fits fairly neatly between two episodes of despotic rule (the reigns of Peter III and Paul I). It therefore might also be termed "liberalizing" simply by contrast to its immediate predecessor and successor.

It should be admitted at once that this presentation cannot presume to be a full-scale reevaluation of issues of reform in Catherinian Russia based on my own fresh research. Rather, it is a meditation on these issues in the light of recent scholarship, most of it Anglo-American. The major historiographical parameters of the discussion may be set, provisionally, by the recent books of David Ransel, Roger Bartlett, J. Michael Hittle, Isabel de Madariaga, Marc Raeff, Robert Jones, John LeDonne, W. Gareth Jones, Gary Marker, and the late Arcadius Kahan.[1] The appearance of so many seminal works on the period in such a brief interval offers impressive testimony to the vigor of scholarship in this field, even as it may hint at an erosion of consensus concerning basic issues. Such controversy is not new for Catherine's reputation, the contradictory qualities of which surfaced almost as soon as she ascended the throne.[2]

The liberalizing character of Catherine's reign was proclaimed at home and abroad almost from its inception and, from a policy perspective, could be seen in retrospect as a continuation of some of Peter III's policies. In fact, the outpouring of favorable publicity for the new monarch and her regime may smack of prearrangement and perhaps some degree of media manipulation, like that seen recently at the start of the governments of Andropov and Gorbachev. Within a month of Catherine's accession, for example, English periodicals printed enthusiastic accounts of her personal qualities and political prospects, concluding that "she has long been the delight of the people over whom she now reigns; she has studied their genius, and will make their good her principal care. . . ."[3] Before the end of the year an anonymous "Extract of a Letter from a Gentleman at Petersburgh" castigated Peter III's gross ineptitude, denied any "intrigues or unfair methods" behind Catherine's seizure of power, and celebrated the good sense of the people of Russia for "placing on the throne one of the worthiest princesses that ever swayed a sceptre."[4]

By contrast, another nameless English commentator opined that the nature of the coup had combined with Catherine's lack of a hereditary title to create a peculiar situation: "the most absolute power on earth, is now held by an elective monarch."[5] These sentiments were quite in line with the "election" rhetoric of Catherine's early manifestoes, which may also remind us of those issued by Vasilii Shuiskii and Mikhail Romanov upon their accession. Yet the same English commentator drew additional lessons from Russia's recent political traditions:

> The power of the tsars, though absolute and uncontrollable in its exercise, is extremely weak in its foundation. There is not perhaps in Europe a government, which depends so much on the good-will and affection of those that are governed, and which requires a greater degree of vigilance and a steadier hand. The regular succession which has been so often broken, and the great change of manners, which in less than a century has been introduced, have left in Russia a weakness amidst all the appearance of strength, and a great facility to sudden and dangerous revolutions.[6]

Indeed, the way that Catherine gained the throne exerted great influence on policies and policymaking throughout her reign. She never forgot her sovereign illegitimacy; neither did her son, the future Paul I. Her political illegitimacy, however, need not be seen as entirely negative for her statecraft. It probably energized her governing activity in an effort to prove that she was worthy of her lofty position. Perhaps it also informed the caution and restraint she displayed in many situations—valuable qualities for any politician. Perhaps, too, it served as a constant reminder of the importance of fundamental political principles, which she once summed up as "circumstance, conjecture, and conjuncture"—principles that she took to heart.[7]

Proclaimed "by the Grace of God, Empress, and Autocratix, [independent ruler] of all the Russias, etc.," Catherine came into power with a mixture of ideas about how to rule her adopted realm.[8] If, as her title's gloss implied, "autocratix" denoted nothing specific about the new ruler's relationship to her subjects, two main models of rulership were at hand: Petrine and Montesquieuian. The Petrine legacy meant unlimited government, or "absolute sovereignty" as Isabel de Madariaga has explained it: government not constrained by "fundamental laws." This Petrine despotism was contrasted unfavorably by Catherine to Montesquieu's "true monarchy," which rested upon fundamental laws more or less limiting the ruler's authority: the law of succession, "intermediary powers" in the form of social orders or estates, and "channels" for the legal transmission of sovereign authority. No third form of rule appealed to Catherine, who resolutely condemned the aristocrat oligarchs (verkhovniki) of 1730 for their affront to national political tradition.[9]

Catherine obviously preferred the Montesquieuian model. But its adaptation to Russia encountered enormous difficulties from the absence (or extreme weakness) of social estates, her own inability to alter the succession because of her status as a usurper (and Paul's competing right to the throne), and the weak development of local institutions, especially legal institutions and media of expression. These obstacles were further complicated by the pervasive presence of serfdom and the sheer size (and vulnerable frontiers) of the Russian Empire that put a premium on centralized, military-style administration and demanded an active, expansive foreign policy. For all these reasons the process of reform under Catherine proved sporadic and erratic, gradual and lengthy. Acutely aware of the dangers of revolution in the Russian context— either a palace coup mounted by elite elements such as the guards regiments or a jacquerie such as the Pugachevshchina (the Pugachev Revolt)—the empress had to feel her way toward liberalizing reforms.

Catherine's principal political aims upon coming to the throne focused on (1) peace and security, (2) order and stability, (3) promotion of legality and consensus, and (4) notions of progress, westernization, modernization, enlightenment, and social and economic development.[10] The priority of these many aims changed over time, of course, sometimes as a result of events beyond her control. Sometimes there might have been fundamental conflicts between the different aims. The search for security in regard to Poland, for example, led to civil war there and then to international war that spawned major internal complications in the form of the plague and the Pugachevshchina, all of which undermined such ideals as westernization, modernization, and enlightenment. It seems somewhat ironic that Catherine should be called the Great for, among other reasons, presiding over a major territorial expansion of the Russian Empire, inasmuch as expansion ranked low on her scale of priorities in seizing the throne. Expansion entailed problems—costs and complications—as well as glory and gains in territory and population. Order and stability clashed in certain respects with notions of enlightenment and social and economic development, at least as those notions were exemplified in revolutionary France after 1789. Furthermore, her efforts at fostering legality and consensus were undercut, it may be contended, by her preoccupation with foreign policy and her own government's lack of order and stability from roughly the mid-1780s. She did not succeed in codifying the laws, a task that she ambitiously undertook early in her reign. Neither did she complete a proposed reform of the Senate, upon which she fitfully worked from the late 1780s. The same can be said of the draft charter for the state peasants, never published in her lifetime.[11]

Neither Catherine nor her government could consistently pursue successfully liberalizing policies in all relevant spheres. Moreover, her highly personal style of rulership led to severe problems of coordination and follow-through, particularly late in her career, when energetic lieutenants like Viazemskii, Potemkin, and the Panins had left the scene, while such holdovers as Bezborodko and Zavadovskii wrestled with the overweening influence of Zubov's clique. Perhaps her government suffered from some of the same infirmities as Brezhnev's last years of tenure: tired blood in the primary leader and inadequate preparations for the succession.

The succession was an issue on which Catherine's Montesquieuian devotion to legality gave her no practical guidance. And yet ensuring the succession was crucial to the further development of many of her liberalizing reforms, for she was certainly aware that Paul did not share many of her fundamental principles. It is doubly ironic, to be sure, that Paul should have instituted a new order of succession in opposition to his mother's practice, particularly since he could not benefit from it himself. Catherine's putative "testament" was reaffirmed posthumously by partisans such as the Zubov brothers, who used it to overthrow Paul in her name for the benefit of her beloved grandson.[12]

In politics it is a truism that means may be as important as ends, which have an astonishing capacity to change under the impact of the means adopted for their achievement. If Catherine's initial aims may be tentatively termed "liberalizing," then what about her means? Her devotion to Montesquieu certainly seems to fit under the rubric of "liberalizing."[13] She began her rule by attending several sessions of the Senate, something her predecessors had rarely done, and she debated the establishment of a new imperial council at the same time, a project that she eventually postponed until 1768, when the first Turkish war confronted her with a host of new challenges. Both these cautious initiatives, together with her appointment of numerous commissions to explore significant issues and institutions (nobility, church estates, the armed forces, the Ukraine, commerce and finance, public health), attested to her determination to conduct a government of consensus that would involve wider circles of the noble and bureaucratic elite in the formulation of policies and their implementation.

In her selection of high government personnel, the empress likewise displayed liberalizing discernment in appointing such new men to high office as Nikita and Petr Panin, Aleksandr Viazemskii, Petr Rumiantsev, Grigorii Teplov, Zakhar and Ivan Chernyshev, Jakob Sievers, Grigorii and Fedor Orlov, Aleksandr Cherkassov, Mikhail Volkonskii, and Petr Saltykov. All these men were well educated for the time, all had experience abroad, and all could be expected to sympathize with Catherine's policies of building consensus in support of peaceful, enlightened imperial aims and institutions. All also appreciated her practice of consultation and cautious implementation of new policies, such as immigration of foreign colonists, economic and financial changes, and reform of the armed forces. Catherine appeared to be repudiating the militaristic excesses of her late husband without compromising the public prestige of the armed forces.

Even her vigorous reaction to suspected and actual plots—the Gur'evs and Khrushchevs in 1762, the Mirovich affair in 1764—did not necessarily violate Montesquieuian concepts of government. The first could be interpreted as showing exemplary restraint, the second as displaying both restraint (in the investigation and trial) and swift resolution of a blatant threat. One wonders what her lieutenants thought of her quiet restoration of the political police. Did they see it as a violation of Montesquieu's precepts or simply as prudent precaution and precedent? In any event, she kept that institution under firm central control and downplayed its public role.

The piecemeal reforms of Catherine's first five years may easily fit under the rubric of "liberalizing" in the sense that they were formulated and implemented in close consultation with a variety of elite officials, working as individuals or as members of commissions. Besides, at least one innovation of this period, the Free Economic Society, offered a new forum for public discussion of new issues, even ticklish matters such as peasant property rights. None of the reforms challenged any entrenched groups, and most spread government patronage to at least a slightly broader circle of the elite, raising the prestige of provincial officialdom in particular. Dividing the Senate into six departments (two in Moscow) had the merit of allowing some aristocrats to stay in their beloved old capital and increasing the membership of that prestigious body without adding to its autonomy or authority.[14] Her reinforcement of the office of procurator-general by the addition of procurators at the province (*provintsiia*) level also supported attempts to rationalize the provincial administration by clarifying the governors' duties and diminishing the military element in everyday administration.

Establishment of the Commission on Commerce in 1763 provided another new focus, albeit not a public one, for broad discussion of state economic policies. Catherine's championship of liberalizing initiatives in the regulation of industrial and commercial activities, hired instead of bondaged labor, the export of grains, and revision of tariff rates for imports all held significant implications for the socioeconomic role of the merchantry and for her professed goal of creating a third estate or "middling sort of people" in Russia. Economic stimulation could be expected to facilitate other liberalizing reforms in the social and political sphere—carefully tailored reforms initiated at the top, of course.[15]

The various welfare-oriented reforms of this period, such as establishment of the Moscow Foundling Home, reorganization of the central medical administration, and the appointment of a commission on town planning, all reflected the emphasis on peaceful, "enlightened" yet pragmatic efforts to address long-standing social problems. Catherine may well have been aware of the criticism of the philosophes for neglecting practical affairs, the contention that they were impractical dreamers and utopians; hence, she endeavored to show that she could apply abstract ideas to actual problems. Her own inoculation against smallpox in 1768 offered an especially dramatic and highly publicized case of personal zeal in pursuit of useful measures against a dreadful disease.

The Legislative Commission of 1767-68 brought many of these same issues into a broader, more public arena. This undertaking in many ways amounted to Catherine's most ambitious, most risk-laden effort at liberalization. It involved more individuals and more diverse social groups in the public discussion of major issues, many with political implications. It was highly publicized in Russia and abroad; Catherine's own *Great Instruction* was quickly translated into all the main European languages (and to such less-known tongues as modern Greek, Swedish, and Rumanian).[16] Certainly it was the most widely representative body to meet publicly in Russia. It generated an enormous volume of documentation on an amazing array of subjects, and its nineteen subcommittees compiled numerous proposals for particular reforms. Withal, this lode of materials provided the empress with information on virtually every conceivable topic that legislation might ever address. No doubt the selection of deputies, the compilation of *nakazy* (instructions, cahiers), the plenary sessions, and the work of the subcommissions all stimulated political discussion and debate on an unprecedented scale in time of peace. This was the politics of consensus writ large.

Yet, the comparative barrenness of the Legislative Commission in producing perceptible change in the short run, the postponement of plenary sessions with the outbreak of the Turkish War, and the confused proceedings of both plenary and subcommittee meetings, all multiplied the threat of raising impossible expectations amid an atmosphere of incipient societal antagonism. The issue of serfdom, specifically peasant attacks on noble landlords, surfaced explosively in 1767, to Catherine's considerable consternation. She started to see what monsters could arise from the morass of serfdom and how morbidly sensitive about it even "enlightened" aristocrats could be. It was a sobering discovery, with huge implications for all sorts of other reforms.[17]

The Legislative Commission's constructive efforts were largely overshadowed in the short run by the multidimensional crisis of 1768-75 erupting from the Russo-Turkish War and first partition of Poland, the disastrous plague of 1770-72, and the horrendous Pugachevshchina, not to mention the problems attendant upon Catherine's estrangement from Grigorii Orlov, the decline of the Panin "party," and Paul's majority and marriage. It seems no accident that Catherine instituted her imperial council as a standing institution at the start of this siege of crises and that she attended it quite frequently for the first few years. Conciliar government henceforth became a frequent mode of administration for her.

Catherine's second burst of "legislomania," as she jokingly called it, drew heavily upon the materials generated by the Legislative Commission to formulate the Guberniia (Provincial) Reform of 1775, the Police Code of 1782, and the twin charters of 1785. The work of the commission on public schools and her issuance of the decree on private presses were both linked in a general way to these reforms, which may be termed "liberalizing" in the sense that they all aimed to encourage a greater measure of initiative and self-directed activity on the part of responsible elements of society, the nobility above all.

The general thrust of these enactments was to create Montesquieuian "intermediary bodies" in the shape of a consolidated nobility, restructured urban estates, and a redefined and refurbished system of courts. Six types of noble status by origin were recognized, and the nobility's corporate organization was reiterated. The townsmen were likewise classed into six categories and were offered an expanded role in urban governance. Elective service in local government became an important feature of Russian life.

It is difficult to quantify the results of these reforms in bringing new persons into local government. One estimate counted 15,000 new officials employed after 1775 (out of a total of 27,000 in 1796), with 10,608 of them elected—4,053 nobles, 3,851 townsmen, and 2,704 peasants. Another estimated the proliferation of offices to be on the order of fourfold.[18] Whatever the actual magnitude was, it certainly amounted to a substantial increase by the end of Catherine's reign. The new configuration of local government lasted for decades, even though the implementation of the new institutions encountered numerous difficulties.

Although Catherine's charter for the state peasants remained in draft form, the legislation of 1775 and after eased the possibilities of peasant enrollment in urban society. Recent unpublished research on the Moscow region has discovered a surprisingly large number of manumitted serfs joining the Moscow urban community (*posad*) in the last decades of the century.[19]

Catherine's periodic reception of delegations from noble assemblies and municipal organizations demonstrated publicly her approval of the new bodies; so did her trip to Mogilev and the western *guberniias* (provinces) in 1780.[20] Indeed, she was certainly the best traveled Russian sovereign since Peter the Great. Unlike Peter the Great's journeys, all of hers were conducted in time of peace. Her ten lengthy journeys as empress covered thousands of miles and stretched over some forty-two months in all. Most of them were highly publicized in the Russian press and widely reported abroad. She devoted much greater attention to civil government than did any sovereign before or later. She showed amazing attention to a vast variety of concerns, from new quarantine regulations in 1786 to an ordinance in 1784 that forbade the flying of hot air balloons from March 1 to December 1.[21]

This flurry of reforms evoked admiration outside Russia as well as within. An anonymous British commentator in 1785 offered this ambivalent assessment:

> The efforts of the Czarina for the introduction of liberty among her people, have not been wholly in vain. But a long series of years must intervene before a succession of sovereigns who sit precariously on a despotic and military throne, can effect so mighty a revolution as the rise of the people on the ruins of their powerful and lordly chieftains; for it is impossible to retain numerous and immense provinces, but by allowing men their own laws, and giving power to their ancient chiefs. Yet what can be done for this end by human genius, is done by the Empress. Privileges are awarded to all who have borne arms, the number of which it is in the power of the crown to increase almost to any amount; rights and immunities granted to the tenants or possessors of the Imperial demesnes, with the contagious example of the advantages accruing to the landlord from so wise and liberal a policy; and, above all, the introduction of the arts of civilization, and the light of literature, will gradually introduce into the great Russian empire liberty and industry, and all that exalts and adorns life.[22]

Apparently this appraisal had in mind the presumed results of the Guberniia Reform and the charters to the nobility and to the towns, the experiments on imperial estates such as those pursued by Jakob Sievers, and the expansion of the armed forces. It should also be remembered that Catherine was the most literate sovereign ever to sit on the Russian throne, that she herself directly patronized many kinds of publications, and that book publishing enjoyed enormous expansion throughout her reign.[23] All these activities contributed to indirect or long-term political modernization as discussed by Alexander Yanov.

The last decade of Catherine's reign witnessed a decided decline of liberalizing initiatives, for several reasons. An unbroken string of costly, albeit successful, foreign wars with the Ottoman Empire (1787-92), Sweden (1788-90), Poland (1792, 1794), and Persia (1796) and the challenge of revolutionary France preempted her attention and directed resources away from domestic affairs. Financial stringency constrained many branches of the state administration, even the court.[24] Furthermore, the empress appears to have lost confidence in the prospect of significant additional administrative reform. She noted to herself at the start of the second Turkish war:

> Use the winter of 1787 and the beginning of 1788 to compose the charters on the Senate and the Senate's procedures and instruction, do this with application and honest industry; if however the information and criticism reveal barriers and tedious or wily difficulties, then put the whole work

in a deep drawer, for we do not see for whose sake I labor and will not my labors, care and warm concern for the good of the empire be in vain, for I do see that I cannot make my frame of mind hereditary.[25]

Apparently Catherine never did complete the documents in question, and the position of the Senate within her reformed government remained in limbo. Her premonitory insight into the possibly transitory impact of her political outlook proved both right and wrong: right in its forecast of Paul's effort to reverse some of her policies, wrong in its pessimism about the long-term effect and repute of her reign. Try as he might, Paul could not undo basic features of her reign, such as the preeminent position of the nobility, an expansive economic policy, and the consolidation of control over the western and southern borderlands. Indeed, the supreme irony occurred in the Zubovs' presenting themselves as "constitutionalist" defenders of Catherinian tradition against Pauline "despotism." Alexander I, her favorite grandson and favored successor, proclaimed posthumously his grandmother's return to grace and perhaps consciously imitated her governing style.

What about the "repressive" episodes with Radishchev and Novikov? Do these show backsliding on the part of the obviously aging empress in an effort to repudiate her earlier ideals? Only to a limited degree, in my judgment. Both episodes puzzled and bewildered Catherine more than they frightened her. She could not fathom what either man intended by his publications. In particular, she could not separate rhetorical excess from reformist aspiration, and she tended to detect a clandestine foreign hand—"Martinist" or Prussian/Rosicrucian—behind each publisher.[26] Both also alerted her to the practical problems of controlling the newly expanded publication media, a problem that would bedevil her successors more than her.[27] Nonetheless, despite the tense atmosphere of wartime, she followed legal procedures in investigating both cases, and she showed restraint in the final sentencing of both men. That these cases cost her much mental turmoil and some self-doubt appears highly probable, at least on the basis of her private remarks to her secretary Aleksandr Khrapovitskii.[28]

Catherine's vehement reaction to revolutionary events in France can scarcely be exaggerated. Certainly it conditioned her treatment of Radishchev and Novikov. Indeed, it revealed how deeply she was convinced that Russia had become a truly European state and society. In some respects she foresaw the revolutionary/reactionary cataclysms of nineteenth-century Europe. To her confidant Melchior Grimm, who had been chased out of revolutionary Paris, she confided on February 11, 1794:

If France overcomes these (misfortunes) she will be more vigorous than ever; she will be submissive and docile as a lamb; but for this is needed a superior man, agile and courageous beyond his contemporaries and even, perhaps beyond the century itself; has he been born, or not yet, will he come? Everything depends on this; if such a man is found, he will halt with his foot any further decline and it will be stopped wherever he is found: in France or elsewhere.[29]

Perhaps this was a prediction of Napoleon's ascendancy, perhaps not. But she certainly recognized that the whole climate of European politics had changed and not for the better. "O God, I don't dare say all that I think," she wrote Grimm seven months later, "but unfortunately I had predicted to the Prince of Nassau and to many others, four years in advance, everything that happened to Louis XVI; sometimes my vision for the moment flashes into the future like a rocket and focuses upon only a single characteristic."[30] Despotic, demagogic power was not her idea of a bright political future for France or Europe or Russia. The democratic revolution in France had unleashed forces that her kind of cautious liberalizing statecraft could scarcely counter.

Even so, in whatever world Catherine entered on November 6, 1796, she would have had reason to reflect positively on the liberalizing achievements of her impressive reign. She had presided over Russia's full-fledged entry into European culture and community. She had demonstrated the benefits of a non-despotic style of leadership. She had left a dauntingly difficult act to follow.

NOTES

1. David L. Ransel, *The Politics of Catherinian Russia: The Panin Party* (New Haven, Conn., 1975); Roger Bartlett, *Human Capital: The Settlement of Foreigners in Russia, 1762-1804* (Cambridge, Mass., 1979); J. Michael Hittle, *The Service City: State and Townsmen in Russia, 1600-1800* (Cambridge, Mass., 1979); Isabel de Madariaga, *Russia in the Age of Catherine the Great* (New Haven, Conn., 1981); Marc Raeff, *The Well-Ordered Police State: Social and Institutional Change through Law in the Germanies and Russia, 1600-1800* (New Haven, Conn., 1983); Robert E. Jones, *Provincial Development in Russia: Catherine II and Jakob Sievers* (New Brunswick, N.J., 1984); John P. LeDonne, *Ruling Russia: Politics and Administration in the Age of Absolutism, 1762-1796* (Princeton, N.J., 1984); W. Gareth Jones, *Nikolay Novikov, Enlightener of Russia* (Cambridge, Mass., 1984); Gary Marker, *Publishing, Printing, and the Origins of Intellectual Life in Russia, 1700-1800* (Princeton, N.J., 1985); Arcadius Kahan, *The Plough, the Hammer, and the Knout: An Economic History of Eighteenth-Century Russia* (Chicago, 1985).

2. N. Dashkevich, *Literaturnyia izobrazheniia imperatritsy Ekateriny II-i i eia tsarstvovaniia* (Kiev, 1898), pp. 6-10, 22-24.

3. *The Court Magazine* (London), August, 1762, p. 566; *The London Magazine,* August, 1762, p. 436.

4. *The London Magazine,* December, 1762, p. 655.

5. *The Annual Register, or a View of the History, Politicks, and Literature of the Year 1762,* 2d ed. (London, 1766), p. 20.

6. Ibid., p. 17.

7. N. Barsukov, ed., *Dnevnik A. V. Khrapovitskago 1782-1793* (St. Petersburg, 1874), p. 4.

8. For the English translation of her manifesto of July 12/23, 1762, see *The Daily Advertiser* (London), August 26, 1762.

9. Isabel de Madariaga, "Catherine II and Montesquieu between Prince M. M. Shcherbatov and Denis Diderot," *L'Età dei lumi, Studi storici sul settecento europeo in Onore di Franco Venturi,* 2 vols. (Naples, 1985), 2:615, 620-23; de Madariaga, "Autocracy and Sovereignty," *Canadian-American Slavic Studies* 16 (1982):369-87.

10. The Earl of Buckinghamshire, the first English envoy to observe Catherine's government closely, privately predicted at the very start of her reign (November, 1762), "When the hurry, the unavoidable consequence of a revolution is over, she has every talent to make this a great and powerful country." After leaving Russia some two years later, he offered an admiring appraisal of her reform program: "It is impossible to consider the general tenour of her conduct, since she placed herself upon the throne, without tracing evident marks of a laudable ambition to distinguish herself; to make her subjects happy at home and respectable abroad; to encourage arts, sciences, and commerce; to form by a liberal education the young nobility of both sexes; to extend in a great degree the same advantages to inferior ranks; to improve the public revenue without oppressing individuals; to check the tyranny with which the clergy distressed their vassals, and to introduce that ease of society, that urbanity and general good breeding which prevail in other European nations; in a word, to transmit her name with glory to posterity, and by the use she makes of empire to palliate the means by which she has acquired it." A. D. Collyer, ed., *The Despatches and Correspondence of John, Second Earl of Buckinghamshire, Ambassador to the Court of Catherine II of Russia 1762-1765,* 2 vols. (London, 1900-2), 1:87; 2:273-74. For a sterling analysis of Catherine's motivations, see David M. Griffiths, "To Live Forever: Catherine II, Voltaire and the Pursuit of Immortality," in *Russia and the World of the Eighteenth Century,* ed. Roger P. Bartlett et al. (Columbus, Ohio, 1988), pp. 446-68.

11. de Madariaga, *Russia,* pp. 299, 307.

12. N. Ia. Eidel'man, *Gran' vekov* (Moscow, 1982), pp. 50-52; G. A. Likhotkin, *Sil'ven Mareshal' i "Zaveshchanie Ekateriny II" (K istorii odnoi literaturnoi mistifikatsii)* (Leningrad, 1974), pp. 5-14.

13. Karen Malvey Rasmussen, "Catherine II and Peter I: The Idea of a

Just Monarch: The Evolution of an Attitude in Catherinian Russia" (Ph.D. dissertation, University of California, Berkeley, 1973), pp. 57-90.

14. John P. LeDonne, "Appointments to the Russian Senate 1762-1796," *Cahiers du monde russe et soviétique* 16 (1975):27-56.

15. Victor Kamendrowsky, "State and Economy in Catherinian Russia: The Dismantling of the Mercantile System of Peter the Great" (Ph.D. dissertation, University of North Carolina, 1982), chaps. 3-6.

16. William E. Butler, "The Nakaz of Empress Catherine the Great," *American Book Collector* 16 (1966):18-21; A. Florovskii, "Shvedskii perevod 'Nakaza' Ekateriny II," *Zapiski russkago istoricheskago obshchestva v Prage 1* (1927):149-52; de Madariaga, "Autocracy and Sovereignty." pp. 381-82.

At least one foreign observer appreciated the scope of Catherine's legislative initiative: "With respect to internal policy, the Empress of Russia has undertaken a great and arduous task, and worthy of an exalted mind. The laws of this vast empire were voluminous to a degree of the greatest absurdity, were perplexed, insufficient, in many cases contradictory, and so loaded with precedents, reports, cases, and opinions, that they afforded an eternal scene of altercation, and were scarcely to be reconciled or understood by the very professors of them. The particular laws of the different provinces were also continually interfering and clashing, and caused such confusion, that the whole presented an endless chaos, and effaced almost every trace of original system or design. This Augean stable the empress has determined to clean; to which purpose she summoned deputies from every province in the empire, to attend her at Moscow, there to form an entire and new code of laws, for the government of the whole. The success attending this patriotic attempt, will we hope, make a part of the subject of our future observations." *The Annual Register, or a View of the History, Politicks, and Literature of the Year 1767* (London, 1768), p. 10.

17. See her note of around 1767, *Osmnadtsatyi vek,* 4 vols. (Moscow, 1869), 3:390-92. A curious echo of these debates found its way into the foreign press, as reported in *The Scots Magazine* (Edinburgh), November, 1768, p. 603: "We find by letters from Petersburg, that debates ran pretty high amongst the deputies appointed to form a new code of laws for the Russian empire, on the question, 'Whether the good of the state requires, that the bondage to which the peasants are subject, be entirely abolished, or that it should still subsist under some restrictions?' The example of the peasants of England and Holland, and that of the peasants of Poland, Hungary, and Denmark, are alledged on this occasion, in opposition the one to the other. Those of the deputies who have at heart the maintenance of the sacred rights of humanity, are for giving the peasantry an entire liberty, like to that of the rest of the inhabitants: 'The husbandman (say they) being the most useful of all subjects, what pretence can there be for making his condition worse than that of the others? To render it such, is certainly to commit the most cruel injustice.' "

18. Robert E. Jones, *The Emancipation of the Russian Nobility 1762-1785* (Princeton, N.J., 1973), pp. 227, 233; LeDonne, *Ruling Russia,* p. 101; Hittle,

The Service City, pp. 213-30. But on the late and confused formation of true estates in Russia, see the provocative discussion by Gregory L. Freeze, "The *Soslovie* (Estate) Paradigm and Russian Social History," *American Historical Review* 91 (1986):11-36.

19. Daniel Morrison, " 'Trading Peasants' and Urbanization in Eighteenth-Century Russia: The Central Industrial Region" (Ph.D. dissertation, Columbia University, 1981), p. 220.

20. "Dnevnaia zapiska puteshestviia Imperatritsy Ekateriny v Mogilev," in *Sbornik Imperatorskago russkago istoricheskago obshchestva,* 148 vols. (St. Petersburg, 1867), 1:384-410 (hereafter *SIRIO*).

21. John T. Alexander, "The Journeys of Empress Catherine II," unpublished paper; *Polnoe sobranie zakonov Rossiiskoi imperii,* 1st series (St. Petersburg, 1830), vol. 22, no. 15,973 (April 4, 1784); vol. 22, no. 16,390 (May 6, 1786).

22. *The Scots Magazine,* September, 1785, p. 422.

23. Roger P. Bartlett, "J. J. Sievers and the Russian Peasantry under Catherine II," *Jahrbücher für Geschichte Osteuropas* 32 (1984):16-33; John P. LeDonne, "Outlines of Russian Military Administration 1762-1796, Part II: The High Command," *Jahrbücher für Geschichte Osteuropas* 33 (1985):175-204; Richard S. Wortman, *The Development of a Russian Legal Consciousness* (Chicago, 1976), pp. 25-26; George L. Yaney, *The Systematization of Russian Government: Social Evolution in the Domestic Administration of Imperial Russia, 1711-1905* (Urbana, Ill., 1973), pp. 74-76; Marker, *Publishing,* pp. 68, 106.

24. Kahan, *Plough, Hammer, and Knout,* pp. 337, 344-46, 348.

25. Quoted by Marc Raeff, "The Empress and the Vinerian Professor: Catherine II's Projects of Government Reforms and Blackstone's *Commentaries,*" *Oxford Slavonic Papers* 7 (1974):38, 41.

26. Jones, *Novikov,* pp. 206-14.

27. Marker, *Publishing,* pp. 221-28; Marianna Tax Choldin, *A Fence around the Empire: Russian Censorship of Western Ideas under the Tsars* (Durham, N.C., 1985).

28. Barsukov, *Dnevnik Khrapovitskago,* pp. 338-40, 344, 397, 399-400, 404, 406, 411-13, 430.

29. *SIRIO,* 23:592.

30. Ibid., p. 610.

Reformability in the Age of Reform and Counterreform, 1855-94

WALTER M. PINTNER

If ever there was a time in the history of pre-revolutionary Russia when it seemed that the nation was undergoing substantial change without a major internal or external crisis, it was, of course, during the Great Reforms of the early years of Alexander II's reign. The word "change" is preferable because "reform" suggests a reformulation according to a recognized set of standards. Certainly for some of the men involved in the process there was a model, that of western Europe. They had a vision of Russia adopting the whole range of social, economic, and political institutions of other mid-nineteenth-century European nations. But that was by no means a universally accepted agenda, and whether or not that actually happened to any significant extent is open to serious question.

Russia abolished serfdom, as had the rest of Europe in the previous half-century.[1] But Russian serfdom — really full slavery — was entirely different from what had existed in most of Europe. So too was the post-emancipation settlement, measured by the social, economic, and juridical position of the former serfs. The new legal system was certainly Western, but it applied only to a relatively small portion of the population since the peasantry was largely excluded. The military reforms of 1874 introduced a system of short-term service and general, but hardly universal, conscription to build up a trained reserve, again modeled on the armies of western Europe. How much the Russian army of the post-reform years actually came to resemble those models is still open to question.[2]

One can argue that all of these measures were important first steps in a direction that in the reasonably near future would produce approximate convergence with the rest of Europe. That is what one group of Russian reformers hoped to accomplish. Such convergence, however, would require appropriate subsequent steps in the same direction, steps that failed to materialize in the era of counterreform. This, in one way or the other, has been the thrust of much of the liberal historiography and, with some changes in emphasis, the Marxist tradition as well.

Another way of looking at the Great Reforms is to think of them as important changes, but not necessarily moving Russia in a direction determined by Western standards. Were they designed to do that in the minds of many of those involved? Probably not in the case of the conservative nationalists or even Alexander II himself. Even if the aim were to westernize Russia, one must ask whether that was at all possible and, if so, which aspects of Russian society and to what degree? Approaching the period of reform with these questions in mind may also raise doubts about the conventional notion of "counterreform" in the 1880s. Perhaps the locomotive of westernization was not actually forced off the track by Alexander III, because it had never really been on it at all or at least had been grinding to a halt even before the red signal had been raised on its pole. Was it the reactionary views of Alexander III or the realities of Russian life that ended the era of the Great Reforms?

Since the term "reform" will be used in this essay to refer to movement in the direction of limiting the autocracy and involving some sort of participation by other elements of society in the governmental process, it is this aspect of the familiar story that should be examined most carefully. It is almost but not quite true that the issue of changing the central political structure was ignored as too sensitive to address. Both the Valuev memorandum of 1863 and the better-known plan of Loris-Melikov in 1881 envisaged a role for elected advisory bodies drawn from a limited electorate, but nothing came of either proposal.[3] It is useful, however, to consider what the prerequisites were for movement in the direction of a more Western—that is, middle-class based—political system and what the Great Reforms did to facilitate or hinder that development. A reformable Russia means a Russia with the minimum social base for a reformed political system. Did the Great Reforms facilitate the development of the minimum? And did the Counterreform undo that progress?

One of the basic facts about the Great Reforms is that they were state measures taken primarily for state purposes, although there was certainly no unanimity of views as to what the state needed. The views of a "radical" reform-minded bureaucrat like Nikolai Miliutin and a traditional conservative like Iakov I. Rostovtsev were hardly the same, but they shared one crucially important notion. Reform was to be accomplished through the use of autocratic power exercised by the bureaucracy.

Political reform, in the sense of limiting autocratic power through the participation of other elements in society, was out. One might even argue that there was no counterreform in the political sense because there was no political reform in the first place.

The reform legislation was primarily the product of the ideas and activity of a group of "enlightened bureaucrats," noblemen in origin and in legal status to be sure, but men devoted exclusively to their careers as professional state servants.[4] In the later years of Nicholas's reign, they had learned the problems of the nation firsthand in the process of collecting statistics and particularly in the attempt to carry out the changes in the administration of the state peasants initiated by Count Kiselev with the full support of Nicholas I. To a much lesser degree, the reforms were the result of ideas developed and supported by liberal members of the nobility, particularly in Tver', and even less or not at all the product of radicals like Alexander Herzen.[5] The enlightened bureaucrats—believing that reform should come from the center and should be designed by experts and that the nobility as a whole was basically hostile to emancipation—strongly and successfully resisted attempts by the liberal gentry to play a role in the elaboration of the emancipation. Richard Wortman has shown that these "experts" in the bureaucracy played a major role in the legal reforms as well. But he also has shown that they needed the support of influential courtiers, who after the emancipation had become convinced of the need for legal reforms to help maintain their own interests on the land.[6]

The Great Reforms definitely were not the result of popular pressure because there was no substantial segment of Russian society capable of or inclined to exert that pressure in the 1860s. The central problem is: did the reforms initiate a major social transformation of Russia that laid the basis for the subsequent important changes, those very political changes that did not come in the 1860s because the autocracy did not want to make them and there was no one to force it to make them?

The greatest of the reforms was, of course, the emancipation of the privately owned serfs. Political change was inconceivable without it because slavery was morally unacceptable to the vast majority of educated Europeans, including Russians, in the second half of the nineteenth century. Those who would have participated in a politically reformed Russian governmental system would never have accepted the existence of serfdom. More important is the question of whether or not the emancipation, and particularly the emancipation as it was actually designed and implemented, contributed to the growth of a class of citizens that was prepared to participate in government and had an interest in avoiding revolutionary upheaval. The answer, of course, is no. The emancipation settlement was designed as much as possible to preserve the traditional order in the countryside and to discourage peasants leaving the village from entering other walks of life. The heavy economic burdens imposed on the villages on a collective basis added to the already great obstacles to social mobility. The emancipation strengthened and tended to preserve the already well-developed division of Russia into two societies, westernized and traditional, rather than weakening it.

Viewed from the perspective of possible political reform in the future, the net impact of emancipation was positive since emancipation was a prerequisite for any political change. It did not, however, go beyond that and even created new barriers, most notably the legal recognition of the village commune. It thus created a new problem and reinforced old ones with which any future reformers would have to deal.

The measure generally labeled as "most successful" was the legal reorganization that, among other things, established the independent judiciary, trial by jury, and the justices of the peace. Without question these measures did a great deal to put the Russian legal system more on a par with those in the rest of Europe. Under the new system, ordinary non-peasant citizens could operate with reasonable confidence that contracts were enforceable and criminal law would function in a fair and equitable way. They were much less subject to the whims of arbitrary authority than before the reforms, at least as long as they stayed away from sensitive political issues.

Two major qualifications exposed the weaknesses of the new legal system. It excluded the overwhelming peasant majority of the population for the vast majority of everyday legal matters, leaving the village to operate according to "customary law." Whether or not there actually was such a thing as customary law, this feature of the reforms clearly reinforced the separation between the peasantry and the educated segment of Russian society. Like the provisions of the emancipation settlement, the legal reforms slowed the integration of the peasants into modern Russian life.

Perhaps even more important from our point of view is the tension the new judicial system created between itself and the autocracy. Although it may be possible to imagine a *Rechtsstaat* in which monarchs retain all legislative authority for themselves but allow the system to operate without interference, changing the laws whenever they wish but never interfering in specific instances, in practice the outcome will more likely be tension. This was precisely the situation that existed in Russia even before the 1864 judicial reforms. The *Svod Zakonov* (Digest of the Laws), promulgated in 1835 as the law of the land, proclaimed in

Article 1 that "the Emperor of Russia is an autocratic and unlimited monarch. God Himself commands that his supreme authority be obeyed not only from fear, but also from conscience." Article 47 continued in the same vein: "The Russian Empire is governed on the firm basis of positive laws, statutes, and establishments emanating from the autocratic power." Yet Article 47 also proclaimed the principle of conformity to law (*zakonnost'*).[7]

None of the tsars was ever willing, no matter how much they spoke of the "rule of law," to concede any limitation on their autocratic power, even to the extent of establishing clear and consistent procedures for legislation. Such procedures were viewed, probably correctly, as the first step in the direction of actual limits on autocratic power. The result was that it was the "will of the Tsar, whether expressed through formal legislation or through an imperial command, personal ukaz, or even oral communication that had the force of the law."[8]

Given such a situation, the result of the legal reforms of 1864 must be viewed as anomalous. They unquestionably gave the modern, educated segment of Russian society the mechanisms of European jurisprudence. The legal implications of actions in most areas were now reasonably predictable. The legal profession developed and attempted to adhere to universal—that is, general European—standards of conduct and professionalism. By the end of the century, this group had become an important segment of the growing Russian middle class.

As Wortman pointed out some years ago, however, the legal profession did not become a mainstay of the existing social and political order as might have been expected. On the contrary, many legal professionals became spokesmen for the opposition to the state, albeit largely of the more moderate opposition. This opposition stemmed from the conflict between their professional commitment to the ideal of a society based on law and the retention and exercise of arbitrary power by the tsar, who did not hesitate to interfere in areas considered sensitive or threatening.[9] Thus the ultimate impact of the legal reforms was not, as it might have been, to develop new sources of support for an existing but evolving social and political order, but to add one more element—a very articulate and influential one—to the many elements in Russian society which were becoming increasingly estranged from the traditional status quo.

The years of the Great Reforms brought no alteration in the formal structure of the autocracy, which remained unchanged until after the 1905 Revolution. Nevertheless, the government could not, and did not, remain unaffected by changes in the nature of Russian society that developed in the course of the nineteenth century. Particularly important was the gradual alteration in character and background of the men who occupied high positions in the ministries, the State Council, and other important agencies of the central government.

The social composition of the higher civil service had changed only moderately between 1800 and mid-century. It was still dominated by men of noble background, but the life experience of those men had been revolutionized. Instead of retired military officers who had little or no institutionalized education — except perhaps as teenagers at the Corps of Pages or the Cadet School — mid-nineteenth-century officials were usually men who had had formal education either at the Lycée at Tsarskoe Selo, the Imperial School of Jurisprudence, or one of the Russian universities. Their education was specifically designed to prepare them for state civil service. Almost all of these institutions had been founded in the first quarter of the century, and their charters mandated that graduates be given very substantial preference when entering civil service. This advantage for graduates made it a virtual necessity for individuals to obtain formal training if they were to have any real hope of successful bureaucratic careers.[10]

From the mid-nineteenth century onward, men trained to work in accordance with formal structures and rules and to apply specialized knowledge to solving problems were not only in the Ministry of Justice, where Wortman has made the case so thoroughly, but throughout the higher levels of officialdom. They were less likely than their military-trained predecessors to think only of unthinking obedience to the autocrat. As we have seen, the role of a special segment of this new officialdom, the enlightened bureaucrats, was crucial in developing and implementing the Great Reforms. This small group of enlightened bureaucrats lost influence, and most of them retired from service during the reign of Alexander III. The importance of the professionalized bureaucracy as a whole, however, did not disappear with the end of the reform era but continued through the years of counterreform under Alexander III down to the end of the old regime.

Alexander III found it extremely difficult—and in crucial cases, failed— to undo the reform measures much as he and his chief advisers apparently wished to. Autocrat though he was, he could not significantly change the judicial reforms; the professionalism of the ministers of justice and their subordinates prevented it. There were apparently no others available to draft the desired statutes, or at least Alexander was unwilling to embark on the total shakeup of personnel required to find them.[11]

Perhaps even more striking is the fact that the *zemstvo* emerged very largely unscathed from an attempt to abolish its substantial independence from the administrative hierarchy of the central government. The *zemstvos* were organs of rural local self-government established as part of the Great Reforms, largely as a concession to the more liberal-minded members of the landed nobility. They were multiclass organizations including representatives of both the peasantry and the nobility of a given locality, but from their inception they were dominated by the nobility. Peasants saw participation in the zemstvo bodies as an expensive burden they could ill afford.

Central government agencies and their representatives in the provinces regarded the zemstvo system as a rival for both authority and financial resources and were generally hostile to it. The zemstvo became the focus for moderate political opposition to the autocracy. Many of the liberal nobility who were members of zemstvo bodies saw them as the first building blocks in a system of representation that would eventually become a national parliament. The professional staff of the zemstvo in each province—doctors, agronomists, statisticians, and the like, who often were called the "third element"—tended to be more radical than the noble landowners who hired them. Many were populist socialists who saw zemstvo employment as an opportunity to "do good" and also make a modest living.

Neither the political aspirations of the noble zemstvo leadership, the "second element," nor the socialist tendencies of the zemstvo professionals were acceptable to Alexander III and his major advisors. It is therefore particularly surprising that the zemstvo statute of 1890, which started out as a plan to place the zemstvo firmly under the control of the central governmental ministries, emerged from the State Council and was confirmed by the tsar in a form which left the independence of the zemstvo bodies substantially intact. Peasant representation was indeed restricted, but it had never been very significant in any case. The change thus cannot be regarded as a significant counterreform.

Exactly why Alexander III chose to accept the State Council's version of the proposed statute, which did not conform to his presumed wishes, is not clear. He was under no legal requirement to do so; his power was de jure unlimited. Perhaps the complexities of zemstvo regulations were beyond him, or perhaps he simply accepted what his minister of the interior, Durnovo, had agreed to without carefully assessing whether or not it was consistent with his own views.[12]

Only in the case of the most famous of the major counterreforms, the Land Captain Statute of 1889, did Alexander insist on having his way.[13] The statute abolished the justices of the peace and created a new type of official, the land captain, to exercise both administrative and judicial authority over the peasant population. Despite the lengthy and complex arguments and discussions in the State Council, Alexander III on this occasion demanded that his own version of the statute be enacted, and, of course, it was. When faced with a clear-cut order from the tsar, the State Council members did not think of opposition. It was only on matters of procedure and bureaucratic status that they resisted. The high-ranking officials in the State Council had no constituency except their fellow bureaucrats. Nobles though they were, they did not represent the "noble interest" or any other.[14]

The Land Captain Statute represented a revival of the principle of seeking "good men" and giving them power to set things right; it replaced the countervailing notion of rationally organized institutions established from either above or below which would act according to fixed, publicly known rules. The practice of delegating the arbitrary authority of the monarch to trusted individuals to carry out specific tasks or govern specific areas was the traditional pattern of Russian administration and was not seriously challenged until the time of Michael Speranskii, working under both Alexander I and Nicholas I in the first half of the nineteenth century.

Speranskii attempted to introduce rational, predictable bureaucratic procedures and earned the enmity of men like the historian Nikolai M. Karamzin, who believed such a change would destroy what he saw as the traditionally warm personal relationship between the autocrat and the loyal nobility which served him. Under Nicholas I, Speranskii succeeded in codifying Russian law for the first time since 1649, a major step in the direction of the rule of law because it became possible to know with relative ease what the law actually was on a given question. In actual practice, however, Nicholas I, despite his many statements favoring the rule of law, tended to act by appointing trusted associates to positions of nearly unlimited authority (that is, he used "good men").

In *The Urge to Mobilize,* George Yaney called the Land Captain Statute a victory of "line over staff" over "staff over line." But he also showed that the attempt to rely on "good men" very quickly failed and "staff" reasserted itself over "line"; in other words, administrative agencies subordinate to ministries reasserted their power over the land captains in short order.[15]

The military reforms of 1874 were, on their face, perhaps the least political of all the Great Reforms, none of which was explicitly so, except perhaps the zemstvos. The military reforms introduced a number of important practical measures to improve the strength, quality, and efficiency of the Russian armed forces. Most important was the introduction—in theory—of universal, short-term military service with a large reserve force, on the model of the systems well established in western Europe. Aside from the emancipation itself, the military reforms certainly had the most widespread impact on the population. In theory, after 1874 all young men could expect to spend some years in a new environment (under the old system, dating back to the time of Peter the Great or even before, only an unfortunate handful of peasant youths were conscripted for very long terms of service). In practice, there were many exemptions because the army was not financially able to mobilize and train all of the recruits available. Furthermore, John Bushnell has argued with considerable persuasiveness that the military environment in which the peasant recruit found himself was not nearly so different from the traditional village as we have tended to assume.[16]

Nevertheless, contemporaries saw considerable social if not political significance in the new system because it was "class blind." The length of compulsory service was determined by level of education and not social origin. Certainly most nobles were educated and served short terms, while most peasants were illiterate and served much longer terms. But the new law ended the exemptions from compulsory military service that the nobility had enjoyed since 1762, and it was a major step in the process that emptied virtually all substantive meaning from formal noble status by the end of the century. Conservatives therefore bitterly opposed that feature of the military reform. The principle of universal liability for service was based on liberal ideology. It was not required to accomplish the strictly military purposes of the reform since exempting nobles and possibly other privileged groups from compulsory service would not have significantly reduced the recruit pool. It suggested in law the idea that all subjects of the emperor were also citizens of the empire and shared some sort of equality.[17]

The architect of the reform, Dmitrii Miliutin, certainly saw the reform as something more than a technical military program. As long as he was minister of war, literacy programs for recruits were stressed as part of an effort to educate and uplift the population in general and to bring an end to the split in Russian society between the westernized elite and the tradition-bound peasant masses. After he left office in 1881, the literacy programs were dropped, only to be revived much later. Miliutin's successor as minister of war, Petr Vannovskii (1881-98), doubted the value of literacy for soldiers. He saw the dangers of their reading the "wrong thing" as greater than any possible gains in military efficiency. Despite its truly radical content, the military reform in practice did little to end the division of Russian society and integrate the peasantry into the rapidly developing urban industrial society.[18]

On the basis of this brief survey, what can be said about the nature of reform and counterreform in the age of the Great Reforms? First of all the reforms clearly did much to prepare for and, indeed, make possible the social and economic progress that occurred in the last third of the nineteenth century and the first few years of the twentieth. The economic development that began to accelerate in the 1880s would have been greatly hampered if not entirely prevented had the peasants not been, at least to a limited extent, free to move in response to new economic opportunity. Similarly, the most important part of the educated population of Russia, the nobility, was freed from an unproductive and parasitic role as rural landlords, and many adopted more useful urban professions.[19] The end of serfdom to a significant degree made possible the formation of Russia's first true "middle class," drawn much more from the nobility than from former peasants. Similarly, the legal reforms greatly facilitated economic growth by introducing reliable and enforceable civil law and encouraging a more modern business ethic. At the same time they fostered the growth of the legal profession, a significant element of the middle class.

The most political of the reforms, the creation of the zemstvos, also made some contribution to social change and economic development, but one much harder to pin down, much less quantify. Rural Russia was studied in detail in the post-1864 years by zemstvo specialists, and some important new services were provided to the peasantry. These had some impact on rural life by the end of the century, although it is impossible to measure it accurately. Much though not all of this development was the result of zemstvo work. The educated personnel performing medical, veterinary, agricultural, and other services formed a relatively small portion of the new middle class, but it was an articulate and disproportionately influential one.

As suggested above the general effects of the military reforms on society have been little studied, but the evidence currently available suggests they were probably quite limited. Efforts to improve officer training seem to have failed, on one hand, to convert the Russian officer corps into a truly modern and professional cadre and, on the other hand, to preserve its traditional prestige in society at large. It can even be argued that the state, which had been strongly oriented to the military both in values and in budgetary terms, had become significantly demilitarized by the end of the century.[20]

On the whole then the Great Reforms had major significance for the social organization and the economic progress of Russia. Without them, or with less extensive changes, developments in crucial areas would certainly have been much slower, and Russia's position as a major

European power would have been even more seriously threatened earlier than it actually was. Russia's experience would have been more like that of Ottoman Turkey or China.

What then of counterreform? Was Russia prevented from proceeding with political modernization—movement in the direction of limiting the autocracy and involving more of the population in the governmental process—by some clearly recognizable force of counterreform, one that can perhaps be identified both earlier and later in the course of Russian and Soviet history? The counterreforms of the reign of Alexander III were less than that. They did not so much undo the Great Reforms as they failed to continue strengthening the monarchy in the context of the new social and economic realities, which the era of the Great Reforms had made possible and which were emerging rapidly in the late nineteenth century. Efforts by moderate, middle-class elements to participate in the political system were harshly rebuffed by both Alexander III and his successor, Nicholas II. This situation has been pointed out many times and is usually, and correctly, described as resulting in the growing isolation of the state from all segments of society, an isolation which eventually permitted the collapse of the monarchy in 1917.

Why did it happen that way? Purely personal factors cannot be ignored. Both Alexander III and Nicholas II believed firmly and stubbornly in the validity and moral correctness of the tradition of Russian absolutism. We can only speculate what difference it could have made if Alexander III had been tutored by a La Harpe rather than a Pobedonostsev. However, the mere fact that Alexander II, the "great reformer," entrusted his son, the future Alexander III, to an arch-conservative rather than to an enlightened bureaucrat suggests we are dealing with a very strong tradition and not just the personal idiosyncrasies of Alexander III and Nicholas II.

The basic Russian governmental tradition certainly was *autocratic,* and for centuries it had worked very well indeed from the state's point of view. It brought Russia from the status of a remote and insignificant principality to that of a major—and at times even the most important— European power. It is hardly surprising the Russian monarchs, with no real exceptions, not only practiced but believed in the autocratic system. Even after the rest of Europe had adopted various modifications of their own monarchical traditions, none of which was ever so autocratic as Russia's, the Russian autocracy remained unchanged. Because Russia really was different from western Europe in size, culture, and social and economic development, it was very simple for those already strongly predisposed by position and training to believe in autocracy to justify it. This tradition and viewpoint shaped not only the tsars themselves but the entire state apparatus. Power, authority, and rewards came from above. The modernizing bureaucrats—from Speranskii through the Miliutin brothers to Stolypin—all wanted to use the power and authority of the autocracy to accomplish their aims and to overcome their opposition. Even the radical Alexander Herzen thought the way to reform was to persuade the tsar to do the right thing.

Given this situation at the top, counterreform was virtually automatic and inevitable. The purpose of state-sponsored changes like the Great Reforms was to create the basis for Russia's continued existence as a great power by establishing minimum preconditions for social and economic development. Once that has been achieved, why should we expect a regime with such an autocratic tradition to abandon the basic principle on which it is founded?

To a limited extent, the Great Reforms did permit and encourage the growth of the social elements essential to a Western-style political system. But, in the context of a government firmly committed to the traditional autocratic ideology, such a development produced increased instability, represented, for example, by lawyers opposing rather than supporting the existing system. Thus should it not be said that the crucial element in the 1880s and 1890s was not counterreform, but the normal Russian state system confronted by increasingly frustrated, newly emerging groups in society? Eventually, when faced with a major crisis in 1905, the autocracy made grudging concessions but never really abandoned its belief in the old principles.

Of course, one can go back over the course of Russian history and say, what if? What if Anna had accepted the conditions originally imposed on her in 1730? Or, much more relevant to the focus of this essay, what if Alexander II had not died in 1881 and Loris-Melikov's proposals had been promulgated? One can never know the answer to such questions. Possibly the elected advisory body proposed by Loris-Melikov might have thrived and emerged a few decades later as a full-fledged parliament representing, to some degree, all segments of the population and enjoying real power. It is not beyond the realm of one's imagination. Russia had a substantial and growing middle class and many highly educated and talented people who believed in the kind of political system that such an institution represented. On the other hand, there was growing discontent among the lower classes that would have been difficult to deal with quickly.

But above all, I find it hard to imagine that the monarch and the bureaucracy would have permitted such an institution to develop. Nothing in their tradition or in their conduct before and after 1881 suggests to me that would have been a likely outcome. The tradition of the

Russian monarchy was not to share power with its supporters but to expect, demand, and usually get their obedience. Thus, to the extent the government of the U.S.S.R. today continues to manifest elements of the Imperial and Muscovite Russian political tradition, there seem to be few grounds on which hope for political reform can be based.

NOTES

1. Jerome Blum, *The End of the Old Order in Rural Europe* (Princeton, N.J., 1978).

2. John Bushnell, "Peasants in Uniform: The Tsarist Army as a Peasant Society," *Journal of Social History* 13 (1980):565-76.

3. Marc Raeff, *Plans for Political Reform in Imperial Russia, 1730-1905* (Englewood Cliffs, N.J., 1966), pp. 121-40.

4. W. Bruce Lincoln, *In the Vanguard of Reform: Russian Enlightened Bureaucrats 1825-1861* (DeKalb, Ill., 1982).

5. Terence Emmons, *The Russian Landed Gentry and the Peasant Emancipation of 1861* (Cambridge, 1968).

6. Richard Wortman, *The Development of a Russian Legal Consciousness* (Chicago, 1976), pp. 3-6.

7. Heide W. Whelan, *Alexander III and the State Council: Bureaucracy and Counter-Reform in Late Imperial Russia* (New Brunswick, N.J., 1982), pp. 47-48.

8. Ibid., p. 50.

9. Wortman, *Development,* pp. 1-6, 269-89.

10. Walter M. Pintner, "The Evolution of Civil Officialdom, 1755-1855," in *Russian Officialdom: The Bureaucratization of Russian Society from the Seventeenth to the Twentieth Century,* ed. Walter M. Pintner and Don Karl Rowney (Chapel Hill, N.C., 1980), pp. 190-226; Lincoln, *Vanguard,* pp. 10-12.

11. Whelan, *Alexander III,* pp. 159-70. Helju Bennett has also argued convincingly that the operation of the *chin* (rank) system and the system of honors and awards restricted access to the monarch and his ability to appoint whomever he wished to high office, *"Chiny, Ordena,* and Officialdom," in *Russian Officialdom,* ed. Pintner and Rowney, pp. 162-89.

12. On the zemstvo statute of 1890, see Whelan, *Alexander III,* pp. 189-96. On the zemstvo in general, see Terence Emmons and Wayne S. Vucinich, eds., *The Zemstvo in Russia: An Experiment in Local Self-Government* (Cambridge, 1982), especially Emmons, "The Zemstvo in Historical Perspective," pp. 423-43.

13. The legislative history of the measure is highly complex and is discussed at length in George Yaney, *The Urge to Mobilize: Agrarian Reform in Russia, 1861-1930* (Urbana, Ill., 1982), pp. 49-97, and in Whelan, *Alexander III,* pp. 171-88.

14. Whelan, *Alexander III,* pp. 186-87.

15. On Speranskii's work see, Marc Raeff, *Michael Speransky, Statesman of Imperial Russia* (The Hague, 1957), chaps. 2, 11; on Nikolai M. Karamzin, *Karamzin's Memoir on Ancient and Modern Russia,* ed. and trans. Richard Pipes (Cambridge, Mass., 1959), pp. 75-92; on Nicholas I, Nicholas V. Riasanovsky, *Nicholas I and Official Nationality in Russia, 1825-1855* (Berkeley and Los Angeles, 1959), chap. 4; Yaney, *Urge to Mobilize,* p. 113.

16. Bushnell, "Peasants in Uniform."

17. Robert F. Baumann, "The Debate over Universal Military Service in Russia, 1870-1874" (Ph.D. dissertation, Yale University, 1982).

18. John Bushnell, *Mutiny Amid Repression: Russian Soldiers in the Revolution of 1905-1906* (Bloomington, Ind., 1985), pp. 8-9; see also his "Peasants in Uniform."

19. Seymour Becker, *Nobility and Privilege under the Last Tsars* (DeKalb, Ill., 1985), chaps. 2, 6.

20. Walter M. Pintner, "The Burden of Defense in Imperial Russia, 1725-1914," *Russian Review* 42 (1984):231-59.

Reform during Revolution: Governing the Provinces in 1917

DANIEL T. ORLOVSKY

In Russian history the concept "reform" has always been associated with the government's domestic policy. Usually, this was policy enunciated by some combination of the tsar, court advisers, and bureaucratic institutions, though outside social influences on the reform process also existed. Reform was most often used as a signifier for an activist domestic policy designed either to correct some administrative weakness or to transform existing institutions. The various reshufflings of the provincial administrative apparatus from Catherine the Great through the 1840s may be seen as an example of the first type. An example of the second is the judicial reform of 1864 that created wholly new institutions and paved the way for a new Russian "legal consciousness."

Both kinds of reform were evident during the revolution in 1917. The Provisional Government had a voluminous legislative agenda, much of it meant to elaborate on reforms already passed in the era of the Great Reforms or under Witte or Stolypin. Much of this was the material of basic domestic policy, though, to be sure, political conflict in the Duma, the State Council, and the bureaucracy itself made it increasingly difficult for the government or the parties to pass new legislation. The revolution was a true catalyst for this kind of reform as the Provisional Government moved quickly to complete work that had been languishing on tsarist dockets for decades. Suddenly, it was possible to resolve, at least on paper, everything from the formation of joint stock companies and land redistribution to the nature of the alphabet. The bureaucracy, most of it inherited from the old regime, had a clear field to issue edicts, given the Duma's demise and the fact that the Provisional Government was "answerable only to the revolution."

Reform or an activist domestic policy, however, is rarely enough during a revolution. It cannot satisfy the desires of either the social groups making the revolution or the political leaders and ideologists who head the revolutionary parties and government. In the Russian case, reform was so deeply associated with failed aspirations, bureaucratic hegemony, and those in the middle of the political spectrum — Kadets, Octobrists and the like — that the term itself became unusable in the new revolutionary discourse. Leftists and even the Kadets of the first Provisional Government cabinet could attempt reform in the transformational mode, but, as the months passed in 1917, it became increasingly necessary for them to appear to be revolutionaries and not reformers. Thus, the Mensheviks could dominate a new Ministry of Labor and try to implement a variety of social and labor policies clearly meant to transform labor relations. Workers, however, considered these policies hostile to their class interest and favorable to the bourgeoisie. Workers viewed the Menshevik desire to instill labor discipline as counterrevolutionary. The Social Revolutionaries (SRs) in the Ministry of Agriculture under Chernov had a similar experience with the peasants. The fact that Mensheviks or SRs even spoke of reform was held against them by the urban and rural masses and used against them by the Bolsheviks.

In a sense, the left, or at least its members who served in the Provisional Government and soviets, were the prisoners of their own revolutionary rhetoric and their status as revolutionaries. Once in power they had to make policy and administer the inherited empire. Attempting to hold on to power overshadowed implementing new reform legislation. Success was something of a lottery, since the government had to deal with not only severe dislocations and social pressures but also the subtler influence of inherited institutions and attitudes. The entire range of pressures placed upon reformers and revolutionaries of all political persuasions in 1917 may be seen clearly in the example of provincial administration.

The fate of the Provisional Government is usually linked to World War I and to labor and agrarian questions. Yet no less important was the matter of governing the provinces, for here the problems of social mobilization and national integration were particularly acute. The survival of the Provisional Government and any hope of implementing revolutionary policies depended almost entirely on its ability to administer the provinces. Survival and state-building were inseparable in the revolutionary situation. The Provisional Government had to meet and harness the multitiered social revolution and its various institutional expressions in the provinces and simultaneously dispense with the problematic legacy of the old regime. This included the state's long-standing inability to penetrate to the *volost'* (rural governing unit made up of several villages) and village levels, the failure to construct at those levels all-estate units of administration that took cognizance of the vitality of new social groups, and the problems of administrative parallelism and ambiguous command relationships between central ministries and their provincial apparatus. Finally, there was the matter of the *zemstvos* (organs of local self-government created in 1864) and town dumas and their place in relation to the state bureaucracy.

Reform of provincial administration cut across the social, political, economic, and cultural components of the revolution. The Provisional Government devoted considerable energy and resources to reform and even to transform the provincial administration, but the results were meager. What makes reform of provincial administration in 1917 especially interesting is the fact that all the major parties of the Provisional Government (Kadets, Mensheviks, SRs, and Popular Socialists) supported it in principle and worked to establish it against the rival claims of the soviets and other popular grass-roots institutions of 1917.

Provincial institutions of all sorts—state, public, quasi-public, and professional, all the way down to the village level—were the focal point for the struggle over state power and rival visions of the revolution. These institutions and social groups displayed a common antipathy to capitalism, which they juxtaposed to their own non-propertied "democracy" as a source of social energy. These provincial institutions were the stronghold of the lower middle strata both in the towns and in the countryside—upwardly mobile peasants, *meshchane* (lower strata of the urban population), cooperative workers, the "third element" (salaried zemstvo employees), clerks, and proto-professionals, who supplied the skills and energy necessary to complement the formidable revolutionary energies of blue-collar workers, peasants, soldiers, and sailors. The lower middle strata used these provincial institutions to complete their own social revolution that had its roots in the earlier revolutionary era of 1905-7. Much of the fate of the Provisional Government hinged on its ability to connect with the lower middle strata and to integrate it into the process of revolutionary state-building. On the surface, this should have been a natural marriage, given the background of so many of the Provisional Government leaders and their strong commitment to "self-government," the cooperatives, and the like. The marriage, however, never took place for the reasons described below.

It is no exaggeration to claim the cornerstone of the Provisional Government's domestic policy, as stated by the first cabinet and sustained by all three coalitions, was the transformation of provincial administration. The watchword was "self-government," that long cherished abstraction whose pedigree went back centuries as part of the history-mythology of the struggle between state and society. Self-government was to be the operational principle and organizational form of statehood. Self-government would be anchored in the new zemstvos and town dumas elected by universal suffrage. These organs were to absorb, and thus eliminate, the police and administrative authority of the bureaucracy; by implication at least, they also were to assume control over the provincial organs of the central ministries. Further, the state was to realize the dreams of several generations of bureaucratic reformers, zemstvo activists, and publicists by extending its reach via self-government to the volost' and settlement levels and, eventually, to the villages of rural Russia and those borderlands where zemstvos had not been created in 1864.

The February Revolution intensified the process of democratization and the development of social movements that shaped the emerging institutions of the revolutionary state. The social movement of the lower middle strata took root in state and public institutions alike.

Reports from most provinces about the reception of the February Revolution and the initial steps to reestablish authority described a carnival-like atmosphere of role reversals as well as concrete initiatives that echoed the development of dual power in Petrograd.[1] The public expressed joy and support for the Provisional Government, arrested high provincial officeholders and police who could be found, and elected temporary executive committees of public organizations or public safety.[2]

The committees of public organizations took power from the civil governors, their chanceries, and the provincial directorates. Like the situation in Petrograd, however, their power was to be temporary, to be held until the promised transformation of provincial state authority and self-government.[3] As would be the case when the Bolsheviks came to power in October, neither the central Provisional Government nor the provincial activists sanctioned the destruction of the inherited apparatus, which continued operations within the new revolutionary state.

Prince L'vov in his capacity as minister of internal affairs—the official who commanded the provincial administration—issued his famous March 5 decree that sanctioned the replacement of civil governors by provincial and district zemstvo executive board chairmen, who were to take the title of commissar.[4] This has often been cited as an example of Provisional Government conservatism—the appointment of men to commissar posts who represented propertied Russia and were often more "hateful" to the lower classes than the governors themselves. The executive boards, however, were L'vov's natural constituency, going back to the Union of Zemstvos and the Zemgor during the three war years prior to the revolution. Also, the democratic revolution in the zemstvos and municipalities quickly swept away most of these early commissars. They would be replaced by local representatives of the democracy with the Provisional Government's sanction.

Since the political power in the zemstvos and dumas had not yet shifted in the first days of the revolution, and since the government was committed in principle to self-government, it was only natural for L'vov to issue such a decree. It at least gave power to the administrative authority of the zemstvos and dumas rather than to the purely estate-based assemblies. The situation was too uncertain and information too scarce for the central government to have known about lower-ranking zemstvo and duma employees and activists as potential commissars. Their time would come in the weeks immediately following the March 5 decree. L'vov's decree also required the inherited apparatus of the old regime to remain in place and to continue operations under the new commissars.

On the surface, the committees of public organizations brought together people of the same social, educational, and career profile as were to be found in the Temporary Duma Committee and the Provisional Government cabinet — members of the Duma's centrist parties, the local intelligentsia, professionals, all manner of representatives from the lower middle strata, and representatives of the provincial commercial and manufacturing classes. Yet there were some important differences. The provincials were more deeply rooted in zemstvo, duma, and public organization work and less in the higher-status urban professions of Petrograd. They were also less likely to represent propertied Russia, despite the presence of noble landowners in the localities. The landowners were far outnumbered by the lower middle strata, and in any case they were identified with the old regime and thus were not considered suitable representatives in the new governing institutions of "democratic" Russia. There were representatives of the commercial and industrial interests, but, as in Petrograd, these remained a powerful and influential minority, which would soon be eclipsed by the more radical lower middle strata.

During the first weeks of the revolution, it was the more prominent and higher-ranking representatives of the public organizations and professions who took the lead in establishing the committees of public organizations. But the social and occupational stratification, which had existed since 1905 and had proceeded apace during the years leading to 1917, would eventually make itself apparent in the nature of dual power in the provinces as well as in the shifting leadership of the public committees, zemstvos, dumas, and similar bodies. In the provinces, the state-building process would reveal the richness and diversity of social life as well as deeply rooted class antagonisms.

From the beginning of the revolution, dual power in the provinces was never as rigidly defined as in Petrograd. Representatives of "the democracy," as soviet and non-propertied social groups and organizations were known, frequently held simultaneous posts in the committees of public organizations, the zemstvos, dumas, *and* the soviets. Sometimes they were also provincial commissars or their assistants.[5] Executive authority in the provinces was rooted in a variety of local and often stubbornly independent institutions. It was one of the revolution's profound ironies that the Provisional Government chose to place so much stock in the concept of commissars, who would begin to resemble the hated civil governors of the old regime.

The new Ministry of Internal Affairs (MVD) clearly defined its goal for the provincial administration during the spring of 1917.[6] Prince L'vov's ministry embodied the aspirations of the first Provisional Government cabinet to transform provincial institutions under the banner of "self-government." The ministry's self-image, as reflected in its official history in the spring of 1917, was derived largely from its legislative work on provincial administration. To accomplish the reform, the ministry created a new Section on the Affairs of Local Administration under the direction of V. N. Shreter, a young docent at the Moscow Commercial School.[7]

The MVD first described its mission in traditional terms: "to direct all policy of internal administration." But the ministry and the new section were to direct it "towards revolutionary ends," to destroy the surviving practices and habits (*navyki*) of the former "*prikaz* (bureaucratic)-police regime." The section aimed to build quickly "in place of the old institutions and order new institutions and methods of administration consonant with the demands of a legal order and the legal consciousness (*pravosoznanie*) of a broad mass of the population." The revolutionary MVD attacked the old regime for its narrow bureaucratism and hostility to "all conscious and rational organization and activity emanating from society." The MVD saw a need to rebuild power at the center and to create a network of local agents, the provincial and district commissars, who would have the support (*doverie*) of a broad mass of the population and would work in close contact with local social organizations.[8]

The MVD viewed its most serious problem as the "planned, rational, reconstruction of the entire system of local self-government on the basis of universal suffrage." It therefore gave the local self-governing units responsibility for both economic and administrative matters.[9] Self-government would be conducted with the "necessary independence of government supervision (*nadzor*)" but within the boundaries of "lawful necessity (*zakonomernost'*)." The Provisional Government and Ministry of Internal Affairs thus envisaged a transformation of the institutions and moral foundations of provincial administration as well as the destruction of police and bureaucratic hegemony in the localities and in the nation as a whole.

Provisional Government legislative acts in the spring of 1917 called for the transfer of all police functions to organs of self-government. The police of revolutionary Russia were now known as militia. Further, in an attempt to establish separation of powers and public control over revolutionary administration, the government passed a law calling for the creation of administrative courts. These would adjudicate conflicts between the state, self-government institutions, individual citizens, and various public organizations. They would also help to define the abstract category of supervision (nadzor), the powers of provincial and district commissars, and the precise relationship between the state and self-government organs.[10]

The MVD viewed the new zemstvos as capable of cultural work in the countryside that would lead to a "full rebirth of the entire provincial way of life (*uklad*)." It was to be based on a new foundation of democratic organs incorporating local initiative, education of a broad mass of the population in state affairs, and local development. All of this was to be accomplished in "the spirit of justice and freedom." The ministry painted anarchy as the worst enemy of its vision of transformation, and it believed its task was to raise consciousness of this threat in the provinces. To accomplish this, it planned to replace high-ranking representatives of the old regime with those possessing "social authority" in the localities.[11]

The program was bold and aimed at transformation, but could the Provisional Government make it work? There were several major roadblocks. First, the program was abstract—a compendium of ideals and ideal types based on faith in the creative capacities of the *"narod"* (toiling masses) in the provinces. The language of Provisional Government declarations and subsequent legislation reveals no concern with the concrete social structure of the provinces or municipalities. All was masked under the label of "universal suffrage"; scant attention was given even to the key concept of "democratization." In short, the legislation aimed to deny the reality not only of class conflict but of any conflict between the multilayered propertied and laboring groups in the provinces. The Provisional Government consequently would have trouble identifying its potential allies in the provinces and capitalizing on the social movements that rippled through provincial life during 1917.

Second, the program paid little attention to the concrete institutional developments within the provinces. The Provisional Government and MVD stuck to the program based on self-government and the zemstvos and dumas without considering the integration of volost' committees, cooperatives, trade union organizations, land and food supply committees, war industry committees, and even the soviets into the revolutionary state structure. Now to be sure, Provisional Government ideology ran counter to any notion of absorbing into the state such purely "social" units as the cooperatives, and indeed the cooperatives themselves would have fought a direct takeover. Even many moderate socialists viewed the soviets as "class" organs, unsuitable building blocks in the new state. But the volost' and the land and food supply committees were state sanctioned, and the soviets and other organs comprised the infrastructure necessary to the state-building enterprise. The Provisional Government fostered overlapping jurisdictions and confusion as to the real meaning of the state in the provinces, which contributed greatly to its ultimate weakness as revolutionary power. Despite some positive steps—with the cooperatives, for example—the Provisional Government ultimately failed to capitalize on the revolution of the lower middle strata, the social group most closely linked to the nascent infrastructure and ripest for cooptation and mobilization into the state-building process.

Finally, the Provisional Government paid scant attention to the concrete administrative problems and traditions inherited from the old regime. For example, the MVD declined to integrate the old ministerial offices into the zemstvos and dumas until the latter were reelected under the new laws. This left the localities partially dependent on the old regime offices, which now functioned under even less central control than had been the case prior to February. The Provisional Government was reluctant to enact the kind of symbolic absorption of old into new that the Bolsheviks would accomplish soon after October, 1917. Also, as already mentioned, the Provisional Government put tremendous stock in the office of commissar in the hope that *individuals* could exert moral authority as representatives of the revolutionary will of the people. These officeholders increasingly came to represent local constituencies, which was by itself not a bad thing. But since these constituencies were the very ones that the government had failed to mobilize for itself, the commissars could hardly act as reliable agents of central state authority. Furthermore, the office of commissar renewed the kind of personal authority so prominent in the political culture and administrative institutions of the autocracy. This undermined the moral foundation of commissar power. The Provisional Government appeared condemned to repeat the past as it strove to overcome it.

The Provisional Government failed to define adequately the relationship between state and self-government organs, and, thus, between state and society. Despite the large amount of Provisional Government legislation—and it must be said that they enacted more than the autocracy had been able to pass during the preceding two decades—self-government remained an elusive concept. Clarification depended to some extent on the decision about the nature of the state itself that was reserved for the Constituent Assembly, but the Provisional Government made no clear statement to match the Bolshevik declaration of January, 1918, that the soviets were now *the* provincial administration of the revolutionary state.

Provincial administration under the Provisional Government had to take into account the already exisiting and now rapidly growing infrastructure, which ranged from the smallest volost' committees and units of the Peasant Union up through the cooperatives, land and food supply committees, zemstvos and dumas, war industries committees, and committees of public organizations. Despite the apparent Provisional Government commitment to these kinds of organizations as elements in state-building and as responsible agents in such areas as supply, the government dwelled on the role of the commissars and their relationship to the abstract notion of "self-government." This is evident in the reports from the First Conference of Provincial Commissars, held in Petrograd, April 22-24, 1917.[12]

Prince L'vov and S. M. Leont'ev opened the conference with a summary of the legislative work in progress in the MVD's Special Council on the Reform of Local Administration. Leont'ev announced general principles had been worked out for a draft statute on provincial and district commissars. He described all the projects as temporary until the final decisions of the Constituent Assembly.

The commissars themselves expressed the ambiguity of their position.[13] At the meeting, the majority of commissars took the position that each was a representative of government authority, in fact, "the sole representative supported in his activity by the confidence of the population and acting in harmony with local public organizations." A minority took the position that their anointment by the Provisional Government did not entitle them as individuals to embody the state. Equating individual power and state power appeared to them to be hauntingly similar to the bureaucratic state power of the old regime's governors they had so recently opposed. These men argued that the representative of government authority in the provinces should be a collegial body elected by the local executive committees and other local public organizations.

The conference recognized the local committees of public organizations were also in some sense bearers of state authority, but their diverse composition, and the fact that they were to give way to the new zemstvos and dumas, led the conference to conclude it was impossible to define precisely any sort of general formula for the relationship between commissars and the executive committees of the committees of public organizations. Instead, the conference appointed a subcommittee to present a formula for the relationship at the evening meeting.

This subcommittee made the following recommendations, which clearly attempted to limit the power of commissars:

> Inasmuch as at the present time and down to the reorganization of the organs of local self-government, the provincial Commissar, along with supervision (*nadzor*), bears also the function of active administration and carries out the task of state construction in various localities in unity with public organizations, it is necessary to supplement the draft bill on Commissars with the following points: (1) In all measures bearing on the local life of the province the Commissar acts in unity with the provincial committee of public organizations. (2) The provincial Commissar is appointed by the Provisional Government in agreement with the provincial committee of public organizations.[14]

After the discussion of the draft statute, a majority of the conference went on record as *opposing* the projected rights of the commissar to conduct inspections of self-government institutions.

Again, this is evidence of the early grass-roots desire to break with the administrative culture and practices of the past. There had been too much abuse of the inspection authority in the past, they argued, and in most cases such inspections had failed in their aim of uncovering abuses. The representatives argued that inspections had disrupted normal operations and had bred enormous ill will between state and society.

At the next session on April 23, Leont'ev presented the MVD plan for new provincial councils that would merge all administrative units not transferred to self-government institutions or abolished. The provincial council would constitute a collegial body divided into four sections: general, administrative, agricultural, and economic. The MVD also proposed an executive office attached to the commissar (much like the old chanceries) to carry out executive functions. The conference majority rejected both of these proposals, preferring instead to abolish all remaining government offices at the time state functions were trans-

ferred to self-government units. After some debate, the conference decided to maintain all existing government offices that were still performing their duties until the reform of self-government was complete.[15]

Again, this first conference of provincial commissars, unlike a later
meeting held in August, 1917, expressed ambivalence or even hostility
to their own power as representatives of the state. The commissars did
not wish to assume the old administration's tutelage over self-government and public organizations. There seems to have been a genuine
belief on the part of these lower middle strata activists that the organized
and democratic society of the localities could assume the functions of
state power without interference from Petrograd. They had not yet
experienced the frustrations of organizing that state power in the face
of local political and social conflicts and the dispersal of authority among
the grass-roots organizations in the provinces.

During 1917, the exact distribution of power in a given province, as
well as in the districts or volosti, varied greatly. The MVD and other
ministries possessing provincial apparatus had difficulty obtaining ac-
curate information about local politics and subordinate provincial institutions. It was also difficult to communicate central government intentions. A June 5, 1917, MVD memorandum to the Provisional
Government noted that in some provinces the provincial commissar
governed with the aid of the committee of public organizations whereas
in others it was the reverse.[16] The ministry noted also that self-government and public institutions in some provinces were sacrificing state
interests to their own local concerns.

This necessitated a ministry statement that provincial administration
consisted of *both* self-government and state institutions. The purity of
the original Provisional Government commitment to self-government
as the foundation of state power was thus tainted by the tacit admission
that state institutions were in fact necessary to control organs of self-
government. This subtle shift in emphasis foreshadowed the Bolshevik
post-October, state-building experience, including the creation of the
so-called party-state and the imposition of state and Party control over
the soviets, trade unions, factory committees, and the like.

The MVD also reviewed its earlier commitments to give financial
support to those public committees fulfilling state functions and argued
for the right of commissars to issue edicts having the force of law. The
ministry further argued that the filling of all 690 district commissar
positions would be prohibitively expensive, and it asked for extra money
from the cabinet to accomplish the task.[17] In the late spring and summer,
the state-controller attempted to determine whether the committees of
public organizations were receiving allotted state funds and, more im-

portant, were using them for state purposes. There had been numerous reports these funds had been filtered to a variety of social organizations, including the soviets.[18] That the funds would have gone to the soviets is not surprising, given the intimate links between the members of public committees, the soviets, and other public organizations.

The complexities of the situation in the provinces were revealed in a June 30, 1917, report from the Voronezh Provincial Executive Committee of Public Organizations.[19] The report claimed that the old regime's provincial directorate was still in existence but, unlike the executive committee, was incompatible with the revolution. The executive committee declared the directorate "hostile" (*vrednyi*) and transferred all its relevant departments to the Provincial Zemstvo Executive Board. The executive committee also reported that the chancery of the old regime's governor was now serving the provincial commissar of the Provisional Government, but that many of its functions would be more properly executed by the executive committee (particularly in the areas of public order and law enforcement).

The report went on to claim that since the Committee of Public Organizations needed an adequate chancery, "we will use all personnel of the Provincial Directorate except those Councillors already dismissed and those officials of the medicine, construction and veterinary section who are not needed."[20] These specialists were to be transferred to the Zemstvo Executive Board. The director and assistant director of the new chancery were none other than the previous director and secretary of the old regime's provincial directorate. This, the committee argued, was in agreement with the April 1, 1917, edict of Assistant MVD Shchepkin ordering committees of public organizations to use the old regime's administrative personnel (*deloproizvoditeli*). Finally, the committee indicated it was creating an instructional-cultural desk to organize lecture meetings, disburse literature (essentially propaganda about the revolution), and enlighten the population about upcoming elections.

This work was emphasized again in a September memorandum from the MVD's Department of General Affairs to the Provisional Government cabinet.[21] Here the MVD reported that it had created within the Section on the Affairs of Local Administration a special cadre of "volunteer workers" to organize the political leadership of the new local administration institutions and to solve problems as they arose in the localities. The department claimed to have twenty-five men engaged in this work and requested funds for four more. The Provisional Government in its own haphazard way thus adopted the approach later to be so well orchestrated by the Bolsheviks—namely, the use of agents of personal power sent out to organize local government and mediate conflicts in the provinces. The idea of personal power—embodied in such offices as commissar and later Party Secretary and in the variety of special plenipotentiaries and "instructors" sent out by both the Provisional Government and Bolsheviks—transcended the formal transfers of power and periodizations of the revolutionary process.

The Provisional Government's MVD maintained that its flirtation with personal agents and strong executive authority had nothing whatsoever to do with the old regime's practices or ideology. According to its own doctrine, government representatives were to exist in the provinces to check on the legality (*zakonnost'*) of local self-government, a legitimate revolutionary function that had nothing in common with traditional tutelage (*opeka*).[22] The same idea lay behind the MVD's notion of police reform.

As early as March 19, Assistant Minister of Internal Affairs S. D. Urusov[23] reviewed the Provisional Government's intention to turn over all police functions to self-government organs and to permit these organs to choose local police chiefs. According to Urusov, there would be no interference from the central government in police matters, including appointments. Even the old regime's police might serve the new order, according to Urusov, if the self-government organs so desired. Urusov also emphasized the government's commitment not to persecute anyone for political beliefs: "The repressive power of government would only be applied when beliefs manifested themselves in concrete actions directed against our renewed structure. But that would be handled under regular criminal codes. Political repression (*sysk*) is removed from the government's arsenal."[24]

During the spring and early summer of 1917, the MVD continued to write the provincial reform legislation, and it began to carry out the first elections to city dumas under universal suffrage. Preparations were also made for the upcoming elections in August and September to the new volost' zemstvos, the introduction of zemstvos into non-Russian areas, the opening of administrative courts, and, above all, the integration of a variety of public and social organizations into the state structure.

The MVD changed hands in early July with the resignation of Prince L'vov and the appointment of the Georgian Menshevik, I. G. Tseretelli. Tseretelli lasted three weeks and was replaced in the new coalition by the (right-wing) SR, N. D. Avksent'ev.[25] While minister of internal affairs, Avksent'ev maintained his position as chair of the Executive Committee of the All-Russian Soviet of Peasant Deputies. His new MVD team, including V. A. Khizhniakov and Prince G. D. Sidamon-Eristov, represented a direct link with the social movement of the lower middle strata and the organizations of "democratic" Russia going back to the Union of Unions and the 1905 Revolution. This was a further step in the power shift toward Moscow and toward the third-element-dominated public institutions and professional organizations of the provinces.

In July and August, 1917, a conflict emerged between the Ministry of Internal Affairs and the Ministry of Agriculture (MZ). This began with Tseretelli's circulars aimed at the independent activities of the MZ's provincial agents and land committees. The Menshevik minister of internal affairs was upholding the power of the state and private property, while the MZ was supporting grass-roots revolutionary action in place of land reform. The contours of the issues were evident at two congresses held in Petrograd at the end of July and in early August. The first was a congress of MZ representatives attached to the land committees, and the second was another congress of MVD provincial commissars.[26] The concerns expressed at both these meetings reveal the distance both the central government and local officeholders had moved away from the March, 1917, ideal of self-government. They also reveal the extent to which the lower middle strata specialists and their institutions had been absorbed into the fabric of the state.

Kerenskii opened the meeting of MZ representatives to the land committees in late July with a speech notable mainly for its claim that class interests had to be sacrificed "to the interests of the state." This was aimed at the actions and aspirations of the land committees, which had sanctioned land seizures and viewed themselves as protectors of the peasant "class." The ministry representatives clamored for legislation to implement the Main Land Committee's directives and program regulating land relations and increasing land under cultivation. Some representatives argued against the MZ projects, claiming that they were too vague. Others drew attention to the April Provisional Government laws giving the land committees the right to make adjustments at the local level according to existing laws and Provisional Government edicts. Unfortunately, the government had never issued these guiding edicts. The representatives emphasized that the peasants were "conscious of the revolution and of their own needs" and that they "instinctively want order and legality." The land committees, they argued, had held back the tide of peasant unrest, and now the government (here read MVD) and the landowners wanted to prosecute land committee members (here read lower middle strata specialists and intelligentsia) for violations of the old laws. The committees, they argued, were caught in the middle, with no clear direction from the central government.

A sense of urgency was clear as delegates stated their belief that the two years it might take for the government to pass and implement agrarian reform was far too long. Instead, land had to be turned over to the committees for immediate distribution. Minister of Agriculture Chernov, in a long speech, spoke of the difficulty in getting MZ legislation through the Provisional Government cabinet. Everything, he complained, had to be discussed endlessly in inter-institutional conferences held in the midst of governmental crises. The result was the process had to begin anew, with a new cast of characters in the cabinet and ministries.

Assistant Minister of Agriculture B. Vikhliaev lectured on the impact of Tseretelli's July 16 decree, showing that in Poltava, for example, medium-sized plots not in use were placed in the land fund and distributed to those with inadequate land or a modest holding. In Penza, such land was used to satisfy the needs of the entire peasantry. Ministry officials reminded the representatives that they too were central government officials and that they had to keep in mind state interests as opposed to the narrow interests of the localities.

Yet these MZ officials were clearly men of the provinces whose conception of state interest was intimately tied to agrarian arrangements in their localities. In the crucible of the revolution, such individuals were *becoming* the state. The MZ representatives themselves demanded a voice and participation in provincial and district zemstvo executive boards and in the Main Land Committee. The rising tide of MZ specialists in the provinces was part of the larger social revolution of the lower middle strata.

The conference of MVD provincial commissars that opened on August 5 revealed other institutional conflicts and a crisis of power in the provinces. Kerenskii again claimed that local administration (by which he presumably meant state administration as opposed to self-government) had suffered immeasurably in the revolution and had in fact disappeared without a trace. Something, he argued, had to replace it, and "we call on you and the local population to build statehood (*gosudarstvennost'*)." Kerenskii expansively claimed, "My comrades and the MVD together will end the anarchy." Avksent'ev then added that in organizing power in the provinces the government was focusing on the commissars as bearers of the will of the central government, enforcers of legality in all provincial institutions, old and new, and ensurers of the population's civil security.[27]

The commissars then responded. A group, whose spokesperson was the Kadet N. M. Kishkin (chair of the Moscow Committee of Social Organizations), appealed for an end to dual power in the provinces and the construction of one united administrative apparatus. Voronezh Commissar B. A. Keller spoke of the healthy signs of the birth of robust and true democratic organs in the countryside and the desire of the peasantry to help save the country. M. A. Sukovkin of Kiev argued the commissars could not depend on the committees of public organizations because there were such severe differences of opinion within them as well as among representatives of the various ministries in the provinces. He proposed an old idea that predated even the February Revolution, namely, the creation of a special council attached to the provincial commissar that would bring together the representatives of all the central ministries. He also complained that Ministry of Justice representatives and the militia acted inadequately and indecisively and that these functionaries should be brought into the projected council to give the commissar control over their activities.

Commissars from a variety of provinces echoed each other's claims that the commissars were the representatives of the state in the provinces until such time as the new organs of self-government were fully in place. They argued that the commissars (unlike the soviets) were above class interests and that they had to be linked organically to the institutions of provincial society. Commissars had to be nominated by these local bodies and only ratified by the central MVD. Upon creation of the new organs of self-government—a process already well underway by the summer of 1917, prior to the official reelection of zemstvo assemblies and executive boards by universal suffrage—ad hoc provincial institutions were to be dismantled and the soviets removed from participation in administration of the provinces. This, of course, was a tacit admission of the fact that the soviets and other public organizations were very much involved in administering "the state" during the summer of 1917. The commissars conceded that the soviets could continue to exist as Party, class, or professional organs.[28]

The commissar of the Trans-Caspian region, Count Dorrer, pointed out that every ministry was attempting to build its own apparatus in the provinces and that their agents were free of the supervision of the commissar, whom they viewed as the representative of only the MVD and not the state or even the Provisional Government.[29] Numerous commissars argued appointment of commissars from the center would be regarded in the provinces as counterrevolutionary or reactionary. This was really a claim for localizing state power. There was a strong sense expressed at the meeting that the government's legislation on commissars was symbolic support of state power and that opposition to the existence of these powerful, but provincially rooted, state agents was purely utopian. The commissars believed commissar power was a necessity during war and revolution.

Assistant Minister of Internal Affairs V. A. Khizhniakov, himself a former commissar, offered his full support to these officeholders, but he claimed that the draft MVD project on commissars was not entirely satisfactory to the ministry because it had been prepared under previous ministry leadership. It would require reworking and, indeed, would not be issued until late September. The government argued the commissars must have supervision (nadzor) rights over all ministries and their personnel. The commissar's office was a Provisional Government, and not strictly MVD, position that was to be guided by general state considerations. Avksent'ev maintained that the search for "good people" for these positions required special gifts and that provincial society and interests could not always be relied upon in such matters.

In the ensuing discussion of legislative projects, two views emerged: the powerful commissar was temporary until the establishment of revolutionary self-government; the powerful commissar must continue to exist even after the creation of self-government. A majority found that the MVD project (presented by Shreter) showed inadequate faith in the provincial population and that the MVD vision of commissars resembled all too closely the governors of the old regime. According to this view, it was preferable to see the newly elected duma and zemstvo executive board chairs in the role of primary mediators between society and the central government. Prince Sidamon-Eristov, assistant minister of internal affairs and chief of the militia, argued that under no circumstances could local militia inspectors be elected. Discipline and subordination of militia personnel to the central government had to be maintained. For Sidamon-Eristov, the *central government* represented the will of the revolutionary people.[30]

A vote taken on the militia project resulted in thirty-one for subordination of the militia inspectors to the commissar, seventeen for subordination of the inspectors to the central Main Directorate of the Militia (Sidamon-Eristov's operation), and twelve for subordination to local self-government. This is yet another example of how revolutionary pressures in the provinces implied the state's cooptation of the political authority and social power generated in the provinces. Again, the result was far removed from the Provisional Government's original idea in March.

On August 8, 1917, the Provisional Government issued a summary of its work on provincial administration through August 1. Here the work of the Special Council on the Reform of Local Administration was reviewed. Once again, the MVD summarized its priorities and concerns: (1) establishment of the volost' and settlement zemstvos, (2) reform of the zemstvo and duma electoral laws and their governing regulations, (3) militia reform, (4) creation of courts of administrative justice, (5) establishment of statutes for provincial and district commissars, (6) reforms of local finances and taxation, and (7) reform of local administration in non-zemstvo areas. The MVD again emphasized its commitment to break with the past and to end the hegemony of both administration and police in the provinces. The review reported that the special council had set up seven commissions on these matters and that by April 15 a set of legislative acts had been presented to transform Russia's local administration.

The foundation of the entire system—much as had been projected under Stolypin and as far back as the Kakhanov Commission—was the all-estate volost' unit: "In accordance with the law on the volost' zemstvo administration, the volost' zemstvo is the nuclear cell not only of self-government *but also of administration,* concentrating in the hands of the entire volost' population the management (by the new zemstvo) of both public economy and administration matters."[31] Politics, economics, and administration thus were to be merged in one all-class unit. The distinction between self-government and administration, between society and the state, was to be eliminated since the new self-government units were to be organs of the state.

The ambiguous position of the commissars and the MVD's inability to establish their position as the Provisional Government's primary agents in the provinces were clear from a number of other August and September decrees as well as from reports that flowed in from the provinces. On August 27, 1917, Avksent'ev issued a circular shoring up commissar power. The commissars were to be in charge of all administration in the provinces.[32] The measure was portrayed as temporary, pending the full "democratization" of self-government. This enhanced the powers of the commissars vis-à-vis the institutions of self-government even before their powers were codified in the final statute in September. Another circular on August 28 ordered the commissars to cooperate with the local food supply organs.[33]

In September and October, 1917, the Provisional Government and the MVD were experiencing more and more difficulty maintaining lines of authority through the commissars. The representatives of the lower middle strata on the provincial executive committees of public organizations and in the soviets began to dismiss commissars or to replace them with lower middle strata individuals who sometimes held multiple positions. The MVD was expanding the power of a group of officeholders whose allegiance to the central government was by no means assured. As far back as July 13, the Provisional Government announced that, in principle, chairs of zemstvo executive boards should not simultaneously hold the office of commissar.[34] The government claimed that this reversal of L'vov's March edict was only an expedient made necessary by the shortage of capable people in the localities.

Some commissars actively opposed central government policy. In early July, for example, the Kursk provincial commissar announced his intention to do all in his power to undermine "the power of the office of Provincial Commissar."[35] In Penza Province, a district commissar announced to the Committee of Public Organizations: "I will execute those laws that bring benefits and do not diverge from general state interests. But when individual laws are antiquated or vague and do harm, the law for me will be my conscience as a revolutionary and the just opinion of the people."[36] The MVD, of course, reprimanded the commissar. It insisted that its officials must implement all laws and that they did not have the right to distinguish between beneficial and harmful laws.[37]

The MVD futilely tried to eliminate multiple officeholding, such as in Kaluga where the provincial commissar, a former attorney, was at the same time chair of the Executive Committee of the Committee of Public Organizations, chair of the Land Committee, and a member of the Soviet.[38] Assistant Minister of Internal Affairs V. V. Khizhniakov issued a circular in mid-September emphasizing the importance of the commissars' supervision of the organs of self-government. This circular went on to emphasize the importance of commissar appointments and stated the MVD would no longer name as commissars those holding posts in other organs with supervisory responsibilities. As commissars, appointees had to work full time for the Provisional Government. The MVD asked all commissars holding such multiple posts to resign them immediately.[39] In an earlier circular, dated August 30, Khizhniakov and the MVD admitted numerous commissars simultaneously were chairs of peasant or worker soviets. To the government, this too was intolerable and the offenders were asked to resign one or the other post. The ministry also declared that commissars could not hold posts in "class, professional or party organizations."[40]

The problems at the provincial level were even more evident in the districts and volosti. From Riazan', for example, came an August report of a conference of district commissars that had voted to take practical and ideological measures against the local Union of Landowners or, in other words, openly to take the side of the peasants in a series of disputes over land and rents.[41] According to the provincial commissar, the offending resolution was pushed through by executive committee activists who dominated the conference of district commissars. The central MVD could only publish "clarifications" in its new journal (see below), demanding that its commissars not take sides in peasant-landowner conflicts.[42] Again, the SR-led MVD demanded that its agents in the provinces—largely populist sympathizers or party members—not take the side of the peasants against the landlords. In another instance, the MVD declared illegal the action of a district commissar who used the militia to bring management to the bargaining table to avert a strike.[43] From Tobol'sk Province came word there were no candidates for the district commissar positions because the towns had no committees of public organizations.[44] The only suitable candidates were nominees of the soviets, but the MVD replied that soviet representatives were unsuitable for the office.

In September, the MVD began to send troubleshooters to the provinces to help with matters of organization and revision. For example, D. F. Sverchkov, a former Menshevik activist in the Union of Clerical Workers and a member of the Kuban' region's food supply board, was named commissar attached to the MVD and was sent to the Don and Ural regions.[45]

Revealing news came from the city of Kaluga, to which the entire provincial administration of Grodno Province had been evacuated shortly after the outbreak of war two years before. Investigation had revealed complete disorder within the Grodno administration. Twenty-one doctors, seventeen paramedics (fel'dshery), and twenty-six midwives had been receiving pay for the two years despite not having worked. The municipal administration of Grodno city had been dispersing funds for its militia, which was no longer functioning in Kaluga, its place of exile. Much has been written about the role of garrisons, unemployed blue-collar workers, and starving peasants in the revolution in the provinces. But, as the Kaluga example illustrates, to these must be added the thousands of lower middle strata personnel, who also were in dire straits financially and who in some cases were languishing in inactivity. Here was a ready pool of support for a workers' and peasants' revolution that promised to supply a livelihood, a chance to continue professional activities, and perhaps status and power as well.

From Simbirsk, the provincial commissar reported that "in most cases and in matters of principle" he was implementing the decisions of the Provincial Executive Committee, established March 20 and dominated by "peasants." The executive committee, in line with MVD circulars and the decisions of the Second Conference of Provincial Commissars, had recently been reorganized to represent the entire "revolutionary democracy," the organizations of which were the proper basis of state power. The new executive committee was dominated by representatives of "democratic" self-government, the soviets, and various peasant organizations. There was barely a trace of commercial or other propertied elements. In late August, the Mogilev Provincial Committee was reorganized similarly.[46]

The MVD attempted to adjudicate all sorts of administrative disputes in the provinces. It upheld the legal authority of volost' committees to take over the functions of pre-revolutionary volost' administrations. It ordered provincial executive committees to steer clear of ordering arrests outside of established legal procedures—especially for violations of executive committee general edicts, a category which the MVD regarded as beyond the power of the committees to issue.

The MVD's local administration journal also reported on regional conferences (s'ezdy) of commissars and representatives from the executive committees and committees of public organization. The MVD supported this growing infrastructure that would persist and continue to grow after the October Revolution. The ministry attempted to insure regular and reliable reporting on political and economic matters from the provinces to Petrograd.[47] It also tried to keep appointments in its own hands and in those of its commissar agents by denying the right of democratized zemstvo assemblies even to nominate candidates for district commissar.[48] The MVD supported Moscow Commissar Kishkin against the Moscow Soviet demand that he, as a Kadet, be removed in the wake of the Kornilov affair. The MVD argued that party membership was insufficient cause as long as the commissar fulfilled "state obligations."

Many communications were received concerning the ad hoc Committees to Save the Revolution, which were created during the Kornilov days. Kerenskii had ordered the shutdown of such committees, but they had continued to flourish as centers of opposition to the central government and as potential levers of power in the revolutionary and state-building processes. In Khar'kov, the Soviet of Workers' and Soldiers' Deputies asked the RevKom (Revolutionary Committee) to remove the commissar and his assistant because the latter had taken Kerenskii at his word and had considered the RevKom no longer legitimate. The commissar threatened to resign unless the Provisional Government supported him, which of course it did, and the MVD steadfastly attempted to thwart the growing influence of the RevKoms.[49] Again, the government could not really control these provincial bodies, and they came to play a major role in transferring power to the Bolsheviks and creating the soviet state.[50]

During its last two months of existence, the Provisional Government's MVD dealt with a variety of other issues in the area of provincial administration. Its decisions and clarifications were sober and followed a certain logic. It shored up the commissars' power in the face of the growing dissolution of social and economic life in the provinces. It attempted to provide some breathing space so the newly democratized organs of self-government could establish themselves as at least partners in state power. It kept the soviets and such offshoots as the revolutionary committees at bay as they intruded more and more in the domain of the state and its functions.

The MVD voice was marked by a curiously legalistic and formal tone as it attempted to justify decisions by logic and precedent, even when some of the precedents predated the establishment of coalition government in May, 1917, or the February Revolution itself. For example, a September 27 circular turned over to the commissars the chairships of all existing commissions and councils formerly chaired by the old regime's governors and vice governors.[51] This decision and a decision to uphold the commissars' rights to issue edicts having the force of law were defended on the basis of the L'vov March 5 decree making the commissars "legal" successors of the tsarist governors.[52] The ministry ruled that commissars might be members of elected zemstvo and duma assemblies (although they could not be officeholders in institutions of self-government). However, the ministry tried to limit commissar power regarding the disposition of land, property, or materials related to the economy. It remained unclear to the end just what authority the commissars had in matters of land relations, food and other supply matters, production, commerce, and the like. Indeed, the authority of the Provisional Government itself was in question, not just because of these issues but also because of the blossoming infrastructure of the revolutionary state—increasing numbers of congresses and conferences of officials, specialists, professionals, and self-government bodies.

In Ekaterinoslav Province, a labor relations case exemplified the Provisional Government's plight.[53] The Provincial Commercial and Industrial Committee, representing traders and factory owners, had gotten into a salary dispute with its white-collar workers and other employees (*sluzhashchie*). The district commissar tried to avert a strike by taking both parties to the local soviet, which had offered mediation. The MVD declared this act illegal and ordered its commissars not only to shun the soviets but to stay out of labor relations altogether. The government also rejected the appeals by several committees of public organizations and commissars for factory owners to continue paying salaries to blue- and white-collar workers who had taken up positions in the soviets. In general, the Provisional Government was opposed to giving any of its money, or any locally generated tax monies, to the soviets. In several instances, the ministry also denied the taxation authority of the committees of public organizations.

By mid-October, the Provisional Government was most concerned about the commissars' right to call in the military to restore order by force and various side projects to "democratize" other branches of provincial administration.[54] In the psychology of the central government's revolutionary officials and certain provincial officeholders, the idea of authority once again came to be associated with strong individuals. The difference was that central government officials tended, as had their tsarist predecessors, to encumber these individuals with legal codes of behavior while the provincial officeholders placed greater stock in charisma and their unfettered ability to make necessary decisions. In the words of one anonymous provincial commissar, who wrote in October about the problem of state authority,

> I am not saying that the Provincial Commissar should be given supreme power in the province (in order to create the kind of state authority needed), but his persona (*lichnost'*) must be elevated by the government to exceptional heights. To make him into a "simple man on the street" (*obyvatel'*) is now impossible. The Provincial Commissar, as guardian of legality, as the state procurator, must stand tall amidst the population so that his figure is always visible to all. To do this is absolutely urgent and necessary.[55]

Such was the Provisional Government's plight concerning the abstract idea of power and its concrete application in the provinces. During the Russian Revolution, all claimants to state power faced similar challenges. Social movements, local power conflict, and traditional patterns of authority and institutions had profoundly shaped the reform process. Party programs and high politics apparently had much less influence on this process. The stage was set for Bolshevik-style state- (and party-) building as well as the debates over centralization and bureaucratization during the civil war. Lenin's regional Party secretaries were already in gestation.

NOTES

1. The Petrograd daily newspapers contained detailed dispatches from the provinces that described the process in the far-flung provincial capitals of the empire. See especially *Birzhevyiia vedemosti*. This same material was used by the soviet historian E. N. Burdzhalov to write his excellent account of the February Revolution in the provinces. See E. N. Burdzhalov, *Vtoraia russkaia revoliutsiia: Moskva, front, periferiia* (Moscow, 1971). See also William G. Rosenberg, "Les libéraux russes et le changement de pouvoir en Mars 1917," *Cahiers du monde russes et soviétique* 9 (1968):46-57.

2. Two recent soviet studies at last have treated the Provisional Govern-

ment and provincial administration in 1917 as topics worthy of serious scholarly analysis. See V. I. Startsev, *Vnutrenniaia politika Vremennogo pravitel'stva pervogo sostava* (Moscow, 1980), pp. 193-207, and A. M. Andreev, *Mestnye sovety i organy burzhuaznoi vlasti (1917 g.)* (Moscow, 1983).

3. Only a few weeks later it would be clear that this temporary authority was to last only until the new zemstvos and town dumas were elected under universal suffrage.

4. Robert P. Browder and Alexander F. Kerensky, eds., *The Russian Provisional Government, 1917: Documents,* 3 vols. (Stanford, 1961), 1:243.

5. Burdzhalov, *Vtoraia russkaia revoliutsiia,* pp. 174-75.

6. *Kratkii ocherk deiatel'nosti Ministerstva vnutrennikh del so vremeni gosudarstvennago perevorota po 1 iulia 1917 g.* (Petrograd, 1917).

7. *Kratkii ocherk deiatel'nosti MVD,* p. 7. This was one of many examples of the Provisional Government's tendency to create new bureaucratic organs within traditional frameworks to solve the crises of the revolution. The new section was under the general supervision of Assistant Minister of Internal Affairs S. M. Leont'ev.

8. Ibid. Even in this early statement, the MVD relied on personal agents, a form of authority always associated with arbitrariness in the programs of the opposition to the old regime, to instill new political and cultural values. See D. T. Orlovsky, *The Limits of Reform: The Ministry of Internal Affairs in Imperial Russia, 1802-1881* (Cambridge, Mass., 1981), and George L. Yaney, *The Urge to Mobilize* (Urbana, Ill., 1982).

9. The formulation was meant to counter tsarist practice, which had always drawn an artificial distinction between the two spheres to deny the zemstvos legitimacy in politics and administration. Ibid.

10. Browder and Kerensky, *Russian Provisional Government,* 1:278. The law was dated May 30, 1917. Ibid., 1:237.

11. *Kratkii ocherk deiatel'nosti MVD,* p. 7.

12. The transcripts are contained in Browder and Kerensky, *Russian Provisional Government,* 1:250-54.

13. Ibid. This ambiguity would only increase during the summer of 1917, as will be seen below from the transcript of the Second Conference of Commissars, held in mid-August.

14. Ibid. Interestingly, point 1 was voted unanimously, whereas point 2 called forth heated debate before approval.

15. The conference ended with a discussion of an MVD plan to install civilian commissars at the front and with a promise to review martial law regulations (ibid.). For material on the social background and political affiliation of Provisional Government commissars, see my forthcoming study, *Russia's Democratic Revolution.*

16. Tsentral'nyi Gosudarstvennyi Istoricheskii Arkhiv SSSR, Leningrad, *fund* (fund) 576, *opis'* (inventory) 25, *delo* (document, item) 627, *list* (folio) 62.

17. Ibid., f. 576, op. 25, d. 627, l. 62.

18. Ibid., f. 576, op. 25, d. 620.

19. Ibid., f. 576, op. 25, d. 610, l. 96.

20. Ibid.

21. Ibid., f. 576, op. 25, d. 610, l. 132.

22. Ibid., f. 576, op. 25, d. 627, l. 60.

23. It should be remembered that Urusov had served as a provincial governor under the old regime; he had enough of a progressive reputation to earn him a post as an assistant minister of internal affairs under Prince L'vov.

24. Interview in *Birzhevye vedemosti,* March 19, 1917.

25. On Avksent'ev, see Oliver Radkey, *The Agrarian Foes of Bolshevism* (New York, 1958), and the important work of Manfred Hildermeier on earlier SR party history, *Die Sozialrevolutionäre Partei Russlands: Agrarsozialismus und modernisierung in Zarenreich (1900-1914)* (Cologne and Vienna, 1978). See also Michael S. Melancon, "The Socialist Revolutionaries from 1902 to February 1917: A Party of the Workers, Peasants and Soldiers" (Ph.D. dissertation, Indiana University, 1984).

26. The reports of both were published in *Delo naroda* (August 2 and 4 for the Ministry of Agriculture representatives and August 5, 6, and 8 for the provincial commissars) and other daily newspapers. The quoted material in the next paragraph is from *Delo naroda,* August 2, 1917.

27. *Delo naroda,* August 5, 1917.

28. Ibid.

29. Ibid., August 6, 1917.

30. Ibid., August 10, 1917.

31. *Vestnik Vremennago pravitel'stva,* August 8, 1917.

32. Ibid., August 28, 1917; *Izvestiia po delam mestnago upravleniia,* no. 1 (September 1, 1917).

33. *Vestnik Vremennago pravitel'stva,* August 28, 1917.

34. Ibid., July 13, 1917.

35. Ibid., July 7, 1917.

36. *Izvestiia po delam mestnago upravleniia,* no. 1 (September 1, 1917).

37. Perhaps the ministry should have adopted a more flexible attitude toward law that was more consistent with the personal authority it was investing in the office of commissar. The Bolsheviks were better able to finesse this conflict between law and personal power since they maintained that they had abolished "bourgeois" law altogether. Personal power—for example, that possessed by Party secretaries during the civil war—fit better with allegiance to a "Party line" or specific edicts from the central government than with legal norms.

38. *Izvestiia po delam mestnago upravleniia,* no. 2 (September 8, 1917).

39. The MVD tacitly recognized that this would be impossible in the districts where holding multiple offices was a fact of life wrought by the social revolution of the lower middle strata. Ibid., no. 3 (September 16, 1917).

40. Ibid., no. 2 (September 8, 1917).

41. Ibid., no. 1 (September 1, 1917).

42. The commissars resolved that, on the ideological front, they would tell

all the peasants that the landowners in the union were reactionary and would tell the small holders, many of whom were peasants, that their interests lay with the "toilers" of the land and not with the landowning "class" (*pomeshchiki*). Ibid. Later the commissar defended himself and the district commissars by claiming this resolution had been passed only under executive committee influence. In fact, argued the commissar to the central MVD, the district officials were thoroughly "state oriented."

43. Ibid., no. 4 (September 23, 1917).

44. Ibid.

45. Ibid., no. 1 (September 1, 1917). Also appointed special commissar was D. I. Deliarov, who was chair of the Vologda Provincial Food Supply Board. He was sent to Kursk and Voronezh provinces.

46. Ibid.

47. Undated circular of Acting Minister of Internal Affairs Saltykov to provincial commissars which demanded weekly telegrams covering social and political life. Ibid., no. 3 (September 16, 1917).

48. The ruling was in response to a query from the Viatka Province commissar. Ibid.

49. Circular of the new Minister of Internal Affairs Nikitin, published in the September 23 issue of *Izvestiia po delam mestnago upravleniia.*

50. See R. G. Tsypkina, *Voenno-Revoliutsionnye Komitety v Oktiabr'skoi revoliutsii (po materialam gubernii Tsentral'nogo promyshlennogo raiona, Urala i Povolzh'ia)* (Moscow, 1980).

51. *Izvestiia po delam mestnago upravleniia,* no. 5 (September 30, 1917).

52. Ibid. The decision concerning commissars' rights to issue edicts was made on the appeal of Tambov activists against the edicts of the newly appointed Commissar Shatov.

53. Ibid., no. 4 (September 23, 1917).

54. For example, see the Bogutskii project to democratize refugee boards, veterinarian and medical branches, laboratories, and the like. Ibid. There was also a proposal to establish new councilors to assist the commissars in their "supervision" role.

55. Ibid., nos. 6-7 (October 14, 1917).

State and Society in the 1920s

LEWIS H. SIEGELBAUM

> Where and how we must now restructure ourselves, reorganize
> ourselves, so that after the retreat we may begin a stubborn
> move forward, we still do not know.
>
> —Lenin, 1922[1]

Reform is once again on the Soviet political agenda, this time with a
vengeance. After years of economic sluggishness, political inaction, and
social malaise, the political leadership under Mikhail Gorbachev is
facing up to the myriad of problems besetting the society and is calling
on the Soviet people to do likewise. Although sources of inspiration
and models for restructuring Soviet society abound, the decade of the
1920s and the New Economic Policy (NEP) with which it is inextricably
connected exercise a peculiar and powerful hold over the collective
imagination. This is understandable. Correctly perceiving many of the
ills afflicting the state and society as stemming from the legacy of
Stalinism, those engaged in the process of *perestroika* (restructuring)
quite naturally are looking for alternatives in the period before Stalin
assumed undisputed power.

   This essay does not assess directly the applicability of the NEP model
to the current situation in the U.S.S.R. Rather, employing two of the
basic building blocks of modern political analysis—state and society—
it seeks to define the historically conditioned ways in which political
authorities interacted with the variety of groups over whom authority
was formally exercised during the years corresponding to the NEP (1921-
29). In outlining this complex and dynamic interplay of state and society,
I draw heavily upon recent scholarship, especially that which has elu-
cidated the social context of party-state policy. At the same time, I have
tried not to ignore institutional questions, the variety of ways the NEP
was perceived by Party leaders, and other no less critical issues that
constituted the main focus for an earlier generation of scholars.

Reproducing the Oppressive State

There is a long and honorable tradition in Russian historiography, going back at least to the mid-nineteenth century, that regards the autocratic state as History's active agent. Whether in celebration of tsarism's supreme unifying authority over Russians and other peoples of the empire, or in condemnation of its suppression of vital social forces, historians frequently have invoked the awesome power of state authority to explain the course of Russian history. The role of autocracy has appeared so obtrusive that some historians have used it to challenge certain basic Marxist tenets. For example, Alexander Gerschenkron argued with evident relish that, in the case of Russia, Marx's understanding of the relationship of base and superstructure had to be reversed: "In reality, the state was the basis and the economy and the social relations connected with it were, to a varying extent the product of the state, and, as such, a superstructure upon a political basis." In the view of Robert Tucker, "Russian history...turned not on class struggle but on the issue of relations between state and society."[2]

Another way of putting this is to say Russian society was weak or, to use a biological metaphor much in vogue in the late nineteenth century, its constituent elements were "immature." It was just such immaturity that could be—and was—used to justify the maintenance of military-bureaucratic rule. According to this view, the proper relationship between state and society was one of tutelage (*opeka*), with the relatively mature bureaucracy protecting society from society's potentially destructive and usually divisive "spontaneity" as well as from foreign threats.

There is more than a faint resemblance here to the later etatism of Stalinist historical literature, a point that many Western historians have noted. Like society as a whole in tsarist times, the toiling masses after 1917 were deemed in need of guardianship by the vanguard party that had captured state power. It is this very assumption, seen by many in the West as a thinly veiled ideological justification for "totalitarianism," that needs to be examined for the 1920s. Was that period merely a prelude to the complete triumph of the state over society—a period in which the state gathered its forces before launching its assault—or can we detect another radically different sort of relationship? Before dealing directly with this question, we must first consider how the transition was made from that relatively mature bureaucracy to Soviet power.

In Antonio Gramsci's classic formulation, tsarist Russia was a country where "the State was everything, civil society was primordial and gelatinous."[3] It thereby fundamentally differed from much of western

Europe, where a certain equilibrium between state and society had been achieved. While Gramsci's distinction may be a useful vantage point from which much of tsarist Russia's history could be surveyed, it obscures the (admittedly) tentative emergence of civil society in the last decades of tsarist power. Under the pressure of capitalist development—itself fostered by the state—society, or rather elements within it, rapidly "matured." The institution of the *zemstvos* (provincial and local assemblies and boards introduced in 1864 to provide a measure of self-government among property holders), professionalization among urban townspeople, the flowering of the arts, and the expansion of an intelligentsia subculture among various nationality groups all point in this direction.

By the early years of the twentieth century, the state proved itself incapable of stifling the demands emanating from the educated public and was barely able to contain popular protest among workers and peasants. In the course of the 1905-7 Revolution, it was compelled to make a number of concessions. The Duma Monarchy, ushered in by the October Manifesto and accompanied by the most ruthless repression, succeeded in restoring order, but only temporarily. Even before the outbreak of World War I, a process of "dual polarization"—civil society against the state, and, within society, the forces from "below" against the educated classes—could be discerned.[4] The war, in effect, removed the last prop of tsarist rule—the peasant-based army—and, in its last hour of need, the state was abandoned by sizeable elements of the landed nobility. The ease with which tsarism was overthrown testifies to how far and fast its power had been eroded. In the absence of any hegemonic class on which it could depend, the succeeding Provisional Government's strategy of reform was doomed from the start. The processes of social polarization and working-class coalescence simply outpaced efforts at compromise and concession.

"Society," then, did not triumph in the October Revolution, but parts of it did. The peasantry won the right to the nobility's land; workers became the favored class in the proletarian dictatorship. Nor was the victory of workers and peasants a triumph over state authority as such, although that is how some may have viewed it. A state that would legitimate their aspirations was a state worthy of support and, at least in the case of workers, participation.

For a short period, it appeared that this organic relationship between the Soviet state and the "toiling masses" might be able to sustain itself and serve as the basis for building the new socialist order. Factory committees, soviets, and the collectivist ethos with which they were suffused seemed to herald the kind of commune-state about which Lenin wrote in *The State and Revolution*. A number of factors, however, militated against such an outcome. First, the disintegration of industry was already far advanced by October. Although many factory committees struggled valiantly to keep enterprises functioning, the breakdown of the transportation system, the departure of many administrative and technical personnel, and the impounding of funds by owners effectively sabotaged their efforts.[5] Working out decisions about who was to produce what and how and coordinating supplies to realize such decisions required considerable skill, patience, and cooperation. These qualities, however, were in short supply. By the time Lenin was asserting "the Russian is a bad worker compared with the advanced peoples" and demanding strict labor discipline in the form of "thousands subordinating their will to the will of one," the hemorrhaging of the proletariat back to the countryside had begun.[6]

Deproletarianization had many causes, but the acute shortage of food in the cities must be ranked at the top. The organization of food supply was a Herculean task that absorbed the energies of both high-ranking state and Party personnel and what was left of the Party's social base. Thousands of future Communist officials received their baptism of fire in the food detachments of the Commissariat of Supply and the Red Army. The "war for grain," as Lenin termed it in May, 1918, inevitably turned into a war against substantial sections of the peasantry. Unlike the military operations against the Whites and interventionist forces, it was a war the Soviet state could not win. As the "state capitalist" policy of monopolizing grain sales—an inheritance from the Provisional Government—was abandoned in favor of *razverstka* (quota assessment) and razverstka turned into requisitioning, the goodwill the state had earned by virtue of the Decree on Land vanished.[7]

Finally, the role of ideology cannot be discounted in the emergence of an authoritarian Bolshevik state. As several scholars have argued, Bolshevism contained two quite distinct if not antithetical visions of the political rule of the working class.[8] One stressed mass participation in the organs of state administration and paid homage to the boldness and creativity of the proletariat. The other, embodied in the vanguardist role assigned to the Party, emphasized the need to combat petty bourgeois and narrow trade unionist alternatives, the transitional and therefore hybrid nature of post-capitalist society, and the purely technical (non-political) nature of economic management and administration.

What occurred during the formative years of the Soviet state was not so much the abandonment of the first vision as its subordination to the requirements of the second. Some initiatives from below—such as the adoption of a piece-rate system of wages by the metalworkers union or the *Subbotnik* ("Communist Saturdays") phenomenon—were acclaimed by Lenin and were incorporated into the arsenal of the state's techniques to raise productivity and "Communist consciousness." By contrast, bitter invective about "petty bourgeois wavering" greeted concern expressed by the Left Communists (and, later, other oppositional and dissident factions) that the state capitalist organization of industry was stifling workers' initiatives and industrial democracy.[9]

Lenin's antipathy to anything that smacked of the petty bourgeoisie was consistent with his admiration for the productive achievements of large-scale industry and state organization, as evidenced by his enthusiasm for GOELRO, the principles of scientific management, and collective and state farming. Lenin dismissed any notion that the leviathan state, so perceptively analyzed by the young Bukharin, was being reproduced in Soviet Russia. So long as state power rested with the "organized expression of the working class"—that is, the Communist party—the working class had nothing to fear from the state.

This argument was advanced not only by Lenin but by Trotsky and Bukharin as well.[10] Their sincerity is not to be doubted, but neither is their capacity for self-delusion. As the civil war drew to a close, the vast chasm between the centralized militarized state and the rest of society, between the theoretical leap into communism and socioeconomic actuality, reached its maximum extent. The Kronstadters' denunciation of the "commissarocracy" and their call for Soviet democracy and freedom for the peasants "to do as they please with all the land" neatly and tragically expressed the gap.[11]

Mountains and Valleys

We now come to one of the few "great turns" of Soviet history, the abandonment of what would retrospectively be known as War Communism and its substitution by the New Economic Policy. The outlines of the new policy as it emerged in 1921 and thereafter are well known—the replacement of the razverstka by a tax in kind (and after 1924, in money), set at substantially lower levels than quota targets had been; legalization of private trade and small-scale industrial production; stabilization of the currency; decentralization of economic decision making down to the level of trusts and their constituent enterprises on the basis of cost accounting (*khozraschet*); and foreign concessions in mining, timber, and oil extraction.

These and other measures were initially characterized by Lenin as a "retreat," and so they were. The state retreated from direct administration of exchange and certain production relations to the "commanding heights" of large-scale industry, banking, and foreign trade. Peasants, Nepmen, petty entrepreneurs, and foreign concessionaires thereby reacquired some of the terrain evacuated by the state. This was essentially a formula or framework for economic recovery, for reestablishing market relations between town and country. Famine—the effect of civil war depredations—delayed its implementation, but recovery was in full swing after the "scissors crisis" of 1923. The decisive questions then became whether the same framework could be used to sustain socialist industrialization (or "reconstruction" in contemporary parlance) and when or whether the state should try to reoccupy the valleys and plains it had vacated.

Much of the politics of the NEP period revolved around these questions. As many historians have pointed out, the course of state policy as defined by Lenin was ambiguous. Already announcing in March, 1922, that the retreat had ended and that the state had begun to regroup its forces for a new offensive, he subsequently backtracked. Eventually, when the extent of the state's dependence on market mechanisms for recovery became apparent, he dropped the language of "retreat" and "attack" altogether. Instead, he talked of the NEP as long-term ("a whole historical epoch ... one or two decades at best"), involving a "long series of gradual transformations into a large-scale socialized economy," and a "radical change in our whole outlook on Socialism," along the lines of "peaceful, organizational, 'cultural' work."[12]

This was hardly a program, still less a blueprint. While imparting to the NEP an ideological legitimacy it had previously lacked, Lenin's last writings remained largely at the level of abstract musings. It thus was left to his successors to borrow, ignore, emphasize, and distort what they chose in advancing their respective programs. The program of the Left Opposition as developed by its most capable economic theorist, E. A. Preobrazhenskii, and Bukharin's prescriptions—dubbed "rightist" by the end of the decade—represent a high-water mark in Marxist discourse on the transition to socialism.

Preobrazhenskii's model was premised on the proletariat's meager inheritance of appropriate skills and habits and the severe limitations the prevailing petty bourgeois mode of agricultural production placed on accumulation for industrialization.[13] "Primary socialist accumulation" thus had to be undertaken chiefly from above, that is, by the state, utilizing the mechanisms of planning, pricing, and taxing to divert funds from consumption to capital investment. It was either that or succumb to the "law of value," whose logic was antithetical to the state economy.

In essence, Preobrazhenskii's understanding of transition was based on his identification of a series of antitheses—from above versus from below, large-scale industry versus small-scale agriculture, planning versus the market, and, finally, the proletarian state versus the non-proletarian classes. Whether such an understanding violated the spirit and principles of the NEP, as Bukharin contended, need not concern us. As already suggested, the NEP was open to a number of interpretations, and there is nothing except Party resolutions to say that the Left's positing of a protracted war of maneuver was any less appropriate than any other view.

Bukharin, of course, denied the existence of these antitheses. There was, he asserted, a compatibility of interests among social groups and between them and the state that could make the NEP mutually beneficial. Unlike its capitalist predecessor, Soviet industrialization need not mean the ruin of the peasantry. On the contrary, it could only succeed by developing the rural sector economically and culturally. This, as Stephen Cohen has emphasized, was not only an economic but also an ethical imperative for Bukharin.[14] The key was to strengthen the alliance (smychka) between town and country by observing strict legality, encouraging credit and consumer cooperatives, providing educational, medical, and cultural services, and tailoring industrial production to the needs of the peasant consumer, which would thereby increase agricultural productivity and, at the same time, create an investment fund that could be used to build up heavy industry at a moderate pace.

Bukharin thus rejected the Left's equations. Socialism would be achieved not by suppressing the market but "through market relations." The proletariat could escape from its isolation on the fortified peaks not by conquering and colonizing the lowlands but by fostering there "the development of a Soviet civil community (obshchestvennost')" based on "all types of voluntary circles, societies . . . and groups for agricultural propaganda, for fighting alcoholism, against smoking, societies for rural amenities, for cooperative assistance and so forth."[15] Finally, the growth of the state sector was not necessarily tantamount to building socialism. On the contrary, if done in haste and without due attention to what was feasible, it could mean "a colossal administrative apparatus" that would be compelled to resort to mass coercion and terror.[16]

Such, in their barest outlines, were the two most carefully constructed models of how the state, from its position on the commanding heights, should relate to the forces "down below." We need not dwell any further on these models, for there exist several excellent accounts that analyze their implications, their common assumptions, and their internal inconsistencies and weaknesses.[17] Neither, in any case, was implemented in its entirety, not even Bukharin's during the period of "high NEP" (1925-26). Limitations imposed by ideological confusion within the Party and the changing fortunes of individual leaders and factions were only two factors. No less important was the resiliency of social forces, only recently examined by historians. While the Party leadership was seeking ways to raise the base up to the superstructure, workers and peasants were making their own imprints on the social landscape.

The New, the Old, and the Very Old

Just as there were two nearly antithetical models of Soviet economic policy in the 1920s, there was also a dual cultural policy, defined as prescriptions for behavior appropriate to a revolutionary society. Historians have used terms such as "authoritarian" versus "collectivist," "revolutionary heroic" versus "utopian," and "instrumentalist" versus "normative" to express this bipolarity.[18] Bolshevism's dual cultural face was reflected in a series of overlapping institutional rivalries—the Komsomol and the Supreme Council of the National Economy (Vesenkha) versus the Commissariat of Enlightenment (Narkompros) for control of educational policy, the All-Union Central Council of Trade Unions versus the Proletkult over the allocation of resources for workers' cultural activities, the Komsomol versus the Women's Section of the Party (Zhenotdel) over the definition of the "new Soviet woman"—as well as clashes within at least some of these institutions. This by no means exhausts the list of antinomies that arose in the 1920s. The movement for establishing a new work culture based on the concept of the scientific organization of labor (NOT) was rent by a division between Kerzhentsev's Time League and Gastev's Central Institute of Labor, and the antireligious movement incorporated both accommodationist and abolitionist tendencies.[19]

Why was there such contentiousness over cultural policy? Partly it was because the stakes appeared so high. Never before had a state undertaken such an immense task, nothing less than the transformation of human behavior via social engineering. Partly it was a throwback to disputes that had arisen in the pre-revolutionary era. These pitted the proponents of Bolshevism's European rationalist heritage against adherents of later avant-garde currents. Although the former, thanks to Lenin's authority, had carried the day, the revolution gave a powerful impetus to avant-garde visions, which were strengthened by the cultural traffic between Russia and the West.[20] Finally, it had to do with the social and cultural contexts, with the fact that, despite the political defeat of the old regime and Bolshevism's numerous other political enemies, the old had not yet disappeared and the new was still being shaped.

Indeed, one could go further and say that, for much of the 1920s, it was not at all clear what constituted "the old" or how much of it should be discarded in the building of the new. Capitalism as an economic system based on the exploitation of wage labor was, of course, anathema. But that did not necessarily mean the Soviet state should dispense with the services of those who had run capitalist industry—the "bourgeois specialists"—or, for that matter, the advanced techniques of industrial production that were being pioneered by the archetypal capitalist Henry Ford. The proletariat was the new ruling class, but since it was still stamped with the attributes of an oppressed class—drunkenness, hooliganism, anti-intellectualism, work-shyness, and the like—its aspirations, even when collectively expressed, did not necessarily have to be translated into state policy. The peasantry, Russia's proverbial "dark masses," needed to be enlightened via cultural revolution so that it too could participate in Soviet power. But did such an agenda necessarily apply to all peasants or only to those who were willing to forsake being a *khoziain* (proprietor)?

Deciding exactly where to draw the limits and how to enforce them was no easy matter. In fact, it was so complex that the Party was severely constrained in its ability to command any of these groups from the height of state power and for that matter, to command the state itself. This point deserves elaboration.

Given the shortage of technically trained Party cadres, the higher organs of economic administration—Vesenkha, Gosplan, and the trusts—were dominated by non-Party specialists. Even at the enterprise level, the "Red directors" were often only nominally in charge since, by the end of the decade, less than one in ten had a higher technical education.[21] The Party could not afford to do without the bourgeois specialists, but, in another sense, it could not afford to rely too much on them. Policy, then, consisted of an almost impossible balancing act: vesting in specialists considerable authority and succoring them against the suspiciousness of lower-ranking Party officials and the wrath of rank-and-file workers, but, at the same time, combating their autonomy and esprit de corps by purging their union leadership and monitoring them both from above and below; encouraging them to identify with Soviet power, but discriminating against their children in terms of access to the Party and, at least until 1926, higher education; paying them high salaries, but denying them certain civil rights.[22] Much the same could be said of the treatment of other professionals, for example, scientists, agronomists, teachers, and those in the legal profession. Only with the Shakhty trial of 1928 and the Cultural Revolution it inaugurated were some of these contradictions resolved, but with predictably disastrous consequences for the professions and the services they could provide.[23]

The relationship between the Party and workers was also vexed, never more so than in the early years of the NEP. E. H. Carr may have gone too far in characterizing the proletariat as the "stepchild" of the NEP, but, notwithstanding the Party's ideological tergiversations, for many proletarians the NEP smacked too much of the old order and was referred to as the "New Exploitation of the Proletariat."[24] Throughout the years 1921-25, industrial life was punctuated with strike activity, usually without the sanction of trade unions, and other manifestations of worker protest. From one point of view, that of the Party leadership, the problem was the replacement of the revolutionary proletariat by a "backward mass" of petty bourgeois and other uprooted elements. It was a problem that could be remedied by political education under the aegis of the vanguard party. This interpretation, so redolent of *opeka* (tutelage), justified the major purge of Party organizations in 1921, the subsequent expulsion of large numbers of "unreliable" members—most of them workers by occupation—and the reliance on appointment of cell secretaries from above. As we shall see, such policies did little to quell worker unrest and eventually were modified.

Of course, it will not do to consider industrial workers as a homogenous mass. Differences of skill and experience (*stazh*), age, gender, ethnicity, family circumstances, and occupation mattered mightily in workers' experiences with and attitudes toward their work, their bosses, the Party, and the state. These differences were not merely remnants of the pre-revolutionary era but were reproduced by the prevailing conditions of the 1920s. For example, the culture of shop and trade solidarity, of jealously guarded craft knowledge, and of numerous rites accompanying the initiation into and celebration of craft practices served to sustain older skilled workers in their dealings with rate- and norm-setters and new recruits into the factory. Such workers were "accustomed to close ranks and stand firm against the foreman, against the boss. The[y] . . . disliked upstarts and bootlickers, those who sought to 'curry favor' and beat down the piece rates, those who whispered to the foreman about fellow workers' idleness. . . ."[25]

These "labor aristocrats" had been the core of the Party's support within the working class. But their support was severely tested by the NEP. They bitterly resented their bosses' high salaries and high-handed manner as well as the Nepmen, speculators, and other "class alien" elements who frequented the restaurants, nightclubs, and high-class shops of the major cities. Threatened by the introduction of various rationalization schemes, assembly-line production, and the narrow and rapid training techniques promoted by the Central Institute of Labor, they most acutely experienced the "crisis of proletarian identity" toward the end of the decade.[26]

At the opposite end of the spectrum of working-class culture were the *otkhodniki,* peasant migrants who flocked to construction sites, the mines, the timber industry, and wherever else a pair of good strong hands was needed. For the most part unskilled and politically illiterate, many clung to their artels, village-based work units that in the eyes of Party and trade union organizers only reinforced their own and Russia's "backwardness." Treated with scorn by more experienced workers and their bosses, they reacted in kind, arriving late (or not at all) to work, sleeping on the job, flitting from one place of work to another, and engaging in "hooligan" attacks against both managers and their fellow workers.

In between these two poles were several other groups of workers— working-class women who struggled, largely unsuccessfully, against displacement by demobilized soldiers, discrimination by employers and their male counterparts, and the indifference of most Party members to their plight; younger apprentices and semiskilled graduates of the factory apprentice schools who, comprising the Komsomol's natural constituency, were often at loggerheads with both management and the trade unions; and the mass of clerks, cleaners, watchmen, and domestic servants who for the most part were the constituency of no organized group and suffered accordingly.

Finally, there was the peasantry which continued to confound the Party's best theoreticians and most ardent activists until the full-scale assault was launched against that class and its defenders at the end of the decade. That the peasantry was beyond the reach of Soviet power for much of the twenties was a function of both the Party's self-denying ordinance with respect to coercion (far from universally observed but still officially mandated) and the resiliency of the village commune. Pre-capitalist in origin, the commune actually faced challenges on two fronts: increased social inequality fostered by opportunities for accumulation that the NEP offered to some peasants, and the attempt to supplant it by village soviets. It managed to withstand both.

On the one hand, the "modernizing" thrust of capitalism, as represented by kulak entrepreneurship and technical progressiveness, was too weakly articulated to seriously disrupt or dominate communal affairs. As alarmed as the Party was about the kulaks, the difficulty investigators experienced in defining just who they were testifies to their elusiveness in reality.[27] On the other hand, Bukharin's dream of "the

development of a Soviet civil community" in the countryside foundered
on the dearth of resources that could be invested in such a project and
on the persistence of mutual suspicion based on a long history of
authoritarian relations between representatives of the state and the local
population.

This is not to suggest that what Soviet authorities confronted in the
countryside was blind tradition, though there undoubtedly was some
of that. It is to assert that the state was not alone in making policy; the
peasants had policies too. When state procurement agents offered them
a decent price for their grain, as was generally the case between 1924
and 1926, they sold it; otherwise, they stored it, turned it into moonshine
(*samogon*), or sold it to private traders. Sometimes they cut back on
its sowing in favor of more lucrative industrial crops. They thus periodically entered the market and withdrew from it, depending on circumstances. When Party recruiters explained that Party membership
was incompatible with worshipping God, they either boycotted the Party
or placed images of Lenin in the icon (Red) corner. When their local
churches were closed and the valuables confiscated, they fell back on
the rites that could be performed in the household or joined one of the
communalist sects that flourished in the countryside.[28]

In this manner, the "old" both resisted and adapted to the "new."
At the same time, the reverse process was occurring. Initially, Soviet
authorities had accommodated all manner of fellow travelers among
the intelligentsia by providing employment for many struggling artists
and writers in the state's propagandistic endeavors. But the affinity of
Russia's cultural avant-garde with European currents—few of which
could be categorized as politically progressive—and the isolation of the
Russian revolution caused a reaction within the Party that spelled doom
for such accommodation. Impatience with the rebellious individualism
of the intelligentsia, a yearning "to achieve unity in the human sciences
'under the banner of Marxism,' "[29] and the desire to inspire and mobilize
the masses for socialist construction eventually tilted the balance in
cultural policy toward authoritarianism, the civil-warlike mentality of
revolutionary heroism, and an instrumentalist view of individual emancipation.

State and Society Revisited

The questions that embroiled Party leaders in the 1920s revolved around
direction and pace. Were the policies inaugurated at the beginning of
the decade leading the country in the direction of socialism, or were
the "capitalist" forces, unleashed by the NEP to stimulate the economy,

actually gaining ground? If the former was the case, could the Party afford to allow the process of socialist reconstruction to proceed at a moderate pace, or, given the likelihood of one or the other capitalist power's launching hostilities against the U.S.S.R., did that pace have to be stepped up?

We know that by the end of the decade these questions were resolved in favor of scrapping the NEP and many of the assumptions on which it rested and initiating the so-called Great Turn. But do we know how and why? The time when an adequate explanation for this denouement could rest entirely on the machinations of Stalin, the ineptitude of his rivals, and other elite phenomena thankfully has passed.[30] Many scholars have focused instead on what was going on beneath the impassioned debates in the Politburo and Central Committee, that is, the impact of state policy on workers and peasants and the ways these classes both shaped and limited policy. This kind of analysis has profound implications for understanding the relationship between state and society. It is not just that the two interacted; they interpenetrated, creating a "spillage" of the one into the other. This was most clearly so in the case of industrial workers.

Despite the deep internal divisions among workers that were discussed above and some improvement in their material circumstances (or, rather, because the sheer physical struggle for survival had passed), all workers had real grievances against the factory system that emerged in the course of the NEP. Even though intra-class conflicts persisted, common subordination to management, the acute shortage of housing, and other problems encountered in their daily lives revived a certain sense of solidarity and militancy among workers. The Party leadership viewed this development with alarm. Having made major concessions to both the peasantry and educated déclassé elements of the population, the Party now was in jeopardy of losing the class in whose name the revolution had been made.

It was then that the Party initiated several revisions that had immense repercussions for Party-worker relations. One was opening the Party ranks to working-class recruitment. This—the so-called Lenin Levy (actually successive recruitment drives in 1924, 1925 and 1927)—vastly increased the size of the Party and the proportion of its members who were workers. Another was the introduction of production conferences at the factory and shop levels designed to elicit suggestions from below about how to raise productivity and curb mismanagement and waste. Finally, there was the decision of August, 1926, to raise wages of workers, particularly in the producer-goods sector where wage levels had remained low relative to consumer-goods industries.[31]

These initiatives were taken in conjunction with a series of campaigns to rationalize production and increase labor productivity. Together, they may be seen as the Party's terms for renegotiating its "historic alliance" with the working class or at least sections thereof. But, as William Chase recently has argued, workers brought their own agenda to the figurative bargaining table.[32] Among those who joined the Party as *lenintsy* (workers recruited into the Party in the mid-1920s) were many who continued to struggle against managerial abuses of authority and complain about the cozy relationship that low-level Party officials enjoyed with their bosses. Workers initially paid little attention to production conferences but, after 1926, increasingly viewed them as an arena in which their economic interests could be defended against their "class enemies." Despite the continual increase in nominal wages, the entire wage system and its linkage with productivity remained a highly contested issue in the trade unions, the Party organizations, and production meetings.

There was, then, considerable tension and risk involved in this alliance. But, at least for the Stalin faction that was about to embark on the destruction of the NEP and its "rightist" supporters, the gains were considerable. It now had coopted a large number of activist cadres into the Party's ranks to complement its own increasingly secure control of the Party apparatus. The workerist posture that this faction assumed in 1928—casting doubt on the loyalty of the technical intelligentsia, raising the alarm about kulaks and resorting to "extraordinary measures" in the countryside, introducing the seven-hour workday, expanding the policy of "pushing up" (*vydvizhenie*) workers into educational institutions and the administrative organs of the Party and state, and adopting the class-against-class position within the Comintern—fed on and sustained this alliance. And when, as a result of the dislocations caused by some of these policies, the relative strength and spirit of the initial recruits flagged, the alliance was once again reconstituted. This time it was the turn of younger workers, the products of the Soviet school of factory life, who formed shock brigades, engaged in socialist competition, eagerly participated in the "socialist transformation of the countryside," and in many cases joined the Party and police apparatuses.

Despite superficial appearances and the rhetoric of the time, these alliances were qualitatively different from the revolutionary prototype of 1917-18. The difference, of course, was in the nature of the Party. It was no longer political but supervisory and administrative, presided over by "an iron guard of energetic, hard-driving, authoritarian men of action who saw in Stalin the indispensable shrewd realist."[33] The "proletarianization" of the Party did not lead to its democratization.

At most, it strained secretarial control over cell organization. Ultimately, however, it provided the leadership with a striking force that could be mobilized as a blunt but still effective weapon against all manner of enemies both within and outside the Party. Chief among the internal enemies were the "Rightists," those who persisted in regarding the NEP as a viable policy. Having acquiesced and even participated in the process by which the machine had crushed the Left Opposition, they in turn found themselves hooted and hounded. As for the external enemies, the peasantry proved the most formidable, but, after several years of brutal struggle, it grudgingly acquiesced to collectivization.

"The state swelled up; the people grew lean." Such was Kliuchevskii's verdict on the territorial expansion of the tsarist state under Peter I. Much the same could be said of the Stalin revolution, except that the swelling was more domestic than international. Moshe Lewin has referred to this process with respect to the peasantry as "statization (*oka-zenivanie*)."[34] The term can be extended to apply to much else within the realm of civil society. But rather than enabling the state to refashion society as the state saw fit, "statization" meant absorbing traditions, habits, and people into the state, rendering it cumbersome and maddeningly inefficient—in short, more backward in some respects than it had been before 1929.

Lest this last point be misinterpreted, it has to be said that not all of society and its ways were absorbed and that, in swelling up, the state also shed some of its procedures. Many of the intellectual pursuits that flourished in the 1920s and were sustained by a plethora of professional associations and societies did not survive; nor did the state's recognition of the laws of economics and economists' models based upon them. In the final analysis, it was precisely this—the state's acknowledgment of and even accommodation to "inconvenient" facts—that distinguished the 1920s from the decade that followed. So long as there was such acknowledgment and accommodation, reform was possible. After 1929, suturing problems with ideological strands—some of which were borrowed from the distant past and others manufactured, as it were, on the run—prevented that possibility. In this sense, *glasnost'* (openness), the watchword of the Gorbachev leadership, is most appropriate to the reformist agenda that has been set.

NOTES

1. V. I. Lenin, *Polnoe sobranie sochinenii*, 5th ed., 55 vols. (Moscow, 1958-65), 45:302 (hereafter *PSS*).

2. Alexander Gerschenkron, "Soviet Marxism and Absolutism," *Slavic Re-*

view 30 (1971):865; Robert C. Tucker, "The Image of Dual Russia," in his *The Soviet Political Mind: Studies in Stalinism and Post-Stalin Change* (New York, 1963), p. 78.

3. Antonio Gramsci, *Selections from the Prison Notebooks of Antonio Gramsci,* ed. and trans. Quintin Hoare and Geoffrey Newell Smith (New York, 1971), p. 238.

4. Leopold Haimson, "The Problem of Social Stability in Urban Russia, 1905-1917," *Slavic Review* 33 (1964):619-42; ibid., 34 (1965):1-22.

5. William Rosenberg, "Russian Labor and Bolshevik Power after October," *Slavic Review* 44 (1986):213-38; Rosenberg, "Workers and Workers Control in the Russian Revolution," *History Workshop* 5 (1978):89-97; Carmen Sirianni, *Workers Control and Socialist Democracy: The Soviet Experience* (London, 1982), pp. 95-158.

6. Lenin, "Ocherednye zadachi sovetskoi vlasti," *PSS,* 34:187, 189-90.

7. Lars T. Lih, "Bolshevik *Razverstka* and War Communism," *Slavic Review* 45 (1986):673-88. See also, Bertrand Mark Patenaude, "Bolshevism in Retreat: The Transition to the NEP," Ph.D. dissertation, Stanford University, 1987, especially Part I.

8. See, for example, Sirianni, *Workers Control,* chaps. 7-9; Philip Corrigan, Harvie Ramsay, and Derek Sayer, *Socialist Construction and Marxist Theory: Bolshevism and Its Critique* (New York and London, 1978), pp. 24-65; and Neil Harding, "Socialism, Society and the Organic Labor State," in *The State in Socialist Society,* ed. Neil Harding (Albany, N.Y., 1984), pp 15-38.

9. Lenin, *PSS,* 36:273-74, 293-306.

10. L. D. Trotsky, *Terrorism and Communism* (Ann Arbor, Mich., 1961), pp. 134 ff; N. I. Bukharin, *The Politics and Economics of the Transition Period* (London, 1979), pp. 117-18.

11. Israel Getzler, *Kronstadt 1917-1921: The Fate of a Soviet Democracy* (Cambridge, 1983), pp. 204, 213-14.

12. Lenin, *PSS,* 44:6; 45:372-76. For discussions of these reassessments, see E. H. Carr, *The Bolshevik Revolution,* 3 vols. (London, 1966), 2:274-79; Moshe Lewin, *Lenin's Last Struggle* (London, 1975), pp. 23-39; and Lewin, *Political Undercurrents in Soviet Economic Debates* (Princeton, N.J., 1974), pp. 75-87.

13. I am following here the interpretation of Mark Harrison, "Soviet Primary Accumulation Processes: Some Unresolved Problems," *Science and Society* 45 (1981-82):387-408.

14. Stephen F. Cohen, *Bukharin and the Bolshevik Revolution* (New York, 1974), pp. 171-73.

15. N. I. Bukharin, "O nekotorykh zadachakh nashei raboty v derevne," *Bol'shevik,* no. 7-8 (1924):23, quoted in Harrison, "Soviet Primary Accumulation," p. 401.

16. See Lewin, *Political Undercurrents,* pp. 61-63.

17. Alexander Erlich, *The Soviet Industrialization Debate, 1924-1928* (Cambridge, Mass., 1960); Lewin, *Political Undercurrents,* pp. 33-48; Alec Nove, *An Economic History of the U.S.S.R.* (London, 1969), pp. 119-35.

18. See respectively Robert C. Williams, "The Nationalization of Early Soviet Culture," *Russian History/Histoire Russe* 9 (1982):157-71; James C. McClelland, "The Utopian and the Heroic: Divergent Paths to the Communist Educational Ideal," in *Bolshevik Culture,* ed. Abbott Gleason, Peter Kenez, and Richard Stites (Bloomington, Ind., 1985), pp. 114-30; and Gail Lapidus, *Women in Soviet Society* (Berkeley, 1978), pp. 73-82.

19. For these clashes, see respectively Sheila Fitzpatrick, *Education and Social Mobility in the Soviet Union, 1921-1934* (Cambridge, 1979), chaps. 3, 6; John Hatch, "The Politics of Mass Culture: Workers, Communists, and Proletkul't in the Development of Workers' Clubs, 1921-1925," *Russian History/Histoire Russe* 13 (1986):119-48; Barbara Evans Clements, "The Birth of the New Soviet Woman," in *Bolshevik Culture,* ed. Gleason, Kenez, and Stites, pp. 230-33; Zenovia Sochor, "Soviet Taylorism Revisited," *Soviet Studies* 33 (1981):246-64; and Joan Delaney, "The Origins of Soviet Antireligious Organization," in *Aspects of Religion in the Soviet Union, 1917-1967,* ed. Richard Marshall, Jr. (Chicago, 1971), pp. 103-29.

20. Williams, "Nationalization of Early Soviet Culture," pp. 159-60.

21. *Ratsionalizatsiia proizvodstva,* no. 9-10 (1930):48-50.

22. Kendall E. Bailes, *Technology and Society under Lenin and Stalin* (Princeton, N.J., 1978), pp. 44-82.

23. See Sheila Fitzpatrick, ed., *Cultural Revolution in Russia, 1928-1931* (Bloomington, Ind., 1978).

24. E. H. Carr, *The Interregnum, 1923-1924* (London, 1969), p. 47.

25. G. Lebedev, "Vziat' novyi kurs," *Molodaia gvardiia,* no. 16 (1929):52.

26. Hiroaki Kuromiya, "The Crisis of Proletarian Identity in the Soviet Factory, 1928-1929," *Slavic Review* 44 (1985):280-97; Kuromiya, *Stalin's Industrial Revolution: Politics and Workers, 1928-1932* (Cambridge, 1988), pp. 78-107.

27. See Moshe Lewin, "Who Was the Soviet Kulak?" in his *The Making of the Soviet System: Essays in the Social History of Interwar Russia* (New York, 1985), pp. 121-41.

28. On *sektantstvo,* see I. Morozov, "Sovremennoe sostoianie sektantstva v SSSR," in *Voinstvuiushchee bezbozhie v SSSR za 15 let. Sbornik,* ed. M. Enisherlov, A. Lukachevskii, and M. Mitin (Moscow, 1932), pp. 139-156, and I. A. Malakhova, "Religioznoe sektantstvo v Tambovskoi oblasti v posleoktiabr'skii period i v nashi dni," *Voprosy istorii religii i ateizma* 9 (1961):77-112. The comment of Richard Stites is apposite here: "There was not only much *dvoiverie* in rural Russia in the 1920s, but *tvoiverie* and perhaps even *mnogoverie.*" Richard Stites, *Revolutionary Dreams: Utopian Vision and Experimental Life in the Russian Revolution* (New York, 1988), p. 122.

29. David Joravsky, "Cultural Revolution and the Fortress Mentality," in *Bolshevik Culture,* ed. Gleason, Kenez, and Stites, p. 108.

30. The standard Soviet position previously avoided the question by extending the life of the NEP well into the 1930s and viewing its passing as a "logical" (*zakonomernyi*) process. See the concluding article to a two-year discussion, "K itogam obsuzhdeniia problem novoi ekonomicheskoi politiki,"

Voprosy istorii KPSS, no. 12 (1968):81-91, particularly p. 86. See also V. I. Kuz'min, "NEP i sotsialisticheskaia rekonstrukstiia narodnogo khoziaistva," in *Novaia eknomicheskaia politika, voprosy teorii i istorii,* ed. M. P. Kim et al. (Moscow, 1974), pp. 20-35, and V. P. Dmitrenko, "Problemy NEPa v sovetskoi istoriografii 60-70kh godov," ibid., especially pp. 300-1. For some recent views, see " 'Kruglyi stol': Sovetskii soiuz v 20-e gody," *Voprosy istorii,* no. 9 (1988):3-58.

31. John Hatch, "The 'Lenin Levy' and the Social Origins of Stalinism: Workers and the Communist Party in Moscow, 1921-1928," *Slavic Review* (forthcoming); William Chase, *Workers, Society and the Soviet State: Labor and Life in Moscow, 1918-1929* (Urbana, Ill., 1987), pp. 264-87; E. H. Carr and R. W. Davies, *Foundations of a Planned Economy, 1926-1929,* 2 vols. (London, 1969-71), 1:556-69.

32. Chase, *Workers, Society and the Soviet State,* pp. 277-82; see also Chase, "The Dialectics of Production Meetings, 1923-29," *Russian History/Histoire Russe* 13 (1986):149-85.

33. Lewin, *Making of the Soviet System,* p. 25.

34. Ibid., p. 228.

Khrushchev and Detente: Reform in the International Context

WILLIAM TAUBMAN

This chapter is one of three in this volume discussing Khrushchev and reform after Stalin. It has been shaped by both its context and what literary scholars might call its "subtext." Its subtext is Yanov's point of view as reflected in the "Conference Proposal: Is the Soviet Union Reformable? Russia and the West at the End of the Twentieth Century" and in his important and provocative book, *The Drama of the Soviet 1960s: A Lost Reform.*[1] The issue of whether Russia is reformable, along with the related issue of the role of the West in encouraging or inhibiting Russian reform, hinges, especially for the Khrushchev era, on answers to at least five general questions. This chapter begins by posing those questions, particularly as they apply to the Khrushchev era, and by noting what seems to be Yanov's answer to each of them. I then provide my own answers for the period between Stalin's death in 1953 and Khrushchev's ouster from power in 1964.

The first question is whether a particular reform attempt was a major effort at genuine reform. Although qualified, Yanov's answer for the Khrushchev era is generally affirmative. As such, it contrasts sharply with the prevailing view in both the West and the Soviet Union. The official Soviet charge against Khrushchev has been that he was, to use the stock Soviet phrase, a "harebrained schemer." Merle Fainsod once argued that Khrushchev was hardly a reformer at all.[2] Yanov recognizes, of course, key contradictions and inconsistencies in Khrushchev's policies, not to mention a series of important "political blunders," including the Cuban missile crisis.[3] But in contrast with other observers, Yanov portrays Khrushchev as a leader with a relatively coherent vision of far-reaching domestic and foreign change and the linkage between them.

The second general question is whether a given reformer had what the conference proposal calls "a realistic and comprehensive reformist strategy."[4] Yanov finds it "very hard to believe that Khrushchev had a carefully planned, comprehensive political strategy"; certainly he "proved incapable of consolidating his allies politically and making permanent the changes resulting from his reforms." But Yanov also cannot believe that Khrushchev's various moves—"the Link Reform, the emergence of a new rural elite, the triumph of rural managers . . . , the retreat of the military, the division of Soviet prefects into two hierarchies"—were "mere coincidence." "There had to be some meaning," to these and other moves; indeed, Yanov contends that as time passed "Khrushchev seemed to have matured as a reformist leader, with his perceptions changed, his strategies evolved."[5]

The third question looms large in Yanov's study of Khrushchev: whether the failure of reform was a foregone conclusion or a near miss. That issue is important not only in its own right but because it bears on a fourth issue, the role of the West in the outcome of Russian reform. The conference proposal poses the issue this way: "If Russian reformist efforts were, in many cases, conducted in an adverse international environment . . . or if none had the benefit of active Western support, the question of the success or failure of reform efforts . . . might indeed be seen as directly contingent on Russian-Western relations."[6] But if, leaving the West out of it for a moment, the failure of reform were a foregone conclusion, then it hardly matters whether the international environment was adverse or the West offered assistance.

Yanov portrays Khrushchev's ouster as far from foreordained. According to him, "the major cause of failure" of the "reform attempt of the 1960s" was "the adverse international environment." "What Khrushchev needed most was not miracles," but "simply *time*."[7] Moreover, it was easily within the power (although not at all the imagination) of the West to give Khrushchev the time he needed. All Khrushchev "might have needed from the West [was] what Brezhnev got so easily at the beginning of the next decade," namely, a thaw in East-West relations, including a Berlin agreement, a presidential visit to Moscow, and the promise of big Western loans to the U.S.S.R.[8] What Khrushchev got instead from Washington was the Kennedy administration's massive military buildup which, occurring just when the Soviet leader was trying to tame his own military, forced him "to fight a struggle on two fronts— against his own *and* the Western military-industrial complexes."[9]

Linked to the Western impact on Russian reform efforts is the fifth issue: whether the West has a stake in the reformers' success. The conference proposal assumes we do, especially in the nuclear age when an indefinite continuation of the present regime, or even worse its replacement by a xenophobic, right-wing, Russophile leadership, could lead to catastrophe. Likewise, Yanov assumes a Western stake in Khrushchev's success: "There can be little doubt that if Admiral Burke's doctrine of minimum deterrence had prevailed in U.S. military planning circles at the time of the Soviet establishment crisis (thus giving Khrushchev *sufficient* grounds for defending a similar strategic policy against the Soviet military), the arms race of the 1970s could have been averted."[10]

The issue, however, is more complicated than that. The Western stake depends on exactly what the West is being asked to do and what it costs to do it. It also hinges on answers to the other questions noted above. Is the Soviet leader needing Western support a genuine reformer? Does the leader have a political strategy and a chance to succeed? Will Western assistance really make a difference? An American shift to minimum deterrence, for example, would have marked a revolution in U.S. nuclear strategy, carrying with it great risks as well as possible benefits. Would such a shift really have provided "sufficient grounds" for facing down the Soviet generals?

Let me provide my own answers to these five questions for the Khrushchev era. Did Khrushchev undertake a major effort at genuine reform? His reformist record is, as I see it, both mixed and contradictory. To evaluate his credentials as a *velikii reformator* (great reformer), one must consider both his domestic and foreign policies. My conclusion is Khrushchev was, indeed, a genuine reformer at home, but his foreign policies were far more ambiguous—in part just *because* he championed internal change.

To Khrushchev's everlasting credit, he freed millions of innocent people from Stalin's prison camps and improved the lives of millions more. Several people recently told me in Moscow he had saved their lives and had provided them with pensions to live on and apartments to live in. If Khrushchev had done nothing more than this, he would deserve great praise. But he did much more. Yanov writes, for example, that Khrushchev adopted "a fundamentally new strategy" centering around "the philosophy of consumerism."[11] Yet the question remains just how far Khrushchev's consumerism went in fact as opposed to rhetoric.[12] Yanov contends that with Khrushchev's new "philosophical-historical formula," "the way was open for comprehensive economic reform as well as general liberalization, for which the formula provided the philosophical foundation."[13] Yanov's argument is that the Link Reform was in effect de-Stalinizing the countryside, that Khrushchev's bifurcation of the Party in 1962 undermined counterreformist Party prefects, and that economic decentralization was under serious discussion as well. But these and other changes still were a far cry from "comprehensive economic reform" and "general liberalization" as those terms are understood in pluralist Western societies.

To be sure, the points just made add up to saying that the glass of domestic reform was half-empty, to which the obvious riposte is that it was half-full. Khrushchev's domestic program was, indeed, positive on the whole. But can the same be said about his foreign policy, including his pursuit of detente? Khrushchev drastically cut Soviet troop strength and held down conventional arms spending, even when doing so required confronting the Soviet military-industrial complex. But did he also adopt the nuclear doctrine of minimum deterrence, as Yanov contends? "Otherwise," Yanov continues, "it would be impossible to explain how Khrushchev, when faced with the undeniable fact of American strategic superiority (which, according to Robert McNamara, should have 'scared the hell' out of a Soviet Secretary of Defense) could have vehemently advocated the reduction of Soviet military expenditures as well as its conventional forces until his last day in office."[14]

It is this deduction which allows Yanov to speculate that if Khrushchev had remained in office and if the United States had matched his moderation (for example, by offering to forego its nuclear advantage in return for Moscow's yielding up its conventional superiority), then the world might have been spared the post-1964 arms race. But such evidence as exists suggests Khrushchev himself insisted on developing the very ICBMs which Brezhnev and company later deployed.[15] Not only that, but he counted on that ICBM buildup, which he exaggerated far beyond its actual extent, to change the world balance of power in the U.S.S.R.'s favor. These two apparently contradictory trend lines (conventional forces decreasing while strategic forces increased) are in fact interdependent; Khrushchev's nuclear messianism helps explain his complacency regarding conventional forces.

The same faith in the political and psychological uses of nuclear weapons undergirded Khrushchev's remarkably belligerent pursuit of detente. Khrushchev sought a new and more stable relationship with the West and especially the United States. But the limits of his new approach, the efforts at expansion which accompanied it, and, above all, the contradictory way he wooed the West, all undermined his own policy. Take, for example, the key issues of Germany and Berlin which were the centerpiece of East-West negotiations during the Khrushchev years. However one explains Khrushchev's on-again, off-again pressure on Berlin—whether intended to stabilize East Germany, destabilize West Germany, deny nuclear weapons to Bonn, or some combination of these and other aims—the fact is the Soviet leader demanded, under the threat of nuclear annihilation, that the Western powers give up key rights in Berlin.

Just ten years after Khrushchev triggered the 1961 confrontation, his successors accepted a Berlin agreement which preserved those Western rights. Of course, it was not only the Soviet side which changed its position between 1961 and 1971. A crucial part of the 1971 Berlin bargain was the very recognition of East Germany which the Western powers had denied Khrushchev. But if the West offered that concession in 1971, it was partly because Brezhnev conceded what Khrushchev had not, and also because Brezhnev did not accompany his diplomacy with the sort of threats and ultimatums which obscured Khrushchev's partially peaceful purpose.

Twice within three years, Khrushchev set deadlines for the abrogation of Western rights in Berlin, only to retreat later on. More times than that, he threatened the nuclear destruction of West European countries which resisted his pressure. Khrushchev insisted on interpreting Western defense of Western rights as a threat to the Soviet Union; he ended up threatening retaliation against moves his own policy had provoked. If one views, as I do, the Cuban missile crisis as an extension of Khrushchev's Berlin policy, then that policy seems even more reckless. Compare Khrushchev's imprudence to Stalin's caution, even during the 1948 Berlin crisis. It is paradoxical that while Khrushchev's version of peaceful coexistence was more far-reaching and long-lasting than Stalin's, Khrushchev's was pursued in a way that disguised the difference.

In other areas of foreign policy, Khrushchev, compared with Stalin, not only intensified East-West competition but extended its scope as well. Throughout the Third World, especially in the Middle East, Khrushchev contested Western predominance with new energy and tenacity. Of course, the very fact that it was Western positions in these areas he sought to undermine confirms that the U.S.S.R. was not the only power with global aspirations. But if our purpose is to gauge Khrushchev's reformist credentials, as well as the stake the West had in his success, then the ambiguities of his foreign policy must be weighed in the balance.

Did Khrushchev have a political strategy? If there is a pattern to his political moves, it seems one of self-destruction rather than consolidation of power. Yanov is right to point out that Khrushchev did not alienate absolutely every possible constituency, as some accounts of his demise have claimed. But he certainly alienated those which were most powerful at the time. Having contemplated Khrushchev's character with some care, I am not sure he was personally capable of conceiving a long-term strategy—which is why I am also skeptical of Adam Ulam's contention that Khrushchev placed missiles in Cuba as part of a grand design to deny nuclear weapons to both the Germans and the Chinese.[16]

Yet, despite the shortcomings of his political strategy, Khrushchev might have prevailed. Yanov correctly points out that dumping the top man in the Kremlin is a risky business requiring the unanimity of his peers. If any of them had balked, the rest might not have dared. What might have deterred one or more of them? Precisely the sort of foreign policy successes that Yanov describes. Ulam, too, believes that "had Khrushchev been able to display some domestic and foreign successes, it is quite possible that he could have gone on with his reforms."[17] Carl Linden emphasizes the corrosive effect of failures on Khrushchev's power and prestige, particularly since such power and prestige "were, to a far greater extent than Stalin's, dependent on the success of his policies."[18] Kennedy's massive arms buildup was devastating to Khrushchev's standing. If Khrushchev had received from the Americans what Brezhnev did ten years later, his position would have been strengthened. But to grant this is also to raise the question of why the West acted as it did. And that takes us back to those elements of foreign policy that turned the West against him.

Khrushchev's bullying tactics over Berlin and Cuba were, I believe, designed to force the Western powers to the negotiating table and then into agreements. But their ultimate effect was to harden Western resistance. The Kennedy buildup cannot be understood apart from the three years of Soviet threats and ultimatums which preceded it, nor can Kennedy's unwillingness to "help out" Khrushchev with the lesser moves Yanov imagines. This is not to say the buildup or the unwillingness was merely a reaction to Soviet behavior; both reflected internal American developments as well. But I would go further than *explaining* American resistance to Khrushchev in this way. I would go so far as to *endorse* it. Whatever his real motives were, Khrushchev demanded of Western leaders what none should have been willing to accept, namely, that they respond to his threats with concessions. Concessions extracted in this way might well have tempted Khrushchev to try for more until, at some point, a confrontation going beyond the Cuban missile crisis was provoked. Eisenhower and Kennedy were quite right to resist Khrushchev's threats and ultimatums even though that resistance weakened him at home. One who lives by the tactics of superpower intimidation must be prepared to die when another superpower responds in kind.

And yet—granting that Khrushchev's aggressiveness made it nearly impossible for the West to support him—there is an important prior question: to what extent, if any, did Western behavior give rise to Khrushchev's aggressiveness? If Khrushchev at his most belligerent was reacting largely to previous Western actions, then the issue of the Western stake in his success looks very different. It might even be said the West was partly responsible for the fact that its stake in him was so small.

The short answer to this prior question is that Western policies did indeed shape Khrushchev's. The paradox is that the West as a whole, and particularly the United States, simultaneously threatened and appeased Khrushchev, thus leading him to pursue detente in a way that virtually guaranteed its failure. But this incoherence of Khrushchev-style detente was also a product of domestic Soviet factors, including the very reformist course Khrushchev was following.

"When Stalin died," Khrushchev remarks in his memoirs, "we felt terribly vulnerable." Stalin's successors faced what Khrushchev called "a plateful" of domestic and foreign problems at a time when the leadership itself was bitterly divided. Moreover, Khrushchev and his colleagues assumed, typically although incorrectly, that the Western leaders knew all about Soviet troubles. The West knew, according to Khrushchev, that "the leadership Stalin had left behind was no good because it was composed of people who had too many differences among them. The capitalists knew that we were still engaged in the reconstruction of our war-ravaged economy and could ill afford the additional burden of heavy defense costs." Khrushchev further assumed that Western diplomacy in the early post-Stalin period was designed to exploit Soviet vulnerability. Even a seemingly conciliatory proposal, like Churchill's for a summit conference in 1953, was made "before we were really ready . . . in order to wring some concessions out of Stalin's successors before we had our feet firmly on the ground."[19] More ominous still was a four-part challenge, reminiscent of the early Reagan years, which Eisenhower and Dulles flung at Moscow in 1953 and 1954: harsh anti-Soviet rhetoric, a far-reaching strategic buildup, alliances designed to encircle the Soviets, and "covert operations" seemingly intended to destabilize Soviet clients and perhaps even the U.S.S.R. itself.[20]

The most serious aspect of this situation in Soviet eyes was probably the strategic nuclear imbalance and its potential political and psychological significance. Although the Soviets had broken the U.S. atomic monopoly in 1949—several years earlier than had been predicted in the West—and had exploded their first hydrogen device about the same time as the Americans did, the United States was far ahead in nuclear weapons that could be delivered on the other side's homeland, and it maintained its lead during the Eisenhower era. Only after Stalin's death, two leading Western experts report, did the Soviet leaders begin "to grapple in earnest with the impact of nuclear and long-range weapons on military strategy and organization." Only in 1954 did nuclear weapons begin "to be integrated into Soviet armed forces and taken into account in military training." The first Soviet nuclear strike forces, which became operational during this period, were strictly of regional range. As late as 1955, the U.S.S.R. possessed no operational intercontinental weapons, whether missiles or bombers, to match the 1,309 U.S. intercontinental bombers and more than 500 U.S. and NATO regional-range, "forward-based" planes and missiles (weapons based around the periphery of the U.S.S.R. and capable of hitting Soviet targets).[21]

Nor was the Eisenhower administration shy about threatening to use these awesome weapons. Besides promising to retaliate massively against Soviet aggression at a time and place of Washington's own choosing, Dulles practiced "brinksmanship" to make his threats seem real. The administration threatened to use nuclear weapons in Korea, assumed it would use them in Indochina had Eisenhower decided to try to save the French at Dien Bien Phu, and apparently came close to using them in crises over Quemoy and Matsu. The fact that President Eisenhower himself was deeply ambivalent about nuclear weapons—believing that their use might be suicidal but that he must be prepared to employ them no differently from conventional weapons—was not clear to the Soviets, at least not in 1953-54.[22] The point is not that Khrushchev and his colleagues feared an atomic attack, especially a nuclear bolt from the blue, but rather that they felt vulnerable to the very sort of nuclear blackmail to which Khrushchev would subject the Western powers when the first sputnik and the specter of Soviet ICBMs gave him the opportunity to do so.

The Eisenhower administration's strategy of encircling the U.S.S.R. with pacts and alliances (CENTO and SEATO, in addition to NATO) was designed to deter Soviet attack on or subversion of its neighbors. Many in the West quickly came to see Dulles's "pactomania" as a liability rather than a contribution to deterrence. But the irony was largely lost on the Soviets, especially given the nuclear weapons based on the territory of America's allies. As for covert operations, they included overthrow of governments sympathetic, or potentially friendly, to the U.S.S.R.—such as Iran in 1953 and Guatemala in 1954—infiltration of former refugees back into Eastern Europe, and extensive and obvious aerial reconnaissance missions over the U.S.S.R. and other communist states. In retrospect, it is clear the Soviet empire was far too strong to be threatened by these largely ineffectual American efforts to roll it back. But at the time, those efforts must have seemed more menacing than they do now, especially in the light of upheavals in East Germany in 1953 and in Hungary and Poland in 1956.[23]

What was the Soviet reaction to these Western pressures? The first response, the prime movers of which seem to have been Malenkov and Beria, was a burst of conciliatory moves in the first months after Stalin's death. After an interval of hard-line policies, Khrushchev pressed hard for "peaceful coexistence" with the West, particularly the United States. None of these moves was unambiguously a response to Western behavior. They marked a retreat from exposed political-military positions which Stalin's successors probably would have undertaken no matter what the West did. They positioned the U.S.S.R. to compete more effectively with the United States. They also reflected an awareness that the West was vulnerable to peace campaigns.

If post-Stalinist foreign policy changes were a result of Western pressures, one might have expected Western leaders to explore the new possibilities for agreements. To a degree, they did so. There was, after all, a four-power foreign ministers' conference in Berlin in 1954 and the Geneva summit in 1955. But on the whole, the West, led by the United States, resisted high-level talks. John Foster Dulles was the chief resister, ably assisted and at times even exceeded in zeal by West German Chancellor Konrad Adenauer. Dulles delayed the Geneva summit as long as possible and stalled again when Khrushchev began pressing for a new summit in 1958.

I believe the prime reason for Khrushchev's Berlin ultimatums, as well as for the bloodcurdling nuclear threats he issued in connection with his German policy, was to force the West into serious talks on a whole range of issues. In that sense, the very Khrushchevian belligerence that alarmed the West was indeed a response to its own policies. There was another, very different aspect of Western behavior that also encouraged Khrushchev to bluster and bluff. President Eisenhower had a tendency—also characteristic of British Prime Minister Harold Macmillan—to try to convince the Soviet leader that he sincerely, even desperately, desired to avoid nuclear war and would therefore bend over backward to work out a modus vivendi with the Russians. This is not to imply that Eisenhower was a woolly headed idealist when he was not being led by the nose by Dulles. Recent research has confirmed that Eisenhower was Dulles's boss and not vice versa and that Ike was deeply sceptical about any enduring settlement with Moscow.[24] But the president was also alarmed about the consequences of nuclear war, and he communicated this feeling to Khrushchev. That led Khrushchev to think that a combination of war scares and peace proposals could force the U.S.-led West to the negotiating table.

John F. Kennedy's Soviet policy manifested a similar incoherence with correspondingly unfortunate results for Khrushchev as well as the United States. Kennedy resisted Khrushchev's pressure for talks, while at the same time he launched the arms buildup that proved so awkward for Khrushchev. On the other hand, Kennedy's indecision at the Bay of Pigs and his behavior at the Vienna summit meeting convinced Khrushchev that the young president could be pushed around. Once again, Khrushchev was tempted to try to bully his way into detente.

Have we not, then, come full circle? Having argued that Khrushchev's aggressive pursuit of detente turned the West against him, have I not established that the West provoked his belligerence in the first place? Not so, for reasons to be cited in a moment. Moreover, even if this were the case, it would not allow us easily to imagine a very different American policy. A U.S. policy that was stronger, steadier, and any less threatening than Eisenhower's and Kennedy's was politically almost impossible given American conditions at the time.

More important, Khrushchev's belligerent approach must also be traced to domestic determinants, including his efforts at reform. Khrushchev's own background and personality were one determinant. All the main features of Khrushchev's chip-on-the-shoulder version of detente were characteristic of him "personally," in contrast to his much more conservative colleagues.[25] Another domestic factor was the ideological lens through which Khrushchev viewed the Western behavior he encountered. No matter what Western leaders did, that lens would have conveyed the impression that the West was both threatening and vulnerable at the same time. For such, according to Marxist-Leninist ideology which Khrushchev took with great seriousness, is the nature of capitalist states with all their built-in hostility toward communism and their crippling "contradictions." And such, according to Khrushchev's own experience in the dog-eat-dog milieu of the Kremlin, was the nature of almost any political adversary. The only safe way to deal with Western leaders, Khrushchev's every instinct told him, was from strength. Moreover, that lesson was reinforced by his dilemma as a reformer.

As a leader whose reforms confronted powerful resistance at home, Khrushchev was tempted, in George Breslauer's phrase, to "build his authority" abroad.[26] Despite all its dangers and despite his own unfamiliarity with it, the outside world seemed easier to manage than the U.S.S.R. itself. Khrushchev needed foreign policy victories demonstrating the world was safe for reform at home. But he had to score his successes "from strength," without making the kind of concessions or suffering the sorts of setbacks that would render him vulnerable to his Soviet critics. The trouble was that just such strength was lacking, especially in the crucial strategic nuclear realm. Khrushchev therefore tried to bluster and bluff his way toward detente, even though that way led to foreign policy disasters which further weakened his position at home.

The story of reform in the Khrushchev era and the West's role in relation to it does not lend itself to any neat conclusion. Almost all the questions with which I began have complicated or ambiguous answers in the case of Khrushchev. If the same pattern applies to other reforms in Russian and Soviet history, the issue of whether Russia is reformable is even more difficult than it seems. If Gorbachev's current reform attempt follows a similar pattern, the future will be painful as well.

NOTES

1. "Conference Proposal: Is the Soviet Union Reformable? Russia and the West at the End of the Twentieth Century" (Prepared for the Conference on Reform in Russia and the Soviet Union, University of Michigan, April 4-6, 1986); Alexander Yanov, *The Drama of the Soviet 1960s: A Lost Reform* (Berkeley, 1984).

2. See Fainsod's description of the "the new model of Khrushchevian totalitarianism" in Merle Fainsod, *How Russia Is Ruled,* rev. ed. (Cambridge, Mass., 1963), pp. 580-86.

3. Yanov, *Drama,* p. 79.

4. "Conference Proposal," p. 3.

5. Yanov, *Drama,* pp. 79, 95-97, 110.

6. "Conference Proposal," p. 3.

7. Ibid., pp. xiv, 103 (emphasis in the original).

8. Ibid., p. 106.

9. Ibid., p. 97.

10. Ibid., p. 104 (emphasis added).

11. Ibid., p. 77.

12. See, for example, George W. Breslauer, *Khrushchev and Brezhnev as Leaders: Building Authority in Soviet Politics* (London, 1982), pp. 27-31.

13. Yanov, *Drama,* p. 78.

14. Ibid., p. 104.

15. See Robert P. Berman and John C. Baker, *Soviet Strategic Forces: Requirements and Responses* (Washington, 1982), p. 82.

16. For elaboration and documentation of this and other points that are simply asserted in this paper, see my forthcoming political biography of Nikita Khrushchev. Ulam's notion of a grand design is in Adam B. Ulam, *The Rivals: America and Russia since World War II* (New York, 1971), pp. 299-340.

17. Adam B. Ulam, *A History of Soviet Russia* (New York, 1976), p. 249.

18. Carl Linden, *Khrushchev and the Soviet Leadership, 1957-1964* (Baltimore, 1966), p. 15.

19. Nikita S. Khrushchev, *Khrushchev Remembers: The Last Testament* trans. and ed. Strobe Talbott (Boston, 1974), pp. 12, 194, 212, 362.

20. For details, see John Lewis Gaddis, *Strategies of Containment* (New York, 1982), pp. 127-63.

21. Berman and Baker, *Soviet Strategic Forces,* pp. 41-43.

22. See Gaddis, *Strategies of Containment,* pp. 148-52, 167-71.

23. Ibid., pp. 157-59.

24. See, especially, Fred I. Greenstein, *Eisenhower: The Hidden-Hand Presidency* (New York, 1984).

25. This point, in particular, is stressed in my forthcoming book.

26. See Breslauer, *Khrushchev and Brezhnev as Leaders,* especially pp. 3-23.

In the Grip of the Adversarial Paradigm: The Case of Nikita Sergeevich Khrushchev in Retrospect

ALEXANDER YANOV

My essays in this volume are based on a set of assumptions that sharply deviate from conventional wisdom, both liberal and conservative. Not only their conclusions, but their very terms and definitions may sound alien to an unaccustomed ear.

Some people on the conservative extreme of the political spectrum in America assume that Soviet Russia is implacably hostile to the West because of its communist ideology. Others who see the world in terms of *realpolitik* consider the geopolitical interests of the superpowers irreconcilable. Still others in the liberal camp believe that, in the face of common annihilation in the nuclear age, there is enough common ground to work out some accommodation. These differences notwithstanding, most Americans, including scholars, perceive Russia as an adversary.

What, however, if this adversarial paradigm itself is no more than a transient convention? There were times after all when a similar convention held that Catholics were implacable enemies of Protestants. There were times when the differences between them were universally perceived as irreconcilable. They are still perceived as such by many in, say, Northern Ireland. Yet the rest of the world thinks of this formerly powerful and sacred convention as bigotry. Moreover, there were people who thought of it as bigotry even in the sixteenth century, at the height of Protestant Reformation and Catholic Counterreformation when believers died readily for the sacred convention.

Let me state from the outset that the current adversarial paradigm seems no more sacred to me than the conventions of the past. Assuming that there is a future in the nuclear world, people may think of it in this future as bigotry (except perhaps in Northern Ireland).

The alternative, non-adversarial paradigm is based on the assumption that Russia can be an implacable enemy of the West all right, but it can be its ally as well. And this difference, crucial for the survival of humanity, depends for the most part on us, not on Russia. Or, more precisely, it depends on whether Russia is able to make its belated breakthrough into political modernity which, as history proves, it cannot make without the help of the international community.

Russia is not always ready for such a breakthrough. In fact, most of the time it is not. Its readiness or unreadiness for it, however, has little to do with ideology or geopolitics. It has to do with the nature of its ruling political regime. Russia cannot make the breakthrough under counterreformist dictatorial regimes, like Nicholas I's or Stalin's, which clearly prefer guns to butter and are bent on grand expansion, whether communist or non-communist. Nor can Russia make it under petty expansionist regimes of political stagnation, like Elizabeth I's or Brezhnev's, which try to have both guns and butter. Russia can make it only under regimes of reform, like Aleksey Adashev's or Nikita Khrushchev's, which distinctly favor butter over guns and, being overwhelmingly absorbed in domestic restructuring, quit territorial expansion altogether. Reform in Russia is hence extraordinarily important—as a window into political modernity.

For centuries it has been handicapped in its perpetual struggle to join the European family of nations—by its own dualistic and polarized political culture and by the tragic fact that its conservative and reactionary forces have successfully neutralized the reformist ones. This is why all its reforms either faded away into dead zones of political stagnation, as did Khrushchev's in the 1960s, or were directly reversed by brutal counterreforms, as was Stolypin's in the 1910s. This is why the non-adversarial paradigm presupposes that only a tactful and coherent intervention of the world intellectual community may perhaps tip this unstable balance of forces in Russia in favor of reform and cure the Sick Man of Europe of its protracted disease.

Communism does not have much to do with this disease. Russia's ancient pattern of political change wasn't altered by it at all. Soviet Russia remains as trapped in the vicious cycle of its reforms and counterreforms as its Petersburg mother and Muscovite grandmother were. It wasn't communism that made Russia sick. In fact, it was the other way around: Russia caught the left-wing extremist disease because it was sick. As long as its pattern of change remains as it has been for centuries, Russia may still catch the right-wing extremist disease as well.[1]

If so, the recovery of the Sick Man of Europe requires more than transcending communism. It requires transcending its dualistic political heritage—precisely what Russia's reformers proved unable to accomplish by their efforts alone. As I see it, that is the true Russian challenge facing us at the end of the second Christian millennium. To meet it, we need a profound and competent strategy for Russia's recovery, going beyond the struggle against communism and certainly beyond the assumption Russia is inevitably the adversary. What may help is the perception of Russia as a dangerous, volatile, and yet curable patient who requires complex and well-thought-out treatment.

I am aware that this image of a doctor-patient relationship between the superpowers may sound not only alien but bizarre as well. But is the comparison any stranger than the current mad era of peace on the brink of annihilation? Both our conventional attitudes toward Russia and the present nuclear confrontation seem to spring from an unwavering allegiance to the antiquated formulas of the adversarial paradigm derived from the pre-nuclear age.

This paradigm presupposes that Russia's political establishment is essentially monolithic and united in pursuit of common goals. My essays, however, portray Russia as a nation divided and its establishment as continually split between groups or interests oriented toward dismantling its political heritage and those intent on perpetuating it. In fact, they suggest the existence of two Russias—European and Byzantine—and thus two establishments, one of which is indeed an irreconcilable enemy of the West and the other its potential ally. Any international strategy for Russia's recovery in our era of peace on the brink of annihilation must include cooperation between the Western intellectual community and Russia's reformist establishment in its perpetual fight against its extremist enemies—and ours.

The adversarial paradigm further presupposes that Soviet foreign policy is a perfectly consistent operation oriented toward world domination and capable of changing its tactics but not its basic objective. In my essays, however, I suggest a pattern of Soviet foreign policy in which each new regime invariably negates the objectives of its predecessor. In other words, the only consistency in Soviet foreign policy is its inconsistency. Moreover, given the antagonistic nature of Russia's political process that follows logically from its dualistic political heritage, Russian foreign policy *cannot* be consistent in principle. Gorbachev's current de-Brezhnevization of Soviet foreign policy is the most recent example. Russian foreign policy has always followed this pattern of inconsistency, not only in its Soviet period but in its Muscovite and Petersburg periods as well.

Western politicians hardly even suspect the existence of this historical pattern of inconsistency in Russian foreign policy, presumably because the scholarly community has never brought it to their attention. Instead, they tend to assume Russia is the adversary, the Soviet establishment is essentially monolithic, and Soviet foreign policy is a consistent enterprise. This is why they always display so much confusion and ambivalence when, in violation of the stereotypes of the adversarial paradigm, Russia opens up for radical reform. The remarks of Governor Cuomo of New York on the eve of his departure for Moscow in September, 1987, summarize these attitudes extremely well.[2] Like most Americans, the governor seems to be of two minds about Gorbachev's reforms. On the one hand, he *wants* them to succeed. Yet, on the other, he *fears* their success, for it might make America's number one enemy even more formidable. In the nuclear age, such ambivalence which springs from the adversarial paradigm is perilous.

One reason for the confusion in Western thinking is the conventional definition of "reform" as some amendment of faulty governmental practices. Such a definition certainly makes sense in the Western historical context in which, for example, the Stuarts regained their throne in 1660 and the Bourbons in 1815 but could not restore the ancien régime. It simply does not apply to Russian history, where the process of political development is in principle *reversible;* where the ancien régime is reestablished regularly, only on a higher military-technological level; where peasants' lands may be taken back from them; where even serfdom, abolished by a reform in 1861, was restored by a counterreform in 1929; and where all the amendments of faulty governmental practices were perpetually erased by counteramendments—to such an extent that new generations of reformers had to start the same reforms from scratch decades or centuries later, only to have them erased by new generations of counterreformers.

Such a pattern of political change, unknown in the West, calls for a very different definition of Russian "reform," for seeing it as an attempt to open the system for political modernization and thus to free the nation from its antiquated political heritage. In other words, "reform" in Russia means altering the very nature of political change and eliminating the pattern of failed and reversed reforms that has dominated Russian political history for five hundred years, since Russia became a nation-state.

From this, it follows that the only possibility for Russia's recovery and thus for humanity to escape nuclear confrontation lies in the success of the current reform campaign in the Soviet Union, because Soviet domestic and foreign policies are inextricably linked. Whether detente is, in principle, good or bad is beside the point. The real question to ask instead is: with whom in Moscow is detente possible? As Henry Kissinger discovered in the 1970s, the attempt to achieve detente with Brezhnev's regime of stagnation was doomed from the start.

Finally, the non-adversarial paradigm assumes that the success of reformers in Russia depends greatly on the response of the West, particularly the United States. Gorbachev's desperate struggle against his— and our—enemies in Moscow will fail, as all others did, if we in America sit and watch it as ambivalent observers. In this sense, Soviet foreign policy to a crucial extent is made in Washington. The following examination of Khrushchev's reforms will illustrate my points in much greater detail.

Khrushchev's Reforms

To begin, let me state that, contrary to William Taubman's assertion, I have never portrayed Nikita Khrushchev as "a leader with a relatively coherent vision of far-reaching domestic and foreign change."[3] In my book on the 1960s, I stated repeatedly that, like virtually all the well-known reform leaders in Russia, Khrushchev *lacked* a comprehensive strategy of reform.[4] Writing about the crucial period of reform after the Cuban crisis, I concluded, "Still not a coherent policy-maker, he had been *intuitively* groping for the essential truth that one cannot base the reform of society on anti-reformist forces."[5] His reformist intuition, however, was remarkable indeed.

This apparently minor distinction is very important—especially in light of Taubman's argument that Western support for Russian reform must be predicated on the reformist leader's "political strategy and . . . chance to succeed."[6] If these are absent, "it hardly matters whether the international environment was adverse or the West offered assistance."[7] As I suggested earlier, reformist leaders in Russia have never been in possession of a coherent political strategy. Consequently none, including Khrushchev, had a chance to succeed *without* the assistance of the international community, including assistance in working out such a strategy.

Here is the nucleus of my disagreement with the conventional Western view that Russia can be reformed either by the application of external pressure, as conservatives assert, or by just leaving it alone, as liberals think. A historical examination of Russia's experience with reform suggests the contrary; Russia cannot make it into the European family of nations on its own, whether pressured or not. This simple conclusion must change our entire perspective on not only Russia's past but also our own future.

It was easy to ignore this particular Russian predicament in, say, the 1680s, when it was vegetating on the margins of Europe as a third-rate barbarian state. It is impossible to ignore it today, when we are confronted with an unreformed nuclear giant. This is especially true given that Russia will always be capable of matching the West in military-industrial terms—at a terrible price to itself—and that military technology races ahead oblivious of Russia's predicament and threatens to become uncontrollable.

Nonetheless, in the half-millennium since it became a nation-state, we know of a significant number of Russia's "openings" into political modernity, which testify beyond a reasonable doubt to its reformist potential. At the heart of this reformist potential lies its middle class, slowly rising in spite of many historical setbacks. That all of these reformist openings were eventually closed tells us in no uncertain terms, however, that the conservative and reactionary forces in Russia—or, in my terms, the forces of stagnation and counterreform—are stronger than its reformist potential.

This is why Russia's middle class needs help from outside.[8] This is the essential and perhaps undeniable fact that shapes the real choices for America's Soviet policy, as I see it. We can either help Russia's middle class overcome the resistance of its conservative and reactionary rivals and thus give the Sick Man of Europe a chance to recover, or leave him to his own fate and thus ensure an uncontrollable nuclear race, with all its potentially fatal consequences.

This is the perspective from which I see Khrushchev's desperate struggle on two fronts—in fact, on three, if we recall that Chinese militants of his time not only were in many respects the mouthpiece of his domestic opposition but also loomed large as archrivals in his own religious camp. After all, he was the only politician in this century to be accused of two equally unforgivable and seemingly incompatible sins: being both a Red Hitler (by the American popular press)[9] *and* an appeasing capitulationist, a Red Neville Chamberlain as it were (by Chinese militants).[10] In retrospect, it is obvious he was doomed by this overwhelming combination of odds against him.

Yet it is fascinating to watch, reconstructing his actions, just how far he got in his effort to modernize the world's last empire. He was a premodern politician, a graduate of the Stalinist academy of terror. The dilemmas facing him were too intractable for the simple solutions for which he was trained, and his time in power was too short to find the right constituency for reform in the complex maze of post-Stalinist society. In the beginning he did not even know he needed it. Later he did not know where to look for it. When he finally found it, it appeared too weak to sustain him in power. He changed his decisions so many times and sowed so much confusion in innocent sovietological souls that he was bound to create the impression of being a "harebrained schemer" in Western minds—a view that presupposes a Soviet reformist leader must know what he is doing. But he did not, at least not in the beginning. Like Gorbachev in his own first days in power, Khrushchev believed in the magic power of socialism, which in his view was hampered and made impotent by a murderous tyrant who tried to rule "with an axe" and thus chained the creative potential of his beloved creed. So he set out to remove the chains and to right the wrongs, naively believing this was all that socialist Russia needed to be propelled into the future and to leave the obsolete capitalist world far behind.

From the start, he was convinced Russia needed a strong and efficient managerial corps—or, to put it better, a "knightly order"—and at first he thought he had found it in the Party professionals. He also hated bureaucracy and bureaucrats with all his heart. And above all, as a true Marxist, he believed in the primacy of "production" over politics and ideology. This was at the foundation of his creed. In his February, 1956, non-secret speech he proclaimed, "Our Soviet apparatus must have its roots in production work, it must subordinate its work to the interests of production."[11] Finally, as a true Russian reformer, he believed in the necessity of preventing forever the emergence of a new dictatorship, and he said so: "From the podium of the Congress we declare: the party must take all the necessary steps so that the path of the cult of personality is closed forever."[12]

Unlike Stalin, he did not expect World War III and did not want the differences between the two worlds to be settled on the battlefield. To show its allegedly miraculous qualities, socialism needed only time and peace. That's why Khrushchev wanted detente with the West, not confrontation. He didn't suspect it would be as impossible to obtain as the miracle of "socialist production" was. Armed with such meager and naive intellectual ammunition, he embarked on the thorny path of Russian reform, which was to bring him disappointment, humiliation, and disgrace.

In retrospect, the most fascinating thing about Khrushchev was his ability to reopen the system so that the right solutions sooner or later presented themselves on their own and the necessary power base for reform constituted itself spontaneously, without direction or command. In fact, it was he who was constantly late in grasping the implications of his own actions and embracing their consequences. Time *was* his problem.

Let me give a few examples. Khrushchev spent five years trying to strengthen and restructure the MTS (Machine Tractor Stations), although abolishing them altogether was what was really required. In September, 1953, he threw 100,000 specialists into the MTS which dramatically changed their educational level. He abolished the agricultural departments of regional Party committees and gave each MTS its own regional secretary in residence. He abolished the position of MTS deputy director for political work—in line with his contempt for the ideological "priesthood." He took the job of appointing MTS directors out of the hands of first the Federal Ministry and then the republican ministries and gave it to the provincial Party committees—in line with his desire to see in the Party professionals the managerial corps for which he yearned. He increased the wages of the MTS tractor drivers and granted them insurance and retirement benefits, in effect elevating the status of qualified agricultural labor to that of industrial labor. He put the MTS on *khozraschet* (self-supporting basis). Five years later, he finally came to the conclusion that none of this made any sense. The institution was abolished, and its privileged workers were thrown into the amorphous mass of unqualified labor in the *kolkhozy* (collective farms) and *sovkhozy* (state farms).

Once again Khrushchev did not envisage the social consequences of his actions, for what he did, in effect, was create a peasant elite which certainly would not be satisfied with the organization of labor and payment in the kolkhozy and would immediately start a spontaneous movement for the de-Stalinization of Soviet agriculture, resulting eventually in Ivan Khudenko's Akchi—the ultimate alternative to Stalin's kolkhozy. The succession of events is clear. In 1958 the MTS were abolished; in 1959 the Link movement (which, under Gorbachev, is called *"podriad,"* that is, contract) began. What it did for Khrushchev was the same thing that 1905 did for Stolypin: it put him in a position to set the elite of the Russian peasantry free from the "commune." Yet it required five more years before, on August 5, 1964, Khrushchev finally understood the implications of his decision taken in 1958 and fully embraced its sociopolitical consequences.

Similarly, for nine years, he tinkered with the rural regional Party committees, trying to mold out of them a managerial corps—perhaps his main preoccupation in domestic politics in all these years. Only after March, 1962, when the production administrations (the institutional stronghold of the rural managerial class) were created, did he finally see the difference between Party professionals and professional managers. As soon as he saw it, however, he did not hesitate much longer. His utter disgust for and ultimate disappointment with Party professionals prompted the radical decision of November, 1962, to abolish the regional Party committees altogether, as was done four years earlier with the MTS. As a result, Soviet agriculture was positioned—alas, only a few weeks before his ouster—for a decisive breakthrough, its final de-Stalinization (which was, of course, smothered under Brezhnev's regime of stagnation and regenerated under Gorbachev's regime of reform—a perfect example of the antagonistic nature of the Russian political process).

What is really fascinating about Khrushchev's domestic reforms is not so much each of them separately, however significant they may have seemed at the time, but their sum total, taken in its dynamics, in its sociopolitical evolution, and in its potential. It is the general direction in which Russia was moving under him that was really promising. I would argue that this was a movement toward political modernity and that the window of opportunity was abruptly and awkwardly shut under Brezhnev, when, according to Mikhail Gorbachev, "in the life of the society stagnation (*zastoinye iavleniia*) surfaced . . . and a curious state of mind prevailed: how to make things better without changing anything whatsoever."[13]

The story of Khrushchev's policies in agriculture would not be complete were it not contrasted with the policies of stagnation implemented after the regime change of October, 1964. After a few years, no trace, naturally enough, was left of the great breakthrough engineered under the reform regime, with its many torturous delays, disappointments, and popular initiatives. The regional Party committees were reestablished, the production administrations abolished, the process of differentiating the peasantry arrested, the Link movement—the agricultural equivalent of "minimum deterrence" in defense policy—crushed, the Akchi experiment demolished, and Khudenko imprisoned, for life as it turned out. The de-Stalinization of agriculture was abandoned.

The alternative solution proposed by the leaders of the ensuing stagnation was similarly primitive in both defense and agricultural policy. The only device they knew was simple: to throw money at the problem. The results were disastrous in both cases.

Khrushchev perhaps never had even a hundred ICBMs. Arnold Horelick and Myron Rush insist in their classic work, *Strategic Power and Soviet Foreign Policy,* that what he really had was a "handful" of them.[14] This is what the strategy of minimum deterrence dictated. Brezhnev's regime change naturally entailed a complete change in defense policy. From 1965 on, the Soviet Union would be guided by a strategy of achieving "nuclear parity" with the other superpower. Apart from being, like beauty, in the eye of the beholder, nuclear parity produced a permanent tension with America and eventually invited Ronald Reagan into the White House with his so-called Star Wars project, which, if not stopped, may mean a political disaster for Russia at the end of the twentieth century.

The agricultural disaster was more immediate and explicit. As D. Gale Johnson noted in 1982, "In fact, there is some basis for arguing that the agricultural situation confronting Yuri Andropov is less satisfactory than the one Brezhnev inherited from Khrushchev."[15] The sums thrown into the bottomless pit of the kolkhoz system have indeed been prodigious. Total direct farm investment in the U.S.S.R. in 1970-77 was 6.3 times higher than its value in the United States. In 1977 alone, Soviet farm investment was the equivalent of 78 billion dollars compared with U.S. farm investment of roughly 10.5 billion. And for all this, according to Douglas B. Diamond and W. Lee Davis, labor productivity in Soviet agriculture actually fell in comparative terms from 7 percent of the U.S. level in the mid-1960s to about 5.5 percent in the mid-1970s.[16] I have argued elsewhere that

> these huge sums of money were primarily intended—in line with the desires of the Party professionals—to eliminate the Link alternative. They were to be used to show that the kolkhoz system was viable in the form in which it had existed since Stalin's time, and thereby solidify the power of the little Stalins over the countryside. . . . the Brezhnevist strategy is perhaps best described as a bribe paid to the provincial elites—a gigantic state subsidy which would make it possible for them to suppress the link movement, and thereby halt completely the process of de-Stalinization of the countryside.[17]

This example clearly testifies to the differences among recent Soviet regimes and to the confusion among Western sovietologists over the meaning of reform in Russia.

Let us turn to industry for a moment. We see under Khrushchev essentially the same pattern—an inability to grasp immediately the political consequences of his own socioeconomic changes, delayed responses, and yet ever increasing openness to modernization. Similarly, we see under Brezhnev a pattern of reform being gradually dismantled.

The foundation for what is known as the Kosygin industrial management reform was laid under Khrushchev. It was a result of the same constant Khrushchevian search for an efficient managerial elite that permeated his changes in agriculture. True, Khrushchev was late here, just as in agriculture. The first tentative turn toward real managerial autonomy capable of capturing the imagination of the urban middle managerial class only took place, judging from the emergence of Evsei

Liberman's piece, in September, 1962. The salvo of reformist articles in *Pravda*,[18] which may have been the harbingers of a new era in industrial management, all appeared in 1964. Khrushchev's famous speech outlining the fundamental turn of the Soviet economy toward consumerism—the speech in which he "out-Malenkoved Malenkov"—was delivered at the end of September, 1964, a few weeks before his fall.[19]

No doubt Kosygin managed to use the Khrushchev reformist momentum to his advantage. An abridged version of managerial autonomy was introduced in 1965. The difference was only that Kosygin's version did not have the slightest chance of success, if only because Khrushchev's plan of managerial autonomy was to take place against the background of the significant weakening of the central economic bureaucracy, which was primarily interested in blocking managerial autonomy, while Kosygin's "reform" was introduced after this bureaucracy was restored in all its power and glory, dooming the whole enterprise from the start. It was to wither away into political stagnation. Similarly, Brezhnev's own scheme, with its emphasis on production associations, dissolved a few years later; everything these men so much as touched appeared to turn out the opposite of what they intended.[20]

Let us go from here to the politics of domestic reform under Khrushchev. As one might expect, the pattern is no different from the one in agriculture and industry. The two major reformist changes of the 1950s were not understood as preparatory. Threatened as Khrushchev was at the time with political annihilation, his immediate purpose in demolishing the central economic bureaucracy in May, 1957, was to undermine the political base of his rivals in the post-Stalin oligarchy. The immediate purpose of the "constitutional crisis" he created in June, 1957, in the face of a palace coup engineered against him by the majority of the oligarchy, was political survival. Yet the real significance of the first change was it created a vacuum in industrial management that eventually had to be filled by either Party professionals or the middle managerial class. Thus what Khrushchev really established in May, 1957, was a potential political arena for a fight between the "service nobility" of Party professionals and the nascent and inarticulate Russian middle class of the 1950s. True, this fight could not have unfolded immediately, for the very ideas of managerial autonomy and of "horizontal" relations between enterprises and the "socialist market" did not exist yet. They would be born only in the early 1960s.

For the time being a compromise had to be found. The Party professionals had to be rewarded for the support they had given Khrushchev.

The bureaucrats of the disbanded Central Economic Administration had to be employed somewhere. "Leninist norms" had to be upheld. The compromise was the artificial restoration of the "Leninist" local economic councils of the 1920s, the *sovnarkhozy*. This gave everyone what they wanted. The Party professionals got control over local industrial management, the bureaucrats got provincial offices, and the middle class got the first embryonic form of institutional representation. The sovnarkhozy were not a solution to the problem, however, any more than the Virgin Lands Program had been a solution for the miserable state of agriculture. They were a convenient way to put off a real solution. The problem of industrial management in the 1950s thus remained unfinished business for Khrushchev. He acted here no differently than in the cases of the MTS, the regional Party committees, or the Link movement.

It was the same way with the "constitutional crisis" of June, 1957. What was really accomplished there was much more significant and promising than the sheer political survival of reform. A post-dictatorial oligarchy was ruined with Khrushchev's famous battle cry: "I was elected by the Plenum of the Central Committee and therefore it is up to it to make the decision. As the Plenum decides, so be it."[21] His position again set up an institutional arena for the upcoming combat between the "service nobility" and the middle class to determine which would win the status of the managerial corps of the nation.

All this happened in 1957. Again, it took years for Khrushchev to make his choice. Only in the early 1960s did he finally understand that his original faith in the power of socialism to propel the country into the future as soon as it was freed from dictatorial abuse was flawed and primitive. Powerful vested interests in society sabotaged change and resisted reform, not because they were poor socialists but because their power and status derived from the very economic system he was trying to dismantle.

To overcome this resistance, it was not enough to denounce the cult of personality or even to crush the Central Economic Administration, for it was rooted much deeper. It permeated his very own power base, the one which helped him overcome the post-dictatorial oligarchy. His allies of 1957, the military, hated the idea of a consumerist turn in the economy. His former allies among the professional ideologists—the "Soviet priesthood" as I call them—struggled to uphold the Stalinist "general line" of the Party. And, above all, the Party professionals, Khrushchev's hope and pride, turned out to be unreliable and thoroughly corrupt.

Of course, they could always be purged. In fact, a gigantic bloodless purge was conducted in 1960-61 in which up to 40 percent of the corps of Party professionals was eliminated—a turnover approximately on the scale of Gorbachev's first-year purge. But even the new Party professionals, his own people, were up in arms over a radical agricultural reform that threatened to undermine their status and power. Did these people, then, actually represent the efficient managerial corps for which he longed? He appeared to be replacing old wolves with younger ones.

At this point, Khrushchev was faced with the most painful choice of his career. The old alliance that brought him to power in 1957 and, in his eyes, symbolized the reform appeared to be anti-reformist. If the reform were to continue, it had to be conducted against the old alliance. This was a very dangerous path, all the more so since a new power base had to be formed, and this required time. A frightening transitional period was inevitable, during which he would have to walk a tightrope across the precipice separating his old power base from his new one. There was no guarantee he would be able to make it. It is to Khrushchev's everlasting credit that he had the courage to try.

The imperative of political survival dictated that, during the transitional period, his former allies, still his only power base, were to be maximally weakened so that they would fight each other instead of challenging him. In 1959, he established the Strategic Forces (*Spetsial'nogo Naznacheniia*) and gave them a special privileged status, thus creating an arena for struggle between the young rocket generals and the old conventional-forces marshals. In November, 1962, he divided the provincial Party committees so that the rural secretaries would fight the urban ones. In 1964, he turned to the liberal intelligentsia to set it against the "priesthood." At the same time, the debate on managerial autonomy was raging in the press, and the new "knightly order" was being prepared to take charge of the nation when the time came.

Whether or not all of this presented itself clearly in Khrushchev's mind, his actions in the early 1960s speak for themselves. In this period, Khrushchev performed an inestimable service to any future Soviet reformer: he identified the domestic alliance of anti-reformist forces by attacking them one by one.

The first to stand in the way of the radical consumerist reorientation of the economy was, of course, the military-industrial complex, the "steel-eaters." They got their just desserts: "I understand that some of our comrades have developed a hunger for metal. [However,] the prosperity of the state is determined by the quantity of commodities man receives and consumes ... and the degree of satisfaction of all his needs. ... Therefore, we should not behave like a flounder, which can see only in one direction."[22] Nine months later, he would address them even more sharply, accusing them of wearing "steel blinders" and not knowing how to do anything except shout "Steel! Steel!"[23] He would declare in London that "Soviet heavy industry has been built. In the future, light and heavy industry will be developed at the same pace."[24] Later, he would continue this line of thought in Moscow: "We will now reduce the expenditures on defense . . . and direct this money into the production of mineral fertilizers."[25]

Let me continue this list in George Breslauer's words:

> In April 1963 he delivered a hard-hitting speech . . . declaring that the Soviet economy could produce "nothing but rockets." At the December 1963 and February 1964 Plenums, he argued vehemently for massive investments in the chemical industry, paid for by cuts in the defense budget for 1964, possible future troop reductions and "slowing down growth in certain branches of industry." In Summer/Fall 1964 Khrushchev went still further, announcing plans for a major new program of investment in means of production [capital goods] for light industry, agriculture, and the sectors of heavy industry which service consumer-oriented sectors of the economy. Little wonder that at this time he was sending his son-in-law, Aleksei Adzhubei, to West Germany to sound out the prospect of a further reduction in international tensions. For Khrushchev's investment priorities had by then become sufficiently reallocative that a major international thaw would facilitate the reduction in defense expenditures that the consumer investment program required.[26]

This was the point Carl Linden called "a virtual revolution in regime planning."[27]

Khrushchev issued this daring challenge to the "steel-eaters" right in the face of the most massive American nuclear armaments program ever, practically a 1960s equivalent of SDI. By the early 1960s, at precisely the time when Khrushchev threw down the gauntlet to the Soviet military, "United States strategic missile programs were operating in high gear: in fiscal 1963 alone the long-range missile forces almost tripled, according to Secretary McNamara, and they were programmed to double again the following year. The Soviet ICBM force grew far less rapidly in these years, so that by April, 1964, the American force was more than four times as large as the Soviet."[28] America seemed to be clearly developing a first-strike capability.

Why the United States would so consistently try to undermine a Soviet reformist leader, thus practically shutting one of the rare Russian windows into political modernity and inviting a ferocious arms race, is a mystery in itself. Why it would do that again with Star Wars, as if its leaders, like the Bourbons, had learned nothing in a quarter-century of fierce arms racing, is an even greater mystery. But the greatest mystery of all is Khrushchev's strange behavior. In the face of such an ominous threat, how could he make a case for the consumer reorientation of the Soviet economy to be paid for by cuts in the defense budget and troop reductions?

Don't we know by now what the standard superpower response is to a missile gap, real or imagined? We know how Stalin's dictatorship responded to the American strategic monopoly in the late 1940s: a crash program to "rearm Russia" by augmenting Soviet conventional forces to an almost unheard-of peacetime level of nearly six million men. Similarly, upon taking office in January, 1961, the Kennedy administration responded to an alleged missile gap by instituting a crash program of "rearming America." The Brezhnev regime reacted likewise in the late 1960s to a gap in America's favor. So, too, did the Reagan administration respond to fill an alleged "window of vulnerability" in the early 1980s. All superpower administrations in the second half of the twentieth century responded similarly to "gaps"—all but one. To quote Horelick and Rush again, "There is no evidence that Khrushchev decided during these years to make a serious bid to overcome the lead of the United States in strategic forces."[29] Why not?[30]

Another confrontation was not long in coming—this time with the "Soviet priesthood," as I call them, or the "hidebound dogmatists," as Khrushchev once referred to them. He struggled for years against their Stalinist "general line" that prescribed the imperative of the preponderance of heavy industry—group A in Soviet planning jargon—over the consumer-goods industry—group B. In 1958, at the time of the abolition of the MTS when Khrushchev first came out with his chemical program and unsuccessfully asked President Eisenhower for a loan, he was unable to devise a persuasive ideological justification for it. He then retreated before seemingly insurmountable opposition to his "heresy." The program withered away. Once again, it required five years for him to make the intellectual breakthrough needed.

How simple it seems now! Yet for Khrushchev it was an extraordinary intellectual coup de theatre. This is its essence:

> The program of chemicalization (*khimizatsiia*) of the economy includes both the sphere of production and that of consumption, and it cannot be said that it relates only to group B or group A. One thing is indisputable: the chemical industry synthesizes the interests of the state in the development of heavy industry [and] the interests of the Soviet people in the rapid increase in the production of consumer goods. . . . *Only hidebound dogmatists can see in this a deviation from the general line.* . . . There can be now no counterposing of group A and group B anymore.[31]

The people he now referred to as "hidebound dogmatists" were, like the military, his former allies of long standing. They were the "Oktia-brist" party of the Soviet cultural establishment.[32] He was betraying them before the eyes of the nation, as he had done two years earlier with the military. More than that, he was allying himself with their bitter opponents, the "Novyi Mirist" party, whose main point for years was precisely the same Khrushchev was now making—that there was an anti-reformist party in the Soviet establishment. If the drive toward political modernity were to continue, his alliance with the "hidebound dogmatists" would have to be broken, just as he was about to break his alliance with the Chinese because they were the mouthpiece for the "Soviet priesthood." When Khrushchev's assistants were conducting negotiations with the "Novyi Mirist" party in May, 1964, to secure its support against the Chinese and the "hidebound dogmatists," it was a clear sign that he finally had made his choice between *Novyi Mir* and *Oktiabr'*.[33]

For years he played a treacherous game with the liberal intelligentsia. He used it in his campaigns of de-Stalinization and then reversed his position under pressure from the "priesthood." Now, for the first time, he needed it as an ally—as a part of a new power base, the general outlines of which were beginning to take shape. But there was no time; he was as dramatically late in this as he was in industry and agriculture (yet the ground was laid for Gorbachev's turning to the intelligentsia for help after 1985).

Nowhere was this more apparent than in the countryside. The new rural managerial elite had directly confronted and beaten the Party professionals by November, 1962, when the regional Party committees were abolished. It allied itself with the new peasant elite, thus reducing the former bosses of the regions to the status of "superfluous people." I have described this breathtaking spectacle in the chapter of my book entitled "The End of a Party Affair":

> I saw this dramatic role reversal with my own eyes, and I bear witness that nothing of the kind was conceivable under Soviet rule before Khrush-chev. The former Olympians who just yesterday had raised people up and cast them down into the abyss of oblivion, who had held in their hands all the threads of life, now lay around under foot, needed by no one, confused, impotent—having lost, it seems, not only status and power, but their very role in life. The official journal *Partiinaia zhizn'*, usually as dull as an autumn rain, suddenly found its tongue, exposing these fallen gods in sarcastic language: "The practice of economic lead-ership which was widespread at one time, and which suffered from over-blown rhetoric and a superficial approach to the problems of production,

gave rise in some people to the incorrect notion that political leadership of the economy was nothing other than leadership 'in general and on the whole.' " . . . They did not know how to do anything else. Even if they were educated, they had long since lost their qualifications. What they knew how to do was no longer needed, and what was necessary they did not know how to do. This was the drama of a whole class of people who before our eyes were transformed from the lords of life into a kind of *lumpens*.[34]

This was a clear sign that Khrushchev was betraying his former allies, the Party professionals, just as he had done with the military a year ago and would do with the "priesthood" a year later. In his eyes, they were no longer the future managerial corps of the nation. At least in his heart, the middle managerial class must have won the battle for this decisive role. It is only in light of this dramatic metamorphosis that the real significance of the new Party constitution, the bylaws of 1961, becomes fully comprehensible. It limited the tenure of Party professionals, which was a mortal blow not only to the existing corps— doomed to be out of circulation in the course of a single decade—but to the very ethos of Party professionalism itself. Who would like to devote his or her life to "Party work" if it could not last more than three or five years? This permanent rotation of personnel applied to the state leaders as well. The only elite not subject to this implacable rotation was the managerial corps.

Imagine if these bylaws had remained in force for at least one decade. What would have happened? Would not a stable and competent middle management class of the 1970s have confronted a shifting, destabilized, and demoralized crowd of Party amateurs, who would suffer the same fate which had already overtaken the former bosses of the rural districts? If this reform had been given a chance, would we not have perhaps faced quite a different Soviet Union in 1970s, instead of the treacherous and corrupt Brezhnevist superpower?

I make no claim that these changes amounted to a "comprehensive economic reform and general liberalization."[35] All I am saying is it must have been clear by the early 1960s that we were dealing with a potential breakthrough into political modernity—so rare in Russian history— which "opened the way" to a comprehensive economic reform and general liberalization, and that the Russian middle class had a rare chance to prevail over the "service nobility." Since its success depended on the support of the international community, we all lost when Khrushchev was brutally denied such support.

Russia got two decades of economic impotence, cultural paralysis, and moral degradation. It lost many of its best sons and daughters in the exodus that ensued. It allowed Chernobyl' to happen. The world got two decades of an era of peace on the brink of war. There was an inept Brezhnev-Kissinger detente, shot through with confrontations and marked by the most grandiose nuclear buildup in history, thus compromising the very idea of detente. The legacy of the Brezhnev era lies in the fact that Cubans are still in Africa and Poland is still a powder keg. There is still a gigantic and wasteful arms race that has become a permanent institution, greatly increasing the domestic political clout of the military machines in each superpower. The idea of Star Wars has been revived and threatens to make all these hideous developments irreversible. What I am saying, then, is that there was an opportunity to prevent all of this, if the West had helped Khrushchev replace the Soviet "service nobility" with the middle class in the 1960s. Luckily, we have another opportunity to reverse these developments in the 1990s, if we assist Gorbachev in doing the same—by weakening the iron grip of the adversarial paradigm on American politicians.

I have no doubt that Gorbachev, like his predecessors, is not a coherent policymaker and that he doesn't have a conscious, let alone coherent, strategy for elevating the middle class. Furthermore, I believe that he, like Khrushchev, is bound to bungle things, if we remain oblivious to this drama. But, much as Khrushchev did, Gorbachev is likely to find his way intuitively when confronted with the ineptitude, corruption, and sabotage of his present allies. He will have to look for alternative solutions, he will have to face dangerous choices, and he might eventually make the right decisions—if we do not cut the ground out from under him, as we did with Khrushchev.

In discussing Khrushchev's foreign policy, Taubman refers to his "bullying tactics over Berlin and Cuba."[36] But Khrushchev did not start his foreign policy adventures with "bullying tactics." In the beginning, his intellectual ammunition in the international arena was just as infantile as it was in domestic affairs. The towering figure of the "murderous tyrant" explained everything for him: it was Stalin's fault Russia did not have detente with the West. He set out to clean up the Augean stables of the dictatorship, apparently not having even the remotest inkling that, just as in domestic politics, he was dealing with deeply entrenched vested interests rather than with a simple misunderstanding created by Stalin's brutal policies.

For an entire generation, Russia was a somber, ascetic garrison-state empire, totally divorced from civilization and bent on grand territorial expansion. Even in a state of absolute strategic inferiority, it managed to swallow the whole of Eastern Europe with a population of 111 million people. It entertained territorial claims on Turkey; maintained its troops and bases in Austria, Finland, and China; and threatened to overthrow Tito in Yugoslavia, undermine Israel, and protract the stalemate in Korea into infinity. It was engulfed in a fortress mentality. It lived not in a postwar but in a prewar world—in preparation for the ultimate showdown with the West, World War III.

As if by a miracle, all of this was erased after Stalin's death. The stalemate in Korea was broken, territorial claims on Turkey dropped, diplomatic relations with Yugoslavia and Israel reestablished, Soviet bases in China and Finland surrendered, Soviet troops in Austria withdrawn, the Soviet military cut down to size, the dogma of the inevitability of World War III cancelled, the fortress mentality dispelled, and the death camps emptied. Not one square inch of new territory under direct Moscow control was added to the empire during the entire Khrushchev decade. What more could the West possibly need to be convinced that Moscow was indeed in the process of a radical de-Stalinization of its foreign policy?

For years, Western negotiators in Geneva tried to talk Stalin into a verifiable agreement on disarmament, both nuclear and conventional, with on-site inspections as its centerpiece. For years, Stalin turned them down flat. They were about to lose faith in negotiations with Moscow when, on May 10, 1955, Khrushchev gave them everything they asked for. Here it was on the table, the West's very own program of disarmament complete with on-site inspections—*proposed by the Soviets.*

One can fully understand the French negotiator who exclaimed in disbelief: "The whole thing looks too good to be true!" The British negotiator seemed bewildered: "The proposals [of the West] have now been largely, and in some cases entirely, adapted by the Soviet Union and made its own proposals." The reaction of the U.S. negotiator was more balanced: "The Soviet Union seems to be using ideas and language which are similar in many respects to the views put forward for many years by the United States."[37] If all this failed to persuade American policymakers that Soviet foreign policy had been turned 180 degrees, then nothing short of an anti-communist revolution could. And indeed it failed. Khrushchev was in for a disappointment in the West no less cruel than what was in store for him in his domestic policies.

This is how James Reston described in the *New York Times* the U.S. response to its own ideas and language put on the table by a Soviet reformer:

A revolution has taken place in American official thinking. . . . What [the Secretary of Air Force Donald A. Quarles] made clear was that the U.S. was not thinking at all about a disarmament system . . . that the U.S. was going to rest its security, not on the solution of power but on the retention of overwhelming air-atomic power . . . not on fullproof inspection system but on mutual surveillance. So when the Russians ask whether, if they accept our alarm system of inspection, we will adopt their system of banning and destroying all weapons of mass destruction, the answer is "no." . . . The whole basis of American thinking on these questions changed. . . .[38]

This is how the adversarial paradigm worked: the instant a Soviet reformer accepted American ideas and language, America assumed the rejectionist position of his former boss, the "murderous tyrant." How was Khrushchev supposed to interpret this extraordinary reversal of roles? Even Taubman himself, who in 1988 still doubted that Khrushchev's foreign policy was indeed reformist, shows us quite vividly this brutal process of the education of Nikita Sergeevich: "More ominous still was a four-part challenge, reminiscent of the early Reagan years, which Eisenhower and Dulles flung at Moscow in 1953 and 1954: harsh anti-Soviet rhetoric, a far-reaching strategic buildup, alliances designed to encircle the Soviets and 'covert operations' seemingly intended to destabilize Soviet clients and perhaps even the U.S.S.R. itself."[39] Add to this, "Nor was the Eisenhower administration shy about threatening to use these awesome weapons. Besides promising to retaliate massively against Soviet aggression at a time and place of Washington's own choosing, Dulles practiced 'brinkmanship' to make his threats seem real."[40]

These people behaved as if Stalin were still alive and the empire were still bent on grandiose territorial expansion. In response to a series of conciliatory moves, they employed horrifying "bullying tactics" and "the very sort of nuclear blackmail to which Khrushchev would subject the Western powers when the first sputnik and the specter of Soviet ICBMs gave him the opportunity to do so."[41]

There was a difference though. Whereas Khrushchev's bullying was designed, according to Taubman, to "force the Western powers to the negotiating table and then into agreements,"[42] American bullying was oriented toward the *extinction* of everything Khrushchev held dear. As Robert E. White noted, "Diplomacy can find no common ground when the aim of one side is to eliminate the other side; that condition is called war."[43]

Be that as it may, the West's absolute refusal to recognize a regime change in Moscow must have been obvious to everyone not blinded by the adversarial paradigm. It ought to have had the same effect on Khrushchev as the stubborn resistance of the Soviet "steel-eaters" to his consumer orientation and the sabotage of his chemical program by the "hidebound dogmatists." There must have been no doubt in his mind that he was faced with a *united front of powerful anti-reformist interests,* foreign as well as domestic. Condemned as he was to fight on two fronts, he must have concluded it was naive to assume conciliatory moves would ever bring results. Only a show of force, only a response in kind could be expected to work. If he wanted to make a reformist breakthrough, he would have to struggle for it tooth and nail, mercilessly and unscrupulously using the very methods the Americans used against him. He was a quick learner, Nikita Sergeevich, and the lessons he was taught so cruelly in Dulles's school of rejectionism, nuclear blackmail, and rollback were not wasted on him.

Among the most intractable problems Khrushchev faced was Germany. Taubman presents the conventional view of the German problem, but there is another side to this issue he seems not to have noticed. Germany was indeed the powder keg of the 1950s, the likeliest place for superpower confrontation. The most terrible thing about it was that, much like the Arab-Israeli conflict of today, it seemed to have no plausible solution. The West's insistence on Germany's reunification was as unacceptable to Khrushchev as Stalin's insistence on its neutralization was to the West. It was an impasse. Reading the American and British press of the 1950s, one is struck by their unprecedented intellectual sterility: no one even envisaged a satisfactory solution to the German problem.

Yet the problem was solved. Germany now seems to be the least likely place for superpower confrontation. The collaboration, or detente if you will, between the two Germanies has safely survived the chills of the early Reagan years. No one expects any trouble from these quarters.

How did this miracle come to pass? Who found the elusive solution? Khrushchev's approach to the German problem challenged both the "reunification" and "neutralization" concepts and proved the only one possible under the circumstances. It may have been brutal, but history has proved it has worked. Incidentally, the Solidarity movement in Poland could hardly have come about, nor any Eastern European aspirations for greater independence from Russia, had there been a reunified Germany in any form. Thus, Khrushchev's solution to the German problem also alleviated the tragic dilemma of Eastern European history, that of being caught in the crossfire of Russo-German rivalry. It seems Solidarity activists and other East European dissidents owe Khrushchev at least a few kind words, for he was the one who not only proclaimed but *secured* the concept of two Germanies and thus made their aspirations possible.

To be sure, some nasty and brutal things had to be done to secure this concept—like the "ugly wall" in Berlin, which appealed to Khrushchev no more than to anyone else and which he tried to avoid by issuing his threats. But when all alternatives were exhausted, when it was clear that he would not get the West to accept the only possible solution to the German problem either by threats or by negotiation, he had the courage to take responsibility for one of the ugliest monuments in European history. After the erection of the wall, the conflict did wither away, never again, one hopes, to be resurrected. Let us then remember not only his threats over Berlin but also his solution to the German problem.

Other facets of Khrushchev's foreign policy also deserve reexamination. As President Eisenhower privately noted, if the U.S.S.R. violated American airspace by secret intelligence-gathering overflights, as the United States did repeatedly, "it might start a nuclear war."[44] In Khrushchev's case, it did not. On the contrary, according to Ambassador Llewellyn Thompson's report, Khrushchev pleaded with him behind closed doors, "*This U-2 thing has put me in a terrible spot. You have to get me out of it.*"[45] No one came to the rescue, of course. Khrushchev never fully recovered from this blow to his prestige. This we know from Khrushchev himself. He told Dr. A. McGhee Harvey in 1969, "From the time Gary Powers was shot down in a U-2 over the Soviet Union I was no longer in full control."[46]

As to the deployment of Soviet missiles in Cuba, Taubman appears not to remember that it was, among other things, a response in kind to the deployment of Jupiter missiles in Turkey, no farther from the Soviet heartland than Cuba is from the American. Has anyone ever heard of a Turkish missile crisis that put the world on the brink of nuclear disaster? Why is it that we are so ready to accept a double standard? That while we endorse Dulles's responses in kind we are so intolerant of Khrushchev's? The public may not understand such subtleties, but should the experts follow it?

This is not to deny that the deployment of missiles in Cuba was a blunder, even if it was a response in kind and an act of sheer political survival, like Khrushchev's actions during the "constitutional crisis" of June, 1957. He did not understand the American mentality and did not anticipate the strength of Kennedy's reaction; nor did he even remotely imagine the breathtaking significance which would be attributed to his action. Even so, he found the courage to withdraw in a direct superpower confrontation. Although he unquestionably behaved like a statesman in this instance and not like a bully, the whole episode demonstrated a lack of subtlety and sophistication. But why should we expect subtlety and sophistication from a pre-modern politician in the modern world? Was it not amazing a man with such a background was able to reverse Stalinist foreign policy so completely that he quit territorial expansion altogether (replacing it with expansion of influence — entirely in line with U.S. policies), refused to participate in the nuclear arms race, eliminated the German problem from the agenda of superpower confrontation, and found a remedy for Russia's perennial predicament?

Is it not even more amazing that most Western intellectuals, not to speak of politicians, so completely misunderstood him? It was Thomas H. Rigby who in 1963 proposed the analogy "between the post-1957 Khrushchev and the pre-1937 Stalin."[47] It was Merle Fainsod who, also in 1963, wrote that "Khrushchev, like Stalin before him, tolerates no derogation of his own authority, permits no opposition to raise its head within the Party, and insists that the Party function as a unit in executing his will."[48] Less than a year later, this alleged new dictator was fired.[49]

It is time to demonstrate our own subtlety and sophistication. This means, among other things, to stop thinking up excuses for the monumental error American politicians made between 1953 and 1964, to stop quarreling with Khrushchev from a position of the adversarial paradigm, and to start examining his foreign and domestic policy from the perspective of the Russian reform he so dramatically, so courageously, and so blunderingly presented to the world, because there is a new reformist opportunity to attend to. Misunderstanding Khrushchev's reformist policies, we are bound to misconstrue Gorbachev's.

NOTES

1. My latest book, *The Russian Challenge and the Year 2000* (Oxford, 1987), explores, among other things, the plans and strategies of the extremist forces in contemporary Russia for a fascist transformation by the year 2000.

2. *New York Times,* September 20, 1987.

3. William Taubman, "Khrushchev and Detente: Reform in the International Context," herein, p. 144.

4. See, for example, p. 79 in Alexander Yanov, *The Drama of the Soviet 1960s: A Lost Reform* (Berkeley, 1984).

5. Ibid., p. 110.

6. Taubman, "Khrushchev and Detente," herein, p. 146.

7. Ibid., p. 145.

8. But certainly not direct or publicized help, since we are still dealing with a medieval, arrogant, and religious state where help from the "heretics" backfires. See my essay, "Is Sovietology Reformable?" herein.

9. See, for example, Natan H. Mager and Jaques Katel's *Conquest without*

War (New York, 1961), which states that Khrushchev's speeches were "the contemporary equivalent of *Mein Kampf*" (p. 3). See also H. Overstreet's *The War Called Peace* (New York, 1961), and the *National Review* during the Khrushchev years.

10. Here is only one example from *Renmin Ribao* (The Peoples' Daily) of February 29, 1964: "In international relations, Khrushchev's revisionism practices capitulation to U.S. imperialism; in the imperialist and capitalist countries it practices capitulation to the reactionary ruling circles; in the socialist countries it encourages the development of capitalist forces."

11. N. S. Khrushchev, "Main Report of the Central Committee," in *Current Soviet Policies II: The Documentary Record of the Communist Party Congress and Its Aftermath* (New York, 1957), p. 47.

12. *XXII S'ezd Kommunisticheskoi partii Sovetskogo Soiuza, Stenograficheskii otchet*, 2 vols. (Moscow, 1962), 1:253.

13. *Pravda*, February 26, 1986.

14. Arnold L. Horelick and Myron Rush, *Strategic Power and Soviet Foreign Policy* (Chicago, 1966), pp. 36-37.

15. D. Gale Johnson, "Prospects for Soviet Agriculture in the 1980s," in *Soviet Economy in the 1980s: Problems and Prospects*, 2 vols. (Washington, D.C., 1981), 2:7.

16. Douglas B. Diamond and W. Lee Davis, "Comparative Growth in Output and Productivity in the U.S. and U.S.S.R. Agriculture," in *Soviet Economy in a Time of Change*, 2 vols. (Washington, 1979), 2:21.

17. Yanov, *Drama*, p. 115.

18. A. Arzumanian, *Pravda*, August 17, 1962; O. Volkov, ibid., August 23, 1962; and V. Shkatov, ibid., September 1, 1962.

19. Harry Schwartz, *The Soviet Economy since Stalin* (Philadelphia, 1965), describes it as "one of the most important and revealing speeches of Khrushchev's long career" (p. 185).

20. This rotten and corrupt regime, for which every one in today's Moscow seems to have nothing but contempt, was hailed by some of us as a triumph of "stabilization" and "normalcy," even "institutional pluralism," as opposed to Khrushchev's "harebrained scheming." "I already argued," Jerry Hough has written, "that since the removal of Khrushchev, the Soviet political system has come to develop a number of characteristics associated by American political scientists of the 1960s with the essence of pluralism." Jerry Hough, *The Soviet Union and Social Science Theory* (Cambridge, Mass., 1977), p. 69. Indeed, Hough's entire "model of institutional pluralism is explicitly focused on the Brezhnev period" (ibid., p. 12), when "the Soviet leadership seems to have made the Soviet Union closer to the spirit of pluralist model of American political science than is the United States" (ibid., p. 10).

21. *XXII S'ezd*, 1:106.

22. N. S. Khrushchev, *Stroitel'stvo kommunizma v SSSR i razvitie sel'skogo khoziaistva*, 8 vols. (Moscow, 1962), 4:290.

23. Ibid., 7:362.

24. *New York Times*, May 21, 1961.

25. Khrushchev, *Stroitel'stvo,* 8:51.

26. George Breslauer, *Khrushchev and Brezhnev as Leaders* (Boston, 1982), p. 96.

27. Carl A. Linden, *Khrushchev and the Soviet Leadership* (Baltimore, 1966), p. 198.

28. Horelick and Rush, *Strategic Power,* p. 155.

29. This conclusion contrasts sharply with Taubman's assertion that "such evidence as exists suggests it was Khrushchev himself who insisted on developing the very ICBMs which Brezhnev and company later deployed." Taubman, "Khrushchev and Detente," herein, p. 147. Let me emphasize, however, that Horelick and Rush were not alone in arguing that Khrushchev refused to participate in the strategic arms race. Lincoln P. Bloomfield, Walter C. Clemens, and Franklyn Griffiths made the same point in *Khrushchev and the Arms Race* (Cambridge, Mass., 1966), and Joseph L. Nogee and Robert H. Donaldson still held this opinion in 1984 in *Soviet Foreign Policy since World War II* (New York, 1984).

30. In the quarter-century since then, not one sovietologist, to my knowledge, has seriously attempted to answer this crucial question, except by referring to the first generation of Soviet ICBMs as "too big and cumbersome." Without answering it, however, it seems to be impossible to distinguish between the defense policies of Soviet reform and those of stagnation.

31. Khrushchev, *Stroitel'stvo,* 8:449-51 (emphasis added).

32. *Oktiabr',* headed by Vsevolod Kochetov, was the chief guardian of Stalin's torch, the defender of the "general line," and the main antagonist of the liberal *Novyi Mir* in the Soviet literary establishment. For more detail, see Yanov, *Drama,* pp. 40-48.

33. On negotiations with intellectuals about the common cause against the Chinese, see Dina R. Spechler, *Permitted Dissent in the USSR* (New York, 1982), pp. 236, and Abraham Rothberg, *The Heirs of Stalin: Dissidence and the Soviet Regime, 1953-1970* (Ithaca, N.Y., 1972), p. 136.

34. Yanov, *Drama,* p. 89.

35. Taubman, "Khrushchev and Detente," herein, p. 146.

36. Ibid., p. 149.

37. Philip Noel-Baker, *The Arms Race* (London, 1958), pp. 21-22.

38. *New York Times,* September 6, 1955, p. 8.

39. Taubman, "Khrushchev and Detente," herein, p. 150.

40. Ibid., p. 151.

41. Ibid.

42. Ibid., p. 149.

43. Robert E. White. "Respect the Arias Proposal," *New York Times,* September 21, 1987.

44. Excerpts from Michael R. Beschluss's book *Mayday* in *US News and World Report,* March 24, 1986, p. 36.

45. Ibid., p. 45.

46. "A 1969 Conversation with Khrushchev: The Beginning of His Fall from Power," *Life,* December 18, 1970, p. 488.

47. Thomas H. Rigby, "The Extent and Limits of Authority (a Rejoinder to Carl Linden)," *Problems of Communism* 12 (September-October, 1963):36-40.

48. Merle Fainsod, *How Russia Is Ruled* (Cambridge, Mass., 1963), p. 583.

49. Let me add that Khrushchev could hardly be expected to understand the American mentality. Sovietologists, on the other hand, were supposed to understand *his* mentality, but they did not. If they had, there would perhaps not have been a Berlin crisis nor a Cuban one either. Rigby and Fainsod, however, were writing in 1963. Taubman wrote his paper in 1988. Nevertheless, he concluded that although "Khrushchev was, indeed, a genuine reformer at home . . . his foreign policies were far more ambiguous." Taubman, "Khrushchev and Detente," herein, p. 146.

Reform of the Soviet Military under Khrushchev and the Role of America's Strategic Modernization

GEORGE F. MINDE II
and
MICHAEL HENNESSEY

The scope of this essay is limited to the policies pursued by Khrushchev in relation to the Soviet military. In this context, "reform" is defined as any restructuring of the Soviet military that would allow resources previously committed to the defense sector to be reallocated to the civilian economy. Although military "reform" and "reductions" are not identical, they are related in that a successful reform would permit a reduction in military spending. Given the considerable drain on Soviet resources represented by military expenditures, currently estimated to be between 12 and 17 percent of Soviet gross domestic product,[1] even a minor reduction in military spending could translate into a substantial windfall for those branches of the Soviet economy that are not part of the military-industrial complex. Such a reallocation of resources from the military to the civilian sector of the economy, while perhaps not necessary for economic reform, would certainly facilitate such a policy.[2]

This essay argues Khrushchev attempted to transform the Soviet military from a large, conventional army into a more economical modern force. His government accomplished this objective with large-scale troop reductions and the acquisition of a relatively less expensive nuclear force capable of deterring a "preventive war" on the part of the West. Khrushchev pursued the buildup of the Soviet nuclear forces with the same sense of economy. Missile deployments were not as rapid as Soviet capabilities would have allowed, nor were they considered great enough by many within the Soviet military.[3] Khrushchev deployed missiles sufficient for deterrence instead of attempting to engage the United States in an arms race.

Khrushchev's efforts at military reform can be divided into three periods or "phases": an initial phase (1955-57) in which there was a consensus between Khrushchev and the military on the nature and scope of the reforms; a middle phase (1957-59) in which Khrushchev attempted to recreate the original consensus by imposing political controls on the military; and a final phase (1960-64) in which he abandoned attempts to reach agreement with the military elites and attempted to impose reforms through decisions of the national government.[4] Each of these phases or periods is marked by differing internal and external circumstances that alternately favored or hindered Khrushchev's reformist program.

Manpower Reductions: The First Round

The period of Khrushchev's initial reformist efforts was characterized by relatively little conflict between Khrushchev and the military; the military appears largely to have supported Khrushchev's initial reforms. These consisted of a series of reductions in the size of the armed forces. The reductions in military manpower during this period were quite extensive. Between 1955 and 1959 the Soviet armed forces shrank from 5,763,000 troops to 3,623,000, or a reduction of slightly over a third of overall strength, instituted in a series of three troop cuts announced successively in August, 1955 (640,000); May, 1956 (1,200,000); and January, 1958 (300,000). The cuts were instituted mostly through the reduction of Soviet unit strengths from full manning levels to cadre strength; they were justified on the basis of the "relaxation of tension" in U.S.-Soviet relations.[5]

During this initial phase of reforms, a unique combination of circumstances favored Khrushchev's efforts. The international situation had greatly improved between February and December of 1955 through such events as the Geneva conference and Adenauer's visit to Moscow.[6] November and December, 1955, saw the explosion of the first two large Soviet hydrogen bombs, making the policy of deterrence Malenkov spoke of in 1953 and 1954 a real option rather than some vision of an indefinite future.[7] Furthermore, the ground forces themselves felt the need for some change in the unit structure, which had remained virtually unchanged since the end of demobilization following World War II.[8] Minister of Defense Marshal Zhukov began a reorganization of the ground forces in 1955 in which motorization of the infantry was completed and the last mechanized and horse cavalry divisions were eliminated; one of the results of this reorganization was fewer infantry in

Soviet military formations, a change which helped lessen the impact of the reductions.[9]

To evaluate the significance of the manpower reductions, it is necessary first to evaluate various explanations for the reductions to see if they were indeed "forced" upon the Soviet leadership as some have claimed. The reason for doing so should be apparent: if the reforms were necessitated by resource constraints of one kind or another, one would expect they would have been reversed when these restraints were removed.

Three explanations are commonly given for these troop reductions. The "traditionalist" view is that a decline in the draft-age manpower pool caused by the low Soviet birthrate of World War II necessitated a reduction in the size of the armed forces: "In the mid-1950s, there were approximately 5 million men in the Soviet Armed Forces. When the low birth rate of World War II began to have its impact upon the number of men available for the Armed Forces, the Party leadership considered it necessary to explain to the world why reductions in military manpower were taking place."[10]

Khrushchev's initial manpower reductions, however, did not correspond to any decline in the size of the Soviet draft pool; rather, at the time these cuts were being made, the draft pool was expanding to its largest size in the post-Stalin era. The low birthrate of the war years did not have an impact until 1961—when the 1942 male cohorts became eligible for military service—and the 19- to 21-year-old male contingents did not drop below the 1955 levels until 1963. Thus, the manpower reductions of 1955 through 1958 anticipated the decline in the draft pool by five to eight years.

Furthermore, the magnitude of the cuts was far greater than any necessitated by the decline in the draft pool. Judging from the disparity between the size of the Soviet armed forces and the 19- to 21-male-age group, it would have been possible for the Soviet Union to support an army numbering at least four million throughout the "lean years" of 1963-65.[11] An even larger army could have been maintained if the Soviet Union had decided to extend enlistments from three to four years, as it had done during the Berlin crisis of 1961.

The second explanation for Khrushchev's manpower reductions was that the troop cuts were an attempt to alleviate an impending labor shortage.[12] The extensive growth in the Soviet labor pool had been due to rural-urban immigration and the increasing participation of women in the work force. Presumably, both sources were drying up. By 1960, half of the population lived in cities, and women already comprised nearly half the labor force (46 percent in 1955 and 47 percent in 1960).[13]

The work force, however, continued to grow extensively during this period. During the Seven-Year Plan, the Soviet population of working age was expected to increase by 6.7 million, and the chairman of the State Committee for Labor and Wages stated in February, 1960, that the troop reductions announced by Khrushchev the month before had not been considered as a source of manpower in the plan.[14] A campaign to increase female participation in the work force led to an additional 6 million women entering the economy during the period 1955-59, and another 12.4 million women entering the labor force during the period 1960-65. The Soviet labor force expanded at approximately the same rate between 1950 and 1970: by 22.7 percent during 1951-55, 24.2 percent during 1956-60, 23.6 percent during 1961-65, and 24.2 percent during 1966-70.[15] Thus, troop reductions do not appear to have been a response to a sudden decline in the labor supply.

The final explanation for the troop reductions is that they were made in order to release funds for the buildup of the Soviet rocket forces.[16] Given the secretive nature of the Soviet government, arguments based on the level of Soviet military expenditures are somewhat suspect. During the period 1955-58, however, Soviet manpower costs declined from 7.4 to 5.2 billion "new" rubles, in other words, by 2.2 billion rubles. Over the same period, overall defense expenditures declined by 3.1 billion rubles. Even by 1960, defense expenditures were still 1.5 billion rubles below the 1955 level.[17] Although the reductions in manpower certainly helped cushion the large increase in Soviet defense spending following the large-scale deployment of ICBMs and the Berlin crisis of 1961, a large portion of the savings from the 1955-58 cuts appears to have been redirected toward the civilian economy.

The reductions in military manpower implemented under Khrushchev during 1955-57 thus appear to have been the result of conscious choice on the part of Khrushchev and the Soviet leadership rather than an unpleasant alternative forced upon them by circumstances beyond their control. They were reformist in the military sphere, significantly altering the Soviet force structure—reducing the size and importance of the army relative to the air force and air defense forces and, to a lesser extent, the navy. The role of the air defense forces, especially, was increased.[18] Research also continued on both tactical and strategic missiles that were to become the basis of greater changes in the Soviet force structure in Khrushchev's later years. Khrushchev's military policy during this period also had a reformist impact on the overall Soviet economy, since it resulted in an apparent decline in military expenditures both in real terms and in proportion to the rest of the economy. The consensus between Khrushchev and the military which had allowed these initial reforms did not continue, however. By the close of 1956, opposition to Khrushchev's military policies had already begun. Khrushchev's relations with the military thus entered their second stage in early 1957.

Resurgence of the Main Political Administration

Khrushchev's initial manpower reductions had fostered a favorable internal situation, and the relative success of a policy of detente abroad (the "Spirit of Geneva") fostered Khrushchev's initial manpower reductions. By late 1956, the delicate political balance which had supported his early reforms had begun to erode. The events in Poland and especially Hungary had cost him severely in prestige. The December Plenum of the Party Central Committee was held without a single mention of Khrushchev. After the start of the new year, the subject of American war preparations began to appear again in the Soviet press, which had been silent on the topic since the Party debates of 1954-55.[19]

There are also signs that opposition to Khrushchev's policies was developing within the military. By mid-1957, the reorganization of the ground forces had largely run its course; their structure had been changed to make best use of the stock of hardware which had been built up since World War II, and most divisions had already been reduced to cadre strength. Further reductions beyond those already announced in 1956 would have forced the army either to begin disbanding entire divisions or to reduce further the quantity of infantry in the divisions, thus making the latter unbalanced as fighting forces.[20] Speaking in India in June, 1957, Zhukov referred to both the initial and subsequent phases of a war—a formula often used later by military leaders in opposition to the reductions Khrushchev announced in January, 1960.[21]

From the military perspective, there had also been a drastic change in the situation due to the increasing nuclearization of the U.S. and other NATO armies. Originally, U.S. interest in the tactical uses of nuclear weapons had been primarily theoretical in nature; studies of the effects of nuclear weapons on the battlefield had begun around 1949 and continued through the early 1950s with such programs as Project VISTA at the California Institute of Technology. Beginning with Eisenhower's "New Look" in 1953, however, U.S. interest began to take a more practical turn. Field tests for the "Atomic Field Army-1 1956" (ATFA-1) were begun in late 1954 utilizing the 1st Armored Division and the 47th Infantry. This and the "PENTANNA" study of 1955 finally culminated in October, 1956, when the army unveiled the Pentomic division, a formation specifically designed to fight and win under nuclear conditions.[22] In addition, other NATO countries such as Belgium and the Federal Republic of Germany began to adopt the Pentomic structure for their divisions. NATO as a whole adopted a posture of forward defense, envisioning the use of tactical nuclear weapons in East Germany in a series of delaying actions.[23]

Not only did NATO develop the theory for fighting a nuclear war in Europe, but the alliance also began to deploy the weapon systems which were to make it possible. These included the Honest John and the Corporal missiles introduced in 1956, with ranges of twenty and seventy-five miles, respectively, and the eight-inch nuclear cannon and the Redstone missile fielded in 1958.[24] The United States and the NATO countries appeared to be adopting a military doctrine based on the assumption that conflict conducted with nuclear weapons was winnable; simultaneously, they were adopting a force structure aimed at reaching the capacity to fight such a war. To make matters worse, this policy was accompanied by relatively little talk of the destructiveness of such a war that Khrushchev often mentioned. The West's apparent willingness to risk nuclear war was reflected in an increasingly provocative U.S. foreign policy. Leaving aside Dulles's rhetoric of "rollback" and "brinksmanship," studies show that beginning in 1955-56 the United States began to resort increasingly to the use of "shows of force" involving nuclear weapons as a diplomatic tool in dealing with the Soviet Union.[25]

Given the international environment developing in 1957, there was ample reason for the Soviet military to doubt the wisdom of continuing Khrushchev's reforms. For the U.S.S.R. to continue a policy of unilateral military reductions while the West was increasing its military strength could eventually threaten the security of the Soviet Union. There thus developed an increasing discrepancy between the policies pursued by Khrushchev and the military's duty of providing an adequate defense for the Soviet state. It was under these conditions of increasing stress in military-political relations that Khrushchev's military reforms then entered their second phase.[26]

Public debate of military issues is somewhat limited in countries having a truly professional army.[27] The question of the proportion of the nation's resources to be allocated to the military — military doctrine, in Soviet parlance — is largely determined by civilian political elites. The question of the strategy under which these resources will be used, however, is left largely to the armed forces as the sole possessor of "military expertise." Civilian elites have relatively little role in determining military strategy.[28] When the military began to oppose his policies, Khrushchev attempted to bridge this gap between the military and the political spheres. The tactics he used included the removal of Zhukov, the appointment of former associates to high military posts, and the reimposition of controls through the Main Political Administration. By these means, he tried to influence the development of military strategy so it would support his policies.

The dismissal of Marshal Zhukov as minister of defense was the first indication of this new phase. The official explanation for Zhukov's removal in October of 1957 centered around charges that he was undermining the work of the Main Political Administration and accusations of "Bonapartism," in other words, that he was planning a "South American-style military take-over."[29] Timothy Colton, however, has done an excellent job of refuting these allegations.[30] Since these charges were dismissed, one is faced with the task of determining if Zhukov was removed for personal reasons or because of policy disagreements.

There are good reasons for believing that it was the latter. Prior to his removal, Zhukov had anticipated many of the issues that would later become bones of contention between Khrushchev and the military. Although Zhukov noted the increased importance of the air force in his speech to the Twentieth Party Congress in 1956, he still acknowledged the ground forces would play the decisive role in a future conflict. In addition, he repeatedly stated future wars would involve nuclear weapons, an idea which the military later developed into the justification for its requirement for a large army to absorb the losses involved in such a conflict. Finally, his comments on the initial and subsequent course of a war likewise implied the outcome of the war would not be determined in the initial phase—again implying a requirement for a large army able to absorb initial losses and still prevail.[31] Khrushchev had also set a precedent for relieving military commanders who disagreed with him over military doctrine when he dismissed Admiral Kuznetsov in 1956.[32]

Khrushchev had additional incentive for demoting Zhukov from his unique position in the Soviet hierarchy. Marshal Zhukov's role in World War II had given him great prestige within the officer corps and broad influence outside of it. Immediately after replacing Marshal Vasil'evskii as minister of defense, he had begun "exercising the prerogatives of a political figure" by such acts as the Hearst interview in February of 1955 and by accompanying Khrushchev and Bulganin to Geneva.[33] His stature was increased by his elevation to candidate membership in the Presidium in 1956, followed by full membership after the "Anti-Party Group" incident in June, 1957.[34] The military had in Zhukov far more than a spokesman who could claim "expert knowledge" if called in for consultation. As a full member of the Presidium, Zhukov had the opportunity to question current military policy, whereas previously the army had been far more limited in its ability to "force the issue" on any policy disagreement. Although not a political rival to Khrushchev in his own right, Zhukov would have been a powerful addition to any new Party faction opposing Khrushchev's military policy. For this reason, it could have become increasingly difficult for Khrushchev to undertake any new reforms while Zhukov retained his position on the Presidium.[35]

After removing Zhukov, Khrushchev attempted to gain a more favorable hearing in the higher military councils by promoting several officers with whom he had served during the war—the so-called Stalingrad Group.[36] The best example of the rise of this group was the appointment of Marshal Malinovskii, who had served with Khrushchev on the southern and Stalingrad fronts, to replace Zhukov as minister of defense. Another of Khrushchev's men was Marshal Moskalenko, who had served on the southwest and Stalingrad fronts from 1941-43; Moskalenko became commander of the Moscow Military District shortly after Stalin's death, held Beria following the latter's arrest in June, 1953, participated in Beria's court martial, and became commander of the Strategic Rocket Forces in 1960, a post which he held until 1962. Still another was Marshal Konev, who served with Khrushchev on the First Ukrainian Front. Konev was Zhukov's major rival within the military; Konev replaced him as deputy minister of war and commander-in-chief of the ground forces in 1946 after Stalin removed him from those posts. While Konev did not benefit directly from Khrushchev's rise to power, he was the military man most supportive of Khrushchev's bid for military glory starting in 1955.[37] In addition to the appointments of the Stalingrad group, Khrushchev worked to "rejuvenate" the officer corps, demobilizing thousands of elderly officers and promoting new ones with more technical backgrounds in the hope that these "modernists" would support his reforms and ideas of military strategy.

At about the same time as Zhukov's downfall, the Party began a sustained effort to increase the power of the Main Political Administration (MPA).[38] The MPA is often seen as playing a watchdog role, overseeing the loyalty of the armed forces; however, given the high membership of the officer corps in the Party or the Komsomol (86 percent in 1952, higher in later years), this was not necessary.[39] The MPA itself recognized this. In early 1955, Major General Moskovskii, editor of *Red Star* (*Krasnaia Zvezda*) and senior officer in the MPA, wrote, "One of the most important measures taken by the Party and government in recent years concerning the Soviet armed forces is the further strengthening of single command. This still further raised the authority of commanders and improved discipline and order in the troops. Our army and navy have experienced cadres of officers and generals supremely devoted to the motherland. . . ." He also made a reference to the armed forces as the "faithful defenders of the state interests of our motherland."[40] The MPA's influence began to decline under Marshal Vasil'evskii and continued to decline under Zhukov.

In an attempt to quell any opposition to Khrushchev's military program, the Party began to reverse this trend in 1957. A series of reforms increased the MPA's role. First the "Instructions to the Organizations of the CPSU in the Soviet Army and Navy," made public in May, 1957, called for "further growth in the activity and militancy of Party organizations, [and] the strengthening of their influence over all aspects of the life and activity of the troops." This program contained a call for the extension of *kritika/samokritika* (criticism/self-criticism) to include command decisions made by officers. This practice, which had been discouraged by Zhukov, could sanction criticism of officers who held to "old" ideas. Immediately before Zhukov's removal, the Party Plenum adopted the "Resolution on the Improvement of Party-political Work in the Soviet Army and Navy," reinforcing the previous instructions.[41] In December, 1957, independent political study by officers in effect since 1953 was rescinded and replaced with a formal program requiring fifty hours of instruction a year.[42] In January, 1958, the MPA head, Colonel General Zheltov, was accused of having been lax in his duties and was replaced by Marshal (then General) Golikov. In April, the plenum passed the "Statute on the MPA," attempting to centralize it and make it more independent of the Ministry of Defense; the "Statute on Military Councils," attempting to enhance the power of that organization; and the "Change in the Instructions to the Party Organizations in the Soviet Army and Navy." In October, the plenum adopted the "Statute on the Political Organs in the Soviet Army and Navy," increasing the authority of the political organs and again instructing them to increase their influence over all aspects of military activity and to introduce "Leninist norms" into military life.[43] In the midst of all this, the Soviet government announced in January, 1958, a troop reduction of 300,000 to take place over the next year.[44]

The military's initial reaction was relatively quiet. Two articles published in February and March, 1958, stressed the need for "boldness and initiative" on the part of officers and the military's role in World War II—apparently to make the point that the armed forces were the "faithful defenders of the interests of the motherland." In late summer the military began to assert itself more strongly. An article in *Krasnaia Zvezda* in August cited cases of rude treatment of unit commanders by political officers and the need for strengthening the role of commanders.[45] Shortly after this, the naval journal *Sovetskii Flot* began a series of articles which stressed the need for increased authority and training for officers. Finally, Minister of Defense Malinovskii entered the fray in an article in *Krasnaia Zvezda* on November 1 which called for less MPA interference in training and other military activities: "All activities of commanders, political organs, and Party organizations aimed at carrying out the decisions of the October plenum must be viewed in light of their inseparability from those practical tasks which are carried out by our forces . . . of strengthening the combat capability and readiness of the army and navy."[46] Marshals Zakharov and Grechko made similiar statements criticizing the MPA's activities. Faced with resistance from both Malinovskii and the lower military echelons, the Party began to limit the role of the MPA. By early 1959, many of the most obtrusive Party controls were eliminated.

Khrushchev's efforts, then, had mixed success during this period. The pace of troop reductions was slowed. The reductions announced in January, 1956, were completed in 1957; another smaller reduction of 300,000 troops was implemented in 1958; and no further cuts were announced for 1959. The removal of Zhukov did eliminate a powerful opponent of Khrushchev's reforms; Zhukov could have been invaluable to any political opposition, such as Frol Kozlov's which emerged in 1960. The promotion of the Stalingrad Group, however, did not have its desired effect. Although the majority of this group remained quiet during Khrushchev's attempt to expand the role of the MPA, it became his most vociferous critic during the manpower debates of 1960-64.[47] The common interests of the military and the officer corps weighed more heavily on their minds than any personal loyalty they may have felt toward Khrushchev.

The more serious threat to military professionalism was Khrushchev's attempt to increase the role of the MPA. Practically all of the new controls introduced in 1957-58 were removed in 1959. Even if these new measures had remained in place, however, they still would have failed in their purpose of controlling the military for numerous reasons. First of all, although the MPA's influence increased, the MPA did not actually participate in formal decision making except on military councils at the service, military district/fleet, and army levels. Even there, regular army officers outnumbered representatives of the MPA or the Party, and participation by local Party officials was "sporadic at best."[48] The monitoring capability of political officers at these and other levels was suspect for a number of reasons, not least of which was the experience shared with the regular officers. A large number of political officers had served as at least platoon leaders prior to work in the MPA, while many worked at higher levels—such as Golikov, the new MPA chief, who had served as a deputy commander and commander of a front during the war. The MPA had ceased to function as monitoring agency by the time Khrushchev came to power, and it had essentially become a part of the overall administration of the armed forces.[49] To reverse this would have required far more radical reforms than those undertaken during 1957 and 1958. On the whole, Khrushchev accomplished little during this period other than eliminating direct military representation on the Presidium in the person of Zhukov.

Manpower Reductions, Round Two

In late 1959, Khrushchev adopted a different strategy. Rather than attempting to shape the military's views through the MPA, he publicly made calls for military reductions and attempted to implement them directly through the Supreme Soviet. Debate between the military and Khrushchev moved from the relatively closed pages of the military press to the halls of the Supreme Soviet and the Party Plenum.

During this period, Khrushchev made major drives to decrease Soviet conventional forces in 1960 and 1963, and Kennedy launched the massive American strategic buildup in 1961. The period also marked the beginning of significant Soviet ICBM deployments in 1960. The decision leading to this step was apparently made in the months immediately preceding the Twenty-first Party Congress in February, 1959. Previously, the Soviet Union had decided to deploy only a token number of the first-generation SS-6 "Sapwood" ICBMs.[50] It appeared that this low rate of production would continue, since the initial wording of the control figures for the Seven-Year Plan proposed by Khrushchev in November, 1958, included the statement, "The production of intercontinental ballistic rockets has been successfully organized." In the final version of the control figures approved by the congress, however, this was changed to "The *series* production of intercontinental ballistic rockets has been successfully organized," implying a change to mass production of missiles or an increased rate of deployment.[51] The increased Soviet ICBM deployments detected in 1961 support the view that the Soviet government decided to increase production at this time.[52]

At this time, Khrushchev also appears to have adopted a policy of "minimum deterrence," that is, building only a sufficient number of missiles to deter a U.S. strike rather than striving for numerical superiority or even parity. The American experience with the first-generation Atlas and Titan missiles—the SS-7 "Saddler" and SS-8 "Sasin" bore closer resemblence to them than to the U.S. Minuteman—showed that it was possible to deploy a large number of liquid-fueled ICBMs rapidly. The rapid Soviet deployment of ICBMs also lends credence to the "capability-based" National Intelligence Estimates of 1958 and 1959, which gave the Soviets credit for being able to deploy 500 ICBMs within a period of three years.[53] Yet, from 1961 to 1965 actual deployment was held at an artificially low rate, numbering between 15 and 40 missiles each year with the exception of 1963. This very limited pattern of deployment, especially during 1964 and 1965 after the Kennedy buildup, demonstrates that Khrushchev was not interested in playing a "numbers game" with the West.

The military reductions he proposed to the Supreme Soviet on January 14, 1960, revealed Khrushchev's new tack. The internal situation at this time was favorable. His meat program appeared to be doing well, with Riazan' and several other oblasts reporting a doubling or tripling of their production.[54] Agriculture had faltered slightly under a drought, but the shortfall had not been catastrophic; industrial production had increased by over 11 percent in 1959 rather than the modest 7.7 percent goal set in the Seven-Year Plan.[55]

In his January 14 speech, Khrushchev announced to the Supreme Soviet the creation of the Strategic Rocket Forces.[56] While these forces may have existed more in name than in fact because of the small number of Soviet ICBMs, this step created at least the image of progress in lessening the strategic imbalance. Moreover, the large-scale production of ICBMs, decided upon prior to the Twenty-first Party Congress the preceding January, would soon begin to bear fruit. Relations with the United States appeared to be entering a new period of detente with Khrushchev's visit to the United States in September, 1959, and plans for President Eisenhower's return trip the following June. Overall, Khrushchev appears to have been at the height of his career in early 1960.

Khrushchev utilized this political "high ground" to announce to the Supreme Soviet a proposal to reduce the Soviet armed forces by a further 1,200,000 men, from 3,623,000 to 2,423,000 troops. In his speech, he stressed the reduction in the level of international tensions and the predominance of missile forces in any future conflict, stating: "In our time the defense potential of the country is determined, not by the number of our soldiers under arms [and] the number of persons in naval uniform . . . [but] by the total firepower and means of delivery available."[57]

In a speech later the same day, Marshal Malinovskii used the opportunity to emphasize the need for retaining strong ground forces;

however, he refrained from opposing Khrushchev's proposals outright: "The rocket troops are indisputably the main arm of our armed forces. However, we understand that it is not possible to solve *all* the tasks of war with any *one* arm of troops. Therefore, proceeding from the thesis that the successful conduct of military operations in modern war is possible only on the basis of the unified use of all means of armed struggle . . . we are retaining all arms of our armed forces at a definite strength and in relevant, sound proportions."[58] Despite the subtle criticism of Khrushchev's reduction implicit in Malinovskii's comments, the proposals were adopted the following day.

The reduction was specifically to include 250,000 officers, between one-third and one-quarter of the Soviet total.[59] This proposal implied a large decrease in the number of cadre divisions—reduced-strength units manned mostly by officers and noncommissioned officers—hampering the call-up of Soviet reserves in case of war. Reportedly a large number of senior officers wrote the Party Plenum stating that they could not guarantee the security of the Soviet Union if the reductions were carried out fully.[60] Publicly, opposition centered around the plight of the officers about to be demobilized. Malinovskii flatly stated four days after the reductions were approved that "the demobilization of officers will be accomplished by various difficulties," and some papers printed articles on the problems faced by those officers demobilized in 1955-57.[61]

Khrushchev's political position began to erode shortly after the reductions were announced. The U-2 incident was followed closely by the promotion of Frol Kozlov to CSPU first secretary on May 4 and a swift reversal of the detente which had begun developing during Khrushchev's visit to the United States the preceding September.[62] As the year went on, it became apparent that Khrushchev's meat program was faltering, and the devastation wrought by the use of "Riazan' methods" began to come to light.[63] The bitter debate centering around the "missile gap" in the U.S. presidential campaign promised a substantial American military buildup—and a corresponding decline in U.S.-Soviet relations—regardless of whether Kennedy or Nixon won the election. And, finally, the dispute with China became public during the meeting of Communist party leaders held in Moscow during November.[64]

The crucial period in deciding the fate of Khrushchev's reforms appears to have been the year immediately following Kennedy's election. The first public criticism of Khrushchev's strategic doctrine came within a week and a half of Kennedy's victory, with the publication of Lieutenant-General Krasil'nikov's article "On the Character of Modern War" in the November 18 issue of *Krasnaia Zvezda*. Krasil'nikov criticized those who believed that the next war would be "a pushbutton war, which would be conducted without mass armies. . . . In the new war, massive multi-million man armies would without a doubt be participating, which would require large reserves of commanding personnel and vast contingents of soldiers." Other comments stated that, although the missile forces were becoming the most important element of the armed forces, this "does not at all mean the minimization of our ground forces."[65] Khrushchev was apparently feeling pressure from other groups besides the military. At a disarmament conference in Moscow, Jerome Wiesner and Walter Rostow—both appointees in the new administration—were approached by Foreign Ministry officials who told them that, if Kennedy went in for a massive rearmament program, the Soviet Union would be forced to react.[66] During January, 1961, several Soviet diplomats warned American officials that, if an agreement on disarmament were not reached soon, Khrushchev's position could be undermined by his internal opponents who, should they come to power, would be far less favorable to the West than Khrushchev was.[67]

The new administration, however, was indifferent to these overtures. In his State of the Union address on January 30, President Kennedy called for a speedup of the Polaris program and missile programs in general and the creation of "a Free World force so powerful as to make any aggression clearly futile."[68] Although Secretary of Defense McNamara stated at an informal news conference on February 6 that a review of intelligence had shown that there was no missile gap, this was quickly denied by Kennedy. The effect of the rhetoric over the "missile gap" in 1960 can be seen in McNamara's private recommendation to Kennedy that the total Minuteman program eventually be limited to only 800 missiles, not because that was the number needed but because that was "the minimum amount with which they might get by Congress."[69]

The acceleration of the Polaris program and Kennedy's quick denial of McNamara's comments of February 6 strengthened Khrushchev's opponents at home. In mid-February, Khrushchev was apparently recalled from an agricultural tour for a Presidium meeting in which his policies were sharply criticized, and his speeches immediately following this meeting were far more militant than those which had preceded it.[70] Kennedy continued to make good his campaign promise to reverse the "missile gap"; on March 28, he announced an expansion of the Minuteman program by 11 percent, from 540 to 600 missiles, and reiterated his intention to give the United States what amounted to a massive ICBM superiority over the Soviet Union.[71] Two months later, on May 25, he announced an increase in American defense spending of $3.4

million.[72] In the meantime, the United States had shown little interest in overtures made by Khrushchev in his April interview with Walter Lippmann, and pressure continued to mount in the Berlin crisis which had begun brewing in late February. During this period, Khrushchev's military policy continued to suffer attack by representatives of the armed forces.[73]

As U.S.-Soviet relations continued to deteriorate through the Vienna summit in June, Khrushchev came under pressure to halt the manpower reductions, which were then only half complete. On July 8, he announced in a speech to graduates of a military academy a suspension of the troop cuts and an increase in the Soviet military budget of 3.144 billion rubles (matching Kennedy's increase of $3.4 billion in May), stating, "These are forced measures, comrades. We are taking them owing to emerging circumstances. . . ."[74]

Although Khrushchev did not respond to further increases in the American military budget announced on July 25, his efforts at military reform were in a shambles by the end of the Berlin crisis. U.S. military expenditures had increased by almost $7 billion, and Kennedy was plainly going to continue the military buildup he had promised in his campaign and his State of the Union address.[75] On the Soviet side, Khrushchev's troop reductions had been suspended indefinitely, even though only half of the planned 1.2 million troops had been demobilized. In addition, Khrushchev had been forced to increase military spending, with most of the additional funds going to the conventional forces he was trying so hard to reduce. Given Kennedy's policies, it is difficult to see how Khrushchev could have preserved his program intact, even without the increased tensions caused by the Berlin crisis and the resumption of Soviet nuclear testing in September.

This partial reversal of Khrushchev's military policy was confirmed at the Twenty-second Party Congress in October. Both Marshal Malinovskii and General Epishev specifically referred to the measures of the previous July. Malinovskii especially noted the increased Soviet emphasis on conventional forces: "Although nuclear weapons will hold the decisive edge in a future war, we are nevertheless coming to a conclusion that the final victory . . . can be achieved only through combined operations by all branches of the armed forces. . . . under modern conditions any future war would be waged, despite enormous losses, by mass, many-millions-strong armed forces."[76] Thus, although Khrushchev was able to fend off any direct challenges to his leadership, he was unable to put his military policy back on course. He no longer had the authority to set military policy that he had had in early 1960.[77]

Numerous articles published the following spring showed continued military opposition to Khrushchev's manpower policies.[78] A demonstration of the strength of this dissent came with the publication in August, 1962, of Sokolovskii's *Military Strategy*—the first major work on Soviet strategy since the late 1920s—which included such statements as, "Soviet military strategy has concluded that, in spite of the extensive introduction of nuclear weapons, as well as the latest types of military equipment, a future war will require mass armed forces." In a direct challenge to the U.S. doctrine embodied in the Pentomic division and a backhanded slap at Khrushchev's view that "the number of greatcoats" did not determine the strength of an army, he asserted, "Consequently, we cannot fail to point out the complete groundlessness of modern bourgeois theories which advocate . . . the idea of waging war with small professional armies highly equipped."[79] The fact that prominent spokesmen for the army openly continued to advocate the need for mass armies—at the same time official Soviet policy maintained that the troop reductions had been only temporarily halted—showed they had support from a relatively strong faction within the Party which opposed Khrushchev's military policies.

The year following the Berlin crisis marked the low point of Khrushchev's influence over military policy. The situation was a stalemate in that opposing factions lacked the power to force an outright abandonment of his policy of minimum deterrence or to gain an increase in the size of the armed forces. This period came to a close at the end of 1962, when relations between the superpowers, at perhaps the lowest point since the Korean War, began to improve. While the Berlin crisis had brought a deterioration in U.S.-Soviet relations, both the United States and the Soviet Union were eager to reduce tensions in the aftermath of the Cuban missile crisis. Several diplomatic initiatives were begun which would bear fruit the following summer. Khrushchev's principal internal opponent, Frol Kozlov, was incapacitated by a stroke in April, and Khrushchev chose this particular time to launch an attack on waste in the defense establishment.[80]

Khrushchev's efforts at military reform, however, began to be overtaken by economic events. The 1962 harvest had been a poor one; furthermore, a drought in Central Asia had allowed wind erosion to destroy several million hectares of farmland in the "virgin lands" areas. By mid-year, it was already apparent 1963 was going to be an agricultural catastrophe, with the winter wheat crop virtually destroyed by drought.[81] According to Breslauer, Khrushchev "had helped build his authority during earlier years by launching grandiose projects and promising unprecedented results. His detailed supervision of agricultural affairs wedded his personal authority closely to that sector."[82] Although such diplomatic successes as the signing of the partial test-ban treaty, "hot-line," and other agreements in the summer of 1963 would normally have strengthened Khrushchev's authority, their effect was largely nullified by the impending agricultural disaster.

The military's rhetoric on the importance of "massive, multi-million man armies" increased in both volume and vehemence during this period, indicating that while its leaders felt a need to defend against a possible resumption of the troop reduction, they felt confident of sufficient support for their views to prevent any reprisals.[83] In his speech to the Supreme Soviet on December 13, Khrushchev called for both specific cuts in the military budget for 1964 and a resumption of the troop reductions suspended two years earlier. Although cuts in the formal military budget were approved three days later, no further mention was made of the issue of military manpower.[84] Articles opposing any further cuts continued to be published in both the military and the general press. Indeed, criticism of Khrushchev's military policy expanded to include his strategy of minimum deterrence; the chief of the general staff, Marshal Biriuzov, wrote in February that victory in modern war would go to the side which "not only masters the new weapons, but which takes the lead in producing missiles."[85] Apparently a sufficient number of Presidium members shared the military's views that, although Khrushchev issued further calls for reductions, none was to be implemented before his "retirement."

Khrushchev, however, continued fighting for his military policies to the very end. In a speech to a joint meeting of the Presidium and the Supreme Soviet on preliminary figures for the upcoming Five-Year Plan less than three weeks before he was removed, he stated, "Whereas the period of the first Five-Year Plans and in the postwar years we laid chief stress on the development of heavy industry as the basis for building up the economy of the entire country and on strengthening its defense capability, now . . . when the defense of the country is at a suitable level, the Party is setting the task of more rapid development of the sectors of the economy that produce consumer goods."[86] His statement that "the defense of the country is at a suitable level" would seem to imply that Khrushchev was even at that late date still seeking military reductions.

How much did the military or the issue of military policy contribute to Khrushchev's downfall? We agree with the majority of authors who place the primary responsibility on his failed economic policies.[87] Wolfe brings up a point not often mentioned, namely, that at the time of Khrushchev's ouster, the economic plans for 1966-70 were just starting to be drawn up.[88] Any delay in the decision to remove him could have tied the country to his agricultural policies, unsuccessful since 1962, for another five years, a consideration that was probably in the minds of those who engineered his "retirement." The issues of military manpower and military doctrine probably did not play much of a role in his removal. At the same time the military profited enormously from his retirement. Despite the nominal cut of 500 million rubles from the defense budget announced by Kosygin in December, 1964, the new leadership committed itself to a policy of strengthening the military. The troop cuts of 1960 were reversed, and the Soviet Union wholeheartedly entered the arms race.[89]

Conclusion

The extent of the changes in Khrushchev's military policy implemented by his successors is readily apparent. Soviet conventional forces increased from 147 divisions in 1965 to over 168 by 1975, and total military manpower increased by over 1 million during the same period. Soviet strategic forces grew from 190 ICBMs to over 1,500 by 1971.[90]

Given the preceding evidence, we can draw several conclusions from Khrushchev's efforts at military reform. First, the international situation is decisive in determining whether or not reform—at least along the lines of minimum deterrence—can occur. Although detente does not guarantee any reduction in the Soviet military, the absence of detente precludes any such reform from taking place. Also, the international environment must continue to be favorable for such a reform to survive; throughout the Khrushchev period there was a negative correlation between U.S.-Soviet tension and Khrushchev's success in his efforts. If the military perceives that the international situation or military balance is deteriorating, it will publicize its views in an attempt to halt any reform or reductions.

Second, would-be reformers must be successful in their domestic policies. Poor economic performance would seriously discredit the responsible faction. In such a situation, the opposition that would inevitably arise would be likely to embrace wholeheartedly the military's criticism of the leader's defense policies. The resulting coalition of military and political opponents would probably be strong enough to preclude any further military reform.

Third, a military reform does not necessarily imply political reform; witness the campaign to increase the role of the MPA in 1958. Eliminating open military opposition through the reimposition of political controls would perhaps facilitate military reform by making it difficult for the army to publicize its views. Any resulting reductions, however, implicitly would be politically counterreformist, regardless of the results achieved.

Khrushchev's experience also carries implications for any plans Gorbachev may have for eventual military reforms. Gorbachev needs to achieve success in his drive for productivity and other campaigns before he can realistically attempt to deal with the military-industrial complex. He must provide some hope that there is, indeed, a possible solution to the Soviet Union's economic woes and also create an "aura of success" associated with his policies before he can garner the support necessary to overcome objections by the military.

Overall U.S.-Soviet relations will play the key role in determining the feasibility of any attempts at military reductions. While the U.S. military buildup may continue, at its present pace it does not represent a serious threat to Soviet security as did Kennedy's in 1961. As long as the U.S. buildup continues to be primarily a matter of force modernization rather than a wholesale increase in the size of the U.S. military, the major external influence on Soviet military policy will come from the diplomatic sector rather than the military balance.

The eventual effect of the Strategic Defense Initiative (SDI), however, remains to be seen. The last technological leap in the arms race—the development of nuclear missiles—made deterrence possible at much less cost, and much of what Khrushchev said about the relative importance of various branches of the military had its echos in NATO's nuclear policies. SDI, on the other hand, promises greater protection but only at much greater cost.

While SDI remains in an experimental stage, its impact on U.S.-Soviet relations could be minimal, assuming that it is eventually used as a bargaining chip for arms accords. As deployment nears, however, the military implications of SDI will predominate. The Soviet Union will be forced to counter, and whichever route it takes—be it a massive ICBM buildup designed to swamp U.S. defenses or the deployment of its own Star Wars—the cost will put a great strain on the Soviet economy. Under such circumstances, the Soviet leadership may decide to shelve any plans for economic and political reform and choose to muddle through under its current system, which is at least predictable. In the absence of an agreement, SDI may become the decisive element in any argument over Soviet military reform, as was President Kennedy's buildup in 1961.

NOTES

1. *Strategic Survey 1984-85* (London, 1985), p. 43.
2. Marshall I. Goldman, "Gorbachev and Economic Reform," *Foreign Affairs* 64 (1985):56-73, particularly pp. 61-62.

3. Thomas W. Wolfe, *Soviet Strategy at the Crossroads* (Cambridge, Mass., 1964), pp. 88-91.

4. Although each of the phases appears to be characterized by distinctly different approaches to reform, they overlap to some extent during the transition from one to the next.

5. Lester A. Sobel, ed., *Russia's Rulers: The Khrushchev Period* (New York, 1971), p. 44; A. A. Gromyko and B. N. Ponomarev, eds., *Soviet Foreign Policy, 1945-1980* (Moscow, 1981), pp. 235, 646-47. See also Earl R. Brubaker, "The Opportunity Costs of Soviet Conscripts," in *Soviet Economic Prospects for the Seventies, Papers Submitted to the Joint Economic Committee, Congress of the United States, 27 June 1973* (Washington, D.C., 1973), Table 3, p. 167; Lincoln P. Bloomfield, Walter C. Clemens, Jr., and Franklyn Griffiths, *Khrushchev and the Arms Race* (Cambridge, Mass., 1966), p. 100; and *The Military Balance 1972-1973* (London, 1972), p. 74.

6. Roy Medvedev, *Khrushchev* (Oxford, 1982), pp. 72-76.

7. David Holloway, *The Soviet Union and the Arms Race* (New Haven, Conn., 1984), pp. 24-25.

8. The strength of the Soviet army dropped from approximately 12 million near the end of World War II to a low of 2.9 million following the completion of demobilization in 1948. Military manpower then began to grow again in 1951, apparently in reaction to the Korean War. Demobilization of these additional forces did not begin until Khrushchev's troop reductions of 1955. See Field Marshal Erich von Manstein, "The Development of the Red Army, 1942-1945," in *The Red Army*, ed. B. H. Liddell Hart (New York, 1956), pp. 140-52, particularly p. 148, and J. G. Godaire, "The Claim of the Soviet Military Establishment," in *Dimensions of Soviet Economic Power: Hearings, Joint Economic Committee, Congress of the United States* (87th Cong., 1st sess.) (Washington, D.C., 1962), p. 43.

9. *Combined Arms Warfare,* instructional booklet printed by the Historian, Command and Staff Department, U.S. Army Armor School (Ft. Knox, Ky.), pp. 144-45. See also Nikita Khrushchev, *Khrushchev Remembers,* ed. Strobe Talbott (Boston, 1974), p. 13, for Zhukov's support of the initial troop reductions.

10. Harriet Fast Scott and William F. Scott, *The Armed Forces of the U.S.S.R.* (Boulder, Colo., 1981), p. 305.

11. In addition to the 19- to 21-year-old male contingent, the Soviet armed forces would include a large number of long-term officers and a smaller number of noncommissioned officers (over 640,000 officers in 1964). See Brubaker, "Opportunity Costs," and Edgar O'Ballance, *The Red Army: A Short History* (New York, 1964), p. 214. In addition, the term of service for the air force, navy, and Strategic Rocket Forces (created after 1959) was four years, not three. These branches accounted for 1,080,000 troops, or about 30 percent of Soviet military strength in 1964. Compare with *The Military Balance, 1964-1965* (London, 1964), pp. 3-5.

12. This argument is most often use to explain the troop reductions of 1960 and 1963. See Jutta Tiedke and Stephan Tiedke, "The Soviet Union's Internal Problems and the Development of the Warsaw Treaty Organization,"

in *Soviet Foreign Policy: Its Social and Economic Conditions,* ed. Egbert Jahn (New York, 1976).

13. Basile Kerblay, *Modern Soviet Society* (New York, 1983), p. 55; Gail Warshofsky Lapidus, *Women in Soviet Society: Equality, Development, and Social Change* (Berkeley and Los Angeles, 1978), p. 166.

14. John F. Kantner, "The Population of the Soviet Union," in *Comparisons of the United States and Soviet Economies: Papers Submitted by Panelists Appearing before the Subcommittee on Economic Statistics of the Joint Economic Committee, Congress of the United States* (Washington, D.C., 1960), p. 33; Tiedtke and Tiedtke, "The Soviet Union's Internal Problems," p. 137.

15. Lapidus, *Women in Soviet Society,* p. 166.

16. George W. Breslauer, *Khrushchev and Brezhnev as Leaders: Building Authority in Soviet Politics* (London, 1982), pp. 69-70.

17. Godaire, "Claim," p. 43; David Shishko, *Defense Budget Interactions Revisited* (The RAND Corporation, P-5882, 1977), Appendix A.

18. Under Khrushchev, the Soviet Union also moved from a program emphasizing a strong surface fleet and replaced it with one concentrating on submarines as the preferred weapon for war "under modern conditions." See Roman Kolkowicz, "The Military," in *Interest Groups in Soviet Politics,* ed. H. Gordon Skilling and Franklyn Griffiths (Princeton, N.J., 1967), and Wolfe, *Soviet Strategy,* pp. 183-86.

19. H. S. Dinerstein, *War and the Soviet Union* (Westport, Conn., 1962), pp. 152-63. See also Robert M. Slusser, "The Presidium Meeting of February 1961: A Reconstruction," in *Revolution and Politics in Russia,* ed. Alexander and Janet Rabinowitch (Bloomington, Ind., 1972), pp. 281-92.

20. Disbanding any of the cadre units would have necessitated the elimination of several officers. For an example of the outcry which could result, see Roman Kolkowicz, *The Soviet Military and the Communist Party* (Princeton, N.J., 1967), pp. 153-55.

21. Dinerstein, *War and the Soviet Union,* p. 220. For the similarity to later opposition, see Matthew Gallagher, "Military Manpower: A Case Study," *Problems of Communism* 13 (May-June, 1964):53-62.

22. Major Robert A. Doughty, *Leavenworth Paper No. 1: The Evolution of U.S. Army Tactical Doctrine, 1946-76* (Fort Leavenworth, Kans., 1979), p. 16.

23. Part of NATO defense plan 14/2 adopted in March, 1957. David C. Isby and Charles Kamps, Jr., *Armies of NATO's Central Front* (London, 1985), p. 15.

24. Robert P. Berman and John C. Baker, *Soviet Strategic Forces: Requirements and Responses* (Washington, D.C., 1982), p. 133.

25. Barry M. Blechman and Stephen S. Kaplan, *Force without War* (Washington, D.C., 1978), pp. 26-36, 94-105, especially Figure 2-1 on p. 31 and Table 4-9 on p. 104. For Khrushchev's views on Dulles's "brinksmanship," see Khrushchev, *Khrushchev Remembers,* pp. 362-64.

26. Public references to policy conflict between Khrushchev and the military are relatively scarce prior to Zhukov's ouster in October, 1957. Some of the differences between Khrushchev and the military are inferred from the re-

movals of Admiral Kuznetsov and Marshal Zhukov and by observing the opposition to Khrushchev's manpower policy in 1960-64.

27. "Professionalism" in the context of this paper refers primarily to the role of the military as the sole source of "expert knowledge" on the "management of violence" (to use Samuel P. Huntington's phrase).

28. According to the text, *Soviet Military Strategy*, military doctrine "determines over-all policy in principle, while military strategy, starting from this over-all policy, develops and investigates concrete problems touching upon the nature of future war, the preparation of a country for war, the organization of the armed forces, and the methods of warfare." V. D. Sokolovskiy, Marshal of the Soviet Union, *Soviet Military Strategy*, ed. Harriet Fast Scott (New York, 1975), p. 40.

On the significance of the distinction between "military doctrine" and "military strategy" in Soviet military debates, see Herbert S. Dinerstein, *The Revolution in Soviet Strategic Thinking* (The RAND Corporation, RM-1927, June 24, 1957), especially pp. 9-12, 14.

29. Kolkowicz, *The Soviet Military*, pp. 134-36; Medvedev, *Khrushchev*, pp. 122-23; Khrushchev, *Khrushchev Remembers*, p. 14.

30. See Timothy Colton, *Commissars, Commanders, and Civilian Authority* (Cambridge, Mass., 1979), pp. 175-95. As evidence against any treasonous activities on the part of Zhukov, Colton points to the fact that he was assigned other work and not retired until March, 1958; that he was never demoted or arrested; that he was allowed to publish his memoirs after Khrushchev's ouster; and that he was given full military honors at his burial in 1974.

31. Dinerstein, *War and the Soviet Union*, pp. 144, 215-16.

32. Medvedev, *Khrushchev*, p. 264, n. 4; Khrushchev, *Khrushchev Remembers*, pp. 26-27.

33. R. L. Garthoff, *The Role of the Military in Recent Soviet Politics* (The RAND Corporation, RM-1638, March, 1956), pp. 26-28.

34. For an example of Zhukov's unorthodox behavior, see Brzezinski and Huntington's discussion of his Leningrad speech of July 1957. Zbigniew Brzezinski and Samuel P. Huntington, *Political Power: USA/USSR* (New York, 1963), pp. 349-50.

35. This could also explain why Khrushchev did not dismiss Marshal Malinovskii as minister of defense when the latter began to oppose his military policies in 1960-61.

36. For discussion of the "Stalingrad Group" and a list of its "members," see Kolkowicz, *The Soviet Military*, pp. 224-78, 362-69. Kolkowicz lists thirty-two "members" of the Stalingrad Group, most of whom rose to high positions under Khrushchev.

37. Ibid., pp. 224-78, 362-69; Garthoff, *The Role of the Military*, pp. 58-72, especially pp. 62-66. Beginning in 1955, several references were made to Khrushchev's role as a political officer during the war, possibly in an attempt to increase his prestige within the military.

38. Different sources give varying dates for the start of this campaign. Kolkowicz places it with the "Resolution of the Improvement of Party-political

Work in the Soviet Army and Navy," adopted by the plenum in October, 1957. Kolkowicz, *The Soviet Military*, pp. 134, 139. Michael Deane states that "a campaign to increase the influence of the Party and the authority of the political officers . . . was launched in February 1958." Michael J. Deane, *Political Control of the Soviet Armed Forces* (New York, 1977), p. 67.

39. Colton, *Commissars*, p. 49. Colton postulates that the MPA and its predecessors played the role of ideological watchdog for only a short time during and after the civil war, and then it took on a new role as part of the overall military administration.

40. Garthoff, *The Role of the Military*, pp. 38-39.

41. Kolkowicz, *The Soviet Military*, pp. 129-34. The quotation is on p. 131.

42. Colton, *Commissars*, p. 73.

43. Kolkowicz, *The Soviet Military*, pp. 137-42.

44. Sobel, *Russia's Rulers*, p. 152.

45. Kolkowicz, *The Soviet Military*, p. 144. The Soviet term for this is *edinonachalie* (one-man command), where the unit commander has full authority and does not have to refer to a commissar or political deputy for authority. See Colton, *Commissars*, pp. 14-15.

46. Quoted in Kolkowicz, *The Soviet Military*, pp. 142-47.

47. For a discussion of this, see Gallagher, "Military Manpower."

48. Colton, *Commissars*, pp. 14, 33.

49. Ibid., pp. 85-114.

50. Some sources give a total deployment of only four of the SS-6 "Sapwoods." See Holloway, *Soviet Union*, p. 43.

51. Leo Gruliow, ed., *Current Soviet Policies III: The Documentary Record of the Extraordinary Twenty-first Congress of the Communist Party of the Soviet Union* (New York, 1960), p. 5.

52. According to testimony by the commander of the Air Research and Development Command, General Bernard A. Schriever, before the Senate Armed Services Committee in February of 1960, "There is a lead-time of anywhere from 24 months to 30 months involved from the time you make the decision to get additional missiles into the inventory until they are actually there." U.S. Congress, Senate Armed Services Committee, *Missiles, Space, and Other Major Defense Matters*, Hearings on February 2, 3, 4, 8, 9 and March 16, 1960 (Washington, D.C., 1960), p. 56.

53. George Lowe, *The Age of Deterrence* (Boston, 1964), pp. 182, 196.

54. Local officials achieved these results only at great cost and through such subterfuges as slaughtering milk cows and breeding stock and illegally procuring cattle from neighboring regions. By 1960, the resources of Riazan' and other regions using the "Riazan' methods" were exhausted. Riazan' itself was able to produce only 30,000 tons of its quota of 180,000 tons. Soviet meat production did not match the 1959 level again until after 1964. Roy Medvedev and Zhores Medvedev, *Khrushchev: The Years in Power* (New York, 1976), pp. 96-101.

55. Speech by Khrushchev to the Supreme Soviet on January 14, 1960, in *Russia's Rulers*, ed. Sobel, p. 202.

56. Arnold Horelick and Myron Rush, *Strategic Power and Soviet Foreign Policy* (Chicago, 1966), p. 72.

57. Kolkowicz, *The Soviet Military,* pp. 150-51.

58. Carl A. Linden, *Khrushchev and the Soviet Leadership, 1957-1964* (Baltimore, 1960), p. 93, n. 3 (emphasis added).

59. O'Ballance, *The Red Army,* p. 214.

60. Medvedev, *Khrushchev,* p. 137.

61. Kolkowicz, *The Soviet Military,* pp. 154-55.

62. Alexander Werth dates the beginning of the decline of detente in 1960 from Christian Herter's hard-line speech in Chicago on April 4, 1960. Alexander Werth, *Russia under Khrushchev* (New York, 1962), pp. 294-311.

63. See note 54.

64. Sobel, *Russia's Rulers,* pp. 185-89.

65. Quoted in Kolkowicz, *The Soviet Military,* p. 160.

66. John Prados, *The Soviet Estimate* (New York, 1982), p. 116.

67. Slusser, "Presidium Meeting," p. 289.

68. Robert M. Slusser, "The Berlin Crises of 1958-59 and 1961," in Blechman and Kaplan, *Force without War,* p. 405.

69. Quoted in Prados, *The Soviet Estimate,* pp. 114-15. Doubt about the validity of American fears of the missile gap were made public as early as January, 1959.

70. Slusser, "Presidium Meeting," pp. 282-88.

71. Robbin F. Laird and Dale R. Herspring, *The Soviet Union and Strategic Arms* (Boulder, Colo., 1984), p. 94.

72. Raymond L. Garthoff, *Soviet Military Policy* (New York, 1966), p. 115.

73. For example, see Colonel A. M. Iovlev's article, "New Technology and Mass Armies," in *Krasnaia Zvezda,* April 5, 1961, quoted in *Current Digest of the Soviet Press* 13, no. 13 (April 26, 1961):8-9.

74. Robert M. Slusser, *The Berlin Crisis of 1961* (Baltimore, 1973), pp. 51-55.

75. Ibid., pp. 80, 370.

76. Charlotte Saikowski and Leo Gruliow, eds., *Current Soviet Policies IV: The Documentary Record of the Twenty-second Congress of the Communist Party of the Soviet Union* (New York, 1962), p. 157.

77. Although sheer speculation, it is possible the decision to increase missile deployments for 1963 was made at this time rather than in the aftermath of the Cuban missile crisis a year later. A decision for increased production at this time would have given Soviet industry more time to react than one made the following November. See also note 52.

78. See, for example, *Current Digest of the Soviet Press* 14, no. 22 (June 27, 1962):14.

79. Sokolovskiy, *Soviet Military Strategy,* p. 207.

80. Kolkowicz, *The Soviet Military,* pp. 292-93.

81. Medvedev and Medvedev, *Khrushchev,* pp. 121ff.

82. Breslauer, *Khrushchev and Brezhnev,* p. 108.

83. Even Epishev, who as head of the MPA was supposedly the primary

defender of the Party within the military, was calling attention to the need for a large conventional army despite—or, rather, as a result of—the "Revolution in Military Affairs," brought about by the development of nuclear weapons. *Voprosy istorii,* no. 2 (1963):10, quoted in Deane, *Political Control,* p. 108. For a detailed discussion of the military manpower debate, see Gallagher, "Military Manpower."

84. Sobel, *Russia's Rulers,* p. 326.

85. Marshal S. Biriuzov, "A New Stage in the Development of the Armed Forces and Tasks of Indoctrinating and Training Troops," *Kommunist Vooruzhennykh Sil,* no. 4 (1964):18, cited in Thomas W. Wolfe, *Soviet Strategic Thought in Transition* (The RAND Corporation, P-2906, 1964), p. 15.

86. Thomas W. Wolfe, *The Impact of Khrushchev's Downfall on Soviet Military Policy and Detente* (The RAND Corporation, P-3010, 1964), p. 9.

87. See Medvedev and Medvedev, *Khrushchev,* p. 169.

88. Wolfe, *Impact,* pp. 8-9.

89. The question still remains: was Khrushchev still fighting for a "minimum deterrent" until the end of his tenure? His assertion in October of 1964 that "the defense of the country is at a suitable level" at a time when the United States had a 4–1 superiority in ICBMs indicates he pursued to the very end a policy aimed at obtaining "sufficiency" rather than superiority or parity. The decision to undertake a massive strategic arms buildup was made by the collective leadership which succeeded him.

90. *Soviet Armed Forces Review Annual,* ed. David R. Jones (Gulf Breeze, Fla., 1977-1986), 2:6-7; Pardos, *The Soviet Estimate,* p. 187.

Gorbachev and the Politics
of System Renewal

TIMOTHY J. COLTON

Mikhail S. Gorbachev has pledged himself to the lofty goal of revitalizing a society of nearly 300 million people. After a hesitant start, he has cast himself as an advocate of far-reaching reforms in the Soviet economy, in communications and culture, and, most fascinatingly, in political institutions. In pursuing change, he generates an electricity absent from the main circuits of Soviet politics for a generation. As supporters rhapsodize about being "born anew in this exciting time of triumph of truth," Gorbachev has gone so far as to profess that the U.S.S.R. has entered a "Renaissance epoch."[1]

We know, however, that, in Russia, as elsewhere, things are not always as they appear. We also know that it is far too soon to reach a final judgment on Gorbachev. The best we can do for now is explain how he and the Soviet elite arrived where they are, examine the main elements of his platform, and assess its prospects.

Change, Succession, and Crisis

Gorbachev and the Action Cycle of Soviet Politics

Gorbachev is best placed in the cycle of action and reaction repeated by the Soviet regime since 1917. Revolutions from below and above, with a lapse in the 1920s, built the Soviet system roughly as we know it. Joseph V. Stalin in the mid-1930s wrenched the Soviet elite toward maintenance of the system. Nikita S. Khrushchev in his ebullient way strove to humanize and adapt Stalin's construction, after which Leonid

Reprinted from Seweryn Bialer and Michael Mandelbaum, eds., *Gorbachev's Russia and American Foreign Policy* (1988), pp. 151-86, by permission of the East-West Forum, a program of the Samuel Bronfsman Foundation, and of the Westview Press, Boulder, Colorado.

I. Brezhnev's approach was one of conservative restoration. Now, under Gorbachev, the reform impulse returns to the fore.

Historical circumstances have made it difficult for Gorbachev to pick up where Khrushchev left off. The institutions Gorbachev intends to modernize were bolted into place by a single-minded tyrant a half-century ago. Stalin's "great retreat" into policy and organizational conservatism coincided with a singularly brutal purge of the Soviet elite. The more plebeian and more malleable managers whom he substituted for the builders of the system were so young that many were to remain in place until the 1980s. Just enough of a relic to be tinged with revolutionary idealism, Khrushchev possessed the decency to begin a reformation after 1953 but lacked the shrewdness and the power to bring it off. He undeified Stalin and emptied the Gulag, only to be entrapped by his own contradictions and humiliated by his own lieutenants. His premature departure left the field to the very managers, then in middle age, whom Stalin had groomed to run his machine without asking questions.

For sheer consistency, Brezhnevism was without equal in Soviet history. Brezhnev had eighteen years in power to Stalin's twenty-nine, but Stalin used up and cast aside his creatures at will, whereas Brezhnev swore by "respect for cadres" and was content to let associates carry on almost into dotage. In policy, where Stalin moved by lurches, Brezhnev inched along one line, conservative and technocratic. From top to bottom, his establishment entered the 1980s in a state of physical exhaustion, fixed in its ways, and vulnerable to attack.

Gorbachev is thus seizing a golden opportunity when he accuses his predecessor of fostering "an artificial stability" and putting in abeyance "the inflow of fresh forces . . . the constant renewal . . . demanded by life." In both personnel and policy, Gorbachev has been able to say that a "forced change" has become unavoidable and that he, Gorbachev, is its agent.[2]

The catalyst of change, as has been the case so often in the past, has been political succession. The choice of a leader is fraught with uncertainty in a one-party state that lacks such institutions as free elections, constitutional limits on terms of office, and impartial courts to settle disputes. The rivals' need to vie for support makes it easier for muffled voices to be heard and for policy to be redirected. With Brezhnev in the 1960s the turn was to no-change. With Gorbachev, as with Khrushchev, the change is to change.

The three mini-successions of 1982 to 1985, and the complications arising from the lingering deaths of Brezhnev, Iurii V. Andropov, and

Konstantin U. Chernenko, shrouded the transition in conspiracy and suspense. But this counted less in the end than that power was grabbed by a younger, stronger General Secretary who was eager to act on the problems that beset his country.

The Crises of Effectiveness and Coherence

Gorbachev has come to portray those problems in stark terms indeed. In speeches in early 1987, he spoke of "the danger of the growth of crisis phenomena" in the U.S.S.R. and of "a condition of stagnation and somnolence, threatening society with ossification and social corrosion." He has since used a clinical analogy that implies a Soviet pathology: "Problems have to be solved and diseases have to be cured. If you drive a disease into an organism's depths, the disease only worsens."[3]

At its origin, "crisis" is a medical term, referring to a turning point at which the patient's health either snaps or recovers. If, strictly speaking, a crisis calls into question survival in the short term, the Soviet Union is not in critical condition. The Party has had little cause to fear overthrow by army coup or crowds in the streets. There has been nothing comparable to the Gulag mutinies of the 1950s or the Polish outbreaks of 1970, 1976, and 1980.[4]

Seweryn Bialer identifies a different phenomenon, one much closer to what Gorbachev seems to have in mind, when he writes of the regime's "crisis of effectiveness."[5] The Soviet system may be said to face such a crisis in several senses. Many of its practical problems have worsened in recent years. There has been a growing awareness of the seriousness and interrelatedness of the problem, but the response of most Soviets has been apathy rather than outrage. And the ineffectiveness of the regime has been weighed not against the traditional aspirations of its citizens alone but also against the performance of other countries, particularly the capitalist democracies.

Ineffectiveness is most easily measured in economics. The familiar story of two decades of waning rates of growth of Soviet national income, technology and productivity, and living standards, with a steeper fall after 1975, need not be repeated here. "Social corrosion," also highly visible, takes forms from alcohol abuse to higher infant mortality, anomie of the Soviet youth, and ethnic conflict. Internal ailments have implications for national security, power, and prestige, so much so that proponents of reform almost always appeal to these values. It is becoming more difficult for the Soviets to sustain their present foreign commitments, much less to expand them as did Brezhnev at his height.

If Western analysts have been alert to the crisis of effectiveness, they have said less about what I would call the emerging "crisis of coherence" of the regime. The issue here is neither the robustness of core institutions nor their efficiency as policy instruments. The crisis of coherence is about integration. It is manifested in the decline in the Soviet state's capacity to bring consistency to disparate behaviors and attitudes, to prevent the transfer of citizens' affection and effort to alternate structures, and to exercise collective wit. It is as slow to ripen as the crisis of effectiveness and as insidious in the long run.

Liberal historians have long identified "two Russias," one official and attached to the mighty state and the other unofficial and popular. Even high Stalinism could not stamp out society's underground life, some of which then gained acceptance during de-Stalinization.[6] In Brezhnev's time, it could be argued, the duality of Soviet society was reasserted. The rulers, eschewing mass terror but unwilling to make the adaptations needed to keep in step with the ruled, permitted, stimulated, and at times forced them to ply extra-systemic channels in order to gratify individual and group desires. By default and stealth, the U.S.S.R. acquired the rudiments of a civil society, but one nestled in the interstices of the state.

The slide toward dualism under Brezhnev might be thought of as a recourse to what Albert Hirschman in his well-known study *Exit, Voice, and Loyalty* calls the "exit option" for dealing with stressful social or political situations. As Hirschman shows, disaffected individuals and their leaders alike may see in escape from such a situation (by migration, for example) an attractive alternative to both passive acquiescence and political action to amend the status quo. The exit option, however, has paradoxical effects. It may keep the peace, yet at the price of depriving the dominant system of the talents of many able persons and of postponing a reckoning with the source of stress.[7]

In the Soviet Union in recent decades, the most egregious displays of exiting behavior have been the spread of the "second economy" (which operates through black markets and non-monetary exchanges) and of official corruption (which feeds on the second economy). The world of ideas saw the rise of dissent in the 1960s and, following its muzzling by the KGB, the creation of a shadow culture, the emigration of leading writers, and the souring of the young on politics. In personal relations, critics write of a seeping increase in "double morality" (*dvoinaia moral'*) and "divided consciousness" (*razdvoennoe soznanie*), in which individuals pay lip service to approved values while scoffing at them in action.

A more elusive symptom of the incoherence of the Soviet system has to do with the system's ability to understand itself and its problems.

The crux of the matter is the impoverishment of communication by means of secrecy, compartmentalization, oversimplification, and sometimes lies. Carried out in the name of political control, this was a badge of Stalinism, decreased but not eliminated afterward. The Brezhnev oligarchy, to be fair, gave experts in the bureaucracy and in think tanks more latitude than before to study and debate discrete issues. Yet it may have made overall coherence less by impeding the aggregation of such issues into larger patterns. It reconciled itself to the microscope of policy analysis but not to the telescope of social debate. Nor did it ever outgrow the reflex to cover up unpalatable facts bred into it under Stalin. When problems flared up in the mid-1970s, one of the Politburo's first reactions was to suppress the most damning statistics, such as those on infant deaths.[8]

The U.S.S.R.'s best and brightest have not reacted well to receiving only snippets of the truth. Most galling under Brezhnev was that, despite the greater technical proficiency and material privileges of the intelligentsia, the rationing of information remained at bottom arbitrary. A Soviet writer in 1981 pictured the intelligentsia as entangled in a web of "magical silences" and uncodified taboos more nettling than those in any primitive society. "They are slippery, and depend on the tastes, temperament, and tactics of the latest 'boss.'. . . They are capable of coming together into a system, but the system so far is incomplete and changes whenever the situation changes."[9]

The point is not so much that thinking persons feel unfairly treated as that haphazard and redundant checks sap their ability to work creatively, and thereby rob the state itself of the capacity to manage an increasingly complex environment. New technologies jar with old methods of control—as in the laboratories where researchers wait for weeks to photocopy materials indexed in seconds on computer screens.[10] The porousness of national frontiers and the globalization of knowledge creates its own kind of anomaly, making it harder to suppress inconvenient truths or to sustain some of the more preposterous myths once accepted unquestioningly.

The art of autobiography is as important to self-knowledge in societies as it is in individuals. By this criterion Brezhnevism let the country down badly. Although nostalgic fiction about the old Russia and memoirs of the Great Patriotic War of 1941-45 were equally in vogue, discussion of many facets of the country's history under Soviet rule was smothered. The halting of de-Stalinization made it virtually impossible to probe the politics of any period from Lenin's death in 1924 to the installation of Brezhnev forty years later. Stalin's barbarisms could be mentioned only elliptically, and the highest clearance was needed to print even the name of Khrushchev, whose years in power were encapsulated in buzzwords such as "subjectivism" and "voluntarism."

Only in art could a Soviet citizen allude to what many feared to be a tragic loss of societal memory. This theme was expressed in some of the best fiction of the late Brezhnev period, most movingly in *And the Day Lasts Longer than a Century,* the 1980 novel by the Kirgiz writer Chingiz Aitmatov. His hero, Edigei Zhangel'din, has partial amnesia because of a war wound, only dimly recalling that he came to live at a Kazakhstan whistle-stop because his peasant parents were uprooted by Stalin's farm collectivization. Aitmatov tells the fable of ancient inhabitants of the area who acquired robot-like slaves by torturing prisoners until their memories were erased. Astride a local burial ground is a launch pad for space vehicles, but the military-manned site is off limits to civilians and its rockets blast off unannounced. State secrecy is thereby reproducing the same kind of cognitive gap that has disabled Edigei and, in its extreme form, reduced the slaves to a subhuman existence.[11]

Memory damage, literary taboos, and the severe limits on social science were all testimony to how the Soviet system in the latter part of the Brezhnev era was being held back by a kind of failure of intelligence. The adaptations required by a mature industrial society were being retarded by the equivalent, for an entire society, of an individual's mental blockages and neuroses. Political innovation, as Hugh Heclo points out, has as a mainspring the ruminations of "men collectively wondering what to do."[12] Whatever its other merits and demerits, Brezhnev's Soviet Union was not good enough at wondering what to do.[13]

The Evolution of Gorbachev's Vision

If Mikhail Gorbachev has begun to deal with Soviet ills, he did not begin from a cogent blueprint for reform. A close ally, Aleksandr N. Iakovlev, has written that when the new rulers asked themselves which course to steer, they found themselves "unprepared to answer, either practically or theoretically."[14] This applies as well to Gorbachev as to anyone.

Gorbachev surely did have qualms about the status quo. They arose, he later said, while he was still the Party leader of Stavropol' Province in the 1970s. Like many who were then working "on the periphery," he said, he "saw the real processes taking place in society and came to feel that it was impossible to go on this way."[15] That negative judgment, however, did not spell out a definitive alternative. Had Gorbachev sought one openly, the aging Brezhnev would never have inducted him into the Party Secretariat in 1978 or into the Politburo two years later. Informal meetings with policy advisers may have helped with Gorbachev's education. So may have Andropov's fumblings toward change in 1982-84, though it is striking how little credit Gorbachev has since given Andropov for anything. But all these experiences were only preparatory. Gorbachev's real apprenticeship in reform occurred on the job.

"Acceleration" and "Putting Things in Order"

It is no slur on Gorbachev to say that at the time that he became General Secretary he was what the Hungarian economist, Janos Kornai, writing of economic change in communist countries, calls a "naive reformer," one who desired improvement yet bandied concepts about without working them through.[16] His main watchword in March, 1985, "acceleration" (uskorenie), was partly meant to exude a new, vigorous style after the pathetic interregnum of Chernenko and the preceding years of plodding government. In substance, it conveyed more interest in society's speed than in its destination.

Gorbachev spoke of acceleration in mostly economic terms: "The main question is how and at what cost the country can attain an acceleration in economic development . . . a quickening of growth tempos."[17] The achievement of his economic goals, he said, would depend primarily on technological modernization, which would be bought by shunting investment into civilian engineering. Since it would take some time for state-of-the-art machinery to be available, the government would have to make efficient use in the meantime of existing human and material resources: "During the first phase of the struggle for more rapid economic development, we can and must get an essential lift by putting things in order, by heightening labor, technological, and state discipline."[18]

"Putting things in order" meant enforcing and intensifying Andropov's crackdown on tardiness and sloppiness at work and on unauthorized revisions of state plans. It was strongly reflected in the May, 1985, decrees curbing the sales of alcohol. The virtues of orderliness and uskorenie were joined with power politics in Gorbachev's personnel policy. Leaders who had been in place for too long, he asserted, had become fat and complacent. They should either fall into line or "simply get out of the way."[19]

Gorbachev's reed-thin margin of victory in the Politburo dictated that his changes begin there. He scored a breakthrough at the April and July, 1985, plenums of the Central Committee, which ushered four new members into the Politburo. Fortified by their votes, he picked off his

adversaries one by one. Grigorii V. Romanov, Premier Nikolai A. Tikhonov, and the Moscow Party leader, Viktor V. Grishin (evidently his
main rival in March, 1985), fell in the first year. Dinmukhammed A.
Kunaev of Kazakhstan and Geidar A. Aliev, the top-ranking first deputy
premier, were retired from the Politburo in 1987. As members of the
Party's old guard were evicted, allies of Gorbachev were moved in. By
the time of Aliev's retirement in October, 1987, eight of the thirteen
full members of the Politburo had been brought into it during Gorbachev's tenure as General Secretary. At intermediate levels, Gorbachev
had had oversight of staffing since 1983. Once in power, and assisted
by a protégé (Georgii P. Razumovskii) who was now head of the Party's
personnel section, he began the biggest cold purge since Stalin.

The early Gorbachev invited innovation in economic and social policy. He was also vaguely receptive to institutional change, at least in
the economy. Beginning in April, 1985, he called for "restructuring
(*perestroika*) of the economic mechanism," which would marry better
central planning with administrative decentralization, along the lines
of experiments begun by Andropov. That summer he asserted that a
new mechanism could be functioning by the end of the year, an innocent
notion that mercifully sank without a trace.[20] Ideas and politics occupied
but a small niche in Gorbachev's early rhetoric. The major exception
was his fervent advocacy of *glasnost*, or openness of reporting and
discussion, but even this took a back seat to the economy. In one speech,
he saluted "our locomotive, our enormous state," hardly an image that
suggested responsiveness by the state to the citizen.[21]

The Greening of Gorbachev

Scholars who surveyed Gorbachev's first year could be forgiven for
seeing some modest potential for economic change but little else.[22] Only
the Twenty-seventh Party Congress, which convened in February, 1986,
gave an inkling that this view was premature. Gorbachev was now
willing to mount a frontal attack on Brezhnev and his illusion of "improving matters without changing anything." He broke new ground by
tying perestroika to all manner of institutions, not only economic, and
by alluding cryptically to improvements in "socialist democracy." On
his main subject, the economy, he used far tougher language than before:
"Our situation now is such that we cannot limit ourselves to partial
improvements—a radical reform (*radikal'naia reforma*) is necessary."
To this end, he demanded reexamination of ideological teachings about
property, planning, and prices.[23]

Gorbachev's most interesting changes of direction occurred after the

Party congress, although most were foreshadowed at it. They were evidently the outgrowth of both private reflection and interaction with events and forces in the public realm.

Two environmental triggers stand out. The first was what Gorbachev came to see as the selfish opposition to his proposed reforms by a bureaucracy that he increasingly characterized as a homogeneous class. The theme surfaced at the June, 1986, plenum of the Central Committee and at a private audience three days later with Soviet literary figures. To the writers, Gorbachev expounded bitterly on the stalling tactics of the entire "managerial stratum" (*upravlencheskii sloi*), which "does not want to lose rights connected with their privileges."

The very existence of a meeting with writers is related to the second change in the environment: Gorbachev's honeymoon with intellectuals whose hopes were being buoyed by glasnost'. In May, 1986, an impromptu insurrection from the ranks toppled the executive of the Union of Cinematographers and elected as head of the union Elem G. Klimov, a director whose best films had been bottled up by the censors under Brezhnev. Gorbachev's first personal intervention was his audience in June with the writers, at which he made a spirited pitch for their support. Several days later, the Union of Writers' congress selected a new, mostly reformist board.

From this point on, several new strands attained prominence in Gorbachev's rhetoric. Most noticeably, he adopted a far more exuberant vocabulary to portray reform, maintaining that change must be nothing short of "revolutionary." He also said with growing conviction that transformations must embrace all segments of society, encompassing "not only the economy but . . . social relations, the political system, the spiritual and ideological sphere."[24]

When he addressed a national conference of social scientists in October, 1986, Gorbachev emphasized yet another far-reaching point, that "new thinking" was a precondition of economic and social advance. Gorbachev's column of revolutionaries needed a road map, and this— and here we have a crucial synapse—could be drawn only in a climate of greater intellectual freedom. "The search for truth must be carried out through the juxtaposition of different points of view, through discussion and debate, through the breaking of former stereotypes. . . . It is necessary that everywhere things be arranged so that the people who are searching, creative, and in the vanguard of restructuring breathe more easily, work more fruitfully, and live better."[25]

The greening of Gorbachev, as it were, culminated in his marathon speech on political change to the January, 1987, plenum of the Central Committee, perhaps the most significant by any Soviet leader since

Khrushchev's 1956 "secret speech" about Stalin. He now argued explicitly that the malaise in the Soviet Union stems, not just from the country's state of hibernation after 1964, as had been the nub of his statements in 1985, but from genetic defects in the Stalinist model that were solidified under Brezhnev. "Theoretical notions about socialism remained largely at the level of the 1930s and 1940s, when our society faced quite different problems"; such "authoritarian" appraisals finally had to be reevaluated. Another high point of his report was his articulation of the idea of *demokratizatsiia,* democratization. "Only through democracy and thanks to democracy," he said in recommending electoral and other reforms, "is reconstruction possible."[26]

In sum, Gorbachev's diagnosis of Soviet problems has become increasingly biting and his prescriptions more ambitious. In a short time, he has moved from a preoccupation with growth rates, discipline, political staffing, and small policy adjustments to endorsement of much more comprehensive changes. "*The business of restructuring,*" he said in January, 1987, of his plans, "*has turned out to be more difficult, and the causes of the problems embedded in our society more profound, than we had imagined earlier.*" The more he and the Party examine the situation, "the more there move into view new, unresolved problems, left over as a legacy from the past."

Gorbachev in Action

Although Gorbachev has been scrupulous about telling the Soviet people that relief from their problems will come only after years of effort, he is well aware that the litmus test of leadership is deeds and results, not high-flown words.[27] It is appropriate to ask how he is faring thus far at converting his slogans into real reforms. The Gorbachev record is mixed. It blends traditional nostrums with ad hoc innovations and, in some fields, with bold attempts to alter major Soviet realities.

Wielding the Personnel Weapon

Aggressive exploitation of the General Secretary's prerogatives in the personnel area may be the least original of Gorbachev's achievements. But it has been indispensable to the creation of a reliable political machine and, in his eyes, to the reinvigoration of Soviet government.

So many heads had rolled by the time the Twenty-seventh Congress opened that 41 percent of the members of the Central Committee were newly elected. By Gorbachev's second anniversary in power, in March, 1987, he had removed 38 percent of the full and candidate members of the Politburo who had been in place when he began. Turnover over two years was 76 percent among the Central Committee secretaries and department heads, 64 percent in the Council of Ministers (73 percent in its Presidium), and 39 percent among regional first secretaries of the Party.[28] Almost all members of the "Dnepropetrovsk mafia" and of the several other subgroups of Brezhnev's coterie were pensioned off. In local districts and towns, some first secretaryships changed incumbents three or more times by early 1987.[29]

The shakeup has been rude by any measure, but it has been especially so when compared to the leisurely pace of elite transition during the previous two decades. In every sector, Gorbachev's rate of hiring and firing has been far more intense than during the Brezhnev-Chernenko eras, and has considerably exceeded turnover during the brief Andropov interlude, when Gorbachev himself was already behind many of the changes, particularly at the provincial level.[30]

Although Gorbachev has behaved deferentially toward some veteran Soviet politicians, he has also brought significant numbers of younger men into positions of responsibility. It is no small accomplishment that in two years the mean age of full and candidate members of the Politburo dropped from sixty-nine to sixty-five years (and to sixty-three years by October, 1987), of Central Committee secretaries and department heads from sixty-eight to sixty-one, and of members of the Council of Ministers from sixty-five to sixty (from sixty-nine to fifty-nine on the Presidium of the Council of Ministers).[31] There has been little rejuvenation at the provincial level, but one survey finds new district and town first secretaries to be on average only forty years old and adds that old-timers' places "are being taken by individuals who would do as their sons."[32]

A final aspect of personnel policy after March of 1985 was its intrusiveness. Gorbachev's new men were not only younger, more energetic, and better educated than the old guard, but they tended to have had fewer involvements with the organizations being placed in their hands. In terms of government departments, this meant that Gorbachev's new managers were either transferred laterally from other agencies or, more typically, had vaulted over several rungs on the job ladder. For positions of authority outside Moscow, Brezhnev's habit of promotion from within the locality was now said to be conducive to the establishment of independent satrapies. Gorbachev made more of an effort to import well-qualified outsiders, the majority from an expanded pool of "Central Committee inspectors." Soviet-style carpetbaggers, they were given marching orders to uproot local "protectionism," graft, and sloth.[33]

Gorbachev may take satisfaction from battering the bureaucracy, but this alone has not solved his problems. The data on turnover suggest, indeed, some second thoughts. When one analyzes Gorbachev's staffing changes over time, in every category they abruptly decline after the spring of 1986.[34] Gorbachev may also be having doubts about the practice of bringing in outsiders. Among regional party bosses in the Russian Republic, 63 percent of those appointed in his second year came from posts within the region and only 25 percent from Moscow; in the first year, only 12 percent were recruited locally with 81 percent coming in from Moscow.[35]

What accounts for this shift? The thinness of Gorbachev's own patronage base has been one reason, attributable to a career dominated by service in a single region (Stavropol') and a single policy area (agriculture). With few exceptions, he has had little luck at installing cronies in positions of influence.[36] He has thus had no alternative to striking accords with relatively independent politicians, most frequently from one of the provincial Party organizations. The newly prominent officials promoted from the Urals and western Siberia form the most conspicuous such group, numbering among them Tikhonov's successor as head of government (Nikolai I. Ryzhkov), the second-ranking Communist Party secretary (Egor K. Ligachev), and the new local Party chiefs in Kazakhstan (Georgii V. Kol'bin) and Moscow (Boris N. El'tsin).

Some degree of slowing down the pace was inevitable as Gorbachev moved down his "hit list" and established commitments to new appointees. He may well have reminded himself that Khrushchev antagonized his own men by constantly holding the threat of disgrace over their heads. He may also have discovered that new agents create enemies as well as enforce dictates—as happened most vividly with the Alma-Ata riots of December, 1986, the aftershock to Kol'bin's replacement of Kunaev in Kazakhstan. The backlash has been greatest when there is an ethnic component (Kunaev is a Kazakh, Kol'bin a Russian) or when the interloper "pushes his way through like a tank," to quote an article on the new breed of local Party secretary.[37]

It now appears that Gorbachev appreciates the danger that a harsh staffing policy can demoralize his entire bureaucracy. He continues to threaten to sack derelict officials "in front of the whole country"—and his May, 1987, ouster of Defense Minister Sergei L. Sokolov for negligence demonstrates his seriousness even toward the military. Gorbachev, however, now also admonishes his supporters that there shall be no "disrespectful attitude toward cadres in general" and no mechanical purging to please superiors or meet artificial circulation quotas.[38] He seems to have come to the conclusion that officials will not do better work simply out of fear and if public policies and larger structures are not also changed.

Economic Activism and Reform

The new leaders' first response to Soviet economic decay was a burst of policy activism that is quite respectable by recent Soviet and comparative yardsticks.[39] After an early emphasis on punitive measures—the most draconian having been the prosecution of corrupt officials and the May, 1986, prohibitions on "unearned income"—emphasis has shifted to more affirmative measures. Gorbachev's Politburo has increased capital investment, given priority to non-military technological modernization, and begun to supply schools and factories with microcomputers. Planners and managers are being pressured harder to deliver goods and services to the consumer. A single inspectorate now performs quality control in 1,500 large manufacturing plants. New rules allow farms to sell at market prices all produce above the requirements of the plan and even 30 percent of their prescribed quotas of meat, milk, eggs, fruit, and vegetables.

The most innovative policies have been those affecting small enterprise, foreign economic ties, and incomes. As of May, 1987, economic activity by individuals and family firms has been legalized for twenty-nine varieties of consumer goods and services. New regulations make the establishment of cooperative businesses easier; they can hire non-relatives and include up to fifty members. Decrees of September, 1986, and January, 1987, authorize a number of industrial entities to trade directly with foreign partners and establish the legal framework for joint commercial ventures on Soviet soil. The first moves were made in September, 1986, to force steep wage differentials based on productivity.

For all its vigor on policy specifics, the Gorbachev leadership in its first two years did not perform a general overhaul of the economic system or breach the traditional canons of state socialism in the manner of marketizers in Hungary and China. Many of the early decisions bore the mark of political compromise—the relaxation of controls on individual enterprise, for instance, requires most entrepreneurs to work normal hours at a state enterprise and allows them to take up their own work only in their spare time. On grand options for reform, a government commission on economic restructuring, chaired by Nikolai V. Talyzin, the new head of Gosplan, did work behind the scenes. The public debate over reform intensified in 1987, some participants even calling for a quick transition to a mixed economy, with minimal state planning, a large private sector, and integration into the global market. But Gorbachev concluded in June, 1987, that only "the first steps at assimilating new management methods" had been made.[40]

Beyond doubt, part of the problem has been with Gorbachev himself. In 1985-86 he forcefully called for higher economic quality, economic decentralization, and new ideas on planning, while simultaneously stressing rapid quantitative growth, administrative recentralization, and orthodox approaches to the plan. Conversely, Gorbachev's expressed views on the economy, as on so many issues, have become steadily more radical and his impatience with halfway solutions has grown. Policy aides, especially his chief economic adviser, Abel G. Aganbegian, have helped bring greater rigor to his economic approach.

After two years of delay, economic reform was given a large boost at a plenum of the Central Committee in June, 1987. It adopted a position paper on reform, approved the first major reform legislation (a "law on the socialist enterprise"), and promoted the new Party secretary for planning, Nikolai N. Sliun'kov, to the Politburo. Most importantly, Gorbachev's outline at the plenum of a "new management mechanism" marked a watershed in leadership thinking about economic change.

Gorbachev's statement was novel for its detailed timetable for the introduction of a reform package, all of the pieces of which are to be in place by 1991. It goes further than before in blaming the Soviet Union's economic stagnation on the Stalinist formula of mobilization from above, rather than only on poor tactics in the 1970s. It grants that reform might produce a temporary diminution of growth rates and observes that much of the low-quality growth in the unreformed system is useless. It dwells at length on agricultural decentralization through "family contracting" and on cooperatives, one of Gorbachev's genuine enthusiasms. Most remarkably, it makes the first forthright admission by any General Secretary of the need to incorporate market relations, based on the uncoerced interplay of supply and demand forces, into the core operations of the Soviet economy. The Soviets, he said, must achieve "the *systematic mastery and management of the market, with due regard for its laws,* and the strengthening and increase in the authority of the ruble," an objective which would be incalculably "more difficult than issuing commands and directives."[41]

There can be little doubt that Gorbachev remains ardently attached to a few irreducible economic components of socialism, chief among them being the predominance of state ownership, some type of planning, and a social safety net. While continuing to urge debate, he has also indicated that there must be limits to debate and change: "Some people have been suggesting things that go beyond the bounds of our system, and in particular that abandon the instrument of the planned economy. We have not gone that road and will never do so, because we are getting ready to strengthen socialism and not to replace it with a different system."[42]

Accordingly, Gorbachev's embrace of the market and its "laws" remains grudging, almost as if he finds it as distasteful a tonic as it is necessary. Although he may have provided a broad template for reform, much of its content remains unclear. It is far from certain what the real roles will be for powerful institutions such as Gosplan, the industrial ministries, and the banks. This is also true of the share of prices to float with supply and demand (there are to be centrally fixed and "negotiated" prices along with market prices), the volume of economic activity to be covered by the state orders (*zakazy*) that will replace physical plans, the place of the so-called state "control figures" (which some suspect will be the old physical targets smuggled in the back door), and the means of inducing competition among producers. It remains to be seen whether Gorbachev fully accepts the ramifications of the tradeoffs—between quality and quantity, individual and collective rights, and dynamism and security—built into his proposals.

As we watch the Soviets wrestle with these enormous issues, we must remember that changes short of total reform can nonetheless make a difference. Manipulations of policy such as the anti-egalitarian decrees on wages will affect tens of millions even if they do not change the economic system. The potential of marketization in the provision of consumer products, services, and food is also important, even if it is unmatched in other sectors. Gorbachev's interest in such a liberalization seems to have grown apace, regardless of where he stands on heavy industry, and he has justified it by invoking Lenin's New Economic Policy of the 1920s, which tolerated private farming and trade. Some spokesmen predict that individuals and cooperatives could account for 15 percent of the Soviet national income within a decade.[43]

As for comprehensive reform, the battle over it is probably barely joined. In Hungary, the most reformist of the East European countries, radical reform was discussed for fifteen years before being introduced in 1968, and two decades later it is still being debated and improved. In China, controversy has been continuous over the last decade and shows no signs of abating. In the Soviet Union, therefore, we can expect the struggle to go through numerous rounds in the 1990s and beyond. The removal of Talyzin from Gosplan in February, 1988, only one month after the new enterprise law began to take effect, is but the opening bell.

The Gorbachev Thaw

The precipitous thaw in communications, intellectual life, and the arts has already had greater impact than the episodic relaxations of the Khrushchev years. Gorbachev's glasnost' has been directed in part at placating interest groups—particularly the cultural and professional elites—and at using "the weapon of openness," as it is unabashedly described, to expose mismanagement and apply pressure to officials and others who resist his program. But the campaign has also been oriented to the neuropsychology of the Soviet system as a whole, to its collective capacity for comprehending its flaws and problems. Glasnost' short-circuits the unofficial communication networks which arise, as Gorbachev said in 1985, when citizens "hear one thing [in the official media] but see another in real life."[44] Most importantly, it gives the regime better antennae for tuning in to the society it governs, recognizing that, as Aleksandr Iakovlev puts it, "contemporary socialism must as a first priority get to know itself."[45]

Gorbachev's first opening gambit in this area was to promote less hidebound officials, from Iakovlev (now a Central Committee secretary and member of the Politburo) down to magazine editors and studio directors.[46] In the media, the newcomers have made tangible improvements in coverage of current events and social issues. The decision, albeit belated, not to stonewall on the Chernobyl' tragedy of April, 1986, was a turning point in the government press's treatment of natural and man-made disasters, about which Soviet citizens were always thought too immature to read. The press now provides more data about who officials are and how they make their decisions. In investigative reporting, taboo after taboo has been shattered—on describing drug addiction, unemployment and hoboism, statistical fraud, police brutality, neglect of invalids and orphans, emigration, and the special stores and clinics for officials, to name only a few. Subjects that were open to public discussion under Brezhnev, and there were many, are now examined with a less wooden protocol. Information about the world outside the Soviet Union can now be presented in a more neutral light.

The leaders have also sought to elicit greater candor and empiricism in the social sciences. Iakovlev has not minced words about the muzzling of sociology and other disciplines under Brezhnev: "enclaves closed to criticism," primitive techniques, the laying waste of theory by "a megatonnage of dogmatism."[47] Social scientists are now promised better statistics, both to improve their work and, as a *Pravda* essay said after the January, 1987, plenum, to win the trust of the public: "If you hide from people information about the general conditions of their own lives . . . you cannot expect their activation either in production or in politics."[48] Even the pages of *Kommunist,* the Party's dishwater-dull theoretical organ, have been opened to real-life controversies.

The effervescence under Gorbachev has been greatest in the arts, where pressure from below has played a greater role. Party policy here now ranges from keen approval of new currents to benign neglect. At Klimov's initiative, a number of movies suppressed by the Brezhnev regime have now been reviewed by a "conflict commission" of film-makers and industry management and given commercial distribution. In literature, works that had been consigned "to the drawer" for years, even decades, have been released in journal and book form. The 1986 upheavals in the cinematographers' and writers' unions have found lesser echoes among composers, architects, and painters.[49] Nor is the ferment only in high culture. Melodiya, the main state studio, now records rock bands reviled only a year or two earlier as the embodiments of Western decadence, and the Party youth league books them on tours. Some of the teenagers attending their concerts now sport purple hair and "heavy metal" gear.

The most stunning product of the thaw is the outburst of historical revisionism. Gorbachev, evidently out of both conviction and political calculation, was at first highly reluctant to encourage it. He implored intellectuals at his June, 1986, meeting with leading writers to stay away from Soviet history, saying it would only "set people at one another's throats." By early 1987, however, he had reluctantly accepted the need to fill in "forgotten names and blank spots" in the country's past.[50] In a carefully crafted speech on the seventieth anniversary of the Russian Revolution in November, 1987, Gorbachev proclaimed Stalin's "enor-mous and unforgivable" guilt for "wholesale repressive measures and acts of lawlessness," while also noting his "incontestable contribution to the building of socialism." He spoke with respect, if not total approval, of opponents of Stalin such as Nikolai I. Bukharin, whose economic and political program in the 1920s bore certain similarities to Gor-bachev's.[51] In February, 1988, in a decision of vast symbolic value, the Soviet Supreme Court legally rehabilitated Bukharin and the other victims of Stalin's last great show trial, in 1938.

The first works in two decades to confront the dark chapters of Soviet history began to appear in 1986, even before Gorbachev expressed his support. "Repentance," Tengiz Abuladze's brilliant anti-totalitarian film, shocked viewers with its surrealistic rendering of a dispute over disin-ternment of the body of a dead dictator, a powerful allegory of de-Stalinization. In February, 1987, the Union of Writers announced that Boris Pasternak had been posthumously reinstated in the union and that his great novel about the Russian Revolution, *Doctor Zhivago,* would finally be published in the U.S.S.R. in 1988, thirty years after it won for its author a Nobel Prize (for which Pasternak was hounded to his death at home). In October plans were revealed to publish in 1988 the late Vasilii Grossman's novel about World War II, *Life and Fate,* which explicitly compares Stalinism to Nazism.

Less sensational, but of enormous moment to Soviet audiences, have been other examples of the new history. A play by Mikhail Shatrov about the 1918 Brest-Litovsk treaty shows Bukharin and other Bolsheviks later to be liquidated by Stalin (and never rehabilitated by Khrushchev) as competent and honest; Stalin is portrayed as a boorish anti-intellectual who wants the Party to be "a closed order of sword-bearers." The terror of the 1930s is brought to life in Anatolii Rybakov's *Children of the Arbat,* which recounts arrests and fear in Moscow, and in Anna Akhmatova's posthumously published poem, "Requiem," telling of her vigil under "the stars of death," in front of the Leningrad prison in which her husband was executed. Vladimir Dudintsev's first novel in thirty years, *White Robes,* chronicles the persecution of geneticists in the late 1940s.[52]

Nikita Khrushchev is also emerging from the shadows. Gorbachev's November, 1987, speech for the first time lauded his role in debunking Stalin and promoting liberalization. Evgenii Evtushenko and other literary lions of the 1950s have recalled Khrushchev's courage and warm heart as well as his petulance and shallowness. An account of his 1957 dismissal of Marshal Georgii K. Zhukov reveals that officers eager to please him stooped so low as to try to slaughter the marshal's horse.[53]

It would be wrong to think that journalists, social scientists, and writers have been given complete freedom of expression. Few of them really believe this to be so. Important areas of taboos have survived— Kremlin politics, the contemporary KGB, and the saintly Lenin head the list. Censorship has not been abolished, and the works of most living émigré writers go unpublished.[54] Publications in the provinces, under the thumb of local bosses, remain far inferior to Moscow. Episodes such as the exclusion in July, 1987, of most reporters from the Chernobyl' trial underline the fact that, when it so wishes, the regime still decides what news is fit to print. And free assembly, a mode of expression taken for granted in the Western democracies, continues to have few defenders in the U.S.S.R.

Glasnost' has also given rise to a predictable backlash. At least a substantial minority of the population—24 percent in one sample of workers—believes it "does more harm than good."[55] Even some liberals are edgy, primarily out of fright that conservatives will be provoked. They have reached, as did Gorbachev in remarks to editors in July, 1987, for the old bromide of anathematizing "antisocialist" views. Critics, Gorbachev said, should question and probe, but "must not undermine socialism."[56] Such remarks are less a guide to the boundaries of debate than a reminder that boundaries continue to exist and, as in the past, it is up to the individual to find them by bumping up against them.

Most worrisome to the leadership has been the inflammatory tone of some of the journal and newspaper articles and letters, as well as television programs, in which participants have traded insults and impugned one another's motives. The problem, as Gorbachev not inaccurately told the editors, is largely one of culture: "We still do not have enough political culture, we still do not have the culture to carry out discussions, to respect the point of view even of a friend or comrade. . . . We are an emotional people."[57] As he surely realizes, a civic culture cannot be built by decree.

Supply Side Politics

Every political system enables some participation and also contains it within agreed-upon limits. In the Soviet Union, the regime's emphasis has always been on the latter part of the equation. Without eliminating restrictions, Gorbachev now wants to shift emphasis. He sees participation in much the way some pro-market economists saw the task of economic recovery in the United States in the early 1980s: as a matter of encouraging increased output by reducing state taxation.

Gorbachev, who gave short shrift to political change in his first months in office, had by 1987 moved "democratization," as he called it, to the top of his agenda. Gorbachev's political reforms, it must be emphasized, would not replicate Western-style democracy. The expansion of political competition and of the involvement of the populace in political decisions would take place, as he envisages it, within the framework of continued single-party rule. Like glasnost' in the media and the arts, Gorbachev's proposed political changes seem to have mostly instrumental value for the new Soviet leadership.

According to Gorbachev, his political changes would heighten the population's sense of identification with the regime and galvanize it to work hard. Order and discipline would be attained "at a higher level, based not on mindless or blind execution of orders but on participation of the members of society in all things." Participatory reform would also provide the authorities with new channels of information about community opinion and subject lower-level administrators to "control from below." Finally, it would act as "a guarantee of the irreversibility of restructuring." This is the most radical rationale, for it can only mean that Gorbachev sees the diffusion of power as a constraint on the regime: it will prevent a future Brezhnev from turning back the clock.[58]

The new approach is being put into effect in more than one way. To telegraph its seriousness, the regime has several times bowed to what it calls, in pre-1917 phraseology, *obshchestvennoe mnenie,* best translated as "educated public opinion." While some of the first concessions were symbolic, as with the August, 1986, decision to hold a contest to redesign an unusually ugly war monument in Moscow, some had real costs. The best example would be the discarding the same month of "the project of the century," the planned southward diversion of Siberian rivers, which was highly unpopular with Russian intellectuals but had been kept alive for twenty-five years by economic ministries.

A major aspect of Gorbachev's "supply side politics" is his encouragement of political activity by non-bureaucratic organizations based on voluntary effort. The Party itself has taken the initiative to establish new, foundation-like associations to foster popular involvement with causes such as preservation of historical buildings, contact with foreign cultures, and care of orphans and war veterans. It has tolerated the proliferation of non-political and political clubs in Moscow and other large cities, some of them with their own publications, without having decided whether to give them permanent legitimacy.[59] The regime has also shown new interest in resuscitating certain state organizations, especially those with a wide discrepancy between ceremonial and actual roles. In this category is the pyramid of government legislatures or "soviets"; a number of suggestions have been aired to make them livelier and less subservient to their executives. A related initiative is the June, 1987, law providing for public discussions and referenda on major issues, while leaving the final say on referenda to the government.

Gorbachev has been most supportive of electoral reform, a major deviation from precedent but one supported in the past by some Soviet scholars and tried in several other communist countries.[60] Gorbachev's wish, unveiled tentatively at the January, 1987, plenum, is for multi-candidate elections, conducted by secret ballot, of deputies to the soviets, Party secretaries, and factory directors and other economic supervisors.

The "economic democracy" provisions are the first to have been enacted. The June, 1987, enterprise law mandates that Soviet employees choose their own bosses, subject to confirmation by higher authority. It was adopted over publicly stated objections that it was legally suspect and politically pretentious.[61] In the soviets, a national experiment with multiple candidates—but not, to repeat, with multiple parties—was conducted in selected districts in June, 1987. Election of secretaries in the Party has been carried out thus far only at the prompting of such strongly pro-Gorbachev local leaders as Boris K. Pugo in Latvia. Intraparty democracy was the main agenda item of a special Nineteenth Party Conference, the first since 1941, in June-July, 1988.

If even partial political reforms are to go ahead, changes must be made in the Soviet system of justice. Arbitrary treatment by the police and courts is hardly an incentive to voluntary participation in public affairs, as the rulers fully understood when they politicized justice after the revolution.

It is intriguing, therefore, to see that a brisk debate about legal and judicial reform has erupted under Gorbachev, with a pronounced intensification, as in so many other fields, after mid-1986. Scholars and journalists (led by two combative legal correspondents, Iurii Feofanov of *Izvestiia* and Arkadii Vaksberg of *Literaturnaia gazeta*) have called for "legal glasnost'," including the publication of crime statistics and of departmental regulations that have the force of law. They have asked probing questions about the virtual disappearance of acquittals from the courts and about sentencing and release procedures, including what one called "telephone law," decisions made by judges after being pressured by officials.[62] At an emotional round table between legal bureaucrats and Moscow writers in late 1986, it was agreed that, "considering the sad experience of the past," legal reform was no less needed than economic reform.[63] More recently, Aleksandr Iakovlev, of the inner leadership, has disparaged the presumption in Soviet theory that the rights of the individual are "a benefaction from on high."[64]

The results to date are inconclusive, although not disheartening. A November, 1986, Party resolution on "socialist legality" gave few details, but only weeks later the U.S.S.R.'s best-known political dissident, Andrei Sakharov, was released from exile. Some two hundred more dissidents were pardoned over the few months. In an extraordinary rebuke, *Pravda* on January 8, 1987, printed an announcement by the head of the KGB, Viktor M. Chebrikov, that KGB agents who had tampered with a journalist's inquiry into corruption in the Ukraine had been fired and the journalist, Viktor Berkhin, exonerated.[65] In early 1988 the "special psychiatric hospitals," in which many dissidents have been confined, were switched from the police to the Health Ministry.

More substantial legal change has not yet progressed beyond the study stage. Gorbachev, a law school graduate who never practised law, told the January, 1987, plenum there should be a revision of the penal code so as to "defend more effectively the interests and rights of citizens." A panel of legal scholars, criminologists, and judges is said to be pondering dilution or excision of the clauses covering "anti-Soviet propaganda" and similar offenses. Also under consideration are proposals for elimination of the death penalty, lifetime appointment of judges, early provision of defense counsel to the accused, and adoption of a quasi-jury system for trials for serious crimes.

As with economics and culture, there is only so much that moderate reformers can do in the area of law without changing the essence of the institutions they wish to save. Gorbachev's assurance in January, 1987, that he would not "break up our political system" will not lay the question to rest. The "mindless obedience" deprecated in his report has been a standing feature of Soviet life since the rise of Stalin, as have mute legislators, snooping policemen, and pliable judges. These things will not be easily superseded, and conservatives will be alarmed if they are. Even reform-minded Soviets have a deeply ingrained fear of the mob and a nervousness that an unraveling of political controls will lead to anarchy.[66]

It may be easier to achieve a consensus of the elite on legal reform than on other measures, since this would extend a trend toward predictability and professionalism in law enforcement that had begun in the 1950s and would benefit more people than it would harm. Multi-candidate elections, however, will detract from elite security and place a strain on many time-honored procedures. Boris Pugo, among others, has argued that meaningful elections in factories and local governments cast doubt on "certain fossilized canons of party practice," most directly the *nomenklatura* system of prior clearance of all staffing decisions by the Party organs.[67] Although he did not say so, it is self-evident that open elections within the Party would not be readily squared with the principle of hierarchy. Gorbachev, who has ruthlessly used appointment from above, has so far brushed the problem aside, declaring that "democratic centralism" will not be tarnished.

As with glasnost', organizational problems probably pale before psychological and cultural ones. An account of the experimental election of a district Party secretary in Moscow is one of many that illustrates the point. Most of the voters were bewildered by the experience, not knowing whether to express themselves and expecting the election to "roll down the rut worn over the decades," whereby "they ask us to vote, and we vote" for the approved candidate. "We are only beginning to learn," the story concluded, "how to nurture our own opinions and to voice them openly and without fear."[68] Mastering that lesson will take as long as any of the changes Gorbachev has set in motion.

Political Dynamics

The Soviet scene several years into Gorbachev's reign abounds in mirage effects. A stroll down a Moscow street turns up signs of change everywhere, but along with it so much that remains as before. Gorbachev has grumbled about those who only talk about reform, creating merely "the illusion of restructuring." It is politics, operating on several levels, that will determine how much progress is real and how much illusory.

Gorbachev's Reform Tendencies

Mikhail Gorbachev has maintained that if he had not happened along, "there would have been someone else" to spearhead reforms.[69] Yet there is no denying his pivotal role thus far. The future of reform will be very much shaped by how he deals with what he thinks and what he learns.

As should be apparent, since coming to power Gorbachev has spoken with more than one voice. If we examine the spectrum of his policies for general principles of action, his program can be seen to incorporate three main tendencies: *policy activism, system reintegration,* and, most weakly, *system change.* All are broadly reformist in spirit, although they entail different kinds of reform.

Pragmatic *policy activism,* the least demanding, has been directed mainly at the regime's crisis of effectiveness. Taking the system's basic machinery as its point of departure, it pulls every available lever and pushes every button to get things done. Typical are Gorbachev's adroit use of the personnel weapon and, in the economy, his Politburo's policy innovations on issues of corruption, technology, foreign trade, and distribution of wages.

System reintegration addresses the Soviet system's crisis of coherence. It is concerned with institutions rather than policies alone, believing the main defect in both to be the inability to unite attitudes and behavior in Soviet society into a logical and functional whole.[70] Gorbachev has been especially troubled by two related manifestations of incoherence under Brezhnev: poor self-knowledge and exiting behavior.

The remedy offered to correct the first flaw has been a strategy of intellectual and cultural *self-discovery.* It has been achieved primarily through a relaxation of political controls over the media, the arts, and the social sciences. To cope with the incoherence that has been expressed as exiting, Gorbachev's response might be seen as an exercise in *system extension.* He seeks to legitimate, and to coopt into the official system, a variety of activities that the rigidity of the state during the last generation has driven out to unofficial structures. The lost souls now being reclaimed include many (though not all) black-market entrepreneurs — who can now work legally and become subject to government licensing, inspection, and taxation — underground artists, and dissidents and semi-dissidents. Supply side politics fits equally well with self-discovery and system extension, inasmuch as it is directed both at finding out about citizens' opinions and at luring some of them into public life.

System change would bring the modification of fundamentals of the Soviet order. On this level, progress under Gorbachev has been slight and the prospect of more is most uncertain. This is a man, when all is said and done, who believes fiercely in the worth of Soviet state socialism, trumpeting it to have "repeatedly and in many ways demonstrated its superiority over capitalism."[71] He has time and again insisted that he wants to modernize the system, not scrap it, and has made the motto "More Socialism!" (*Bol'she sotsializma!*) a propaganda staple. It is abundantly clear that he stands by the Soviet Union's single-party political system, state-dominated economy, and collectivist approach to rights, in which the needs of society and the state take precedence over those of the individual.

This does not mean, however, that Gorbachev is imparting no impetus to change anything essential. If one must accept at face value his reiterations of his faith in "socialism," we must do the same with his assertions, equally plaintive, that major surgery is needed for Soviet socialism to compete and thrive in changing circumstances. These statements have become more common as his education in power has proceeded since March, 1985.

Therefore, while continuing to expound the core values of the regime, Gorbachev has come to interpret some of them, and to connect them to practical considerations, in ways that may point to structural change. His Marxist economics have made room for a more accommodating attitude toward individual and cooperative enterprise and a recognition that forms of market coordination must be grafted onto government planning. His Leninist politics have not prevented him from issuing a searing critique of Soviet political culture or from proposing major changes in rules affecting participation. His organic view of society coexists with other convictions—about the reliance of the whole on the well-being of the individual cells—that are pulling him away from Stalinist absolutism.

If the regime were to institutionalize policy changes that Gorbachev has already made, it is possible that some change would take place in the system. A Party directive decreeing slacker censorship is one thing; a statute protecting freedoms of the press and delineating where state security would override them would be another; independent judges who would hear a complaint about the Party or the police meddling in a journalist's work would be something else again. The first occurred in 1985; the second has been promised; and it is now possible publicly to discuss the third. It is too soon to forecast where the regime will draw the line.

Nor can it be overlooked that some of Gorbachev's present commitments in the areas of policy activism and the reintegration of the political system have been impelling him to consider structural reforms. New policies can raise expectations of change more quickly than they can ameliorate problems. And some problems, including the most pernicious flaws of the command economy, will probably not respond at all to simple policy nostrums.

Attempts to reintegrate the Soviet system by stretching it—bringing back into the official system the moonlighting car repairmen, the Sakharovs, and the novelists who want to write about Stalin's purges—are bound to produce some ripple effects within the larger system. If Gorbachev attempts to dam these up completely, he can count on provoking yet another round of the exiting he wanted to lessen in the first place. If he condones communication with the main system, as has been his wont, he will invite demands for more sweeping changes; so, too, with self-discovery in modes such as freer debate, better statistics, and the rebirth of a national historical memory. Fuller collective awareness of Soviet reality is certain to add to the thrust, at least from highly motivated minorities, toward greater reforms.

A last point to consider concerning Gorbachev's program is how difficult it is to say what is systemic change and what is not. A generation ago, most Western specialists saw terror as innate in the Soviet system. It may have disappeared, but the regime has not. Was this because terror was not essential, because the system invented substitutes for it, or because Stalin's system was in fact qualitatively different from those that followed? There are no easy answers. Consider glasnost' and competitive elections. Does the fact that *Pravda* is now printing comments that would have produced an arrest in 1970 or a death sentence in 1940 mark the passing of something fundamental? Is it integral to Soviet rule that citizens have no say in who governs them, as the clinging to bogus elections for more than six decades suggests, or will life go on more or less as it did before? Will the ability to choose from among several candidates, all cleared by the one party, leave Russians in a totally different situation from Americans who can vote Republican or Democrat? Only empirical study of the changes as they unfold will help us to know.

Patterns of Support and Resistance

The likelihood of Gorabchev's ideas being implemented depends on how they are acted upon elsewhere in the Soviet system and how skillfully he is able to build support and compliance around them. He has not disguised the fact that his program has not met with unanimous approval. At times, he seems almost to revel in this, like the rugged outdoorsman who prefers to hike in a sharp wind. Thus, the question becomes: how strong is the anti-Gorbachev wind, and how much headway is he making against it?

Like all General Secretaries since Stalin, Gorbachev has not been spared the need to adapt his strategy and tactics, if not goals, to the wishes of his coalition partners in the Kremlin. Esoteric signals strongly imply that some in that small group are more Gorbachevian than others. Aleksandr Iakovlev would most likely be at the pole of maximum support for Gorbachev and Egor Ligachev, the de facto second secretary for whom Iakovlev is a rival, would be at the other pole. Speaking on draft laws on economic reform in June, 1987, Gorbachev mentioned "big discussions" in the leadership and said the Politburo "did not make decisions" on most of the drafts, sending them for further staff work. Whether from lack of votes or a failure to reach consensus, the upshot was a delay in vital business.[72] We now know of a far more dramatic episode of dissension at the top: the speech at the October 21, 1987, plenum of the Central Committee by the Moscow Party leader, El'tsin (a candidate member of the Politburo), who attacked his fellow leaders for stalling on perestroika. Three weeks later Gorbachev deposed his erstwhile ally from his Moscow post and condemned him for demagoguery and "putting his personal ambition above the interests of the party."[73] Since El'tsin's fall, Gorbachev has said that the danger to his program from the left, from those who want to push change too fast, is as serious as that from the right.

The El'tsin affair does not alter the fact that, by past standards, Gorbachev has moved quickly to advance his position within the leadership. It took Brezhnev seven years to bring eight individuals into the Politburo, something Gorbachev did in barely more than two years. On the other hand, only four of the newcomers (Iakovlev, Sliun'kov, Viktor P. Nikonov, and Lev N. Zaikov) were without at least the status of candidate member of the Politburo or member of the Secretariat before March, 1985. They are still outnumbered by those who scrambled most of the way to the top on their own—two of the thirteen Politburo members (not counting Gorbachev) promoted under Brezhnev, two under Andropov, and four (of whom Ligachev is one) under Gorbachev. They can be assumed to have a fair degree of independence.

While most of the present leaders will probably defer to Gorbachev on routine issues, on matters of consequence they will make their views heard. The situation, it ought to be underlined, is far from static. Several in the leadership seem to have drifted toward greater radicalism, much as has Gorbachev.[74] And Gorbachev will have a freer hand once he has completed the renovation of the Politburo and brought in more enthusiastic supporters. His early pace suggests that he will not dawdle with this. Gorbachev-era promotees are already more dominant among the Politburo candidates and non-ranking secretaries (four of six and five of five, respectively) than among the voting members of the Politburo.

There is no reason to doubt Gorbachev's contention, persistently made, that the main obstacles to his reforms have been raised, not in the Politburo, but in the bureaucracy below. Resistance is found, he said in April, 1987, "at the level of the Central Committee and the government, in the ministries, republics, and regions."[75] The Soviet press today overflows with anecdotal evidence of economic and other administrators dragging their feet on innovations. Lucid evidence is the difficulty Gorbachev had in arranging the January, 1987, plenum of the Central Committee, which is overwhelmingly composed of Party and government bureaucrats. It had to be postponed three times, Gorbachev said, until the necessary "clarity" could be reached—a revelation made all the more astounding by his statement at the plenum that the committee had been for years an inert rubber stamp.[76]

One should be skeptical, however, of any simplistic image of a bureaucratic monolith, or of Gorbachev and his Kremlin allies as fighting a lonely battle against all odds. Gorbachev himself favored such an image in some of his early statements about the "bureaucratic stratum" and its crassly self-interested hostility to him. But he has since begun speaking of administrators in more differentiated terms. He now identifies bureaucratic supporters as well as nay-sayers, and allows that the latter include "people who are honorable and unselfish but remain the prisoners of old concepts."[77]

This is not to trivialize bureaucratic obstructionism but rather to argue that it be kept in perspective. Absent a crisis in the Party leadership, most bureaucratic foes of reform will work to absorb rather than repel it. Their resistance will take the form of a multitude of uncoordinated, localized actions. They will be motivated, not only by prejudice and privilege, but also by a conviction that they are doing their duty and, more often than not, by a sincere befuddlement about what is expected of them.[78]

Gorbachev is not without an arsenal he can deploy in the bureaucratic arena. He can scold laggards from his bully pulpit and remove them outright if they are defiant. At the Nineteenth Party Conference held in 1988 he was expected to purge the Central Committee of those members who had been least cooperative. He can also bribe individual bureaucratic supporters with offers of promotion and can appeal to them collectively by playing to interests beyond those related to their jobs. The salaried middle class to which they belong should be well served by the stratification of incomes and greater availability of personal services that Gorbachev promises. Like intellectuals, administrators also stand to benefit from a greater leniency and predictability in political control, especially if they are applied to foreign travel.

A perceptive Soviet publicist, Fedor Burlatskii, has noted that the administrator who shuns change is more to be feared than the man in the street, "since he has more influence and more depends on him." Yet the bureaucracy, as Burlatskii said, has no monopoly on conservatism. "A part of the mass [public], passive toward changes, must be considered as a factor braking restructuring."[79]

In understanding this, as other aspects of Gorbachev's policies, we should avoid black-and-white thinking about support and resistance. Gorbachev has more than any previous leader looked at Soviet society as having needs that must be respected: "We cannot make our society dynamic and vital if we do not take interests into account, if there is not a reciprocal link through which interests influence both policy and society."[80] The interests of which Gorbachev has been most solicitous are those of the Soviet middle class, broadly defined, and most emphatically of the intelligentsia, the main beneficiary of cultural liberalization. At the same time, he has tended to look at social interests in highly specific terms, rather than in the crude class categories that pervaded Soviet theory in the past. In addition to his general middle-class bias, Gorbachev's early actions suggest that he is intent on appealing to substrata within large social constituencies.

The multinational character of Soviet society, in which Russians comprise a bare majority, presents Gorbachev with particular problems. Gorbachev's personnel and anti-corruption policies have had greatest effect in the outlying areas, and it is no accident that the most violent outburst against him, in Kazakhstan in 1986, was fueled by grievances over such policies. Glasnost' also is evoking non-Russian (and Russian) resentments on a variety of issues. The demonstrations in the summer of 1987 by Crimean Tatars in Moscow, and by local nationalists in the Baltic republics, would not have been possible without Gorbachev's liberalization. On the other hand, when it comes to the advantages of cultural and political change, most members of the minority groups are not likely to think much differently from the Russian majority. In economics, local politicians of all backgrounds are apt to see a larger role for themselves, mostly in terms of promoting consumer welfare, if management is decentralized. And certain aspects of economic reform, including the toleration of small businesses, may actually be of less profit to most Russians than to modernized minorities with a strong entrepreneurial tradition, such as the Baltic peoples, the Armenians, and the Georgians.

Among socioeconomic groups, it holds as a gross generalization that white-collar employees have the most to gain, and blue-collar workers the most to lose, from Gorbachevism. It is the workers who have been most offended by the rationing of vodka, who will complain most vociferously about increases in food prices, and who have gained the least from the cultural thaw. Surveys show that the bulk of Soviet workers have seen little improvement from economic change thus far and "feel restructuring only in the greater pressure at work."[81] Radical economic reform, if consistently pursued, is certain to bring plant closings and retraining programs. In June, 1987, Gorbachev promised that no workers would be left unemployed, but he also announced the necessity of a "regrouping of the work force," which would redeploy workers out of smokestack industries and into advanced manufacturing and services.[82]

If all these points apply here and now, Gorbachev's reforms have the potential of eventually urging the U.S.S.R. down a path long since traveled by the West, on which economic modernization blurs rather than reinforces class boundaries. Soviet peasants stand to benefit economically from economic reform, and many Soviet workers still have ties with the village. Economic dislocation will affect the middle class as well as the working class—high officials now speak of deep cuts in the administrative staffs of economic agencies and of closing hundreds of unproductive research institutes. Most significantly, the regime's approach to wages and welfare promises to increase stratification and differentiation within class groups, not only between them: "It is precisely the most qualified part of the population, the 'wagons' on which society rides, that will come out ahead of their present situation."[83] These wagons are found in all social classes, including the industrial proletariat.

Gorbachev has on several occasions said (making a point familiar to political sociologists in the West) that attainment of higher levels of education and income magnifies an individual's aspirations for political rights. It should follow that the best-schooled and most affluent groups will most appreciate political reforms. It is interesting that the Soviet leadership seems not entirely comfortable with this logic. How else to explain the totally unexpected provision for election of factory directors and foremen? Better a dose of workplace democracy, Moscow's attitude seems to be, than a working-class revolution.

No Room to Retreat?

Gorbachev, like politicians everywhere, likes to dramatize political choices. Putting on his best television evangelist's face at the January, 1987, Central Committee Plenum, he stated that the course he had charted was absolutely necessary, "for we simply have no other way." "It is impossible for us to retreat and we have nowhere to retreat to."

Many in the Soviet elite, however, assuredly do think it possible to retreat, perhaps to a revivified Stalinism. Nor is the decision as simple as whether to go backward or forward, or even whether to go full- or half-throttle. Doubtless, there are those with influence in the Soviet Union who would prefer to strike off on an entirely different tangent, or to accept some parts of Gorbachev's program and reject others, or even to subside into a reasonably intelligent conservatism, such as that represented by Leonid Brezhnev in the first half of his administration. The longer Gorbachev and his allies are able to exploit the immense organizational resources at their disposal, and the more success their changes bring, the worse it will be for their detractors. Yet Gorbachev can never be rid of them entirely, and he will never be able to forget what the enemies of change did in October, 1964, to another reformist leader, Nikita Khrushchev.

The basic question is whether perestroika will work. Fedor Burlatskii, a Khrushchev reformer for whom Gorbachev has been a godsend, has said that the worst thing for the Soviet Union would be inept and indecisive "microreforms," the creation of "something that is half horse and half grouse, some kind of dinosaur that can neither jump nor fly."[84] Gorbachev clearly fears this as well, and intends to carry out macro-reforms, but his own inhibitions and the many constraints in his political environment may keep him from going far enough. Herein lies a real danger for him. Had he been unambitious, Gorbachev could have gotten away with Brezhnev-style, band-aid solutions for quite some time. Now that he is being almost reckless in the way he challenges elites and vested interests, he probably cannot survive reforms that fail to deliver the goods, especially economically.

Will the Gorbachev reforms be sufficient to alleviate the regime's crisis of effectiveness? In the short term, over the next five years, the odds are overwhelming that they will not. Gorbachev seems conscious of his vulnerability here, as I have noted, and has braced the public for a long wait for improvement and even, most recently, for a dip in economic growth before new structures begin to pay dividends. As time goes, it will be essential to Gorbachev that he continue to show the impressive ability to learn in office he has exhibited so far. This is because, as has been convincingly demonstrated in other communist countries, serious economic and other reforms must constantly be adjusted and affirmed. If Gorbachev persists with his more enlightened cultural policy, and with the ginger political reforms begun in 1987, he will not be alone in being educated by experience. His changes make a credible beginning on curing the Soviet system's crisis of coherence. At a minimum, they will give the leadership and the whole Soviet elite superior intelligence as well as feedback about what they are doing. The dinosaur, finally, will know better whether it can jump or fly, and that knowledge itself is a crucial condition of getting off the ground.

If Gorbachev's economic and other reforms fizzle, if after a period of adjustment things do not improve, if there is an unforeseen policy disaster (most likely to occur in foreign policy)—if worse comes to worst, the balance of political forces may conceivably tip enough to force a retreat. If that happens, two things can be predicted. First, a radical change of compass would be impractical without a change of leader. If it is debatable whether the Soviet system has room to retreat, there is no question that Mikhail Gorbachev has left himself very little. Second, a retreat would not come easily. Gorbachev is giving many in the elite, and millions outside it, a stake in a broadly reformist strategy. Overcoming his coalition would not be impossible, nor would it be but a day's work, and it probably could not be achieved without violence. The possibility cannot be excluded that an enforced retreat, polarizing the political elite and attempting to remobilize a partially emancipated society, would bring about what has so far eluded the Soviet system, a crisis of survival.

NOTES

1. Quotation by Teimuraz Mamaladze in *Izvestiia,* January 31, 1987, p. 3, and by Gorbachev in *Pravda,* May 20, 1987, p. 3.

2. *Pravda,* January 28, 1987, pp. 3-4.

3. Ibid., p. 1; February 26, 1987, p. 1; May 20, 1987, p. 1.

4. For further discussion, using crisis in the narrow sense of a crisis of survival, see Timothy J. Colton, *The Dilemma of Reform in the Soviet Union,* rev. ed. (New York, 1986), pp. 57-61. The terrible camp battles of the 1950s are described in Aleksandr I. Solzhenitsyn, *The Gulag Archipelago 1918-1956,* 3 vols. (New York, 1978), 3:chaps. 10-12.

5. Seweryn Bialer, *The Soviet Paradox: External Expansion, Internal Decline* (New York, 1986), p. 75.

6. See especially Robert C. Tucker's classic essay on "dual Russia," in his *The Soviet Political Mind,* rev. ed. (New York, 1971), pp. 121-42.

7. Albert O. Hirschman, *Exit, Voice, and Loyalty* (Cambridge, Mass., 1970).

8. The frequency of exiting behavior, in defiance of system canons, might be another cause of denial of reality. Corruption is an especially good example. As in eighteenth-century Russia, collective repression of the truth about corruption was resorted to because Russians lived in a world "where no one could maintain moral identity or sense of purpose without denouncing bribery but where no one could function without taking and giving bribes." George L. Yaney, *The Systematization of Russian Government* (Urbana, Ill., 1973), p. 34.

9. Efim Etkind, "Sovetskie tabu," *Sintaksis* (Paris), no. 9 (1981):8.

10. See the account in *Pravda,* September 10, 1986, p. 3.

11. Chingiz Aitmatov, *Sobranie sochinenii,* 3 vols. (Moscow, 1982-84), 2:195-489. In the 1960s Soviet literature as a whole lost the sense of personal wholeness and harmony typical of Stalinist "socialist realism." Novelists now wrote of alienation, disintegration, and confusion. Katerina Clark, *The Soviet Novel: History as Ritual* (Chicago and London, 1981), p. 232.

12. Hugh Heclo, *Modern Social Politics in Britain and Sweden* (New Haven and London, 1974), p. 305.

13. A suggestive parallel might be the plight of Jimmy G., the strong but passive and "unconcerned" amnesiac described by the neurologist Oliver Sack in *The Man Who Mistook His Wife for a Hat and Other Clinical Tales* (New York, 1986), p. 36. It is interesting that some of the best work on memory loss has been done by Russian psychologists.

14. A. Iakovlev, "Dostizhenie kachestvenno novogo sostoianiia sovetskogo obshchestva i obshchestvennye nauki," *Kommunist,* no. 8 (May, 1987):4.

15. *Pravda,* May 20, 1987, p. 1. On the other hand, the unofficial transcript of Gorbachev's June 19, 1986, audience with Soviet writers contains a surprisingly warm reference to the economic situation in Stavropol' in 1969. See Arkhiv samizdata, "Beseda chlenov SP SSSR s M. S. Gorbachevym," AS No. 5785, prepared by Radio Liberty, Munich. All quotations from his remarks in this chapter are from this Russian-language version.

16. Janos Kornai, "The Hungarian Reform Process: Visions, Hopes, and Reality," *Journal of Economic Literature* 24 (December, 1986):1724-26.

17. *Pravda,* April 24, 1985, p. 1.

18. "Nastoichivo dvigat'sia vpered," *Kommunist,* no. 8 (May, 1985):32.

19. Ibid., p. 32.

20. This claim was made in remarks in Minsk, only a summary of which was given in *Pravda,* July 12, 1985, p. 1.

21. "Nastoichivo dvigat'sia vpered," p. 34.

22. See, for example, the statement that Gorbachev's reformism "has nothing in common with liberalism . . . stresses authoritarian rule, discipline, and predictable conformist behavior. Cultural experimentation, not to speak of expanded political rights, has no place in his world." Seweryn Bialer and Joan

Afferica, "The Genesis of Gorbachev's World," *Foreign Affairs* 64 (America and the World issue, 1985):620.

23. Quotations from the congress speech are taken from *Pravda,* February 26, 1986.

24. Ibid., August 2, 1986, p. 1.

25. Ibid., October 2, 1986, p. 1.

26. All quotations here from ibid., January 28, 1987, p. 1; emphasis added.

27. As an example of Gorbachev's cautioning about the time needed to deliver on reforms, see his claim that the population "understands that there are problems with restructuring that will take one, two, and for certain of them even three five-year plans to resolve." Ibid., July 15, 1987, p. 2.

28. I define turnover here as the proportion of all officeholders at the beginning of the measured period who left office during the period due to retirement, demotion, liquidation of the office, or death. Death accounts for less than 5 percent of turnover in every category except the Politburo under Andropov. In a small number of cases, an official moved from one position in a given category to another; these were included in turnover totals. This rule was waived for the membership (including candidate members) of the Politburo, since a seat there confers political status over and above one's administrative position.

29. This last point is in *Pravda,* January 14, 1987, p. 1.

30. Average yearly turnover under Gorbachev, as of March 10, 1987, was 19 percent among Politburo members and candidates, 38 percent among Moscow Party secretaries and department heads, 32 percent in the Council of Ministers, and 20 percent among regional Party bosses. Under Brezhnev (between his last Party congress in March, 1981, and his death), annual turnover was 3, 2, 2, and 6 percent, respectively, and under Chernenko 5, 6, 10, and 10 percent.

Under Andropov, annualized turnover in these four groups was at 15, 25, 16, and 18 percent, far closer to Gorbachev's. But three of the four exits from Andropov's Politburo were by death, and the only outright removal (of A. P. Kirilenko) had apparently been settled when Brezhnev was still alive; all four under Gorbachev were political demotions.

Gorbachev appears to regard his purge as a continuation of the changes begun under Andropov. Officials appointed under Andropov and Chernenko have been far less vulnerable than others. In the Council of Ministers, for example, 76 percent of the Brezhnev holdovers were removed in Gorbachev's first two years, as compared to only 11 percent of those selected after November, 1982.

31. I lack ages for five of the twenty-nine March, 1987, secretaries and department heads, but have them for all others.

32. *Pravda,* January 14, 1987, p. 2.

33. See Colton, *Dilemma of Reform,* pp. 104-5, and Thane Gustafson and Dawn Mann, "Gorbachev's First Year: Building Power and Authority," *Problems of Communism* 35 (May-June, 1986):8-11.

34. If turnover is grouped into six-month intervals ending in September

240 / Gorbachev and the Politics of System Renewal

of 1985, March and September of 1986, and March of 1987, the pattern is striking. In the Politburo, turnover rates (annualized) are 13, 47, 0, and 11 percent in those subperiods; in the Central Committee apparatus 62, 85, 7, and 14 percent; in the Council of Ministers 28, 63, 32, and 28 percent; and among regional Party leaders 26, 30, 10, and 13 percent. Invariably, the most rapid change was in the second half of Gorbachev's first year. There was some recrudescence of change in the second half of his second year, but never to anything like the peak level.

35. Based on information available on the twenty-six new first secretaries named in Gorbachev's first year and the eight in the second year. It should be noted that, although only 12 percent of the first year's secretaries came directly from a position in the region, 54 percent had once held such a position. The pattern in the Council of Ministers is quite different. Of the nine branch economic ministers appointed in Gorbachev's second year, only two were deputies of the outgoing minister, the standard Brezhnev pattern; four held field positions in the ministry and three had most recently been Party officials. For a related discussion, see Thane Gustafson and Dawn Mann, "Gorbachev's Next Gamble," *Problems of Communism* 36 (July-August, 1987):10-16.

36. Four Stavropol' colleagues have been named to the Council of Ministers, but only one (V. S. Murakhovskii, first deputy premier in charge of agriculture) to a major portfolio. None has been named a national Party secretary or department head or to an important position in the KGB. Brezhnev, with his much wider experience, was a far more effective patron in the mid-1960s.

37. *Pravda,* January 14, 1987, p. 2.

38. Quotation from ibid., July 15, 1987, p. 2.

39. Changes up to mid-1986 are summarized in Colton, *Dilemma of Reform,* chap. 4. A good overview by an economist is Philip Hanson, "The Shape of Gorbachev's Economic Reform," *Soviet Economy* 2 (October-December, 1986):313-26. A fine socioeconomic analysis is Peter A. Hauslohner, "Gorbachev's Social Contract," ibid. 3 (January-March, 1987):54-89. Political variables are discussed in Timothy J. Colton, "Approaches to the Politics of Systemic Economic Reform in the Soviet Union," ibid. 3 (April-June, 1987): 145-70.

40. *Pravda,* June 26, 1987, p. 3.

41. Quotations from ibid., June 26, 1987, pp. 1, 3; emphasis added.

42. Ibid., July 15, 1987, p. 2.

43. Hanson, pp. 319-20.

44. *Pravda,* April 24, 1985, p. 2.

45. Iakovlev, p. 10. Compare to Gorbachev's comment to the writers in June, 1986: "We have no [political] opposition, so in what way can we monitor ourselves? Only through criticism and self-criticism and above all through openness. There cannot be a society without openness. We are learning about this."

46. Iakovlev was made head of the Party's propaganda department in July, 1985, secretary for propaganda and cultural affairs in March, 1986 (his responsibilities broadened to include science and social science in January, 1987),

and a full member of the Politburo in June, 1987. Other key appointments, all in 1986, included those of V. G. Zakharov as minister of culture, Iu. P. Voronov as head of the Central Committee's culture department, M. F. Nenashev and A. I. Kamshalov as chiefs of the publishing and film industries, and I. T. Frolov as editor of *Kommunist*. Frolov in 1987 became one of Gorbachev's personal assistants.

47. Iakovlev, pp. 8, 13.

48. T. I. Zaslavskaia in *Pravda,* February 6, 1987, pp 2-3.

49. Many younger painters in Moscow, impatient with their conservative union and with state studios and galleries, have begun experimenting on their own. Since May, 1987, individual painters, other artists, and artisans in Moscow have been allowed to sell their wares at a large weekend arts fair in Izmailovo park. A painter with whom I spoke in September, 1987, said that the opening of the fair was the first time he had felt proud to be a Soviet citizen.

50. *Pravda,* February 14, 1987, pp. 1-2.

51. This speech is in ibid., November 3, 1987.

52. The Shatrov play is in *Novyi mir,* no. 4 (April, 1987) (quotation on p. 27); Rybakov's novel started publication in *Druzhba narodov,* no. 4 (April, 1987); Akhmatova's poem is in *Oktiabr',* no. 3 (March, 1987); Dudintsev's novel is in *Neva,* no. 1 and 2 (January and February, 1987). As with the better-known *Doctor Zhivago,* it is bizarre to think how long some of the literary works here have gone unpublished. Shatrov's was written in 1962, Rybakov's was first slated for printing in 1967, and "Requiem" was completed in 1940!

53. The details about the purge of Zhukov are in "Marshal Zhukov," *Ogonek,* no. 49 (December, 1986):7, and no. 51 (December, 1986):27.

54. See on this point Nancy P. Condee and Vladimir Padunov, "Reforming Soviet Culture/Retrieving Soviet History," *The Nation,* June 13, 1987, p. 816. The newspaper *Moscow News* was reprimanded in September, 1987, for publishing a sympathetic obituary of the émigré novelist, Viktor Nekrasov. And yet, plans seem to be afoot to publish some of the poetry of Joseph Brodsky, the 1987 Nobel Prize laureate in literature, who has been living in exile in the United States for some years.

55. *Izvestiia,* May 5, 1987, p. 2.

56. *Pravda,* July 15, 1987, p. 2.

57. Ibid., p. 1. For particularly acrid press exchanges, see *Izvestiia,* April 20, 1987, p. 4 (about river diversions), and *Sotsialisticheskaia industriia,* May 24, 1987, p. 3, and June 14, 1987, p. 3 (concerning Stalin's poor preparations for World War II).

58. *Pravda,* January 28, 1987, p. 2, and February 26, 1987, pp. 1-2.

59. There were said to be 30,000 such clubs by the beginning of 1988.

60. See Werner G. Hahn, "Electoral Choice in the Soviet Bloc," *Problems of Communism* 36 (March-April, 1987):29-39.

61. See especially *Sotsialisticheskaia industriia,* February 17, 1987, p. 2.

62. Quoted in "V pol'zu spravedlivosti," *Literaturnaia gazeta,* no. 47 (November 19, 1986):13.

63. Arkadii Vaksberg, "Komu eto nuzhno?" ibid., no. 4 (January 21, 1987):12.

64. Iakovlev, p. 17.

65. The Party first secretary in Voroshilovgrad region was then dismissed in February, 1987, and the chief of the Ukrainian KGB, Stepan N. Mukha, several months later.

66. See the essay by the reformist intellectual, Fedor Burlatskii in *Pravda,* July 18, 1987, p. 3. While strongly defending political liberalization, he argues against an unrestricted right of assembly, warning of "how quickly democracy and mob rule interpenetrate." His main example is the activities of *Pamiat'* (Memory), a group of ultra-nationalist Russians who have staged several demonstrations in Moscow, but he also mentions gatherings of Jewish "refuseniks."

67. Ibid., July 8, 1987, p. 2.

68. *Moskovskaia pravda,* July 18, 1987, p. 2.

69. *Pravda,* May 20, 1987, p. 1.

70. This is nothing new. Many in Russia before the revolution worried over essentially the same problem, as is brilliantly argued in Yaney, *The Systematization of Russian Government.*

71. Gorbachev remarks to Margaret Thatcher, *Pravda,* March 31, 1987, p. 2.

72. Ibid., June 13, 1987, p. 1. Compare to his statement to the writers in June, 1986, that "clashes and arguments do occur" in the Politburo.

73. Ibid., November 13, 1987, pp. 1-2. El'tsin's speech and resignation threat were at first considered too explosive to be publicly reported. A TASS bulletin was sent out to Soviet editors, but revoked within minutes.

74. The best example of this is probably Premier Ryzhkov, who in mid-1987 strongly endorsed economic reforms quite a bit more thorough than those he seemed to favor a year or two before.

75. *Pravda,* April 17, 1987, p. 1.

76. Ibid., February 26, 1987, p. 1.

77. Ibid.

78. Soviet surveys suggest that such confusion may be most serious in the administrative apparatus of the Party. See ibid., June 17, 1987, p. 2, which reports that 79 percent of Party secretaries polled in one region "imprecisely understood the distinction" between new and old kinds of economic leadership.

79. Ibid., July 18, 1987, p. 3.

80. Ibid., July 15, 1987, p. 2.

81. *Izvestiia,* May 5, 1987, p. 2.

82. *Pravda,* June 26, 1987, p. 5.

83. Zaslavskaia in *Sotsialisticheskaia industriia,* February 7, 1987, p. 2.

84. *Pravda,* July 18, 1987, p. 3.

Reform in Russia: American Perceptions and U.S. Policy

ALEXANDER DALLIN

American views concerning the prospects of reform in the Soviet Union have typically oscillated between two characteristic but incompatible attitudes. At times, Americans have exuded an irrepressible optimism grounded in an often unexamined belief in the perfectibility of all humanity and all social systems and in the likelihood that, given a chance, people everywhere—the Soviet Union included—would opt for a "better" life and a "better" (that is, either a different or a significantly reformed) system. At other times, there has been a pervasive conviction that, of all regimes, the Soviet system—Marxist-Leninist, atheist, totalitarian, and rooted in Tatar, Byzantine, and Muscovite political culture to boot—was surely beyond redemption and repair.

The optimistic strain can be traced back at least to Woodrow Wilson's war message to Congress, weeks after the tsar had been deposed. He linked (as would later leaders) idealism and ulterior motive in declaring:

> Does not every American feel that assurance has been added to our hope for the future peace of the world by the wonderful and heartening things that have been happening within the last few weeks in Russia? Russia was known by those who knew it best to have been always in fact democratic at heart, in all the vital habits of her thought, in all the intimate relationships of her people that spoke their natural instinct, their habitual attitude towards life. . . . [Now] the great, generous Russian people have been added in all their naive majesty and might to the forces that are fighting for freedom in the world, for justice, and for peace. Here is a fit partner for a league of honour.[1]

Here we have both the belief in Russia's goodness "at heart" and the linkage of Russia's domestic political order to the prospects for world order and peace: two recurrent themes in later years, the former clashing with the view that the Soviet system was a fitting expression of Russia's political culture, and the latter challenged by those who denied a linkage between foreign and domestic affairs.

If the following years of American intervention in Russia added little fondness, some of the humanitarian arguments for helping the needy population through the American Relief Administration were based on the same notion of a good people victimized and on the less vocal hope that they might take things into their own hands.[2]

The Stalin years hardly provided any realistic basis for expecting reform, however defined. Few Americans cared, and even fewer understood, what was going on in the Soviet Union. Across popular fronts, purges, and pacts, events tossed public opinion, media, and officialdom from one position to the other. What reform could there be so long as an evil and omnipotent Stalin was purging and plotting, repressing and aggressing? If in the 1930s a few American "fellow-travelers" or naive observers—journalists and diplomats—took seriously the so-called Stalin Constitution of 1936 and the show trials, few worried whether, and even fewer seriously thought that, the Stalinist system could be reformed. Indeed, what could reformed Stalinism mean: tepid ice? barbed wire with a blooming thistle?

The wartime alliance imposed on the two powers by Hitler did generate a new wave of American hopes regarding Russia's future. Many observers in the United States liked to believe that the Soviet regime's reliance on its population—those to whom Stalin now appealed as "brothers and sisters"—and the ultimately loyal performance of most Soviet citizens were bound to mellow the regime, bring out more authentic attitudes, and help erode the system's uglier and more intolerant, messianic, revolutionary, and expansionist strains. The return to Russian "nationalism" and all-Slavic themes, the reestablishment of the Moscow Patriarchate, and the dissolution of the Communist International seemed to herald the revival of tradition and conservatism, which some in the United States were prepared to welcome as a desirable "reform." A few American commentators thought that, as a reward for victory, Stalin might end collectivization of agriculture or institute other "liberalizing" reforms. Needless to say, such a view revealed a lack of familiarity with Stalin and Stalinism and, more often than not, projected assumptions derived from American politics onto the Soviet scene. That such Soviet "reforms" would have been welcome in America was not in doubt; in fact, some public figures fastened on to the prospect as if it would relieve them of some sense of guilt for collaborating with the Soviet Union in the war.

During the war, the U.S. government did not make any effort to hold lend-lease aid hostage to Soviet "reforms." Perhaps the only attempt to induce changes of domestic policy related to freedom of religion; Franklin D. Roosevelt evidently sensed that lining up with Stalin would be more readily accepted in middle America if he could point to some improvement of conditions in the "atheist" U.S.S.R. in a symbolically important area such as religious tolerance. But under the circumstances the United States did not believe it could—or should—make this a condition for aid in a cause defined as vital to American self-interest. Nor would this have been a case of Soviet "reform" but rather an extracted concession.

The problem came up momentarily at the end of the war when the United States first used its atomic bomb. At Potsdam to meet with Stalin, Harry Truman and Secretary of War Henry L. Stimson discussed (as Stimson put it) "whether we could be safe in sharing the atomic bomb with Russia while she was still a police state and before she put into effect provisions assuring personal rights of liberty to the individual citizen." Curiously, without spelling out what the connection was, they linked civil rights to behavior abroad, as would others on later occasions. Stimson pondered the question and then sent Truman a memorandum on the "control of atomic bombs," which he accompanied with a note: "I have come to the conclusion that it would not be possible to use our possession of the atomic bomb as a direct lever to produce the change [in Soviet attitudes toward individual liberty]. I have become convinced that any demand by us for an internal change in Russia as a condition of sharing in the atomic weapon would be so resented that it would make the objective we have in view less probable." Stimson thought the nuclear problem deserved to be treated on its own merits, even if it could not be linked to human rights in the U.S.S.R.: "I believe that the change in attitude toward the individual in Russia will come slowly and gradually and I am satisfied that we should not delay our approach to Russia in the matter of the atomic bomb until that process has been completed. . . ."[3]

The Cold War served to dispel the optimism that had developed during the common struggle. Now the conceptions and expectations of the American elite and government community concerning the Soviet Union were increasingly shaped by the theories and assumptions of totalitarianism. In their dominant, orthodox form, these theories pessimistically implied a static system: once a totalitarian regime is established, there is no way of altering, ameliorating, or overthrowing it. From 1948 on, the typical observer in the United States—in and out of government—tended to equate Russia's future with *1984*. Reform was out of the question both in theory and in practice. Reports and dispatches from the American embassy in Moscow reiterated time and again that there were no grounds to expect any improvements there; National Security Council estimates—including "assumed probabilities of war . . . through 1952"—stated, "No change in the character of the Soviet regime is to be expected during this period."[4]

There were, however, two variants that pointed in other directions. One was the approach taken by George F. Kennan—first in his famous "X" article and later in other writings. In "The Sources of Soviet Conduct," he first formulated his argument for an American policy of containment, including his belief in a linkage between foreign behavior and Soviet domestic conduct:

> It is entirely possible for the United States to influence by its actions the internal developments, both within Russia and throughout the international Communist movement, by which Russian policy is largely determined. . . . The United States has it in its power . . . to force upon the Kremlin a far greater degree of moderation and circumspection than it has had to observe in recent years, and in this way to promote tendencies which must eventually find their outlet in either the breakup or the gradual mellowing of Soviet power.[5]

Perhaps the prospect of Soviet mellowing was initially intended as a bonus for the pursuit of a policy of containment by the United States. Later, many observers—including Kennan himself—came to adopt a more agnostic attitude in regard to the inevitable effect of containment on Soviet domestic affairs. But just what sort of Russia did the United States favor in the first place? The question reemerged in the early 1950s, at a time when relations between the superpowers had deteriorated further and the prospect of a Soviet-American war was being seriously discussed.

In his "America and the Russian Future," George Kennan put forth a number of cautionary ideas that retain interest: "Perhaps the first thing to get straight here is the sort of Russia there is no use looking for. And such a Russia—the kind we may *not* look for—is easy to describe and envisage, for it would be a capitalistic and liberal-democratic one, with institutions closely resembling those of our own republic." After speculating about the institutions of Russia's future economy, he concludes that, in any event, "there is no reason why the form of Russian economic life, beyond certain major exceptions . . . should be considered a matter of vital concern to the outside world."

What America would wish to see, according to Kennan, would be a Russian government "tolerant, communicative, and forthright" in dealing with other states and peoples; a regime, however organized, that stops short of totalitarianism in the exercise of its authority; and a system which will "refrain from pinning an oppressive yoke on other peoples who have the instinct and the capacity for national self-assertion." Judicious, though perhaps too general to be directly applicable, Kennan's prescription is important in stressing what sort of things the United States has no business concerning itself with:

> There is great good in the Russian national character, and the realities of that country scream out today for a form of administration more considerate of that good. Let us hope that it will come. But when Soviet power has run its course, or when its personalities and spirit begin to change (for the ultimate outcome could be one or the other), let us not hover nervously over the people who come after, applying litmus papers daily to their political complexions to find out whether they answer to our concept of "democratic." Give them time; let them be Russians; let them work out their internal problems in their own manner.[6]

The other, and strikingly different, direction was steered by the State Department's Policy Planning Staff, which under Paul Nitze's direction in 1950 produced the no less famous document known as NSC 68—arguably the most belligerent statement ever of U.S. policy toward the Soviet Union. The Soviet Union, it declared, "seeks to impose its absolute authority over the rest of the world." If the United States had adopted containment as its basic strategy in 1948, now "the intensifying struggle requires us to face the fact that we can expect no lasting abatement of the crisis unless and until a change occurs in the nature of the Soviet system." Here, too, was a clear reassertion of the dichotomy between the innocent people and the "evil men who have enslaved them." But for Nitze the required change in the nature of the Soviet system presumably referred not to reform but to its replacement—not so much for the sake of the population of the Soviet Union as for the ostensible security objectives of the United States (though, self-servingly, the distinction was not always made clear).[7]

To be sure, with the onset of the Korean war, the ambitious commitment to change the nature of the Soviet system, articulated in NSC 68, was virtually ignored. Conveniently, if cogently, the document had added, "Clearly it will not only be less costly but more effective if this change occurs to a maximum extent as a result of internal forces in Soviet society."[8] Nonetheless, it represented an influential mind-set that periodically was to be resurrected and, thirty years later, was to find support in important quarters in the first years of the Reagan administration.

A good deal of incoherence continued to prevail in the American outlook on Russia's future. Activities such as broadcasting were stepped up, on the assumption that the Soviet population wanted and needed to hear from the "free world" to maintain and develop those values they shared with us. And yet the "optimism" implied in the original Kennan thesis did not appear to materialize. Few spoke or wrote of it, and few seem to have been confident that "containment" could bring about a marked alteration of the Soviet regime.

These assumptions were tested when, in the months following Stalin's death in March, 1953, the United States refused to believe that things could "get better" as a consequence of the change of leadership in the Kremlin—let alone that a meaningful and significant reform of the Soviet regime could take place. Government documents of the time reveal a good deal of confusion over what "change" or "reform" might mean. It would be fair to say that the prevalent view was that reform *within* communism was meaningless and reform *of* communism—in other words, its transformation into political democracy—was impossible. Thus, to most political analysts of the day, the problem hardly deserved much thought. This was particularly true in the post-Stalin years as belief in the possibility of a victorious war against the Soviet Union—seriously considered until then—vanished once it was clear what nuclear war would mean.[9] Whatever change was going to occur had to come from within the U.S.S.R.

And yet, some elements of both political pragmatism and optimism proved to have survived when, for the first time, concrete issues arose requiring yes-or-no decisions. The question of cultural exchanges with the Soviet Union and the assumptions and purposes underlying them came to the attention of senior officials of the U.S. government in 1955-56.

While President Dwight D. Eisenhower favored them and Secretary of State John Foster Dulles initially resisted them, presidential assistant Nelson Rockefeller—whose job included the elaboration of psychological warfare activities vis-à-vis the U.S.S.R.—in January, 1955, spelled out the "advantages" of increased contacts with Soviet intellectuals and "potential future leaders": "Their attitudes and convictions can only be changed—gradually—if we can reach them on something approaching a normal, human basis." This was Rockefeller's paraphrase of his own argument in NSC 5505/1, approved by Eisenhower, when later that year he contended that cultural exchange would help implement this policy, whose eventual goal was to "redemocratize" Russia by flooding it with information and ideas.

The notion of long-distance "redemocratizing" could be interpreted either as reflecting a belief in the underlying democratic qualities of the

Soviet population or as an artful euphemism for indoctrination and reeducation. That this was a formula acceptable to not merely "liberal" Republicans like Rockefeller but also arch cold warriors is shown by the transcript of one of Nelson Rockefeller's strategy sessions at Quantico, Virginia, where Stephen Possony, a prominent publicist known for his strongly anti-communist views, argued that it was "necessary to provide the Russian intelligentsia . . . with the necessary wherewithal in this field—to do their thinking for them or at least work up the required documentation."[10]

After discussions at the Geneva meeting of foreign ministers in October and November, 1955, some controversy over exchanges developed within the Eisenhower administration. The FBI feared the exchanges would be used for Soviet espionage; the Department of Defense feared they would weaken the push for a strong defense budget; the Department of Commerce feared they might produce a technology drain; and State Department officials feared they would encourage some U.S. allies to cut defense expenditures if relations with Moscow improved. Among the advocates of exchanges, the optimists favored them as a step on the road to coexistence, while the pessimists wanted them to subvert the Soviet regime. Thirty years later, it is an all-too-familiar tableau.

The National Security Council in February and March, 1956, decided in favor of selective exchanges, which in the most positive option were justified as "favor[ing] evolution of the Soviet society and economy toward peaceful development."[11] Dulles elaborated his rationale for the exchanges in a memorandum on "East-West Exchanges," stating that "for the first time since the end of World War II" internal pressures were forcing a liberalization of the Soviet system. He found that "within the Soviet Union there is increasing education and consequent demand for greater freedom of thought and expression; there is increasing demand for greater personal security than existed under Stalin's police state and there is increasing demand for more consumer goods and better living conditions for the masses of people. The demands referred to must be considerable because the Soviet rulers judge it necessary to take drastic and hazardous measures to seem to meet them." The "basic strategy" of the United States, according to him, must be "to promote within Soviet Russia evolution toward a regime which will abandon predatory policies, which will seek to promote the aspirations of the Russian people rather than the global ambitions of International Communism and which will increasingly rest upon the consent of the governed rather than upon despotic police power."[12]

Later in the same memorandum Dulles added that exchanges were to be part of American policy "designed to weaken International Communism." They were not to be seen as "either an acquiescence in Soviet policy or a recognition that Soviet motives have so changed that they are no longer to be feared." Once again, the assumption underlying the policy was the dichotomy between the evil Soviet system and the good Russian people (the non-Russian nationalities of the U.S.S.R. remained virtually ignored). The proposed "strategy" was a mishmash of foreign policy objectives and the quest for popular self-determination. Without abandoning the totalitarian model, Washington was in practice moving beyond it.

J. Gerrit Gantvoort correctly concludes from his examination of the available evidence that the "cultural iron curtain" was lifted by the United States in the summer of 1956 for the same reason it had been imposed earlier—as part of the struggle against "International Communism." At bottom, reform in Russia had nothing to do with it.

For the years from John F. Kennedy through Jimmy Carter, not all key government documents have as yet become available. However, it is clear that in the post-Stalin years—allowing for all the significant variations within them—the focus shifted to "managing" Soviet-American relations rather than assuming that an early "termination" of the conflict, one way or the other, was apt to take place.[13] "Managing" meant operating on the assumption that relations with the Soviet regime would extend into the indefinite future and might improve once something significant changed on the Soviet side. "Reform" should have been an obvious expectation, especially in the Khrushchev years. In fact, it hardly was.

To be sure, there were occasional discussions, among academics and government officials, whether the United States should seek to "strengthen" one faction (or what was presumed to be a faction) in the Soviet leadership against the other or others, but in the end no serious effort of this sort was ever made. American knowledge of cleavages and alignments in the Kremlin was too tenuous; American understanding of whose positions and future behavior would be in the U.S. national interest was too uncertain; American skill in giving aid and comfort to one individual or group would have been sadly lacking; and American reluctance to get involved in what were at times described as "games among mafiosi" was overwhelming. No one apparently realized that, like it or not, American capabilities, policies, and behavior served as arguments cited by different elements in the Soviet elite in internal disputes. To that extent, the United States was unwittingly a silent actor in Soviet politics—but only to that extent. There was no active American "banking on reform."

In the Brezhnev years, "reform" in the Soviet Union was once again a farfetched idea. To be sure, Henry Kissinger's "web of interdependence" would have endeavored, once more, to generate feedback from the international to the domestic policy realm, but it would have focused—had it been implemented and practiced over some time—largely on stimulating a more restrained and responsible foreign policy. The one area of American "interference" in what to Moscow was (and remains) a matter of domestic jurisdiction was emigration, primarily of Soviet Jews. Since the change of Soviet policy on emigration was clearly motivated by interest in foreign reactions—and foreign trade—this was not properly a case of Soviet "reform."[14]

The Reagan administration came into office with a stronger ideological commitment against "Soviet communism" than any of its predecessors since World War II. While they were by no means universally shared by the new team, Richard Pipes's views most systematically expressed the "essentialist" approach to Soviet problems around the White House.[15]

After having asserted for many years that any possible reform of the Soviet system was bound to be insignificant, trivial, or cosmetic since it would not change the essence of the Soviet system, such premier "essentialists" as Richard Pipes now argued both that (1) a change of the Soviet system must be an objective of the West, and (2) such a change is in fact possible. The principal point, as he himself summed it up, "is that the West, in its own interest, ought to assist those economic and political forces which are at work inside the Communist Bloc undermining the system and pressuring its elites to turn their attention inward. Experience has shown time and again that attempts to restrain Soviet aggressiveness by a combination of rewards and punishments do not accomplish their purpose, because they address the symptoms of the problem, instead of its cause, which is the system itself."[16]

After discussing the tsarist heritage of expansion, Pipes found that "Communist ideology and the interests of the *nomenklatura* [political elite] have reinforced these expansionist traditions, making Russian imperialism more aggressive and more persistent than ever before."[17] He later commented,

> Russia . . . is so vast and complex and so loosely held together that its leaders have always feared and rarely volunteered changes. They have consented to make changes only under duress caused either by humiliations abroad or upheavals at home. This was the case with the reforms of Peter the Great, Alexander II and Nicholas II. . . . The record of Russian history thus strongly suggests, and informed Russian opinion cor-

roborates, that such changes for the better that one can expect in the nature of the Soviet government and in its conduct of foreign relations will come about only from failures, instabilities, and fears of collapse and not from growing confidence and sense of security.[18]

According to Pipes, the minimum reforms needed—which he defines as legality, private enterprise, and decentralization—are impossible so long as the present system exists, until the nomenklatura surrenders some of its authority.[19]

This scheme, however, can scarcely be accepted as a proposal for a reform of the Soviet system. Not only is it self-contradictory—for instance, in calling for the support of those who "pressure the elites for change" within the existing system as well as those who seek "to undermine it"—it is an attempt, however quixotic, to mobilize the Soviet elite to hoist themselves on their own petard. When challenged to reconcile this advocacy with his earlier notion of unchangeable Russia, Pipes argues that strong shocks can indeed induce changes in political cultures, citing Hiroshima and the Holocaust as examples.[20] Many observers will, of course, also wish to contest his argument that only instability and insecurity can bring about desirable changes in the Soviet regime and its policies.

Even in the Reagan administration, however, this was not the prevalent view, especially after 1983. Far more characteristic was an agnostic approach to the possible effect of U.S. policy on the Soviet system. Thus Secretary of State George P. Shultz testified before the Senate Foreign Relations Committee:

True friendship and cooperation will remain out of reach so long as the Soviet system is driven by ideology and national ambition to seek to aggrandize its power and undermine the interests of the democracies. We must resist this Soviet power drive vigorously if there is to be any hope for lasting stability. At the same time, in the thermonuclear age the common interest in survival gives both sides an incentive to moderate the rivalry and to seek, in particular, ways to control nuclear weapons and reduce the risks of war. We cannot know whether such a steady Western policy will, over time, lead to a mellowing of the Soviet system; perhaps not. But the West has the same responsibility in either case: to resist Soviet encroachments firmly while holding the door open to more constructive possibilities.[21]

One recurring source of confusion in American policy debates is a lack of clarity concerning the meaning of "reform." It is useful to distinguish reform from both (1) changes of policy, which require neither structural changes nor redistribution of power and which can readily be reversed; and (2) a replacement of the existing regime, be it by revolt and forcible takeover or by foreign conquest. "Reform," if it is to have a consistent meaning, must denote a significant change *within* the existing system.

This formulation begs the question just how "significant" the changes must be to qualify as reform. There is, in fact, no objective criterion, and observers will legitimately differ in their estimation of the scope and impact of a given set of changes. It is also important to remember that a reform may, but need not, be benign. Moreover, reforms may aim at greater discipline, efficiency, or productivity; they thus may be functional for the "system" without helping the citizen within it. Other reforms may ease the lot of some or all citizens, broaden opportunities, provide for regularized legal procedures and predictable penalties, or open access to ideas or media not previously available. Usually, foreign observers have simply called for the latter. Yet the absence of clarity on this score has been among the reasons for the lack of consistency in the U.S. position concerning reform in the U.S.S.R.

This essay contends that the United States must define, for its own purposes, what kinds of reform in the Soviet Union it favors and why, but that the achievement of such reforms normally should not be an explicit objective of American policy. The United States must, as a matter of both self-interest and common humanity, look with favor on the prospect of certain changes in the Soviet Union. These would surely include changes in institutions, policies, and practices that would lead to the rule of law, would promote and protect pluralism and tolerance, and would require accountability and responsiveness by the powers-that-be.

Some forms of American behavior and policy are apt to some extent to promote or retard, facilitate or complicate, the adoption and implementation of these and other Soviet reforms. But it is not always clear what does and what does not enhance propitious circumstances for such reforms. Favoring such changes in the Soviet system or even wishing to promote them does not by any means require proclaiming them as official objectives of U.S. foreign policy. In fact, often the chances of their implementation may be best when American interest in them is kept unadvertised or, in some instances, "quiet diplomacy" is used.

Regarding Soviet behavior abroad, American concern is proper and legitimate—and here structural reforms are least likely to be either required or relevant. Expansionism is not an organic necessity of the existing system. Reforms within the Soviet Union (for instance, of the governmental apparatus, the policymaking machinery, the economic structure, Soviet responsiveness to popular demands, and policy priorities) are not properly the official business of the United States. Even when they are of supreme interest to the United States, they must not be trumpeted as such. There are both principled and practical reasons for this.

First, as a matter of principle, it must not be the task of any country to change the internal order of another (except insofar as international agreements, such as the Helsinki Accord of 1975, provide legitimate grounds for concern with some aspects of another state's domestic order). If sovereignty has any operational content left, it means precisely this.

Second, there is a powerful pragmatic argument for such a policy: there are reciprocal implications for the United States and its allies if everyone — Moscow (and any terrorists) included — is recognized as having an equal right to try to alter the behavior and institutions of other states.

Third, if we look at the record of the United States in seeking to promote radical changes in other nations, we discover a pattern which is marked by depressing incompetence, lack of realism, naivete, quixotic mismanagement, and all too often a total lack of political or emotional empathy. In regard to the Soviet Union, we have at least fragmentary information on such pathetic endeavors as the "Free Russia Committee," thirty to thirty-five years ago, probably sponsored behind the scenes by appropriate organs of the U.S. government, and similar (or rather, often wildly conflicting) American-sponsored efforts to shape up organizations "representing" separatist nationality groups. With a few noteworthy exceptions, the record of the United States in trying to deal with pressures for reform abroad, whether in friendly or in hostile countries — from Chile to South Africa, from Iran to Pakistan — has been neither enlightened nor encouraging. We do not need U.S. sponsorship of Soviet *contras,* even in the name of reform.

What the United States can do, at the right time and with proper discretion and tact, is to signal Moscow that it would not seek to take advantage of any destabilization the institution of domestic reforms might produce; and that desirable transformations in the Soviet world would be positively received in the United States, which may be an added incentive to proceed with the reforms.

The United States — the government and the public — will do well to be keenly aware of the limits of American power in the reform of the Soviet system as well as others. The United States can and ought to be better informed about the prospects for changes in the U.S.S.R., their scope, significance, and likely consequences. Knowing that it cannot control them, Washington still ought to know what changes it would or would not favor. These are both moral and realistic goals. They may be modest, compared to reshaping or demolishing the adversary superpower, but they are by no means trivial. They might truly improve the conditions for better relations. They are also goals with which the United States can live.

NOTES

1. United States, Department of State, *Foreign Relations of the United States, 1917,* Supplement I (Washington, D.C., 1931), p. 200. Like some later commentators, Wilson went on to say that the tsarist autocracy "was not in fact Russian in origin, character, or purpose."

2. For a balanced assessment, see Benjamin M. Weissman, *Herbert Hoover and Famine Relief to Soviet Russia: 1921-1923* (Stanford, 1974).

3. Henry Stimson to Harry Truman, September 11, 1945, in *Foreign Relations of the United States, 1945* (Washington, D.C., 1968), 2:41.

4. See, for example, *Foreign Relations of the United States, 1948* (Washington, D.C., 1975), 1:667-68; *1949* (1976), 1:339; *1949* (1976), 5:625-27, 659; *1951* (1979), 1:1047.

5. "X" [George F. Kennan], "The Sources of Soviet Conduct," *Foreign Affairs* 25 (July, 1947):566-82, quote on pp. 581-82; Kennan, *American Diplomacy, 1900-1950* (Chicago, 1951), pp. 126ff. See also Kennan, "The X-Article," in his *Memoirs: 1925-1950* (Boston, 1967), chap. 15.

6. George F. Kennan, "America and the Russian Future," *Foreign Affairs* 29 (April, 1951):351-70, quote on p. 356. See also Kennan's *Memoirs: 1950-1963* (Boston, 1972): "Since, as I firmly believed, the best discernible possibility for the evolution of Russian society in the direction we desired lay precisely in just such a liberalization and moderation of Soviet power, and since this, in turn, could hardly be expected to take place if the Soviet leaders became convinced that the United States was committed against them come what may and had lost confidence in any outcome other than their overthrow and total destruction, then to permit them to gain that impression might mean, in the end, to forfeit the last and only chance of avoiding catastrophe" (pp. 101-3).

7. NSC 68 and related documents are in *Foreign Relations of the United States, 1950* (Washington, D.C., 1977), 1:234-92, particularly pp. 237, 242, 244. See also Samuel F. Wells, Jr., "Sounding the Tocsin: NSC 68 and the Soviet Threat," *International Security* 4, no. 2 (1979):116-58, particularly pp. 131-32.

8. NSC 68, Report to the President, April 7, 1950, in *Foreign Relations, 1950,* p. 241.

9. See, however, John Lewis Gaddis, *Strategies of Containment* (Oxford, 1982); Alexander George and Richard Smoke, *Deterrence in American Foreign Policy* (New York, 1974); and Robert Dallek, *The American Style of Foreign Policy* (New York, 1983).

10. For most of the information in this section, I am much obliged to J. Gerrit Gantvoort, who kindly made available to me his unpublished paper, "Lifting the American Iron Curtain: Cultural Exchange and National Security, 1955-56." The Rockefeller memorandum cited above is in Eisenhower Papers, Rockefeller (1), Box 61, Dwight D. Eisenhower Library, Abilene, Kans. The Possony memorandum, "The Purpose, Requirements, and Structure of an American Ideological Program," is in *Declassified Documents Retrospective Collection, 1977* (Washington, 1975–), A-269, p. 219.

11. NSC 5602/1, p. 13, cited in Gantvoort, "Lifting the American Iron Curtain."

12. Dulles draft, May 12, 1956, in Dulles Papers, Subject Series, East-West Contacts, 1956, Box 4, Princeton University Library; became the basis for NSC 5607 (adopted June 28, 1956), partially declassified. For Dulles's views, see also Ole Holsti, "Belief System and National Images: John Foster Dulles and the Soviet Union" (Ph.D. dissertation, Stanford University, 1962), and his contribution to David J. Finlay, Ole R. Holsti, and Richard R. Fagen, *Enemies in Politics* (Chicago, 1967).

13. See a good discussion in John Van Oudenaren, *U.S. Leadership Perceptions of the Soviet Problem since 1945* (Santa Monica, Calif., 1982). On the problems of U.S. policymaking toward the Soviet Union, see also Joseph S. Nye, ed., *The Making of America's Soviet Policy* (New Haven, Conn., 1984).

14. Kissinger claims, in retrospect, that there was an additional element in his calculus: "We were dealing with a system too ideologically hostile for instant conciliation and militarily too powerful to destroy. We had . . . to make arrangements with it that would gain time—time for the inherent stagnation of the Communist system to work its corrosion and to permit the necessity of coexistence based on restraint to be understood." Henry Kissinger, *White House Years* (Boston, 1979), p.123.

15. On "essentialist" and alternative American approaches, see Alexander Dallin and Gail W. Lapidus, "Reagan and the Russians," in *Eagle Defiant,* ed. Kenneth A. Oye, Robert J. Lieber, and Donald Rothchild (Boston, 1983), pp. 199ff.

16. Richard Pipes, *Survival Is Not Enough* (New York, 1984), p. 14.

17. Ibid., p. 42.

18. Ibid., pp. 203-5.

19. Many observers will consider the power attributed to the so-called nomenklatura an exaggeration. This paper does not consider those proposals for "reform" which amount to the disintegration of the U.S.S.R. into separate ethnic entities.

20. Oral remarks by Richard Pipes.

21. Department of State, *Bulletin,* March, 1985, p. 13. This statement is identical with a passage in the George Shultz article, "New Realities and New Ways of Thinking," *Foreign Affairs* 63 (1985):706. As earlier indicated, the success in improving certain human rights practices or securing the release of individual political prisoners, such as Anatolii Shcharanskii, may qualify as "concessions" but scarcely as a "reform."

Is Sovietology Reformable?

ALEXANDER YANOV

At the outset let me make clear that Western strategy for helping Russia make its belated breakthrough into political modernity cannot and should not be *imposed* on Mikhail Sergeevich Gorbachev. Rather, its essence must consist of our being ready to *react adequately* to any socioeconomic or political move the Soviet reformist leadership might make. As I tried to show in my first essay in this volume, it is because we did not have such a strategy that we blew the case of Nikita Sergeevich Khrushchev. The strategy's main objective would be to support Gorbachev's own intuitive drive to uplift the Soviet middle class, thereby directing his reformist energy into the right channels.

If we are able to work out such a grand strategy for an irreversible Russian reform (a task that for centuries has eluded Russia's reformist leaders), we may be in a position to competently judge which practical steps should be taken by the U.S. government at any turn of Soviet reform. Although a few such steps directed at supporting the elevation of the Soviet middle class are proposed later in this essay, they are clearly just bits and pieces of what could be accomplished by, say, an institute of Soviet reform, if such an intellectual forum were ever established in America.

It is no less clear that dismantling the adversarial paradigm or a paradigm change in our vision of Russian reform is a *sine qua non* for any such strategy. And who can possibly initiate such a dramatic breakthrough in the basic attitudes of the American public toward the Soviet reform if not us, experts, members of the sovietological guild? If the point of my piece on Khrushchev was to try to show that a reform in American sovietology is a prerequisite for a successful Soviet reform, it seems logical to ask whether sovietology itself is reformable. Are we capable of what the Soviet intelligentsia is doing in Moscow right now— with such an iconoclastic vigor and passion?

Can we, for instance, when discussing Soviet reform get rid of most of the standard formulas and terms derived from the adversarial paradigm? I am talking about basic terms that betray and shape our very assumptions as to the nature of political change in Russia, terms like "totalitarian dictatorship," or "Soviet regime," or "Soviet ideology," or "Soviet elite." Those terms were born in the context of adversarial relations, and they are operational only in that context. They are no good for a strategy whose central orientation is to assist Soviet reformers in breaking the bond of Russia's political heritage. They are no good, if only because they deprive us of the fundamental component of any strategy—a clear vision of purpose.

Let me give an example. Here is one way we might argue our case before a jury of American politicians (and the American public). What do we want from Russia? To be sure, we would like it to behave in a civilized fashion in both international and domestic policies. The behavior of a political system, however, is only a function of its nature. It is naive to scold a wolf for eating sheep rather than grass. It is no surprise people with common sense refrain from doing this. But is it not just as naive to denounce a pre-modern political system for behaving in an uncivilized manner in the modern world? It simply cannot behave otherwise. Common sense demands a choice. If we are indeed dealing with a "totalitarian" wolf, then all negotiations to make it eat grass rather than sheep are senseless, as the conservatives assert. If we nevertheless conduct such negotiations in hopes of their success, it should logically follow that the people with whom we are sitting down at the negotiating table *are not* representing a totalitarian wolf. It is a case of either-or. The very fact that Western strategy now operates on the basis of both these assumptions—that it is dealing with an evil empire and that negotiations with it are possible—indicates this strategy is *neither constructive nor businesslike.*[1]

For a pre-modern system to start behaving like a civilized one, its political and cultural isolation should be broken, as Petr Chaadaev dreamed a century and a half ago. In short, it must be politically modernized. Consequently, the only Western strategy that makes sense is to facilitate Russia's political modernization, the nucleus of which is the elevation of its middle class—something Khrushchev started and the Hungarians continued.

Such a perspective would immediately bring a clear and articulate purpose to our strategy toward Soviet reform. How useful for *this purpose* are the terms "totalitarian dictatorship" or "Soviet regime"? These terms only serve to confuse the public by lumping together indiscriminately all the different Soviet regimes. By using them, we are virtually doomed to treat similarly the aggressive regime of War Communism and the regime of the New Economic Policy that leaned toward peaceful coexistence; Stalin's terroristic dictatorship bent on grand expansion and Khrushchev's regime of reform seeking accommodation with the West; the petty expansionist Brezhnev regime of decay and stagnation and Gorbachev's *perestroika* promulgating "new thinking" in international relations.

Now is the time to arm ourselves with some more subtle instruments of analysis that would help us distinguish between Soviet regimes working for political modernization of Russia and those working against it. It is imperative that we act now since the political process in Russia is traditionally antagonistic and each new regime invariably negates the basic priorities and objectives of its predecessor.[2] Wouldn't it be much more sensible to introduce into our analysis of Soviet politics a concept like "regime change" that focuses the public's attention on *changes* in the system, instead of "Soviet regime" that focuses this attention on its *adversarial immutability?*

Similarly misleading seems to be the term "Soviet ideology," if only because we may be dealing with a number of distinctly different Soviet ideologies, as I have argued elsewhere.[3] Most misleading, however, is the term "Soviet elite" (or *nomenklatura,* in vulgar usage). In reality we are dealing with a broad and contradictory spectrum of Soviet elites, some of which are agents of political modernization—and in this sense potential allies of the West—while others are agents of stagnation or counterreform and thus our irreconcilable adversaries.

This is how we might have argued our case before a jury of American politicians (and the American public), if we were indeed prepared for a paradigm change. In reality we aren't, however. In reality, we ourselves are too often the prisoners of antiquated conventions, and sovietological perestroika is, alas, far behind the one in Moscow.

I shall try to show how far behind we are, using as an example an extraordinary coincidence. Two books appeared simultaneously in 1984 that seem to summarize coherently for the first time the respective positions of sovietological conservatives and liberals in their dispute over how American policy toward Soviet Russia is to be conducted. One was Richard Pipes's *Survival Is Not Enough* (at the time it was hailed by U.N. Ambassador Jeane J. Kirkpatrick as a "major new study [in which] Professor Pipes's unexampled scholarship illuminates the most important policy questions of our time"),[4] and the other was Timothy Colton's *The Dilemma of Reform in the Soviet Union,* which represents a kind of encyclopedia of sovietological liberalism.[5] Since the books appeared on the eve of Gorbachev's perestroika, we have a terrific opportunity to compare their policy analyses and prognoses with what really happened in Soviet-American relations later. I must add perhaps that, to my knowledge, nothing appearing since then in American sovietological literature contradicts in any substantial way the basic concepts used by Pipes and Colton in their analyses in 1984.

The principal assumptions of these books stand in such opposition to one another that it is as if one had been written, say, by Lenin and the other by Miliukov. Pipes himself does not hide the fact that his evaluation of what is going on in Russia is close to Lenin's. He even uses Lenin's terms to describe it: "Were Lenin alive today, he would very likely conclude that conditions in his country and its empire meet the criteria which he had established for 'revolutionary situations.' Certainly, the Soviet bloc is currently in the throes today of a much graver economic and political crisis than either Russia or Germany had experienced a century ago."[6] It is this very Bolshevik revolutionary situation, the basis of all of Pipes's political analyses and recommendations, that Colton refutes: "Some in the West suggest the U.S.S.R. today is a society in crisis, that it has come to a turning point in which the very continuance of the Soviet order is at stake. The thesis is wrong. It understates the rulers' resources and overstates their problems."[7]

All the rest of the authors' conflicts with one another emerge from this single point. Like Lenin's evaluation of the crisis of Imperial Russia, Pipes's evaluation of Soviet Russia's crisis begins with the standard Bolshevik credo best summarized by the Russian saying, "the grave cures the hunchback": "totalitarian regimes are by definition incapable of evolution from within and impervious to change from without."[8] In Colton's book, the term "totalitarianism" is not used at all. Actually, Pipes's relation to this ironclad "totalitarian" formula, which has reigned in sovietology for decades, is by no means as unambiguous as it might seem. In the same paragraph he himself knocks a hole in the totalitarian formula with his—in Colton's opinion, false—thesis that the "systemic crisis" Soviet Russia is undergoing demands from the Soviet elite, which Pipes calls the nomenklatura, "action of a decisive kind."[9] That means action capable of effecting evolution in a system "incapable of evolution."

Colton has no doubt the post-Stalinist Soviet system is fundamentally different from what it was under Stalin. Pipes cannot seem to decide exactly what he thinks on this point. On the one hand, he asserts that the nomenklatura "so dreads *any change* in the Stalinist system, from which its power and privilege largely derive, that it chooses ever weaker general secretaries as Party leaders."[10] On the other hand, he considers a *"reversion to Stalinism"*[11] as one of the alternatives to the current

Soviet regime, albeit an "unrealistic" one.[12] Further, Pipes talks about "the political and economic system of Stalinism which his successors have retained even as they turned its originator into a virtual non-person,"[13] while at the same time he maintains the "current crisis of Communism" is caused by the nomenklatura's *denial* of Stalinism. The crisis is "due to its vegetating in a kind of no man's land between compulsion and freedom, unable to profit from either."[14] Such an agglomeration of contradictions is unavoidable for an author who simultaneously shares and refutes the totalitarian formula. Colton, naturally, does not have this trouble.

The main difference between the two books, however, is their political recommendations. Pipes, referring to one of the principal founders of Marxism, Friedrich Engels, recommends applying pressure on the Soviet Union by all possible means: "The West would be well advised to do all in its power to assist the indigenous forces making for change in the U.S.S.R. and its client states. . . . by denying to the Soviet bloc various forms of economic aid, it can help intensify the formidable pressures which are being exerted on their creaky economies. This will push them in the direction of general liberalization as well as accommodation with the West."[15] In other words, Pipes proposes to achieve reform by the revolutionary means Engels and Lenin recommended. The classical authorities to whom he refers, however, were thoroughly logical: they had no interest in a "general liberalization" of tsarism or its "accommodation with the West." In recommending "pressure" sufficient to drive Russia's "regime" crisis to the white heat of a revolutionary "systemic" crisis—one in which the very survival of the political and social system is at stake—they had in mind the *destruction* of tsarism, not its reform.

Be that as it may, all these problems are alien to Colton, since he, as we have seen, denies in principle the existence of a crisis in the Soviet system. Correspondingly, all the recommendations of Pipes and like-minded thinkers represent to him irresponsible chatter: "Loose talk about destabilizing the Soviet system is at best a diversion from the practical business of foreign policy, and at worst a flight from reason inviting a comparably immoderate response from Moscow. Economic boycotts, arms buildups, propaganda offensives, intervention on behalf of specific domestic groups, and the like may or may not deter or punish specific Soviet foreign policy decisions. But they have little potential for influencing in a way congenial to Western interests the domestic environment within which such decisions take place."[16]

Moreover, reflecting the general tendency of liberal sovietology, Colton is opposed in principle to any attempts to influence events within Russia.

He sympathetically quotes George Kennan's evaluation of the dilemma: "A choice must be made between the interests of democratization in Russia and the interests of world peace. In the face of this choice there can be only one answer." Colton decisively announces, "The ultimate Western resource for influencing Soviet society is not grain, optical fibers, or gas turbines but the slow-acting magnet of Western culture." Of course, he understands that "altered attitudes and values take generations."[17]

As we know, "the slow-acting magnet of Western culture" also existed throughout the past five centuries of Russian history. Somehow, though, it failed over the course of these twenty generations to exert sufficient influence on the operation of the Russian political system to move it "in a way congenial to Western interests." Otherwise, Colton would not have had to express such vague hopes at the close of the twentieth century. Where is the guarantee, then, that this "magnet" will be able to accomplish in future generations what it could not manage in preceding ones? Where, in other words, is the guarantee that the policy of noninterference recommended by Colton will ever bear fruit? And would it not be fitting to ask ourselves if humanity has the necessary generations at its disposal in this nuclear age of ours? How can we square this with Colton's own prediction that, in the event a new Russian reform fails, the Soviet regime will face an unprecedented crisis as early as the 1990s? As he said in the same book: "If conservatives or reactionaries gain the upper hand in the 1980s, or if bungled reforms come to naught . . . the likelihood would then be high that the 1990s would bring a crisis of legitimacy and far more searching dilemmas for the regime, with its core structures and values open to question and under attack as never before."[18]

It appears that the "slow-working magnet of Western culture" would be too slow to prevent such lamentable developments after all. So what, then, does Colton recommend to prevent them? What should we do "if bungled reforms come to naught" in the 1990s? These crucial questions are not answered in his book. In fact, they are not even asked.

Let's summarize the differences between the conservative and liberal sovietological positions up to this point. Pipes, confidently evaluating the Soviet situation as revolutionary, predicts an upheaval that would put at stake the very continuance of the Soviet order. In contrast, Colton evaluates the situation as moderately distressful and therefore rejects the likelihood of *radical* reform (one which would focus on changing Soviet institutions and beliefs). His favorite model of the Soviet future is one of *moderate* reform focusing on changes in public policy and in the machinery needed to fulfill these changes.

Who was right and who was wrong? Is Soviet order at stake in the late 1980s? It is not. Are Soviet institutions and beliefs in the process of radical change? They are. What, then, is the conclusion the reader must draw as to the prognostic capability of both conservative and liberal positions? Unfortunately, it is rather poor. Both authors appear to be wrong in their basic predictions. What is taking place in Moscow now is precisely a radical reform, the possibility of which has been rejected by both Pipes and Colton. There must be something inadequate with the very instruments of sovietological analyses, both liberal and conservative, if they left the America public in the dark as to the most probable way of Soviet development. When the Soviet reformers met with a similar predicament in their own analyses, they unleashed the *radical* reform — boldly revising the very foundations of the inadequate analyses. So far there is no sign that American sovietology responded in kind. But let's go back to Pipes and Colton.

Up to now, the focus has been on the differences between conservative and liberal sovietology because there seemed to be nothing in common between their positions in the dispute. Yet there appears to be one point on which Pipes and Colton agree. Unfortunately, this single point of agreement seems to spring directly from the adversarial paradigm. Both Pipes and Colton deny the reversibility of the political changes that took place in Russia after the death of Stalin. Both deny, in other words, the possibility of a counterreform. Paradoxically, both deny it for the same reasons.

Despite all his vacillations regarding the "totalitarian" formula and Stalinism, Pipes states explicitly, "Stalinism cannot be restored for any number of reasons, the most weighty of which is the impossibility of running the country's present-day sophisticated industrial plant and military establishment by brute force and in isolation from the rest of the world."[19] Colton agrees: "The economic and social content of the primal Stalinist model also loads the dice against re-Stalinization. . . . It [the Soviet Union] has near-universal literacy, is reasonably settled in its ways and mores, and is far less divorced from world developments and opinion."[20]

It should be noted that what Pipes and Colton have both inadvertently described is Weimar Germany. What would they now have to say if people in the 1920s had attempted to prove the unlikelihood of a Fascist coup in Germany by arguing that it was impossible for a Nazi dictatorship to run a sophisticated industrial plant by brute force? Or by using arguments about Germany's near-universal literacy and reasonably well-established ways and mores? Did all this actually hinder a Fascist coup? Did Hitler really encounter so many difficulties in running

Germany's quite sophisticated industrial plants once the masses had accepted the conditions of the new social contract which he offered them? Was there truly so much resistance once the Germans had agreed to a dictatorial mentality and a new ideology based on asceticism, military prowess, and a deified leader guiding the empire out from the depths of humiliation and up to the shining heights of a thousand-year Reich? Once they began to see themselves as a race of masters and warriors, locked in a mortal struggle to save Germany, they were prepared to accept the rest without question. This is precisely the ideology and mentality the Russian New Right is offering the Soviet people today.

Here is where the danger of indiscriminate use of the term "Soviet ideology" enters in. After years of exaggerated claims about the role of ideology in the Soviet system, we still do not seem to grasp its meta-ideological nature, in other words, its capacity to accommodate any number of sub-ideologies in the same way that the Christian or Islamic meta-ideologies have been able to accommodate a multitude of denominations, each negating the others and calling itself the only "true" Christianity or Islam. We call communism a secular religion, but the obvious implications of this statement seem to escape us. The idea of "denomination change" can be as essential to comprehending the dynamics of Soviet ideology as "regime change" is to comprehending the political dynamics of the Soviet system. What I have in mind in this case is that the ideological justification of a new counterreform, or a new denomination change in Soviet ideology, has been prepared over the last twenty years by Russian nationalist intellectuals, both in Moscow and abroad, whom I call the Russian New Right.

I do not see Russian nationalism as a collection of vague sentiments and emotions that Stalin skillfully used in building his national-communist denomination. I see it rather as a distinct ideology which I, following Nikolai Berdiaev, call the Russian Idea and which is at least as old as Marxism and much more deeply rooted in the Russian psyche. According to available sources, the Russian Idea, which was defeated by Marxism at the beginning of the century, is planning to take its revenge by the year 2000, which coincides, by the way, with Colton's prediction of a systemic crisis in the U.S.S.R. in case "bungled reforms come to naught."

The main point is that the Russian Idea's plan for the year 2000 does not envisage a decisive break with Soviet meta-ideology. Quite the contrary, its strategies are oriented toward a denomination change within it, which presages a rebirth of the siege mentality, a reassertion of imperial status and ascetic values, and a new vision of Russians as a race of masters and warriors locked into a mortal struggle with the worldwide conspiracy of "kike-Freemasons" and "smatterers" who are seeking to enslave the world. In the event the New Right triumphs and the population accepts the terms of its new social contract, the West might be faced with a nuclear-garrison-state empire—something more monstrous than humanity has ever seen. If such a metamorphosis was possible under the conditions of a systemic crisis in twentieth-century Germany, why should it be impossible in Russia?[21]

Here we see something still more striking: both Pipes and Colton, in describing the political situation in Russia in the 1980s and its future prospects, ignore the rebirth of the Russian Idea in the Soviet Union, its ideological evolution, and its plan for the year 2000. That, though, is just half the trouble, as the Russians say. The real trouble starts when both authors identically neglect the long-term patterns of political change in Russia and conceive of a possible future counterreform only as the restoration of Stalinism.

All previous Russian historical catastrophes, however, have differed from Stalin's and each other in all things except their primary func-tion—the violent arrest of political change within the empire and the maximal weakening, sometimes even the complete annihilation, of the emerging middle class. Stalin loved to be compared to Ivan the Terrible or Peter I. Indeed, all these tyrants had much in common: a brutal garrison-state dictatorship, grandiose expansionist schemes, and the re-vitalization of the Russian military-industrial complex. In the ideological sense, however, the leaders of Russia's counterreforms stood in total opposition to each other.

Why, then, in considering the precedents for a new Russian coun-terreform, should we limit ourselves to just one, that of Stalin, to the exclusion of all the others? Is it because they are beyond the pale of our conventions? And how can we—in light of the catastrophic char-acter of the Russian political past—insist on the *irreversibility* of the changes which occurred after the last of its brutal dictatorships? It is really the *reversibility* of political change that sets Russia apart from the history of all other European nations. Russia's total experience with counterreforms decisively rejects the single assertion on which Pipes and Colton agree.

Yet their agreement is entirely in line with the adversarial paradigm which habitually sees the "Soviet regime" as absolute evil. Because of that, a political change in Russia—any change—could naturally be only for the better. It is this unilinear vision that actually distinguishes the adversarial paradigm from its rival. This rival, the non-adversarial paradigm, is sufficiently open-minded to see Russia's political process as a two-way street as it were. According to the non-adversarial paradigm, change in Moscow can be for the worse as well. Or, in other words, the chances for a new radical counterreform in the 1990s are just as good as the chances for the irreversibility of the current radical reform.

As the reader may remember, in 1984 Pipes saw Soviet Russia in the throes of a systemic crisis and Colton denied that there was a crisis at all (while allowing for a systemic crisis in the 1990s in case bungled reforms come to naught). In fact, Soviet leaders themselves admitted frankly that Brezhnev's stagnation did bring the nation to the verge of a crisis (they call it a "pre-crisis situation"). Thus both Pipes and Colton seem to be in trouble again—and again due to the crude, insufficiently differentiated instruments of analysis provided by the aversarial paradigm.

In contrast, its non-adversarial rival seems to be equipped with more subtle analytical instruments that are needed for both evaluating the current stormy events in Moscow and envisaging the possibilities of the future. Just as it allows us to distinguish between the two basic types of political change in Russia—reformist and counterreformist—it gives us an opportunity to distinguish between the basic types of its political crises—regime and systemic.

Regime crises, no matter how sharp and painful they may be, still leave the national leadership with a *choice* of the direction of regime change. This can lead to reforms, which resulted, for example, from the crises of 1801, 1855, 1921, and 1953; or to counterreforms, which followed the crises of 1825 and 1881; or to political stagnation, which ensued in 1613 and 1964. In certain circumstances, the national leadership can force a regime of counterreform on the nation, which happened in the course of the crises of 1796 and 1929.

The other type of Russian political crisis, which I call "systemic," differs from all the previously discussed cases in that it deprives the national leadership of control over the direction of the regime change and thus leaves the system with no choice other than *counterreform*. In a systemic crisis, it is not the regime's fate that is at stake, as in a regime crisis, but rather that of the system itself. Up to this point in Russian history, the only way to avoid its collapse in a systemic crisis situation has been a garrison-state dictatorship.

Systemic crises have been rare in Russia. They have come as the result of either powerful reforms that have threatened to become irreversible—as in the 1550s under Ivan the Terrible—or the extreme spiritual and political exhaustion of the system, when its core structures and values were open to question—as in the 1690s and 1917. Each of *these* systemic changes was a genuine revolution, be it from above or from below.

These Russian revolutions, however, have performed a function directly opposite to that performed by revolutions in the West; they have not destroyed, but rather renewed and perpetuated the system's premodern character. For just this reason I call them "systemic counterreforms." Each systemic counterreform required not only mass terror and grandiose purges of the old elites but also radical changes in the mentality of the new elites. They brought about not only gigantic political and institutional changes, which made Russia practically unrecognizable compared to its former self, but also systemic denomination changes. Each of them marked a catastrophe for the Russian middle class and the return of the system to its original pre-modern parameters—only on a higher level of military-industrial complexity. Each was the result of either the success or failure of a reform.

What follows from this schematic overview of Russia's political crises over the past five centuries is that Pipes was right in asserting that in 1984 the Soviet Union was in crisis. Yet he was wrong in suggesting that this crisis was revolutionary, in other words, systemic. For what indeed occurred in Moscow in 1985 was a regime crisis. The national leadership was given a critical choice. It chose a radical reform. It is undeniable that by now the new reform regime is firmly in charge of the situation.

Although Colton was wrong in denying the crisis condition in 1984, he may still be right in envisaging a systemic crisis in the 1990s. Yet he may again be wrong, according to our overview, in suggesting that such a crisis can only be a result of the failure of reform. As follows from our overview, Russia is in for a crisis in the 1990s regardless of whether Gorbachev's reform is successful or it fails. To imagine Russia can part with its centuries-long political tradition and complete its journey into political modernity without a serious upheaval is beyond both historical precedent and common sense. The crucial difference is only in whether the coming upheaval remains within the limits of a "normal" regime crisis or is destined to turn into a new historical catastrophe for Russia—and perhaps for the world.

According to the non-adversarial paradigm, the outcome of this future crisis depends on whether Russia will meet it with a middle class strong enough, organized enough, and articulate enough to withstand the new extremist assault. The Russian middle class wasn't ready for it in either 1560 or 1917. How to prepare it for the coming showdown with the Russian New Right is a task, as I mentioned earlier, for some serious intellectual forum in America to figure out. I don't know whether the establishment of an institute of Soviet reform is possible in this country. The non-adversarial paradigm suggests, however, that it is absolutely necessary—to focus the Western intellectual potential on the problems of the Soviet middle class.

I would go as far as to assert that it is not MX or Star Wars or any other technological gadgetry, on which our current debate on national security is focused, but the readiness of the Soviet middle class for the year 2000 that will ultimately determine our security in the foreseeable future.

Neither the policy of pressure recommended by Pipes nor the policy of noninterference suggested by Colton orient American politicians (and the public) toward these fundamentals of Soviet reform. Moreover, as our examination of both conservative and liberal creeds showed, their prognostic capabilities are extremely poor, their analytical instruments insufficiently subtle, and their terminological equipment inadequate. In fact, they seem better equipped to challenge each other than the dilemma of Soviet reform. In this sense, they are more ideological than pragmatic. If we remember that the entire conservative-liberal rivalry derives from the adversarial paradigm, there can hardly be any doubt that sovietology is not reformable—until and unless it goes for a paradigm change.

In essence, sovietology faces the same challenge as its own subject. What a breakthrough into political modernity is for Soviet reformers, a breakthrough into a new paradigm is for American sovietology. Both are painful and crises-ridden. Both are impossible without dismounting the high ideological horses and getting down to the practical business of figuring out ways of helping the Soviet middle class. Yet, if the reformability of Russia indeed depends on the reformability of sovietology, the effort seems to be worth making.

Let me offer by way of conclusion two examples which I believe indicate that points of tangency between the two opposing schools of sovietology can perhaps be found on the basis of practical work. If sovietology is indeed sick and tired of its internecine paper war and wants to acquire the legitimate status of a superpower in American intellectual discourse that it deserves, there is no other way to do it except perestroika.

I would try to stay away from the hot topics of the day—like whether Gorbachev has already incapacitated Ligachev or still has a long way to go to accomplish that—however exciting these topics may be. I would also avoid the reanimated cremlinological squabbles about the decisive role of the General Secretary vis-à-vis the nomenklatura or vice versa. I shall only try to show that there may be practical ways to help the Soviet middle class—in the process of which sovietology may perhaps be reformed.

"Theory, my friend, is gray, but the eternal tree of life is ever green," Mephistopheles once explained to Faust. Let us imagine for a moment that we have never heard of any gray theories such as nomenklatura, totalitarianism, or "Soviet regime," that our minds are fresh and open to observations of the Russian tree of life. How would the problem of trade between the U.S.S.R. and the West appear to us then? Would it be reduced to the one single question—to trade or not to trade—which we have been hearing from the experts for years? As soon as we start to look at things from the position of the Soviet middle class, completely different questions immediately arise.

Is it possible to use trade with the Soviet Union to strengthen the reformist elements within the Soviet establishment and accordingly to weaken the counterreformist ones? To put it another way, is it possible to use this trade as leverage for the elevation of the middle class? If this is possible, then how?

I see three principal actors and not a faceless monolithic "Soviet elite" involved in the issue of trade with the West from the Soviet side. The first is the gigantic foreign trade bureaucracy, an important component part of the central economic bureaucracy. It was created as an impermeable barrier between Western corporations and their natural partners in the Soviet Union, the middle managerial class. The latter represents the second of our principal political actors who are vitally concerned with this issue on the Soviet side. The third actor, whose voice may be decisive in the fight between the first two, is the national leadership—including the Politburo, the Central Committee Secretariat, and the General Secretary's staff. Even if the most powerful, it represents an *independent set of interests* in the Soviet establishment. Naturally, these interests are not at all identical with the interests of the central economic bureaucracy, just as they are not identical with those of the middle managerial class.

In the second half of the 1970s sovietological observers recorded the national leadership's hesitation in the struggle between the middle managerial class, demanding direct access to trade with Western corporations, and the central economic bureaucracy, desperately opposing this assault on its prerogatives. The struggle ended in a compromise, connected, it must be assumed, with the collapse of detente at the end of the 1970s. The Soviet middle class did not receive "Hungarian rights" in full measure, but it made a breach in the foreign trade bureaucracy's monopoly: Soviet corporations obtained the right to trade directly with their East European partners. The bridge has recently been widened: a few selected Soviet corporations gained access to direct trade with their Western counterparts.

What is going on in the area of foreign trade in the Soviet Union is reminiscent, at least in one respect, of what happened in medieval Europe. The reformist elements of the middle class have risen up against a bureaucratic hierarchy that was cutting them off from direct contact with the source of their inspiration—the world market—paradoxically repeating the rise of Protestantism against a Catholic hierarchy that was cutting believers off from direct interaction with God. This analogy only looks frivolous. In fact, it simply reflects the pre-modern character of the Soviet political system. But let us go further.

Is the situation of the Soviet middle class in the pre-modern U.S.S.R. hopeless? The Reformation's success in England, Germany, and parts of Eastern Europe would seem to indicate that it is not. This success is also evidence that, in each instance, reformation depended on the position of the national leadership. It succeeded where the national leadership agreed to dismantle the monopoly of the Catholic hierarchy. In no instance did the Reformation lead to the undermining of the national leadership's position, only its reorientation. This is analogous to the way in which foreign trade reform did not undermine the position of the national leadership in Hungary when the "Protestant" middle managerial class there won out over the "Catholic" central economic bureaucracy. The middle managerial class simply took the place of the former bureaucratic hierarchy, entering into the world arena, acquiring new skills, new experience, new responsibility, and new international connections, and thus significantly strengthening its political position within the Hungarian establishment.

The prospect of repeating this experiment in the Soviet Union depends, therefore, on the position of the national leadership. We assume that its position is not rigidly fixed and that, for this reason, the Soviet national leadership is fully free to side with the "Protestants"—as occurred in medieval Europe in the sixteenth century and communist Hungary in the 1970s—should it consider this course of action advantageous to its own group interests. The maximization of Soviet-American trade is obviously one of the leadership's fundamental interests. In this respect, the position of the American national leadership, on whom this maximization depends, unexpectedly becomes decisive in this dispute between the two groups within the Soviet establishment.

That is why the traditional argument over whether to trade or not to trade makes no sense. The question is completely different: it is *with whom* in the Soviet Union should we trade—with the "Catholic hierarchy," thus strengthening the forces of counterreform, or with the "Protestant" middle class, reinforcing the position of reform?[22] The American national leadership could offer to maximize trade and credits on the condition that business be conducted entirely between Soviet and American corporations, without bureaucratic intermediaries. This kind of offer would in no way resemble any kind of political ultimatum. It would not have anything to do with politics at all. It would be motivated exclusively by the hard-nosed business objective of easing the trade process and would, in fact, correspond to the interests of both Soviet and American corporations. At the same time, it would also be pushing the Soviet system in a direction "congenial to Western interests."

This is only one example of a possible American strategy oriented toward supporting the Soviet middle class. I mention it here only because, over the course of many years in Moscow, I had the opportunity to study the problems of the Soviet middle class professionally, trying, as much as possible under the constraints of a censored press, to articulate their group interests. Western sovietology does not have to contend with censorship. It has described, analyzed, catalogued, and packed into tables and statistical computations each and every nuance of Soviet society. Has it really expended all this effort just to have this fabulous wealth of information gather dust on library shelves? If scholars would start to work together on the *practical* problems involved in moving the Soviet system in the direction of political modernization, Western sovietology could have at its disposal dozens of similar strategies. Moreover, in the process of this joint practical work, sovietology could become an effective counter to the Russian New Right—in other words, do its part in preparing the Soviet middle class for the year 2000.

The second example of a constructive strategy is a bit more complex. Konstantin Leont'ev, the most incisive of the Russian conservatives of the past century, insistently advised the then dictator Alexander III in the 1880s not to give himself over to pan-Slavic sentiments and instead to leave Eastern Europe in peace. For Leont'ev, Eastern Europe was a dilemma. Russia had not been able to integrate Poland into its imperial—"Byzantine," as he put it—commonwealth over the course of nearly a century. What would happen if Russia had to handle another half-dozen Polands? Such a course would be fraught with the destruction of Russia's Byzantine culture. From the moment it swallowed Eastern Europe, the empire would be doomed. The middle class, which he so despised as "bourgeois Philistines" and yet so correctly identified as a gravedigger of the Byzantine system, was traditionally much stronger and more articulate in Eastern Europe and would set about its destructive work, dragging its Russian partner in a direction "congenial to Western interests."

Several decades later, another dictator, Joseph Stalin, found himself in no condition to resist the expansionist impulse of Russian counter-reform. He accomplished what the pan-Slavists had urged Alexander III to do, thus committing, from Leont'ev's point of view, the worst blunder. Eastern Europe became the pre-modern empire's westernmost outskirts. If Leont'ev was right, from that moment on, the problem was whether the civilized world would take advantage of this blunder to bring about the political modernization of the empire. The question is, can the powerful potential of the Eastern European middle class be transformed into leverage for the elevation of its Soviet counterpart?

For understandable reasons, the nations which have fallen into Russia's imperial orbit have shown little interest in Leont'ev's dilemma. They wish to break away from the empire's embrace, not concern themselves with its modernization. The Germans in East Berlin in 1953 and the Hungarians in 1956 tried to do this "Polish-style," that is, by a national uprising. This ended, of course, the same way the Polish efforts of the previous century had—in bloody futility. The pre-modern empire does not give in to frontal attack. The Czechs, naively relying on socialist fraternity, tried to escape via the roundabout route of separate democratization in 1968; Soviet tanks crushed their hopes. The pre-modern empire was not to be duped either. The Poles with "Solidarity" tried in 1980 to achieve success where the Czechs had met failure; the result was military dictatorship. Thus was dispelled the last hope that any single imperial province will be able, by its own efforts, to break free of the empire's clutches—without modernization of the imperial center, that is.

This tragic history has a reverse side though. Just as Leont'ev predicted, a "half-dozen Polands" do have an enormous liberalizing potential. Over the course of a few decades, however, they have not yet been able to find a "fulcrum" on which to influence decisively their pre-modern sovereign. But in 1968 it was as if one small province, having learned from its own bitter experience, had inadvertently hit upon Leont'ev's dilemma. This time, Hungary began its process of liberalization not with an uprising and not with a revolutionary attempt at separate democratization, but rather with the elevation of its own "bourgeois Philistines." To do this, it was necessary, first and foremost, to breach the empire's economic model which was set up, as always, to block the middle class's elevation. Without any fanfare, Hungary managed to achieve what both Czechs and Poles had suffered defeat trying. By strengthening its middle class, Hungary in less than two decades has transformed itself into a relatively prosperous and, to the extent possible within the framework of a pre-modern empire, liberal country. Radical economic reform accomplished what neither revolts nor efforts at separate democratization could. Is it any surprise, then, that Hungary has become the first province in the empire which legalized competing political parties, which has an essentially open border with a capitalist state, where censorship has been reduced to a minimum and every citizen has the legal right to travel abroad, and where neither emigration problems, nor food crises, nor lines for consumer goods exist?

It is true that Hungary is in economic trouble now. Still, this is trouble related to the role it assumed in 1968, that of the Soviet trailblazer in the search for a viable model of free-market socialism. Unlike its neighbors to the east, including the Soviet Union itself whose radical reform may well have been impossible without the Hungarian experience, the national leadership in Budapest has publicly recognized that confidence in one-party rule has dwindled and the very viability of socialism is in doubt. Yet it continues its pioneering journey into the unknown. No one, including leaders in Budapest, can be sure at this point where exactly Hungary is heading—perhaps to the Scandinavian social-democratic model, with its heavily welfarized and yet authentically democratic state.

Be that as it may, what distinguishes Hungary from any other socialist state is that it seems to have reached the stage of permanent and irreversible—at least from within—reform. If Russia were ever to reach that stage, it would mean that the entire dilemma of East-West confrontation would be settled.

The problem is how to transmit this Hungarian transformation to Russia. Can Hungary do it alone—by way of example, as has been the case up to now? Or is a stronger, perhaps much stronger, medicine needed? Anyone who knows Russia's dramatic record of failed and reversed reforms would bet that the latter is true. A powerful second reformist center within the empire is needed for Leont'ev's nightmare to come true.

Budapest alone cannot challenge the imperial center. But Warsaw can. Poland has always been the key country of Eastern Europe. A second reformist center might become a reality if Poland would go the "Hungarian" way and, instead of being the powder keg of Europe, would enter into a kind of alliance with Hungary, thus lending empire-wide scope to the search for irreversible reform. In fact, Poland could serve as a magnet for the entire western flank of the empire, including perhaps the three Baltic republics. If could be a signal for the rebirth

of the whole Eastern European middle class as well as for the transformation of the empire into a kind of Euroasian, socialist commonwealth. This would diffuse the threat of a gigantic upheaval in the east
of Europe which, if allowed to happen, would surely bury the radical
reform in Moscow and make the triumph of the Russian New Right
by the year 2000 inevitable.

The only problem is that Poland's military government is not in the
position to lead the nation to an irreversible reform. It has neither the
authority nor the resources, let alone the national consensus needed
for such a breakthrough. This is where the West can help. A "mini-
Marshall plan" for Poland, predicated on the implementation of the
most radical "Hungarian" reform, could perhaps do the trick. Of course,
it would require a new government in Poland based on a national
consensus and possessing the authority to lead the nation, as is the case
in Hungary. Yet the plan would not contain the slightest hint of a
political ultimatum. In this sense, it would be analogous to the suggestion
to maximize Soviet-American trade on the condition that corporations
deal with each other directly.

It would involve only the natural desire of Western creditors to receive
what is due to them and help the borrower avoid bankruptcy. It would
be based purely on the sincere desire to support radical reform throughout the Soviet system. Who on earth would object to that in Gorbachev's
time, except the diehards in the Soviet bloc and, much more important,
those inspired by the adversarial paradigm in America?

These Americans see the Soviet order as absolute evil, just as the
Bolsheviks saw tsarism before 1917. For them, just as for the Bolsheviks,
the extermination of that order is worth any revolutionary upheaval.
Their logic is simple and may seem appealing. They call on American
policy to fulfill the same pressure function with respect to the Soviet
empire that World War I fulfilled for the Petersburg one. Are the empire's
resources not in fact limited? Will its rulers not face a choice between
guns and butter as a result of Western pressure? At some point, driven
to the wall, the Soviets will be forced to decide whether or not to build
new rockets and completely deprive the population of meat, thus running the risk of provoking spontaneous riots and undermining their
own legitimacy. At that point, they calculate, the Soviets will have to
choose meat, unless they want to commit political suicide. Thus the
problem will be solved. There is just one thing this calculation does
not take into account: the pressure of World War I produced *not ben-
eficent reform in tsarist Russia, but a communist, garrison-state dictatorship.*

Speaking in more conventional terms, their recommendation does not take into account that *ideology is also a resource for a pre-modern system,* its most powerful resource at that. Let us assume that under a post-dictatorial ideology the empire's rulers are required either to produce 250 million tons of grain a year or to make massive grain purchases in America to provide their population with meat. Under the alternative ascetic sub-ideology which the Russian Idea offers in the event of a systemic crisis, the empire would not need to produce more than 100 million tons of grain, much less make any purchases abroad, because this particular sub-ideology does not foresee feeding the populace meat at all. In 1953, forty years after the Bolshevik counterreform, the production of meat in Russia had not even attained its 1913 level. For a quarter of a century, the imperative of national survival successfully replaced meat in the garrison-state dictatorship. A dictatorial sub-ideology turned asceticism into a patriotic virtue and consumption into a national sin—and no spontaneous riots were recorded. The dictatorial regime's legitimacy was not subjected to doubt until the death of the dictator.

In other words, the rulers of the pre-modern empire *never* would end up faced with the fatal choice between rockets and meat. Their real choice at the point of a systemic crisis will be, as it has always been in Russian history, something completely different—a choice between a post-dictatorial sub-ideology, which forced them to triple meat production after the dictator's death, and its antipode, a vegetarian sub-ideology of dictatorship, which would allow them to concentrate *all* the system's resources on rocket production.

To summarize, the dilemma facing us vis-à-vis a radical reform in Moscow, on the one hand, and the radical diehards in America, on the other, seems to be the following. If a systemic crisis does happen in Russia at the end of this century, the new Russian extremists might have at least as good a chance to win by the year 2000—with the help of their American counterparts—as the Bolsheviks had by the year 1917. The leaders of Russian radical reforms, however daring and vigorous they might have been, have never been able to prevent the outbreak of such a crisis by their own efforts alone. There is, however, a chance that, having on their side the intellectual potential of the West, they may succeed. Such intellectual support in the West cannot be summoned unless the adversarial paradigm goes. At the time of a Soviet radical reform, it must be reduced to the status of a lunatic fringe— unless we want the year 2000 to catch us by surprise, as 1917 did. No one can accomplish such an awesome paradigm change except us, the sovietological guild—in case we are able to perform the same feat we demand from our subject.

NOTES

1. See, among other evidence, President Reagan's television interview with Barbara Walters on March 24, 1986.

2. It has been the same in both the Muscovite and the Petersburg periods of Russian autocracy. Remember, for example, the de-Ivanization of the system after Ivan the Terrible or its de-Petrinization after Peter I.

3. For more detail, see A. Yanov, *The Drama of the Soviet 1960s: A Lost Reform* (Berkeley, 1984), pp. 127-30.

4. Richard Pipes, *Survival Is Not Enough* (New York, 1984). Several men and women who were influential in the Reagan administration expressed their enthusiastic approval of Pipes's book. The reader may find a short summary of its arguments in Pipes's article, "Can the Soviet Union Reform?" *Foreign Affairs* 63 (Fall, 1984):47-61.

5. Timothy J. Colton, *The Dilemma of Reform in the Soviet Union* (New York, 1984). A second, revised and expanded, edition of Colton's book appeared in 1987, but it doesn't seem fair to Pipes, who did not have a chance to revise his book, to use Colton's revised views, particularly since his essential concept remains intact.

6. Pipes, "Can the Soviet Union Reform?" p. 51.

7. Colton, *Dilemma*, p. 26.

8. Pipes, "Can the Soviet Union Reform?" p. 49.

9. Ibid.

10. Ibid., p. 50 (emphasis added).

11. Ibid., p. 53 (emphasis added).

12. Ibid., p. 54.

13. Ibid., p. 59.

14. Pipes, *Survival,* p. 205.

15. Pipes, "Can the Soviet Union Reform?" p. 61.

16. Colton, *Dilemma,* pp. 98-99.

17. Ibid., p. 99.

18. Ibid., pp. 78-79.

19. Pipes, "Can the Soviet Union Reform?" p. 53.

20. Colton, *Dilemma,* p. 62.

21. For more detail on this, see Alexander Yanov, *The Russian Challenge and the Year 2000* (Oxford, 1987).

22. As to whether the Soviet middle class is indeed vitally interested in further widening direct contacts, see, for example, the piece by Iu. Iakhontov, "Nuzhny, kak vozdukh, priamye kontakty (Direct Contacts Are Needed Like Air)." *Pravda,* September 7, 1987.

Conclusion:
On the Problem of Reform in Russia and the Soviet Union

WILLIAM G. ROSENBERG

With few exceptions, discussions about "reform" in Russia and the Soviet Union have been characterized by a lack of systematic thinking. Our tendency to view the problem of "reform" through the lenses of particular scholarly disciplines naturally imparts a certain unidimensional quality to much of our analysis, even as we recognize that at issue are extremely complex problems concerning the very nature of social transformation and historical change.

Understanding the concept of "reform" itself is difficult enough. As many of the essays here indicate, it is hardly sufficient to think of reform as the enactment of decrees or the issuance of directives, however much we are encouraged to do so by references to "the reforms of Peter the Great," "the Great Reforms of the 1860s," or "Gorbachev's agenda for reform." Properly speaking, reform is a process. In any historical epoch in which significant social transformations are discernible, one can ask what is being reformed and for what purpose, and one can measure the extent of change by contrasting the altered formations and their role to what preceded them; but understanding the process of reform requires taking into account the multidimensional nature of societies themselves, especially the interactive relationships between political organization, socioeconomic structures, culture, and contacts with others. Why and how change actually occurred in particular historical conjunctures—the impulse, extent, and limitations of historically located social transformations, in other words—is thus an exceptionally daunting question in and of itself, let alone using the past as an indicator for the future.

Much of the analysis in this volume understandably focuses on the state. As Alexander Dallin points out, however, the difference between regime change and the structural reformation of the underlying political system is often confused. The former may give the appearance of fundamental change when what is occurring in structural terms is relatively superficial. This hardly means it is unimportant. The changes imposed by Ivan IV and his *oprichnina* clearly proved disastrous for tens of thousands of Russians by altering the ways political institutions functioned, even if, as Robert Crummey indicates, the structural forms of these institutions remained relatively intact. On the other hand, Khrushchev clearly improved the lives and well-being of tens of millions by altering the ways the Soviet party-state functioned, even if few would argue that the Soviet political system was fundamentally restructured as a result of his efforts.

Perhaps surprising to those accustomed to thinking autocrats or dictators have unlimited power, Khrushchev himself may have wanted more than the de-Stalinization of Soviet politics. Like others before him, he found that structural (or systemic) change depends on more than autocratic wishes. What Westerners should have learned from Max Weber about the organic nature of bureaucracies, Russians should know from Marx about the power of particular socioeconomic configurations, "communist" or not. One need not be an economic determinist to appreciate the power of underlying relations of production to constrain the ambitions of state-based reformers, nor a follower of Lévi-Strauss or Durkheim to understand the role culture or social relations in general can play in shaping the parameters of possible change. If revolutions can occur when established institutions and socioeconomic relations lose their functional validity and "break," reform can be effective only if these underlying structures are themselves "bending" or being "bent" from without, no easy task even for able politicians like D. M. Golitsyn, Mikhail Speranskii, Count Loris-Melikov, P. A. Stolypin, or Mikhail Sergeevich Gorbachev.

"Modernization" is a relevant if shopworn concept here, and so is the more slippery concept of "westernization." They alert us to the importance of Russian and Soviet interactions with technologically more developed states in Western Europe and North America, and they describe the processes and direction of changes which bring Russian social formations closer to comparable forms abroad. Commerce and other aspects of economic integration with the West can obviously affect the evolution of Russian and Soviet socioeconomic structures even against the wishes of their agents. When economic or other interactions with the West bring with them new cultural or social values, the stimulus for change can be powerful indeed.

"Westernization," however, can provoke a powerful cultural backlash as well, even if its benefits in, say, military-industrial terms, are accepted as necessary. Here the process of reform becomes inextricably bound with elements of political culture, the values, mentalities, rituals, prejudices, and myths that constitute the vibrant psychological and emotional underpinning to both politics and social order. On one hand, resistance to change can be as much a function of personal insecurity, fear of social dislocation, ideology, religious conviction, and alternative views about the value of life, as concerns about one's material well-being, although these are obviously all related. On the other hand, pressures for reform can come as much from convictions about the cultural penalties of "backwardness" as from concerns about military readiness.

How can we sort all of these matters out in reviewing four hundred years of Russian and Soviet history? Clearly not by drawing grand designs, however stimulating and provocative these may be. Better by way of conclusion to raise briefly one or two questions about the ways different periods of reform may or may not have been affected by these various dimensions of the reform process and to suggest possible consequences in terms of broader patterns of change.

One of the most striking characteristics of early Russian reform efforts had to do with, as Crummey tells us, the ways in which attempts to rationalize state administration clashed with dominant elements of Muscovite social relations and political culture, at least among the nobility. *Mestnichestvo* was clearly more than a customary means of structuring social hierarchy. It involved elements of a deeply localistic (patrimonial) outlook at variance with the very notion of a dominating, centralized state. In the case of both Ivan and Peter, efforts to bring order and (relative) efficiency to a secular state administration by regulating and centralizing government functions had to do with real and imagined military needs, and hence to a combination of circumstance and political vision. Conquering Kazan' was important to Moscow's security and to Ivan's sense of the preeminence of Moscow in the process of Russian state development; defeating Charles and the Turks helped protect Russia's western and southern frontiers but promoted as well, and perhaps more successfully, Peter's own grandiose vision of a secular Russian state equal to its European counterparts. "Reform" in these circumstances was partly regime change and partly the alteration of governing systems, but in both respects it was state-centered, state-serving, and fundamental to the very formation of a "modern" Russian state. It was also far more the consequence of directives from above than of pressures from below (although these also existed). It was imposed by men who perceived the alternative to be military weakness and political fragmentation.

Since this vision was at best only partly shared by broad strata of the gentry and nobility (albeit for different reasons) and was alien in many if not all respects to the peasantry and much of the clergy, the state-building efforts of Ivan and Peter necessarily involved a full-blown assault on traditional social relations, values, and political culture, which could only be mounted with a generous use of force. (One might go so far as to argue that *any* significant program of reform that does not substantially correspond with broad social interests or cultural forms will require a great deal of force from above, however much it serves state interests.) The horrifying brutalities of this early period, like those of the 1930s, are thus more interesting as a matter of method rather than process, and they tell us more about the psychologies of those demanding change than the nature of change itself. By the same token, however, it is little wonder that when the early modern "state-in-the-making" began to weaken, as it almost surely had to do once Russia found itself without a forceful and determined tsar, the brutalities associated with reform could only strengthen residual commitments to traditional social patterns and cultural perspectives. By their very nature, such attachments are not easily relinquished, even if behavior is forcefully altered.

One of the most interesting aspects of the reform process in the eighteenth century is precisely the way in which political culture and entrenched social relationships leavened efforts to modernize further. As David Ransel and John Alexander suggest, "modernity" in this historical context increasingly implied the application of enlightened reason to the ordering of state and social institutions, the recognition that individual or group welfare could best be developed if these institutions were ones of shared or limited power. Also fundamental was a deep appreciation of the importance of compromise, with its implied recognition of legitimate competitive interests and outlooks.

At best, however, such categories of thought remained poorly developed in eighteenth-century Russia. This certainly contributed to the debacles of 1730 and 1767, the affirmation of absolutist structures as legitimate political forms, the consolidation of serfdom, and hence the failure of Russian political modernization in this period to correspond to Western patterns. Without a broad-based recognition of the importance of law as a superordinate agency of social and political constraint and without a corresponding appreciation of its value as a means of mediating conflict—two fundamental aspects of political modernization in the West—the "liberalism" of Catherine II or Alexander I could only mean a "well-ordered police state," in Marc Raeff's phrase: regularity (*poriadok*) instead of despotism (*proizvol*), a rule of decree (*zakon*) rather than law (*pravo*).[1] Again, one should hardly underestimate the relative merits of enlightened as opposed to despotic absolutism, but one needs to bear in mind that order and efficiency can serve good and bad rulers equally well.

By most standards the tsar liberator, Alexander II, can be considered just such a good autocrat, a ruler forced once again to confront the implications of Russia's military inferiority vis-à-vis the West. And once again, as Walter Pintner tells us, the "Great Reforms" of the 1860s were state measures taken primarily for state purposes, even if they also reflected worldwide perceptions of the economic limitations, moral depredations, and political dangers of slavery. Pintner may be correct in arguing that the reforms were not the result of popular pressure, since there was no substantial segment of Russian society able or inclined to exert it, but only if he means that the socioeconomic structures of mid-nineteenth-century Russia were not yet in serious conflict with the autocracy's instruments of rule, only its need for military betterment. Certainly a widespread climate of opinion favored the end of serfdom. A willingness to accept its termination on very favorable terms may well have pervaded the gentry from top to bottom, partly because of the peasantry's own eagerness for freedom.

The mid-century crisis thus reflects the importance of East-West interactions in more than military terms, even if Russia's defeat in the Crimean War was its proximate cause. What was "critical" in the 1860s was not the danger of imminent peasant rebellion, immediate economic collapse, or new military disasters, but a general recognition that Imperial Russia was in danger of "falling further behind" its European counterparts because of antiquated social and state institutions. Without the abolition of serfdom from above, to paraphrase Alexander himself, it would sooner or later occur from below in a manner which might tear the country apart, leave its borders exposed, and preclude the further realization of Russia's own imperial ambitions.

This helps explain one of the most interesting aspects of this period: the fact that the reform process involved the articulation of Western principles and values without their substantial institutional embodiment. Serfs were juridically free, but they were bound to the commune (and the state) almost as tightly as they had been to their owners. Zemstvos resembled democratic organs, but their powers were soon largely restricted to matters of education and welfare, generally within the traditional bounds of local gentry governance. Because of the legal implications of emancipation, the judicial reforms of 1864 necessarily established the preconditions for a rule of law, but these, too, were at variance with traditional patterns of autocratic governance and outlook, and they were partly eclipsed by extrajudicial processes of administrative hearings and sanctions, just as they have been ever since. Recognizing the *necessity* of Western values and procedures as a condition of "modernization," Alexander and others were nonetheless unable (and unwilling) to break traditional forms or even in many respects to bend them very far. In these circumstances it is hardly surprising, as Hans Rogger's recent work has shown, that calls to resolve the "Jewish question"—reforms whose direct benefits to the state were not clearly discernible—got short shrift.[2]

To maintain that Western concepts and values (and especially the concept of law as superordinate authority) were only superficially reflected in the Great Reforms is not to imply, however, that the zemstvos, the new judicial apparatus, changes in the military, and especially the reformation of sociopolitical institutions and relations in the countryside did not themselves generate new and even more fundamental pressures for change. What largely differentiated such pressures during the last decades of the old regime from earlier times of crisis, however, was their structural quality.

As is well known, the post-emancipation countryside was soon developing in a manner basically incompatible with the state's investment needs and what Alexander Gershenkron and others have described as the "prerequisites" of "modern industrialization": capital availability, an elastic and expanding domestic market, and adequate technological and educational resources.[3] At the same time, the zemstvos in many places soon confronted extraordinary problems of social welfare, especially in matters of health and food distribution. These naturally led to institutional confrontation with central authorities and "senseless dreams" about the necessity of sharing power. The judiciary itself, throttled and abused by what Alexander Yanov calls the "counterreforms" of the 1880s, nonetheless developed into a powerful professional corporation whose activities in areas of the economy and commerce were as central to industrial development as they were antagonistic to autocratic prerogatives.

Whether or not a "modern" industrial and commercial order was actually developing in late Imperial Russia through the common forms of Western capitalism, the changes of the 1860s left a legacy of sharpening social conflict and structural contradiction. New social formations, institutions, and a range of corresponding mentalities necessarily became more and more antagonistic to the political, social, and cultural foundations of the traditional order. In such circumstances, the *process* of reform was itself changing character. It was no longer primarily the consequence of more or less coherent conceptions of state-serving changes imposed forcefully from above, but the logical outcome of underlying changes to which the state and its agents could only respond.

With the exception of Daniel Orlovsky's valuable essay, the contributors to this volume pay little attention to these responses or to the great upheavals of 1905 and 1917 related to them. This is partly because careful examinations would require volumes in themselves and partly because these revolutionary moments pose issues about the nature and possibility of reform quite different from those related to relatively stable periods like the 1980s, our point of departure. Revolution by definition implies the failure of societies to reform, whatever the reason. Whether dumas or soviets emerge in the immediate aftermath is less important in addressing the question of "reformability" than the complex conditions which preceded the upheavals themselves. In this respect, although the *Stolypinshchina* and the policies of the Provisional Government in 1917 are of enormous importance and interest—very much deserving careful and comprehensive review—the question of their ultimate impact was essentially mooted by the events of 1914-21 as a whole. For our purposes, the main questions concern the ways in which reform processes themselves may have been affected by these seven years of upheaval.

The obvious point to be stressed is that revolution in Russia was first and foremost a *social* upheaval of staggering proportions, however much the historical literature concentrates on its political dimensions. Its impact on future reform was felt not in the reconfiguration of the state but in the restructuring of social and cultural formations and the realignment (although much less drastically) of traditional social relations. The Bolshevik state soon emerged with far more power than its tsarist predecessor. Within a relatively short period, it was also able to maintain a more effective system of political administration and social control, however great its faults. State-centered and state-serving reforms would now be, of course, conditioned by a radically different ideological system and legitimized by a very different set of social attachments and commitments. Yet the issue of reform again turned on the state's relation to society and especially on the way post-revolutionary social formations continued to reflect traditional cultures and mentalities. The importance of reform for Russia's state development continued to be conditioned by interactions with the West, still more advanced technologically and a very real danger to Soviet interests and security.

From this perspective, to describe the New Economic Policy (NEP) as a "concession to market forces" is essentially to recognize that Lenin and the Bolshevik leadership thought it expedient to halt temporarily their efforts to have the Soviet state control basic socioeconomic relations in the 1920s and allow systemic interactions to determine, again temporarily, the levels of popular well-being. The power of market forces lay in their ability to function *independently* of the state, even if their ultimate threat to Bolshevik state objectives lay in precisely this same freedom. In fact, the extraordinary range of social dislocation in the 1914-21 period made it highly unlikely the market's power would not soon create conditions which, from the Bolsheviks' perspective, would again require forceful state intervention. In the countryside, the expropriation of lands and producers largely responsible for agricultural surpluses drastically reduced the availability of agrarian products for domestic and foreign markets, greatly exacerbating the chronic problem of capital formation. Investments were certainly not stimulated by the decimation of pre-revolutionary commercial and industrial elites, nor was Bolshevik ideology exactly conducive to attracting investment capital from abroad.

At the same time, the very character of social change in the revolutionary period strongly reinforced cultural patterns and social relations inimical to Party goals: a reclusive *mir* (peasant commune), for example, wary of all outside authority; a leveling disposition on the shop floor antagonistic to "experts" as well as traditional managerial authority and factory control; an adherence to customary law as a source of equity and to personal contacts as a means of structuring exchange relations, rather than the more formal (and abstract) values and contractual relations underlying Western jurisprudence and civil law; and a broad identification of state authority in all of its guises with the functions of extraction (taxation) and repression, as it had been historically, rather than as a means to assure rights or promote popular interests.

It is perhaps not too much to say that despite the best efforts of the young Soviet state to legitimize its actions in the people's name, its very form, with few organic links to the popular will, essentially kept it an alien power to many of its subjects after the revolution. Certainly this was the case in the countryside. In this respect, as in others, both Lenin's and Stalin's state systems were structurally linked to Peter's.

As Lewis Siegelbaum suggests in his most insightful contribution, each of the different models for development after the inception of the NEP continued to be predicated on the assumption that Russia itself needed to industrialize to survive, just as earlier reformers had assumed. Similarly, conceptions of "modernity" continued to center on notions of industrial and military parity with (or superiority over) the (capitalist)

West, however much they were now embossed with socialist values. Dispute focused on questions of pace and direction, not the state's ultimate objective.

Underlying concerns about pace and direction, however, were also quite different conceptions of the links between socioeconomic systems, cultures, and Soviet Russia's prospects for development. Although rarely articulated in these terms, the position of the "right" toward the state in this regard was optimistically instrumentalist. Bukharin and others evidenced little doubt that "bourgeois" mentalities and values were derivative of capitalist socioeconomic relations, but they assumed the Party could effectively use state power to bend both to its needs. Those more keenly tuned to history's dialectical complexities understood that cultural patterns and mentalities themselves played an important role in structuring socioeconomic forms and relations, and that each could not help but shape and limit the policies and power of the state itself, even as the state struggled in turn to restructure its underlying social order. From the general perspective of the left, in other words, fundamental contradictions between entrenched (and strengthening) sociocultural interests and the programmatic goals of the Party precluded the orderly and rapid development of a powerful, industrialized, *socialist* state. Given the hostile and competitive world environment, anti-socialist and anti-state mentalities and their root system of "bourgeois" socioeconomic relations had to be forced to wither, if not outright trampled.

The "Great Turn" of 1929-30 was thus a momentous point in Soviet history partly because it once again represented a deliberate effort on the part of the state to restructure fundamental components of society and culture and harness them to its own immediate goals. One should not underestimate the degree to which Stalin and others were able to mobilize broad social strata, in other words, the extent to which the Great Turn was itself a revolution from below. Recent work by Lynne Viola, Sheila Fitzpatrick, Lewis Siegelbaum, and others should put to rest the notion that Stalin changed Russia on his own and entirely from above.[4] On the other hand, and more important for an understanding of the processes of reform, neither should one diminish the inherently subversive power of various systemic residues which themselves helped determine the ultimate outcome of change, even if Stalinist reconstruction successfully met the state's needs in other ways.

The questions of "modern" and "Western" again loom large, since many of these residues remained by nature non-Western and pre-modern, bearing little resemblance to the social and cultural forms underlying industrial development in Western Europe and North America.

As it was earlier, the task of industrial "modernization" under Stalin was only partly a matter of increased production. Just as central was the need to develop alternative and equally functional substitutes for such facilitating structures as the liberal political and legal systems, which had proved so important to industrialization in the West and which continued to be practically and ideologically unacceptable in Russia. In effect, history bequeathed to Stalin, as it had to Witte, the need to contain an extensive and deep structural resistance to "modernity," as the state defined it, and to a modern industrial order, as it was understood in the West, even though the Party's (and Stalin's) goals of a strong and defendable Soviet state were broadly shared.

From this perspective, the structural faults of Soviet social transformation are more than apparent even if one only glances at this complex historical epoch. As collective farms became instruments of collection rather than collective work, in Jerzy Karcz's trenchant formulation, the "beaten" village ultimately responded powerfully if passively.[5] It erected virtually impenetrable sociocultural barriers to the creation of a "modern" agricultural order and culturally structured a near permanent state of agricultural underproduction. Similarly, the implantation of rigid and highly centralized planning, investment, and pricing systems (whose questionable merits in any event were directly related to conditions of great scarcity) helped raise traditional patterns of *blat* (influence, bribery) to an art form, institutionalizing a basically corrosive system of behaviors and values and strengthening the sociocultural foundations of a burgeoning "second" economy. Perhaps above all, the state's intolerance of critical thought and its pervasive (and familiar) use of force again bred deep resistance to its conception of "modernity," restricting technological innovation and change and leaving Russia excessively dependent once again on borrowing from abroad.

The very ambiguity of Soviet-Western interactions was hardly much different from the time of Peter, when Heinrich Fick was sent to Stockholm to study an admired and efficient system of state administration in the very midst of the Russo-Swedish war. That even the most flawed elements in the Stalinist program of industrial transformation during the first five-year plans appeared to be validated by Soviet military success in World War II only served to institutionalize further its structural antipathies and weaknesses, just as victory itself ironically exposed Stalin's successors to the risk of undermining their own political legitimacy if they again attempted systemic reform.

From all that has been said in this volume about the inherent complexities of the reform process in Russia and the Soviet Union, it should by now be apparent that the question of whether one or another of Stalin's successors was a "genuine" reformer confuses the most important issues. One must instead inquire about the perspective Soviet leaders had or have on the relationship between reform and the systemic elements of Soviet society as a whole, the links between social and cultural formations, the country's political structures, and the ability of the U.S.S.R. to compete effectively with the West—the historical index of Russian "modernity" and perhaps the one constant in Russian and Soviet *state* consciousness from Ivan IV to the present.

Since 1953, all Soviet leaders, active or passive, have had in some way to define the Party's role in terms of both indigenous and exogenous pressures for change. As Roman Szporluk has pointed out,[6] the very absorption of Eastern Europe under Soviet control necessarily presented Soviet leaders with alternative models of socioeconomic organization within broadly similar political systems; and as Timothy Colton and others argue in this volume, the evolution of increasingly complex market relations, technologies, interest group politics, and even ideological diversity within the "bloc" has necessarily forced an alteration in state-society relations whether or not Party leaders wanted them to change. This steadily growing pressure from below, reflecting both structural faults in the Soviet system and sociocultural failures of past state-directed and state-centered "modernization," is perhaps the dominant feature of the contemporary reform period, just as it was in the last decades of the old regime.

The energetic and impetuous Khrushchev clearly wanted very much to alter the nature of the Party and the state's relation to society, but as far as we can tell, he fully expected the end of Stalinist abuses alone would be enough to overcome, finally, these broadly constraining elements of Russian and Soviet "backwardness." In a way, as Alexander Yanov implies, Khrushchev's extraordinary naivete did not lie so much in his underappreciation of the systemic connections between politics, culture, and Western economic power; nor did it even rest in his failure to calculate properly Western political resolve or foresee the impact of his own politics on Eastern Europe. It centered, rather, on his failure to understand the ways in which Soviet Russia's own social and political institutions and political culture could constrain and ultimately thwart his own impulses to reform. In retrospect, it is hardly surprising powerful interest groups within the Party resisted his early "restructuring," the kolkhoz could not or would not efficiently absorb the dismantled Machine Tractor Stations (MTS), and Liberman and other economic reformers boosted into prominence found fault with the system itself and its underlying rationalizations.

Khrushchev's weakness was ultimately related not so much to his "harebrained" schemes as to the fact that others understood better than he did that effective change meant more than liberal authoritarianism. It required an assault on the systemic foundations of the Soviet order itself. Since few in the Party's leadership, and perhaps not even Khrushchev himself, were sufficiently confident in their own (or the Party's) ability to go that far, they yielded rather easily to the patterns of resistance that came to dominate the Brezhnev era of "stagnation." They were satisfied that they were still in power and that the Soviet Union was militarily strong.

Certainly, as Yanov insists, the international climate mattered. But while the West's technological superiority and more advanced standard of living were continual incentives for change, the West's hostility was a rationale for continued domestic privation, military expenditure, and hard-line resistance to tinkering with what "worked." The problem was, of course, as Gorbachev and others recognized, that at best the system worked poorly; as Bennett Kovrig has suggested, in comparison even with Hungary—not to mention West Germany or Japan—it barely seemed to be working at all.[7]

It would hardly do to conclude this volume with idle speculations about the future, but the past is inescapably prologue. Whatever its ultimate outcome, perhaps the most significant aspect of *Gorbachev-shchina* is the new Soviet leadership's own apparent perception of the problematic relationship between Soviet state power and the tasks of social and cultural transformation, a perception that seems radically different from the dominant views of the past. If Khrushchev took power with an admirable if limited appreciation of the dysfunctional elements of Stalinist politics, Gorbachev is clearly able to understand the complex problem of Soviet modernization in broad and systemic terms. For him, discipline and order are not simply matters of regulation but include habit, education, and an effective system of economic exchange. Increased productivity is not simply a question of new appointments but depends on the restructuring of industrial relations. Effective allocation of capital resources and the full utilization of labor resources, especially in the countryside, can only occur through a functioning social trust, one in which the state and its objectives are genuinely appreciated, its underlying socialist values internalized in everyday life. Gorbachev thus seems to recognize that *perestroika*—the word "restructuring" is itself significant in this regard—is hardly possible without broad-based social support. His consequent effort through *glasnost'* (openness) to enlist first the support of Soviet Russia's cultural elite—

its young, alert, and "critically thinking intelligentsia," to borrow a term from a previous reform era—is a measure of the degree to which he and others are convinced that this group is the key to lasting socio-cultural change.

In this there are bound to be disappointments, since glasnost' clearly matters to Gorbachev and others not so much to achieve political freedom and civil liberties, valued in the West, but to create a solid social and cultural foundation from which to move ahead. To put the matter differently, political liberalization remains a functional means of improving state-society interactions rather than institutionalizing Western cultural values or political principles. For reasons that should now be apparent, one can hardly expect Soviet Russia in the future to mirror its Western counterparts, nor would many in the world think this desirable. The primary issues for Russia's leadership now as before are material well-being and national security—on terms reflecting Russian or Soviet values rather than Western ones—and the resolution, finally, of their country's historic disadvantages vis-à-vis the outside world. In contrast to the state-centered ways in which these goals were so often pursued in the past, however, the Soviet Union under Gorbachev finally seems to have entered a period of essentially "society-centered" change in which social and cultural formations are being bridged in a way historians might one day regard as key to its success.

NOTES

1. Marc Raeff, *The Well Ordered Police State: Social and Institutional Change through Law in the Germanies and Russia, 1600-1800* (New Haven, Conn., 1983).

2. Hans Rogger, *Jewish Policies and Right-Wing Politics in Imperial Russia* (Berkeley, 1986).

3. See especially Alexander Gershenkron, "Reflections on the Concept of 'Prerequisites' of Modern Industrialization," in his *Economic Backwardness in Historical Perspective* (Cambridge, Mass., 1962).

4. Lynne Viola, *The Best Sons of the Fatherland: Workers in the Vanguard of Soviet Collectivization* (New York, 1986); Sheila Fitzpatrick, *Education and Social Mobility in the Soviet Union, 1921-34* (Cambridge, 1979); Lewis Siegelbaum, *Stakhanovism and the Politics of Productivity in the USSR, 1935-1946* (Cambridge, 1988).

5. J. Karcz, *The Economics of Communist Agriculture: Selected Papers* (Bloomington, Ind., 1979), p. 320.

6. Roman Szporluk, unpublished contribution to conference discussion.

7. Bennett Kovrig, "Hungarian Socialism: The Deceptive Hybrid," unpublished conference paper.

Guide to Further Reading

There is no body of literature focusing on reform which encompasses all the territory covered in this volume. Consequently, this guide highlights works that will help the reader broaden his or her understanding of particular topics. Many of these do not directly address the question of reform; rather, they provide a basis for considering the issues raised in the preceding articles. Of course, the smaller number of books focusing on reform receives special attention.

For convenience, this guide is roughly arranged by time period. Because the available literature on most of these topics is vast, the following suggestions should be regarded as only an introduction to the major secondary sources in English and translated primary sources. Those wishing to pursue detailed study of a particular topic will find bibliographies in most of the works listed below that indicate additional monographic works as well as Russian-language literature. Readers will also find some of the most important and interesting work in periodicals, especially *Slavic Review, Russian Review, Soviet Studies, Survey, Studies in Comparative Communism,* and *Problems of Communism.*

Ivan the Terrible and the Time of Troubles, 1533-1613

A number of classic Russian interpretations of this period are available in English. In *The Tsardom of Moscow, 1547-1682,* 2 vols. (New Haven, Conn., 1959), George Vernadsky, a Russian émigré historian writing in the United States, defends centralization of power as necessary for Russia's survival. A. E. Presniakov, *The Formation of the Great Russian State,* trans. from Russian by A. E. Moorhouse (Chicago, 1970), emphasizes the exploitative and aggressive nature of the Muscovite princes' policies. Also important are the work of the Russian-Soviet historian, M. N. Pokrovsky, *History of Russia from the Earliest Times to the Rise of Commercial Capitalism,* 2 vols., trans. J. D. Clarkson (Bloomington, Ind., 1966), and the relevant sections of V. O. Kliuchevsky, *Course of Russian History,* 5 vols., trans. C. J. Hogarth (New York, 1911-31). Kliuchevsky is considered by many to be the best and most influential Russian historian of the late nineteenth century.

Robert O. Crummey, *The Formation of Muscovy, 1304-1613* (New York, 1987), is an up-to-date general survey of the history of early Muscovy. For studies of Ivan himself and his policies, one might begin with S. F. Platonov's pre-revolutionary work, *Ivan the Terrible,* trans. and ed. Joseph L. Wieczynski (Gulf Breeze, Fla., 1974), and then investigate more modern works such as Bjarne Nørretranders, *The Shaping of Czardom under Ivan Groznyj* (Copenhagen, 1964). For a review of Soviet considerations of Ivan's place in history, see Robert O. Crummey, "Ivan the Terrible," in *Windows on the Russian Past,* ed. Samuel Baron and Nancy Heer (Columbus, Ohio, 1977), pp. 57-74. Examination of what some consider Ivan's reform period can be found in Antony Grabovsky, *The "Chosen Council" of Ivan IV: A Reinterpretation* (Brooklyn, 1969). The unique and fascinating insights attributed to Ivan's contemporary, Prince A. M. Kurbskii, are published in *The Correspondence between Prince A. M. Kurbsky and Tsar Ivan IV of Russia, 1564-1579,* ed. and trans. J. L. I. Fennell (Cambridge, 1955), and in *Prince A. M. Kurbsky's History of Ivan IV,* ed. and trans. J. L. I. Fennell (Cambridge, 1965). The authenticity of Kurbskii's writings has been challenged by Edward L. Keenan in *The Kurbskii-Groznyi Apocrypha: The Seventeenth-Century Genesis of the "Correspondence" Attributed to Prince A. M. Kurbskii and Tsar Ivan IV* (Cambridge, Mass., 1971).

Studies of Boris Godunov and the origins of the Time of Troubles include: S. F. Platonov, *Boris Godunov, Tsar of Russia,* trans. from the Russian by L. Rex Pyles (Gulf Breeze, Fla., 1973); A. M. Kleimola, "Boris Godunov and the Politics of Mestnichestvo," *Slavonic and East European Review* 53 (1975):355-70; and S. Graham, *Boris Godunov* (London, 1933). The foremost study of the Time of Troubles remains S. F. Platonov, *The Time of Troubles: A Historical Study of the Internal Crisis and Social Struggle in Sixteenth- and Seventeenth-Century Muscovy,* trans. John T. Alexander (Lawrence, Kans., 1970).

There are a number of interesting studies of this period focusing on matters other than high politics. On the peasantry, see R. E. F. Smith, *Peasant Farming in Muscovy* (Cambridge, 1977), and the relevant chapters of Jerome Blum, *Lord and Peasant in Russia from the Ninth to the Nineteenth Century* (Princeton, N.J., 1961). See the first section of Paul Avrich, *Russian Rebels 1600-1800* (New York, 1972), on peasant uprisings in the Time of Troubles, and for studies of serfdom and slavery, see Richard Hellie, *Enserfment and Military Change in Muscovy* (Chicago, 1971), and his *Slavery in Russia, 1450-1725* (Chicago, 1982). Two good works on the merchantry in this period are Paul Bushkovitch, *The Merchants of Moscow, 1580-1650* (New York, 1980), and Samuel H. Baron, *Muscovite Russia: Collected Essays* (London, 1980). R. E. F. Smith's and David Christian's *Bread and Salt: A Social and Economic History of Food and Drink in Russia* (Cambridge, 1984), has a fascinating section on the sixteenth and seventeenth centuries. Firsthand accounts of Muscovite Russia are available in Lloyd E. Berry and Robert O. Crummey, *Rude and Barbarous Kingdom: Russia in the Accounts of Sixteenth-Century English Voyagers* (Madison, Wisc., 1968).

The Eighteenth Century

Surprisingly, there are few good studies of Peter the Great's reign available in English. Perhaps the best biography of Peter is still the work of V. O. Kliuchevsky, translated by Liliana Archibald from his *Course of Russian History* as *Peter the Great* (Boston, 1958). A stronger treatment of Peter's foreign policy is found in B. H. Sumner, *Peter the Great and the Emergence of Russia* (London, 1950). A worthwhile and more recent biography is M. S. Anderson, *Peter the Great* (London, 1978). The best work on the church in this period is James Cracraft, *The Church Reform of Peter the Great* (London, 1971). The thoughts of many leading Russian and Soviet historians can be found in Marc Raeff, ed., *Peter the Great: Reformer or Revolutionary?* (Boston, 1963), and in Basil Dmytryshyn, ed., *Modernization of Russia under Peter I and Catherine II* (New York, 1974). Peter's significance for later Russian thinkers is traced in Nicholas Riasanovsky, *The Image of Peter the Great in Russian History and Thought* (New York, 1985), and in X. Gasiorowska, *The Image of Peter the Great in Russian Fiction* (Madison, Wisc., 1979).

There is, as yet, no definitive treatment in English of the so-called Constitutional Crisis of 1730. Two good studies of Empress Anna are Philip Longworth, *The Three Empresses: Catherine I, Anne and Elizabeth of Russia* (London, 1972), and M. Curtiss, *A Forgotten Empress: Anna Ivanovna and Her Era* (New York, 1974). Brenda Meehan-Waters has contributed a study of the high nobility of 1730 in *Autocracy and Aristocracy: The Russian Service Elite of 1730* (New Brunswick, N.J., 1982). James Cracraft has written an interesting article, "The Succession Crisis of 1730: A View from the Inside," *Canadian-American Slavic Studies* 12 (1978):60-85, and James Hassel's piece, "Implementation of the Russian Table of Ranks during the Eighteenth Century," *Slavic*

Review 29 (1970):283-95, is important for understanding the origins of the crisis.

There are a number of good studies of the latter half of the eighteenth century. Three important new works on Catherine the Great's rule are: John LeDonne, *Ruling Russia: Politics and Administration in the Age of Absolutism, 1762-1796* (Princeton, N.J., 1984); Robert Jones, *Provincial Development in Russia: Catherine II and Jakob Sievers* (New Brunswick, N.J., 1984); and Isabel de Madariaga, *Russia in the Age of Catherine the Great* (New Haven, Conn., 1981). This last work contains a particularly extensive bibliography. Eighteenth-century urban life is traced in J. Michael Hittle, *The Service City in Eighteenth Century Russia* (Cambridge, Mass., 1979), and an important series of essays on the serf economy and Russian social order can be found in Arcadius Kahan, *The Plough, the Hammer, and the Knout: An Economic History of Eighteenth-Century Russia* (Chicago, 1985). The development of a newly distinctive noble class is discussed in Marc Raeff, *Origins of the Russian Intelligentsia: The Eighteenth Century Nobility* (New York, 1966). The relationship between crown and nobility is analyzed in David Ransel, *The Politics of Catherinian Russia: The Panin Party* (New Haven, Conn., 1975), and in Robert Jones, *The Emancipation of the Russian Nobility, 1762-85* (Princeton, N.J., 1973). For an understanding of the two most important "dissidents" of the period, read A. Radishchev, *Journey from St. Peterburg to Moscow,* edited with an introduction and notes by R. P. Thaler (Cambridge, Mass., 1958), and W. Gareth Jones, *Nikolay Novikov: Enlightener of Russia* (Cambridge, 1984). The Pugachev revolt is discussed in Paul Avrich, *Russian Rebels 1600-1800* (New York, 1972). See H. Kaplan, *The First Partition of Poland* (New York, 1962), and A. W. Fisher, *The Russian Annexation of the Crimea, 1772-1783* (Cambridge, 1970), for studies of Catherine's foreign policies. Catherine was a highly literate and perceptive individual and many of her writings have been translated. See Catherine the Great, *The Memoirs of Catherine the Great,* ed. D. Maroger, trans. from French by M. Budberg (New York, 1961), and W. F. Reddaway, ed., *Documents of Catherine the Great: The Correspondence with Voltaire and the Instructions of 1767 in the English Text of 1768* (Cambridge, 1931).

For considering the issue of reform in the eighteenth and nineteenth centuries, the reader should find studies of legal and institutional traditions valuable. The best such study for the period through the Judicial Reforms of 1864 is Richard Wortman, *The Development of a Russian Legal Consciousness* (Chicago, 1976). This book is nicely complemented by Michael Cherniavsky, *Tsar and People: Studies in Russian Myths* (New Haven, Conn., 1961). Many of the most important documents from these centuries have been translated and appear in Marc Raeff, ed., *Plans for Political Reform in Imperial Russia, 1730-1905* (Englewood Cliffs, N.J., 1966), and in Basil Dmytryshyn, ed., *Imperial Russia: A Source Book, 1700-1917* (Hinsdale, Ill., 1974).

The Late Nineteenth Century, 1855-1905

Although the reform era itself has not been comprehensively analyzed in English, Werner E. Mosse, *Alexander II and the Modernization of Russia* (New York, 1958), offers a concise overall treatment of the tsar and his reforms. The system Alexander II sought to reform is best analyzed in Nicholas Riasanovsky, *Nicholas I and Official Nationality, 1825-1855* (Berkeley and Los Angeles, 1959). Serfdom, rural life, and agrarian reform are thoroughly discussed in G. T. Robinson, *Rural Russia under the Old Regime: A History of the Landlord-Peasant World and a Prologue to the Peasant Revolution of 1917* (New York, 1932), and in Jerome Blum, *Lord and Peasant in Russia: From the Ninth to the Nineteenth Century* (Princeton, N.J., 1961). Two good works focusing specifically on the peasant emancipation are T. Emmons, *The Russian Landed Gentry and the Peasant Emancipation of 1861* (Cambridge, 1967), and Daniel Field, *The End of Serfdom: Nobility and Bureaucracy in Russia, 1855-1861* (Cambridge, Mass., 1976). For a broader study of the bureaucracy and its role as an agent both for and against reform, see Walter Pintner and Don Karl Rowney, eds., *Russian Officialdom: The Bureaucratization of Russian Society from the Seventeenth to the Twentieth Century* (Chapel Hill, N.C., 1980).

The state's efforts to reimpose tight control over education in Alexander II's reign are discussed in Alan Sinel, *The Classroom and the Chancellory: State Education Reform in Russia under Count Dmitrii Tolstoy* (Cambridge, Mass., 1973). For an account of Alexander's judicial reforms, see Richard Wortman, *The Development of a Russian Legal Consciousness,* mentioned above, and on the zemstvo reforms and their enduring effects, see T. Emmons and Wayne Vucinich, eds., *The Zemstvo in Russia: An Experiment in Local Self-Government* (New York, 1982). The reader might also want to investigate reform attempts earlier in the century by consulting W. Bruce Lincoln, *In the Vanguard of Reform: Russian Enlightened Bureaucrats 1825-1861* (DeKalb, Ill., 1982), and Marc Raeff, *Michael Speransky: Statesman of Imperial Russia* (The Hague, 1957). The best general summary of social and political change during the reigns of the last two Romanovs is Hans Rogger, *Russia in the Age of Modernization and Revolution 1881-1917* (New York, 1983). This book also contains an excellent bibliography arranged by subject.

For analysis of the successes and limitations of Russian industrial growth around the turn of the century, see T. H. Von Laue, *Sergei Witte and the Industrialization of Russia* (New York, 1963). The reactionary nature of Alexander III's rule is best perceived by reading the memoir of his minister, K. P. Pobedonostsev, *Reflections of a Russian Statesman,* trans. from Russian by R. C. Long (London, 1898; reprint, Ann Arbor, Mich., 1965).

The development of the intelligentsia and revolutionary political movements comprises one of the most fascinating chapters of Russian history. The volume of literature on and by the Russian intelligentsia is immense, so the reader is reminded that the following is only an introductory sampling. Two brief surveys on the Russian intelligentsia are A. Yarmolinsky, *Road to Revolution: A Century of Russian Radicalism* (London, 1957), and Philip Pomper, *The Russian Revolutionary Intelligentsia* (New York, 1970). A large and detailed study of populism can be found in Franco Venturi, *Roots of Revolution: A History of the Populist and Socialist Movements in Nineteenth Century Russia,* trans. from Italian by F. Haskell (New York, 1960). The growth of Russian liberalism in the early twentieth century is discussed in G. Fischer's somewhat dated *Russian Liberalism from Gentry to Intelligentsia* (Cambridge, Mass., 1958), and Slavophilism is discussed in Nicholas Riasanovsky, *Russia and the West in the Teachings of the Slavophiles* (Cambridge, Mass., 1952). A number of Isaiah Berlin's well-crafted essays on leading members of the intelligentsia have been compiled in H. Hardy and A. Kelley, eds., *Russian Thinkers,* (New York, 1978). Martin Malia's *Alexander Herzen and the Birth of Russian Socialism* (Cambridge, Mass., 1961) remains the definitive biography of Alexander Herzen, the most important of the mid-century political philosophers and activists. Firsthand accounts of populist activities in the 1870s and 1880s by leading women in the movement have been translated in Barbara Engel and Clifford N. Rosenthal, eds., *Five Sisters: Women against the Tsar* (New York, 1975).

The history of the Russian empire requires consideration of peoples other than the Russians. While much of interest has been written on Jewish and Polish history, scholars are only just now turning needed attention to the empire's other ethnic and national groups. The standard history of Jews in Russia remains S. M. Dubnow, *History of the Jews in Russia and Poland,* 3 vols., trans. from Russian by I. Friedlaender (Philadelphia, 1916-20; reprint, 1946). A more recent history is provided in G. Israel, *The Jews in Russia,* trans. from French by S. L. Chernoff (New York, 1975). A good study of Russian Jews in the eighteenth century is I. Levitats, *The Jewish Community in Russia, 1722-1844*

(New York, 1970). A superb work on the political and national awakening of Russia's Jews is J. Frankel, *Prophecy and Politics: Socialism, Nationalism and the Russian Jews, 1862-1917* (Cambridge, 1981). Ezra Mendelsohn's shorter work, *Class Struggle in the Pale: The Formative Years of the Jewish Workers' Movement in Tsarist Russia* (Cambridge, 1970), nicely complements studies of the Russian working class. A fascinating examination of the tensions between nationalism and socialism in the Soviet period can be found in Zvi Gitelman, *Jewish Nationality and Soviet Politics: The Jewish Sections of the CPSU, 1917-1930* (Princeton, N.J., 1972). Two excellent studies of Russian Poland are P. S. Wandycz, *The Lands of Partitioned Poland, 1795-1918* (Seattle, 1974), which includes discussion of Austrian and Prussian Poland as well, and R. F. Leslie, *Reform and Insurrection in Russian Poland, 1856-1865* (London, 1963).

Revolutions, 1905-21

Russia's first major upheaval of the twentieth century was the Revolution of 1905-7. Teodor Shanin's new volumes, *Russia as a "Developing Society,"* 2 vols. (New Haven, Conn., 1985), especially Vol. 2, *Revolution as a Moment of Truth,* deepen conceptions of the 1905-7 revolutionary period by emphasizing the often overlooked events in the Russian countryside. The enthusiasm and dedication of those manning the St. Petersburg barricades in 1905 is vividly portrayed by a leading participant in Leon Trotsky, *1905* (New York, 1972). John Bushnell has contributed an important study of the tsar's army in *Mutiny amid Repression: Russian Soldiers in the Revolution of 1905-1906* (Bloomington, Ind., 1985). The development of Russian Marxism is discussed in Leopold Haimson, *The Russian Marxists and the Origins of Bolshevism* (Cambridge, Mass., 1955), and in A. K. Wildman, *The Making of a Workers' Revolution: Russian Social Democracy, 1891-1903* (Chicago, 1967). The best analysis of Russia's failed attempt to form a parliamentary monarchy after 1905 is Geoffrey Hosking, *The Russian Constitutional Experiment: Government and Duma, 1907-1914* (London, 1973).

The most comprehensive general account of the revolutions of 1917 and the civil war is still William Chamberlin, *The Russian Revolution,* 2 vols. (New York, 1935). A good, short interpretive look at both the 1917 and Stalinist revolutionary periods is Sheila Fitzpatrick, *The Russian Revolution, 1917-1932* (Oxford, 1984). On the roles of political parties in 1917, see Alexander Rabinowitch, *The Bolsheviks Come to Power: The Revolution of 1917 in Petrograd* (New York, 1976); William

G. Rosenberg, *Liberals in the Russian Revolution* (Princeton, N.J., 1974); and Oliver H. Radkey, *Agrarian Foes of Bolshevism* (New York, 1958). Biographies of leading Bolsheviks include Adam Ulam, *The Bolsheviks: The Intellectual and Political History of the Triumph of Communism in Russia* (New York, 1965), which focuses on Lenin in power; Isaac Deutscher, *The Prophet Armed: Trotsky, 1879-1921* (London, 1954), which is the first book in a three-volume biography of Trotsky; and Robert Tucker, *Stalin as Revolutionary, 1879-1929* (New York, 1973), which presents a convincing psycho-historical analysis. On workers in the revolution, see Diane Koenker, *Moscow Workers and the 1917 Revolution* (Princeton, N.J., 1981), and Steven Smith, *Red Petrograd: Revolution in the Factories, 1917-1918* (Cambridge, 1983). Robert Service focuses on the Bolshevik party administration in the provinces in *The Bolshevik Party in Revolution, 1917-1923* (New York, 1979), and Graeme Gill discusses peasants in 1917 in *Peasant and Government in the Russian Revolution* (London, 1979).

The 1920s

Before focusing on particular post-revolutionary developments, the reader might want to consult general surveys of Soviet politics and history. For years two standard texts on Soviet politics were Leonard Schapiro, *The Communist Party of the Soviet Union* (New York, 1971), and Merle Fainsod, *How Russia Is Ruled,* rev. ed. (Cambridge, Mass., 1967). Fainsod's book has now been extensively revised and updated as Jerry Hough and Merle Fainsod, *How the Soviet Union Is Governed* (Cambridge, Mass., 1979). There is as yet no completely satisfactory comprehensive history of the Soviet period, but Adam Ulam's *A History of Soviet Russia* (New York, 1976), Donald Treadgold's *Twentieth Century Russia,* 5th ed. (Boston, 1981), and Basil Dmytryshyn's *USSR: A Concise History,* 4th ed. (New York, 1984), are quite useful for reference purposes.

As the Soviet Union's first experiment with a mixed economy, the NEP offers valuable lessons for today's reformers. Stephen Cohen's important work, *Bukharin and the Bolshevik Revolution* (New York, 1980), seeks to establish the ideological legitimacy of the mixed economy by focusing on the NEP's leading advocate. The economic and political debates surrounding NEP are outlined in Alexander Erlich, *The Soviet Industrialization Debate, 1924-28* (Cambridge, Mass., 1960), and in Moshe Lewin, *Political Undercurrents in Soviet Economic Debates: From Bukharin to the Modern Reformers* (Princeton, N.J., 1974). The most comprehensive economic history of the 1920s is found in E. H. Carr, *A History of Soviet Russia:* Vol. 4, *The Interregnum, 1923-1924*

(New York, 1954); Vols. 5-7, *Socialism in One Country, 1924-1926* (New York, 1958); Vols. 8-9, *Foundations of a Planned Economy, 1926-1929,* Vol. 8 with R. W. Davies (New York, 1971-72). A more concise but still excellent economic history is Alec Nove, *An Economic History of the USSR* (London, 1969). The Kronstadt revolt, more than any other incident, underscored the need for political and economic change in the early 1920s and the standard account of that uprising is Paul Avrich, *Kronstadt 1921* (Princeton, N.J., 1970).

The period 1917-30 is perhaps most remarkable for the cultural creativity it nourished and then destroyed. Two excellent collections of essays cover many aspects of this "cultural revolution": Abbott Gleason, Peter Kenez, and Richard Stites, eds., *Bolshevik Culture* (Bloomington, Ind., 1985), and Sheila Fitzpatrick, ed., *Cultural Revolution in Russia, 1928-31* (Bloomington, Ind., 1978). Sheila Fitzpatrick, *Lunacharsky: Commissar of Enlightenment* (Cambridge, 1970), also covers many of the important political and cultural issues. The thoughts of many leading Bolsheviks on cultural matters are compiled in William G. Rosenberg, ed., *Bolshevik Visions: First Phase of the Cultural Revolution in Soviet Russia* (Ann Arbor, Mich., 1984). Women's issues received much attention in this period and two fine studies of this subject are Richard Stites, *The Women's Liberation Movement in Russia: Feminism, Nihilism, and Bolshevism, 1860-1930* (Princeton, N.J., 1978), and Barbara Clements, *Bolshevik Feminist: A Life of Alexandra Kollontai* (Bloomington, Ind., 1979). The excitement, contradictions, and tensions of the period are vividly portrayed in the period's literature and in the interaction between the state and the artistic community. The reader interested in exploring this area might best begin with one of the general surveys: Edward J. Brown, *Russian Literature since the Revolution* (New York, 1963), which contains an excellent bibliography; Marc Slonim, *Soviet Russian Literature: Writers and Problems, 1917-1967,* rev. ed. (New York, 1967); Robert Maguire, *Red Virgin Soil: Soviet Literature in the 1920's* (Princeton, N.J., 1968); and Gleb Struve, *Russian Literature under Lenin and Stalin, 1917-1953* (Norman, Okla., 1971).

Again, because consideration of reform calls for an understanding of legal institutions, readers might want to consult legal studies of the Soviet period. See John Hazard, *Settling Disputes in Soviet Society: The Formative Years of Legal Institutions* (New York, 1960), and Harold Berman, *Justice in the USSR* (Cambridge, Mass., 1966).

The Khrushchev Era

Unfortunately, there is no single, comprehensive history of the Khrushchev years. Roy and Zhores Medvedev have written an intelligent and critical appraisal of Khrushchev, focusing on his agricultural policies, in *Khrushchev: The Years in Power,* trans. Andrew Durkin (New York, 1976). Based on his experience as a Soviet journalist, Alexander Yanov positively assesses the ramifications of Khrushchev's policies in *The Drama of the Soviet 1960s: A Lost Reform* (Berkeley, 1984). Perhaps the most thorough analysis of economic reform programs in the 1950s and 1960s is in Abraham Katz, *The Politics of Economic Reform in the Soviet Union* (New York, 1972). Although the title casts doubt on the prognostications of sovietologists, Michel Tatu's book, *Power in the Kremlin: From Khrushchev to Kosygin* (New York, 1969), has thoughtful analysis of the Twenty-second Party Congress, the Cuban missile crisis, and Khrushchev's ouster. A short, journalistic account of Khrushchev's ouster is available in William Hyland and Richard Wallace Shryock, *The Fall of Khrushchev* (New York, 1968). George Breslauer provides detailed analysis of Khrushchev's and Brezhnev's efforts at political consolidation in *Khrushchev and Brezhnev as Leaders: Building Authority in Soviet Politics* (London, 1982).

A number of interesting essays on the Khrushchev period can be found in Stephen F. Cohen et al., eds., *The Soviet Union since Stalin* (Bloomington, Ind., 1980). Contemporary, American analyses of topics from politics to the arts can be found in Abraham Brumberg, ed., *Russia under Khrushchev: An Anthology from Problems of Communism* (New York, 1962). Two biographies concentrating on high politics are Carl Linden, *Khrushchev and the Soviet Leadership, 1957-1964* (Baltimore, 1966), and Edward Crankshaw, *Khrushchev: A Career* (New York, 1966). Khrushchev's ground-breaking "secret speech" given at the Twentieth Party Congress in 1956 is available in translation in Nikita Khrushchev, *The Secret Speech,* trans. Tamara Deutscher (Nottingham, 1976). After his ouster from power, Khrushchev dictated his memoirs which are available as *Khrushchev Remembers,* trans. and ed. by Strobe Talbott (Boston, 1974). For scholarly analysis of one of Khrushchev's major agricultural initiatives, see Martin McCauley, *Khrushchev and the Development of Soviet Agriculture: The Virgin Land Programme, 1953-1964* (New York, 1976). A general overview of the Soviet economy for this period is in Harry Schwartz, *The Soviet Economy since Stalin* (Philadelphia, 1965). An interesting contemporary assessment of Khrushchev's and Kosygin's reformist potentials is in Eugene Zaleski, *Planning Reforms in the Soviet Union 1962-1966: An Analysis of Recent Trends in Economic Organization and Management* (Chapel Hill, N.C., 1967).

On foreign policy issues, the reader might first wish to consult a general text, such as J. Nogee and R. Donaldson, *Soviet Foreign Policy since World War II* (New York, 1984); Adam Ulam, *Expansion and*

Coexistence: A History of Soviet Foreign Policy, 1917-1967 (New York, 1968); or Alvin Rubinstein, *Soviet Foreign Policy since World War II,* 2d ed. (Boston, 1985). A detailed account of events between 1953 and 1960 is available in David J. Dallin, *Soviet Foreign Policy after Stalin* (New York, 1961). There are a number of good works on specific events and aspects of Khrushchev's foreign policy: Robert Slusser, *The Berlin Crisis of 1961: Soviet-American Relations and the Struggle for Power in the Kremlin, June-November, 1961* (Baltimore, 1973); Donald Zagoria, *The Sino-Soviet Conflict 1956-1961* (Princeton, N.J., 1962); and L. Bloomfield, W. Clemens, and F. Griffith, *Khrushchev and the Arms Race, 1954-1964* (Cambridge, Mass., 1966).

The reader interested in exploring the rich history of this period's cultural "thaw" might begin by referring to the general surveys of Soviet Russian literature listed in the section on the 1920s. Studies focusing on the politics of culture in the 1950s and 1960s include Priscilla Johnson, *Khrushchev and the Arts: The Politics of Soviet Culture, 1962-1964* (Cambridge, Mass., 1965); Robert Conquest, *The Pasternak Affair: Courage of Genius, A Documentary Report* (Philadelphia, 1962); and A. Rothberg, *The Heirs of Stalin: Dissidence and the Soviet Regime, 1953-1970* (Ithaca, N.Y., 1972). Much of the literature itself is available in translation. A sampling of this literature might include: Ilya Ehrenburg, *The Thaw,* trans. Manya Harari (London, 1961), which, while not great literature, had a profound impact on Soviet society; Vladimir Dudintsev, *Not by Bread Alone,* trans. Edith Bone (New York, 1957), much talked about in the 1950s and now again under Gorbachev; and Alexander Solzhenitsyn, *One Day in the Life of Ivan Denisovich,* trans. Max Hayward and Ronald Hingley (New York, 1963), probably the most famous and most daring of the era's published novels.

The 1980s and Gorbachev

For the reader to understand the current calls for reform in the Soviet Union, some background on politics and society in the Brezhnev years should prove helpful. A thorough political analysis of Brezhnev's first fifteen years in power can be found in Seweryn Bialer, *Stalin's Successors: Leadership, Stability and Change in the Soviet Union* (Cambridge, 1980). A good collecton of articles on politics in the mid- and late-1960s is Alexander Dallin and Thomas B. Larson, eds., *Soviet Politics since Khrushchev* (Englewood Cliffs, N.J., 1968). The problems inherited by the post-Brezhnev leadership are the focus of Alexander Dallin and Condoleezza Rice, eds., *The Gorbachev Era* (Stanford, 1986); Erik P. Hoffman and Robbin F. Laird, eds., *The Soviet Polity in the Modern*

Era (New York, 1984); and Jerry F. Hough, *Leadership in Transition* (Washington, D.C., 1980). A discussion of the Soviet military's role in politics is in Timothy Colton, *Commissars, Commanders and Civilian Authority: The Structure of Soviet Military Politics* (Cambridge, Mass., 1979).

The best and most comprehensive sociological survey of the Soviet Union in the Brezhnev years is Basil Kerblay, *Modern Soviet Society* (New York, 1983). James Cracraft has compiled a nice composite picture of society in Brezhnev's last years in James Cracraft, ed., *The Soviet Union Today: An Interpretive Guide* (Chicago, 1983). A good study of Soviet society's growing stratification is Mervyn Matthews, *Privilege in the Soviet Union* (Winchester, Mass., 1978), and the best discussion of the status of women is Gail Lapidus, *Women in Soviet Society: Equality, Development and Social Change* (Berkeley and Los Angeles, 1978). A large number of journalistic accounts of Soviet society have also appeared in recent years. Among the best are Hedrick Smith, *The Russians* (New York, 1976); Robert Kaiser, *Russia* (New York, 1976, 1984); and Andrea Lee, *Russian Journal* (New York, 1981). A good account of dissident activities at the end of the Brezhnev period is Ludmilla Alexeyeva, *Soviet Dissent: Contemporary Movements for National, Religious, and Human Rights* (Middletown, Conn., 1985).

The biographies written when Gorbachev took power will probably not have lasting value, but they do provide important background information. Perhaps the best is Archie Brown, "Gorbachev: New Man in the Kremlin," *Problems of Communism* 34 (May-June, 1985):1-23. There is also Thomas G. Butson, *Gorbachev: A Biography* (New York, 1985), and Christian Schmidt-Haver, *Gorbachev: The Path to Power,* with an appendix on the Soviet economy by Maria Huber, trans. Ewald Osers and Chris Romberg, ed. John Man (London, 1986).

Because relations with the United States and arms control in particular can have a significant bearing on Gorbachev's success or failure as a reformer, the reader might want to become better acquainted with these issues. A most readable history and analysis of Soviet-American arms control negotiations is Coit Blacker, *The Reluctant Warriors: The United States, the Soviet Union, and Arms Control* (New York, 1987). Also good is David Holloway, *The Soviet Union and the Arms Race* (New Haven, Conn., 1984). Essays touching on various matters affecting Soviet-American relations, including human rights and Sino-Soviet relations, can be found in Richard A. Melanson, ed., *Neither Cold War nor Detente: Soviet-American Relations in the 1980's* (Charlottesville, Va., 1982).

On the subject of the Soviet economy and reform agenda, many good article-length analyses can be found in the tri-annual publications of the Joint Economic Committee of the U.S. Congress. For a thorough examination of the Brezhnev economic legacy, for example, see U.S. Congress, JEC, *The Soviet Economy in the 1980's: Problems and Prospects* (Washington, D.C., 1982). Other good contemporary studies of the Soviet economy touching on the theme of reform include A. Bergson and H. S. Levine, eds., *The Soviet Economy: Toward the Year 2000* (Winchester, Mass., 1985); Marshall Goldman, *Gorbachev's Challenge: Economic Reform in the Age of High Technology* (New York, 1987), which includes discussion of the Hungarian, East German, and Chinese "models"; and D. Gale Johnson and Karen McConnell Brooks, *Prospects for Soviet Agriculture in the 1980's* (Bloomington, Ind., 1983). Timothy Colton offers extended and important political analysis of possible reform programs in *The Dilemma of Reform in the Soviet Union* (New York, 1984). For an interesting examination of the reformist possibilities in recent environmental programs, see Thane Gustafson, *Reform in Soviet Politics: Lessons of Recent Policies on Land and Water* (Cambridge, 1981). To stay abreast of current developments in the Soviet Union, readers should consult both *The Current Digest of the Soviet Press,* which is published weekly and carries translations of articles from the Soviet press, and the U.S. Government, Foreign Broadcast Information Service [FBIS] Daily Report, Soviet Union, which has daily translations from a range of Soviet media. Short reports and analyses of contemporary events are available in the *Radio Liberty Research Bulletin,* published by Radio Free Europe/Radio Liberty on a weekly basis.

For more information on the possibilities and limitiations of reform models for the Soviet Union, see Zvi Gitelman, *The Diffusion of Political Innovation: From Eastern Europe to the Soviet Union* (Beverly Hills, Calif., 1972). Perhaps the best contemporary survey of the East European economic reforms and economic performance is U.S. Congress, Joint Economic Committee, *East European Economies: Slow Growth in the 1980's,* 3 vols. (Washington, D.C., 1985). Two good explanations of the organization and operation of Hungary's New Economic Mechanism are David Granick, "The Hungarian Reform," in *Comparative Economic Systems, Models and Cases,* 3rd ed., ed. M. Bornstein (Homewood, Ill., 1974), and the chapter on Hungary in Hans-Hermann Hohmann, Michael Kaser, and Karl C. Thalheim, eds., *The New Economic Systems of Eastern Europe* (Berkeley, 1975). For assessments of the Hungarian reform's successes and failures, see Wlodzimierz Brus, "The Eastern European Reforms: What Happened to Them?" *Soviet Studies* 31 (1979):257-67; P. G. Hare, H. K. Radice, and Nigel Swain, eds.,

Hungary: A Decade of Economic Reform (London, 1981); Bela Csikos-Nagy, "The Hungarian Economic Reform after Ten Years," *Soviet Studies* 30 (1978):540-47, together with Hugo Radice, "Csikos-Nagy on the Hungarian Economic Reforms: A Comment," *Soviet Studies* 31 (1979):257-77; and Paul G. Hare, "The Beginnings of Institutional Reform in Hungary," *Soviet Studies* 35 (1983):313-30. A possible East German reform model is explored in the Spring, 1987, issue of *Studies in Comparative Communism* 20, no. 1; and in Gert Leptin and Manfred Melzer, *Economic Reform in East German Industry* (Oxford, 1978). The extensive Chinese economic reforms are analyzed in A. Doak Barnett and Ralph N. Clough, eds., *Modernizing China: Post Mao Reform and Development* (Denver, 1986); Elizabeth Perry and Christine Wong, eds., *The Political Economy of Reform in Post-Mao China* (Cambridge, Mass., 1985); and the now somewhat dated, U.S. Congress, Joint Economic Committee, *China under the Four Modernizations* (Washington, D.C., 1982).

Notes on Contributors

John T. Alexander, professor of history and Soviet and East European Studies at the University of Kansas, received his A.B. from Wesleyan University in 1961 and his M.A. and Ph.D. from Indiana University in 1963 and 1966, respectively. He has taught at the University of Kansas since 1966 and is the translator of S. F. Platonov's *The Time of Troubles* and the author of four books, most recently *Catherine the Great: Life and Legend* (1989). He has also written some twenty journal articles, more than thirty encyclopedia entries, and some fifty book reviews.

Timothy J. Colton is a professor of government at Harvard University. He taught Soviet and comparative politics at the University of Toronto from 1974 to 1989 and was director of its Center for Russian and East European Studies. He is the author of *Commissars, Commanders and Civilian Authority* and *The Dilemma of Reform in the Soviet Union.* His current research involves the process of change under Gorbachev and the government and politics of the city of Moscow since 1917.

Robert O. Crummey is a professor of history and acting dean of the College of Letters and Science at the University of California, Davis. His research centers on the history of early modern Russia, particularly from the late sixteenth to the mid-eighteenth century. His publications focus on two distinct themes: movements of religious dissent and popular protest and the history of the Russian aristocracy. Among them are *The Old Believers and the World of Antichrist* (1970), *Aristocrats and Servitors: The Boyar Elite in Russia, 1613-1689* (1983), and *The Formation of Muscovy, 1304-1613* (1987). At present, he is investigating the cultural history of the Russian Old Believers from the late seventeenth century until recent times.

Alexander Dallin, Raymond A. Spruance Professor of International History and professor of political science at Stanford University, is director of its Center for Russian and East European Studies. He received his graduate training at Columbia University and taught there for some fifteen years. He was president of the American Association for the Advancement of Slavic

Studies and currently serves as president of the International Council for Soviet and East European Studies. He is the author of a number of books and articles on modern Soviet history, Soviet-American relations, and Soviet foreign policy.

Michael Hennessey is a graduate student at the University of Michigan with a special interest in Soviet military policy.

George F. Minde II, a recent graduate of the University of Michigan, is continuing his study of Soviet politics and the military.

Daniel T. Orlovsky is professor of history and chairperson of the Department of History at Southern Methodist University. He is the author of *The Limits of Reform: The Ministry of Internal Affairs in Imperial Russia, 1802-1881* and *Russia's Democratic Revolution: The Provisional Government of 1917 and the Origins of the Soviet State* (forthcoming). His current research involves state-building in the early Soviet period and the role of the lower middle class in the Russian Revolution.

Walter M. Pintner, professor of Russian history at Cornell University, received his Ph.D. from Harvard. Before going to Cornell, he worked for the U.S. Department of State and taught at Princeton. Since 1959, he has made lengthy research visits to Leningrad and Moscow in connection with his work on the administrative, social, and military history of pre-1917 Russia.

David L. Ransel is professor of history at Indiana University and editor of the *American Historical Review.* He is the author of *The Politics of Catherinian Russia: The Panin Party* (1975) and *Mothers of Misery: Child Abandonment in Russia* (1988). He is editor of and contributor to *The Family in Imperial Russia: New Lines of Historical Research* (1978) and was formerly editor of the *Slavic Review.*

William G. Rosenberg is professor of history at the University of Michigan, Ann Arbor. He received his Ph.D. from Harvard University in 1967. His research and writing have focused on the Russian revolutionary period, emphasizing the relationships between political and social change. He has also worked in the later Soviet period, and in 1982 he published with Marilyn B. Young *Transforming Russia and China.* His most recent study, *Strikes and Revolution in Russia,* written with Diane P. Koenker, will be published in 1989.

Lewis H. Siegelbaum is professor of history at Michigan State University where he has taught since 1983. He received his D.Phil. from Oxford University in 1976 and taught for seven years at La Trobe University in Melbourne, Australia. He has published *The Politics of Industrial Mobilization in Russia, 1914-17* (1983) and *Stakhanovism and the Politics of Productivity in the USSR, 1935-1941* (1988), as well as numerous articles on tsarist and Soviet labor history. He is currently writing a book on the NEP years.

William Taubman is Bertrand Snell Professor of Political Science at Amherst

College. He is the author of *The View from Lenin Hills* (1967), *Governing Soviet Cities* (1973), and *Stalin's American Policy* (1982), and the co-author of *Moscow Spring* (1989). He is currently completing a political biography of Nikita Khrushchev. He co-chairs a joint U.S.-Soviet project, which includes a series of scholarly conferences, alternating between the United States and the Soviet Union, on the history of Soviet-American relations since the end of World War II.

Alexander Yanov received his Ph.D. in the history of Russian political thought from the Plekhanov Institute of National Economy in Moscow in 1970. Four years later he was asked to leave the Soviet Union. Since January 1975, he has taught Russian history and Soviet politics at the University of Texas, Austin; University of California, Berkeley; University of Michigan, Ann Arbor; and the Graduate School of the City University of New York. His field of expertise is political change in Russia and the Soviet Union. While in the United States, he has published ten books in three languages on this subject, including *Detente after Brezhnev* (1977), *The Russian New Right* (1978), *The Origins of Autocracy* (1981), *The Drama of the Soviet 1960s: A Lost Reform* (1984), and *The Russian Challenge and the Year 2000* (1987). He is now in the process of writing a new book, *The Choice: The Soviet Union as an Intellectual Challenge.*

Index

Abuladze, Tengiz, 223
Adashev, Aleksei, 157
Adenauer, Konrad, 152, 183
Administrative reform under Ivan IV,
  12, 16-18, 26
Adzhubei, Aleksei, 169
Aganbegian, A. G., 220
Aitmatov, Chingiz, 212
Akhmatova, Anna, 224, 241
Aleksei (son of Peter the Great), 46
Aleksei Mikhailovich, 23
Alexander I: and reform, 3-4; men-
  tioned, 81, 93, 280
Alexander II: Great Reforms of, 86-99;
  and civil service, 91; Ministry of Jus-
  tice of, 91; mentioned, 97, 251, 281,
  282
Alexander III: and *zemstvo,* 91-92; and
  Land Captain Statute, 1889, 92-93; po-
  litical attitudes of, 96; mentioned, 87,
  91, 92, 271
Aliev, G. A., 214
All-Union Central Council of Trade
  Unions, 133
American perceptions: of U.S.S.R., 243-
  55; of Soviet foreign policy, 259-69
Andropov, I. V., 73, 165, 208, 213, 217,
  239
Anna, Empress: and project of the soci-
  ety, 48-50; and project of the 361, 62;
  mentioned, 45, 51, 52, 56, 57, 58, 60,
  97
Apraksin, Fedor, 47
Armenia, 235
Army: reform under Khrushchev, 8; re-

form under Ivan IV, 12, 14-16; and
  military reforms of 1874, 93-94; during 1860s, 95; used by commissars,
  122; used for grain procurement, 129;
  strategic forces, 168; under Khrushchev, 168-70, 182-200; buildup under Brezhnev, 170; reorganization of
  ground forces, 183-86; manpower reductions under Khrushchev, 183-86,
  192-99; and Main Political Administration, 186-92; dismissal of Zhukov,
  188-89; creation of Strategic Rocket
  Forces, 193
Austria, 174
Autocracy and Russian tradition, 96-98
Avksent'ev, N. D., 112, 114, 117, 124

Banditry under Ivan IV, 16
Bay of Pigs, 153
Berdiaev, Nikolai, 264
Beria, L. P., 152, 189
Berkhin, Viktor, 227
Berlin: bargain of 1971, 148; crisis of
  1948, 148; conference in 1954, 152;
  and 1961 crisis, 181, 184, 185, 197;
  mentioned, 147, 149, 173, 177
Bezborodko, A. A., 75
Biriuzov, Marshal S. S., 198
Bolshevik party: and soviets, 107; ideol-
  ogy and society, 129-30; cultural poli-
  cies of, 133-34; and society during
  NEP, 133-34; relations with workers,
  135-36; mentioned, 103, 108, 110,
  111, 112, 120, 122, 124, 224, 274, 283,
  284